ILLINOIS
CONTINUING EDUCATION *for* REAL ESTATE SALESPERSONS & BROKERS

Clarke R. Marquis
Daniel P. Sarrett

Real Estate Education Company
a division of Dearborn Financial Publishing, Inc.

While a great deal of care has been taken to provide accurate and current information, the idea, suggestions, general principles and conclusions presented in this text are subject to local, state and federal laws and regulations, court cases and any revisions of same. The reader is thus urged to consult legal counsel regarding any points of law--this publication should not be used as a substitute for competent legal advice.

Publisher: Carol L. Luitjens
Acquisitions Editor: Margaret M. Maloney
Cover Design: Mary Kushmir

©1992 by Dearborn Financial Publishing, Inc.

Published by Real Estate Education Company/Chicago, a division of Dearborn Financial Publishing, Inc.

All rights reserved. The text of this publication, or any part thereof, may not be reproduced in any manner whatsoever without written permission from the publisher.

Printed in the United States of America

93 94 10 9 8 7 6 5 4 3

Library of Congress Cataloging-in-Publication Data

Marquis, Clarke R.
    Illinois continuing education for real estate salespersons & brokers / Clarke R. Marquis, Daniel P. Sarrett.
       p.   cm.
  ISBN 0-79310-457-2 (pbk.)
  1. Real estate agents--Licenses--Illinois. 2. Real estate business--Law and legislation--Illinois. 3. Real estate agents--education (Continuing education)--Illinois. I. Sarrett, Daniel P.
II. Title.
KFI1482.R4M37 1992
346.77304'37--dc20
[347.7306437]   92-11270
                                                                                  CIP

CONTENTS

PREFACE — Page v

PART I MANDATORY CONTINUING EDUCATION—LICENSE LAW

Chapter

1. **INTRODUCTION** The history of state real estate licensing, testing, and continuing education not only explains their purpose, but also foretells their future. This chapter explains where the profession has been, and it offers a glimpse into the future of professional licensing. In addition, the chapter answers questions relating to the need and qualifications for licensure; it describes the licensing bureaucracy; and it details the handling of licenses, pocket cards, and sponsor cards. — 1

2. **CONTRACTUAL REGULATIONS** Contracts are the hub of the real estate wheel. Surprisingly, however, they are not heavily regulated by license laws and rules. Loss of a commission, though, may be the least of a licensee's concerns in the event of an infraction of these contractual rules and regulations. A detailed look at the *Quinlan Tyson* case and a discussion of "safe fax" are also provided. — 18

3. **OFFICE AND ADVERTISING REGULATIONS** Advertising is the lifeblood of all professional salespeople. In advertising real estate, the consumer's most important investment, the licensee must be knowledgeable of marketing restrictions, which are covered in this chapter. Chapter 3 also provides a primer in the legal aspects of office administration. Branch offices, assumed names, and the responsibility for the activities of non-licensees are just a few of the administrative details covered here. — 38

4. **ESCROW** As the custodian of funds belonging to others, a broker is governed by stringent rules and regulations regarding the handling of and accounting for such deposits. This chapter fully covers these requirements. It also provides a primer in the actual practice of escrow account bookkeeping. — 53

5. **THOU SHALT NOT** Like driving a car without knowing what a red light means, practicing real estate without knowing the rules of the road is dangerous to both the driver (licensee) and pedestrian (consumer). In real estate, however, just one blown stoplight can cost you your driving privileges. Chapter 5 will assure that you know the most important rules of the road. — 71

6. **DISCIPLINARY PROCEDURES AND HEARINGS** What happens when you run a red light? This chapter fully explains how to handle traffic court (or in some instances, felony court) when and if the real estate rules of the road are violated. — 98

CONTENTS

Page

PART II MANDATORY CONTINUING EDUCATION—OTHER TOPICS

7   **FAIR HOUSING** Our children and our children's children deserve to live in a nation free from undeserved bias and discrimination. Until such time as each of us voluntarily affords equal treatment to others, we must at least conform our conduct to the mandates of the law. Chapter 7 provides a foundation for our continuing knowledge and appreciation of both federal and state fair housing laws.   116

8   **AGENCY** Purchasing or selling a property has never been easy; however, the real estate licensee is now facing new challenges as more and more suits are being filed against Illinois registrants relating to disclosure of agency relationships and property defects. This chapter explains in detail what agency disclosure means, who gives it, when, and how. Because the doctrine of *caveat emptor* (buyer beware) is no longer a valid defense for the used-home seller, sellers and their agents must now bear a greater responsibility for property disclosure. This chapter addresses that issue as well.   139

9   **ANTITRUST** Real estate education and training classes available to the real estate practitioner traditionally have been focused on licensing course work, as well as sales-training-type seminars. Increasingly important to the practitioner, however, are a firm understanding of and appreciation for the competitive environment in which one applies one's trade. It is therefore imperative that antitrust education be included in the real estate professional's course curriculum.   165

PART III ELECTIVE CONTINUING EDUCATION TOPICS

10   **FINANCE DEVELOPMENTS** Nothing changes faster in the real estate business than the ways and means of financing the purchase and sale of real property. This chapter will update you on all the latest financing requirements, techniques, and issues, better equipping you to function in today's dynamic real estate environment.   181

11   **TAXATION** One of the two certainties of life (taxation—and death, of course, is the other) is detailed in this chapter. A licensee should stay abreast of the most important and relevant areas of taxation, which are discussed in this chapter.   209

12   **ILLINOIS APPRAISAL LAW** The real estate professional interfaces on a daily basis with many other professionals. The appraiser is one of these. Appraisal is a new ball game, and the licensee should be familiar with the new rules and players.   227

PREFACE

As a result of legislation enacted in 1990, beginning with the renewal of salespersons' licenses in 1993 and brokers' licenses in 1994, twelve (12) hours of completed continuing education will be required for each license renewal. Regulations adopted by the Illinois Department of Professional Regulation prescribe the course parameters, and this text meets the established standards.

The purpose of this text is to provide licensees with a review and an update of selected laws and professional subjects that affect real estate practitioners. It may be used as the principal course material to fulfill the requirement on either a classroom or a correspondence basis.

ABOUT THE AUTHORS

Clarke R. Marquis, JD—Mr. Marquis is the author/editor of *State of Illinois Real Estate License Act, Rules, and Forms; Illinois Real Estate Licensing Examinations Review Manual; Basic Real Estate Transactions Study Guide; Study Guide for Contracts and Conveyances; Study Guide for Advanced Real Estate Principles*; and *Basic Real Estate Transactions Student Workbook*, all published by Real Estate Educational Services, Inc. He developed, along with several other nationally recognized and respected real estate attorneys, authors, and educators, the ASI, ETS and ACT audiocassette *Real Estate License Examination Review Program* published by Prentice-Hall; and he served as a reviewer for the 11th edition of *Modern Real Estate Practice* and the 9th and 10th editions of *Illinois Supplement for Modern Real Estate Practice*, published by Dearborn Financial Publishing, Inc. Professor Marquis received a JD from Loyola University School of Law and is a practicing attorney in St. Charles, Illinois. Besides holding an Illinois broker's license, he is certified by the Illinois Department of Professional Regulation to instruct both prelicensing and continuing education real estate. He has for several years actively taught brokers' and sales courses, and he has served as an associate professor of business law for North Central College, Naperville, Illinois.

Daniel P. Sarrett, MBA, DREI—Mr. Sarrett has been a real estate instructor and a real estate school director since 1974. Mr. Sarrett is the president of Real Estate Education Company and has authored numerous textbooks, training manuals, and papers on various real estate topics. He received a Master of Business Administration degree from Northern Illinois University and holds an Illinois broker's license. Mr. Sarrett was the first Illinois recipient of the Designated Real Estate Educators (DREI), which is awarded by the Real Estate Educators Association to recognize outstanding classroom performance and communication in the art of teaching others.

AUTHORS' ACKNOWLEDGMENTS

Both of us received help from many people, and for this we are thankful. We would, however, like to thank one very special person who, more than any other, made this book possible. Connie Madsen, who has been Clarke R. Marquis's secretarial partner for 19 years, processed our words and served as our grammarian, illustrator, art director, and chief critic. Without her, we would not have succeeded and to her we owe our sincerest gratitude—a raise, time off, and a bonus.

vi   Preface

We would also like to acknowledge the cooperation we have received from the Illinois Department of Professional Regulation and, in particular, from Albert M. Suguitan, Commissioner of Real Estate; Marvin Fricke, member of the Real Estate Administration and Disciplinary Board; and Gilbert Lynn, Supervisor, Auditing Real Estate Investigations. The opinions expressed in this publication are not, however, the official position of the Illinois Department of Professional Regulation or any other Illinois state agency. For contributions to the content of this publication, we would like to thank Dr. John Weidemer, DREI, and John Lukehart.

For their assistance and cooperation in developing the chapter on fair housing, we would like to extend our thanks and appreciation to the Leadership Council for Metropolitan Open Communities, and especially to John Lukehart.

Thanks are also extended to the Illinois Association of REALTORS®; the National Association of REALTORS®; Chicago, Illinois; and Professional Publishing Corporation, San Rafael, California, for use of materials and forms.

TO THE STUDENT

For your ease of study and future reference, each chapter is organized into the following elements:
- chapter overview
- learning objectives
- main body of chapter
- cases to judge
- 10-question multiple-choice diagnostic quiz

We believe that the overview of legal matters in this text will serve a useful role in alerting you to the existence and general nature of the statutes. However, several *cautionary* comments should be emphasized. First, this text is *not* an authoritative source for legal reference. Many aspects of the laws are abstracted and summarized. Furthermore, the laws are amended periodically and are subject to interpretation by the courts. A second caution is that the statutes often are implemented by rules of executive agencies. Thus, licensees should become familiar with such rules. Third, this text does *not* contain a complete or an exhaustive set of statutes affecting real estate. A number of omitted laws could have a direct and an important bearing on a particular real estate activity or problem.

It should be evident, therefore, that the course material is *NOT* designed to develop a professional level of legal knowledge. Its purpose is *familiarization—not development of expertise*. The intent of this material is to help you gain knowledge that should enable you to recognize relevant legal problems, to apply the underlying principles of law to real estate situations, and to seek or recommend legal or other professional counsel when it is appropriate to do so.

In subscribing to the purposes and intentions for which continuing education was adopted by our legislature, we intend this book (and courses adopting its use) to benefit the public by increasing the professional competence of real estate practitioners.

TO THE EDUCATOR

We have designed this book to service not only the readers' need for up-to-date information on important topics covering their daily practice, but also to accommodate the needs of associations, schools, and instructors who ultimately will be the primary source for the delivery of the materials. On February 4, 1992, the rules for continuing education were finally adopted and are now in effect and set forth in Section 1450.175 of the Rules for the Administration of the Real Estate License Act of 1983. Of special note are two requirements of these rules: (1) mixing and matching elective and mandatory subject matters within a given program is not permitted;

and (2) the time allotted for a final examination *may not* be included in calculating the time required for instruction.

As the table of contents indicates, we have divided the material into three parts. Part I, which contains the License Law, may be covered in 3, 6, 9, or 12 hours, or it may be "mixed and matched" with chapters from Part II.

The chapters in Part II cover other mandatory topics. These may be taught independently (as stand-alone courses), or they may be combined with other mandatory topics.

Part III contains electives that may be used to fulfill the six-hour maximum of elective continuing education. The chapters in Part III may be mixed and matched within an elective program, but they may not be combined with mandatory topics.

The structure of this text thus permits many variations for curriculum development. Although the number of options are finite, we think you'll agree that the materials may be worked into as many different programs as the sponsor chooses to produce.

CHAPTER 1

INTRODUCTION
(BITTER MEDICINE)

○ **CHAPTER OVERVIEW**
   The history of state real estate licensing, testing, and continuing education not only explains their purpose, but also foretells their future. This chapter explains where the profession has been, and it offers a glimpse into the future of professional licensing. In addition, the chapter answers questions relating to the need and qualifications for licensure; it describes the licensing bureaucracy; and it details the handling of licenses, pocket cards, and sponsor cards.

○ **LEARNING OBJECTIVES**
   After completing your study of this chapter, you should be able to:
   1) Evaluate the wisdom of the General Assembly in mandating continuing real estate education.
   2) Identify activities that require a real estate license.
   3) List the major exemptions from real estate licensure.
   4) Summarize the nature, scope, and activities of the Illinois General Assembly, the Illinois Department of Professional Regulation (and its Director), the Commissioner of Real Estate, and the Real Estate Administration and Disciplinary Board.
   5) State the purposes of the Real Estate License Administration Fund, Real Estate Research and Education Fund, and Real Estate Recovery Fund.
   6) Assist in assuring the proper handling of licenses, pocket cards, and sponsor cards.
   7) Explain the requirements for corporate and partnership licensing.
   8) Outline the costs of and requirements for becoming a licensed broker or salesperson in the State of Illinois.

○ **5 CASES TO JUDGE**

○ **10-QUESTION DIAGNOSTIC QUIZ**

CHAPTER 1

INTRODUCTION
(BITTER MEDICINE)

In putting together this manuscript, we have talked with hundreds of licensees as to what should be covered, what elective topics were of most interest, and how they felt about continuing education in general and the mandatory topics in particular. Of these conversations, we took particular interest in the conversations we had with the licensees who were "grandfathered" out of the continuing education requirements. These old-timers generally felt that if continuing education were run properly, it would be of significant benefit to both the general public and the participating licensee. They also said that although they wouldn't have the time to attend the mandatory courses, they might register for an elective course that would actually *benefit* their business practice. We're sure the information offered here will be of the utmost benefit to licensees new and old.

Remember being sick as a child? Your mom or dad would offer up some vile-tasting pea-green syrup and confidently say something like, "Honey, I know this medicine tastes bitter, but it will make you feel better." Your authors have such memories, and those visions have guided us from the beginning to the end of this book. We have also endeavored to artificially flavor the text so that the taste is not bad. We're confident that, in the end, this medicine will make you feel better.

LICENSE HISTORY

Few brokers today would recognize their early-1900s progenitors. What today we call a profession was hardly even a true calling less than a century ago. Except for in the metropolitan areas of the country, few individuals could earn a living selling real estate, and therefore, the early-1900s practitioner was generally someone who knew everybody's business (lawyer, banker, barber) and seized the opportunity of making an occasional buck by putting a deal together.

Early license laws required little more than registration and the payment of a fee. As the business became more complex, age and general education requirements were added. Testing followed; however, early tests were aimed primarily at the establishment of literacy and the most rudimentary knowledge of real estate.

Subsequently, states expanded their educational requirements to include real estate education and concurrently upgraded the difficulty of the examination. Along the way the two-tiered system of licensing was adopted whereby only brokers could own and operate a brokerage firm under whom salespersons would be employed.

Although California was the first state to enact a real estate license law, Oregon was the first state to enact a valid one. In 1917, California enacted a real estate license act that was nullified on a technicality by the California Supreme Court. In 1919, California reenacted its real estate license act; however, earlier in 1919, Oregon enacted the country's first valid real estate license law, thereby laying its claim to the country's first valid real estate license act. Tennessee and Michigan also enacted license laws in 1919, and today, all 50 states and the District of Columbia have real estate licensing.

ILLINOIS REAL ESTATE LICENSING
Illinois first adopted a real estate license act in 1921; however, this was not the first endeavor at real estate licensing in Illinois. The City of Chicago licensed real estate agents as early as 1874, and in 1884, the Illinois

Supreme Court entertained its first case in which an unlicensed person was convicted of having practiced real estate without a license.

THE BUREAUCRACY

The Illinois Real Estate License Act of 1983 (as amended at each session of the legislature) is the primary source of law governing participants in the real estate business. The License Act sets forth the basic qualifications and guidelines for real estate salespersons, brokers, appraisers, schools, and instructors.

The License Act either establishes or is intermeshed with several governmental offices, departments, committees, and funds. This section briefly explores the various legislative and administrative offices and bodies, starting with the legislature and continuing through the various funds established by the License Act.

THE GENERAL ASSEMBLY

The legislative power of the State of Illinois is vested in the General Assembly, which is composed of the Senate and House of Representatives. The General Assembly convenes each year on the second Wednesday in January. In addition, special sessions of the two houses may be convened by the proclamation of the presiding officers or the Governor.

The principal activity of the General Assembly is enacting, amending, or repealing laws and adopting appropriation bills. The legislature also acts on amendments to the United States Constitution, proposes and submits amendments to the State Constitution for the consideration of the voters, and, if required, confirms appointments made by the Governor. The General Assembly, then, is the primary source of Illinois real estate license law.

GOVERNOR

The Governor of Illinois is the chief executive of the state and is generally responsible for the administration of the government, exclusive of the administrative responsibilities placed with other elected officials, such as the Attorney General and Secretary of State. The Governor's authority is clearly delineated in the Civil Administrative Code (Chapter 127 of the Illinois Revised Statutes). The Governor is charged with the administration of a large number of departments, semi-independent boards, commissions, and agencies. Of relevance to the real estate practitioner is the Governor's administrative responsibility to appoint:
- the Director of the Department of Professional Regulation
- the Assistant Director of the Department of Professional Regulation
- all nine members of the Real Estate Administration and Disciplinary Board
- all seven members of the Real Estate Appraisal Committee
- all five members of the Real Estate Education Advisory Council

Once appointed, the foregoing officials may only be removed for good cause.

DEPARTMENT OF PROFESSIONAL REGULATION

The Department of Professional Regulation, formerly the Illinois Department of Registration and Education, is charged with the day-to-day administration of the Real Estate License Act. The Department also administers 35 other license acts, issues 147 types of licenses, and licenses/regulates 34 occupations and professions as follows:

- architects
- athletic trainers
- audiologists
- barbers/barber schools
- collection agencies
- cosmetologists/cosmetology schools
- dentists/dental hygienists
- detection of deception

- detectives/private security contractors/private alarm contractors
- embalmers
- estheticians/esthetics schools
- funeral directors
- land sales
- land surveyors
- medical doctors/osteopaths/chiropractors
- nurses
- nursing-home administrators
- occupational therapists
- optometrists
- pharmacists/pharmacies
- physical therapists
- physician's assistants
- podiatrists
- professional boxers and wrestlers
- professional engineers
- professional service corporations
- psychologists
- public accountants
- real estate brokers, salespersons, and appraisers
- roofing contractors
- shorthand reporters
- social workers
- speech-language pathologists
- structural engineers
- veterinarians/veterinary technicians

Altogether, the Department oversees the operations of over 510,000 active Illinois licensees and over 100,000 inactive/inoperative licensees.

Departmental functions are carried out primarily through the Department's Chicago and Springfield offices. The Springfield office, headquarters of the Department, is responsible for general administration and license issuance. The Chicago office is responsible for enforcement and regulation. Most routine inspections and some investigations are completed by employees living in various parts of the state who report to either Chicago or Springfield.

DIRECTOR

Heading up the Department of Professional Regulation is the *Director*. Both the Director and Assistant Director of the Department are, as noted above, appointed by the Governor. Besides having the ultimate responsibility for assuring the smooth operation of each of the boards and committees falling under the Department's jurisdiction, the Director appoints the various chief administrators of each license unit. As will be noted in Chapter 6, the Director is also charged with rendering the final decision in any matters of licensee discipline.

COMMISSIONER

The Director appoints to the position of *Commissioner* of Real Estate a licensed broker, whose license is surrendered to the Department during his or her term of office. The Commissioner reports to the Director and has the following administrative duties:

1. Nonvoting chairperson of the Real Estate Administration and Disciplinary Board;
2. Direct liaison between the Department, the profession, and real estate organizations and associations;
3. Prepares and circulates to licensees such educational and informational material as the Department deems necessary for guidance or assistance to licensees;
4. Appoints any necessary committees to assist in the performance of the Department's functions and duties; and
5. Supervises the Real Estate Unit of the Department.

At the end of 1991, the Real Estate Unit was charged with the responsibility of issuing 17 different licenses and for administering the License Act to 56,432 salespersons, 30,483 brokers, 3,639 corporations, 141 partnerships, 108 real estate schools, 759 instructors, 15 certified and 32 licensed appraisers, 14 continuing education sponsors, 210 continuing education instructors, 40 time-share units, and 70 land sales units.

REAL ESTATE ADMINISTRATION AND DISCIPLINARY BOARD
The Real Estate Administration and Disciplinary Board is composed of nine members who are appointed by the Governor. Appointment to the Board is subject to the following conditions:
1. A member must have been a resident and citizen of the state for at least six years prior to his or her appointment;
2. Six of the members must have been actively engaged as brokers or salespersons or both for at least ten years prior to their appointment; and
3. Three members of the Board must be public members who may not be licensed under the Act nor the spouse of a person holding a real estate license.

The members' terms are four years, but no more than two members' terms expire in any one year. A member may be reappointed for successive terms but may serve no more than eight years in a lifetime.

The major portion of the Board's work involves its participation in the disciplinary process; however, the Board also provides guidance to the Director on questions involving standards of professional conduct, discipline, and licensing examinations. The Department may not discipline a licensee, refuse to grant or renew a license, or reinstate a previously revoked license without consideration of the Board's recommendation.

REAL ESTATE LICENSE ADMINISTRATION FUND
Except for fees deposited in the Real Estate Recovery Fund, the Real Estate Research and Education Fund, and the Department of Central Management Services Printing Revolving Fund, all fees paid to the Department under the Act are deposited in the Real Estate License Administration Fund. This fund pays for the operations of the Department and the Board.

REAL ESTATE RESEARCH AND EDUCATION FUND
The Real Estate Research and Education Fund was created to finance the operations of the Office of Real Estate Research, which is located at the University of Illinois. Besides providing scholarships for minority students interested in pursuing a real estate education, the Fund also provides real estate research grants. Five dollars is collected from each applicant for a new license and from each licensee reinstating an inactive or expired license. Interest earned through deposits in the Recovery Fund also helps to finance this fund.

REAL ESTATE EDUCATION ADVISORY COUNCIL
The Real Estate Education Advisory Council has five members, all appointed by the Governor. Three of the members are members of the Disciplinary Board; one member is a trade organization representative; and the fifth member is a school or continuing education sponsor representative. The Advisory Council is chaired by the Commissioner of Real Estate, who has no vote.

The Advisory Council approves prelicense schools and curricula, continuing education sponsors and curricula, and may make recommendations to the Department relative to the adoption of rules and regulations relating to prelicense and continuing education.

REAL ESTATE RECOVERY FUND
The Real Estate Recovery Fund was established to provide a fund from which payments could be made to consumers who suffer financial losses as a result of a real estate licensee's or a licensee's employee's act. The Recovery Fund is discussed in greater detail in Chapter 6.

Chapter 1 Introduction

WHO NEEDS A LICENSE?

Section 4 of the License Act sets forth the requirements for a license. Anyone who performs any of the following services for another and for compensation must be licensed:

1. Sells, exchanges, purchases, rents, or leases real estate;

> This, the most customary type of brokerage activity, clearly falls within the ordinary understanding of the practice of real estate.

2. Offers to sell, exchange, purchase, rent, or lease real estate;

> Here, the offeror didn't quite get the job done. He or she attempted to sell, exchange, purchase, rent, or lease real estate for another and for compensation, but was for some reason unsuccessful.

3. Negotiates or offers, attempts, or agrees to negotiate the sale, exchange, purchase, rental, or leasing of real estate;

> From the consumer's vantage point, having a negotiator is an important part of the agency relationship. Accordingly, the Act requires negotiators of real estate deals to be licensed, and it bars most professional negotiators from participation in the real estate market.

4. Lists or offers, attempts, or agrees to list real estate for sale, lease, or exchange;

> Listing property is within the typical definition of real estate brokerage. Note that here, offering to list is also covered.

5. Buys, sells, offers to buy or sell, or otherwise deals in options on real estate or improvements thereon;

> An option listing is an arrangement whereby the broker buys an option to purchase real estate at a specified price for a particular term. During the term of the option the broker shows the property and, if possible, negotiates the sale of his or her option to purchase. The seller is not represented, and only the broker and the purchaser of the option from the broker know how much the broker made. This provision closes a loophole through which unlicensed persons could slip--to the consumer's injury. Potential abuses caused net listings to be outlawed in many states (not Illinois); similarly, an option listing should be taken with great care to avoid the appearance of overreaching.

6. Collects, offers, attempts to collect, or agrees to collect rent for the use of real estate;

> The "thug" image of rent collectors should serve to succinctly explain the purpose of this provision.

7. Advertises or represents himself or herself as being engaged in the business of buying, selling, exchanging, renting, or leasing real estate;

> Why would anyone hold himself or herself out as being in the real estate business if he or she weren't? The purpose here is to facilitate the prosecution of a non-licensee who has violated or is about to violate the licensing restrictions.

8. Assists or directs in the procuring of prospects, intended to result in the sale, exchange, lease, or rental of real estate; and/or

> This subsection was principally designed to control rental finding services, which are organizations that, for a fee, sell a list of available apartments and homes that may be rented. Prior to bringing this type of business under control, many firms were selling listings that were outdated and fraudulent and of annoyance and a nuisance to landlords, who would continue to be bothered by phone calls for months after a vacancy had been filled. This subsection also has been held to cover "finders," who bring two parties in touch with one another but do little else. Canvasing by phone or otherwise is also covered by this subsection, thus precluding the office secretary, bookkeeper, or receptionist from being of much assistance to the licensee or prospect.

9. Assists or directs in the negotiating of any transaction intended to result in the sale, exchange, leasing, or rental of real estate.

> Here the non-licensee does not actually participate in the negotiations, but in effect coaches a party in negotiating his or her own deal.

REAL ESTATE
For purposes of the License Act, real estate is rather broadly defined as leaseholds, as well as any other interest or estate in land, whether corporeal (tangible), incorporeal (intangible rights), freehold or nonfreehold, and whether the real estate is situated in this state or elsewhere.

EXEMPTIONS
The License Act (Section 6) sets forth the following exemptions:

> *(1) Any person, partnership or corporation who as owner or lessor shall perform any of the acts described in subsection (4) of Section 4 of this Act with reference to property owned or leased by them, or to the regular employees thereof with respect to the property so owned or leased, where such acts are performed in the regular course of or as an incident to the management, sale or other disposition of such property and the investment therein, provided that such regular employees shall not perform any of the acts described in subsection (4) of Section 4 of this Act in connection with a vocation of selling or leasing any real estate or the improvements thereon not so owned or leased.*
> *(2) An attorney in fact acting under a duly executed and recorded power of attorney to convey real estate from the owner or lessor, or the services rendered by an attorney at law in the performance of the attorney's duty as such attorney at law.*
> *(3) Any person acting as receiver, trustee in bankruptcy, administrator, executor or guardian or while acting under a court order or under the authority of a will or testamentary trust.*
> *(4) Any person acting as a resident manager for the owner or any employee acting as the resident manager for a broker managing an apartment building, duplex, apartment*

complex, when such resident manager resides on the premises, the premises is his primary residence, and such resident manager is engaged in the leasing of the property of which he or she is the resident manager.

(5) Any officer or employee of a federal agency in the conduct of his official duties.

(6) Any officer or employee of the State government or any political subdivision thereof performing his official duties.

(7) Any multiple listing service wholly owned by a not-for-profit organization or association of real estate brokers.

(8) Any not-for-profit referral system or organization of real estate brokers formed for the purpose of referrals of prospects for the sale or purchase of real estate.

(9) Railroads and other public utilities regulated by the State of Illinois, or their subsidiaries or affiliated corporations, or to the officers or regular employees thereof, unless performance of any of the acts described in subsection (4) of Section 4 of this Act is in connection with the sale, purchase, lease or other disposition of real estate or investment therein unrelated to the regulated business activity of such railroad or other public utility or affiliated or subsidiary corporation thereof.

(10) Any newspaper of general circulation in the routine course of selling advertising along with which no related services are provided.

LICENSING

For a complete description of the licensing and testing requirements, see Sections 11 and 12 of the License Act or request a copy of the Department's booklet, "Real Estate Assessment for Licensure Candidate Handbook." The following chart summarizes the fees and other requirements to become licensed as a broker or salesperson in the State of Illinois.

GENERAL REQUIREMENTS	SALESPERSON	BROKER
AGE	21	21
SECONDARY EDUCATION	HIGH SCHOOL OR GED	HIGH SCHOOL OR GED
REAL ESTATE EDUCATION	30 HOURS	60 ADDITIONAL HOURS
EXAM	110 QUESTIONS	120 QUESTIONS
ACTIVE EXPERIENCE	NONE	1 YEAR
FEES		
PROCESSING	$25	$50
R.E. RECOVERY	$10	$10
R.E. RESEARCH	$5	$5
TOTAL	$40	$65

Exceptions to the above requirements: (1) attorneys who are licensed in Illinois must take the examination but may become either salespersons or brokers without any further education and without the one year of active experience required for a broker's license; (2) a person between 18 and 20 with two years of college credit focused in real estate may qualify for the salesperson's license; and (3) a person holding a bachelor's degree with a minor in real estate of at least 30 semester hours of credit in specified subjects satisfies the educational requirements for both license classifications; however, the exams and the one year of experience for a broker's license are required.

LICENSE

A real estate broker's license is pictured below (Figure 1-1). The license is 6.75 inches by 5.25 inches and is identical in size and color (blue) to all other licenses (salesperson's license included) issued by the Department, except for physicians, whose licenses are much larger, more impressive, and more suitable for framing and display. The real estate license, however, must be *conspicuously* displayed in the broker's office. Investigators from the Department routinely check for compliance with this requirement when visiting an office—regardless of the purpose of the visit.

FIG 1-1

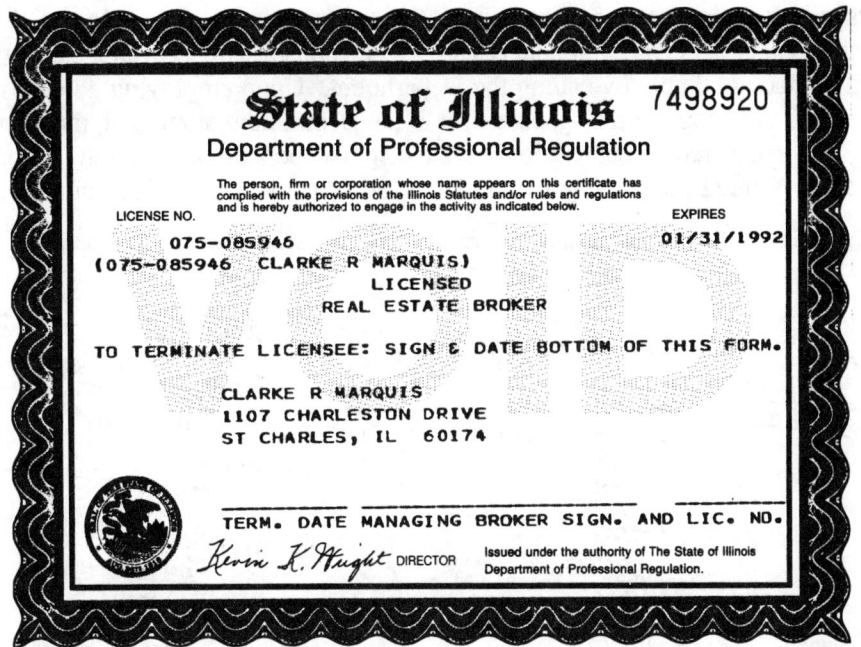

The license is originally issued upon payment of the appropriate fees and will be reissued each time the license is renewed and/or upon transfer to a new sponsoring broker. Upon termination of an employment relationship, it is the responsibility of the sponsoring or managing broker to endorse the original license with the date of termination, and to mail a copy of the terminated license to the Department within two (2) days of termination. The sponsoring broker will want to retain an additional copy for his or her records along with documentation of having sent a copy to the Department. The original license is then given to the terminated associate.

POCKET CARDS

At the time of issuance/reissuance of the license, a pocket card is also issued by the Department. The pocket card is similar to a driver's license—you must have it with you whenever you are engaged in a licensed activity. Upon request of an interested party, you must display the card. If you become embroiled in a heated debate at a closing, one of the interested parties or their representative may "get a leg up" in the debate if they ask to see your pocket card and you are unable to produce it. The interested party thus has several witnesses who can corroborate a complaint to the Department. As seen at the top of the next page (Figure 1-2), the pocket card identifies the licensee, the licensee's sponsor, the license number, and the date the license expires.

10   Chapter 1   Introduction

FIG 1-2

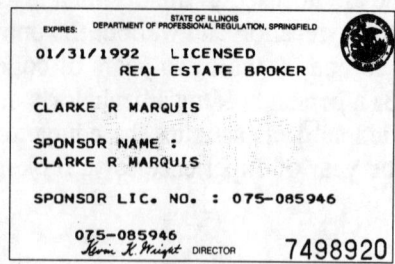

An effective way of assuring that sponsored salespeople and brokers know this rule is to periodically start out office meetings with "Show me your pocket cards!"

SPONSOR CARDS

Sponsor cards are similar in function to the "license applied for" sticker we receive after buying a new car. The "license applied for" sticker entitles us to drive the vehicle while the State is manufacturing our tin license plates. A sponsor card is issued by a sponsoring broker and entitles the salesperson/broker to practice real estate while the State is manufacturing a new license and pocket card. The sponsor card is produced by the State of Illinois in triplicate form and is made available by calling the Department. Upon employing a new associate, the broker must immediately send the third copy of the sponsor card to the Department along with the appropriate supporting documents and fees. The sponsored associate receives the original sponsor card, and the second copy is retained for the broker's records. Pictured below (Figure 1-3) is a sponsor card along with a summary of the foregoing.

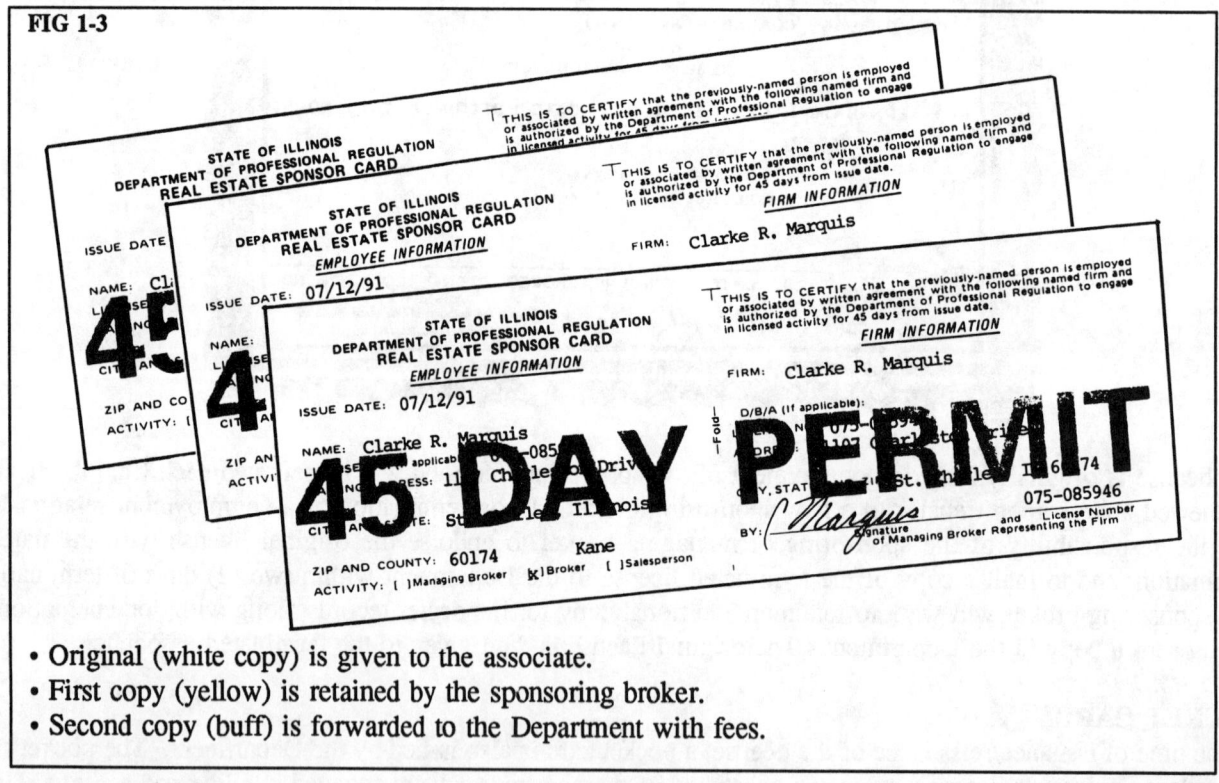

- Original (white copy) is given to the associate.
- First copy (yellow) is retained by the sponsoring broker.
- Second copy (buff) is forwarded to the Department with fees.

The sponsor card is good for forty-five (45) days from the date of issuance. The sponsoring broker should adopt office practices that assure that the license is received or that the associate's employment is terminated if the license is not received and on display within the 45-day period. Compliance with these requirements is also routinely checked by Department investigators.

EMPLOYMENT AGREEMENT

Simultaneously with the issuance of a sponsor card, the associate and broker must enter into an employment contract. The terms of such contract are more fully developed in Chapter 2. The minimum requirements, however, are set forth in Rule 1450.60 and require that each sponsoring broker have a written agreement with each associate that is dated, signed by the parties, and that covers the salient aspects of their relationship, including, but not necessarily limited to, supervision, duties, compensation, and termination. A sample agreement that more than meets these requirements is illustrated on the following two pages (Figures 1-4 and 1-5).

DEBUNKING RECIPROCITY

True reciprocity in real estate licensing does not exist. Many licensees are under the mistaken impression that if they move to one of the 11 states that have real estate license reciprocity with Illinois, then they may immediately restart their careers in the sister state. What does exist is a type of reciprocity that permits an *out-of-state* licensee to practice in one state while residing in another state. Once the licensee moves to the sister state, he or she would have to fully qualify anew for licensing. Some states will recognize education and experience acquired outside the state, and others will not. Therefore, if you are planning a move to another state and your decision to relocate hinges on whether you may quickly reenter the real estate business, you are strongly encouraged to contact the appropriate state licensing authority for information on shortcutting the licensing requirements. The only shortcut that is available in Illinois is that the experience necessary to sit for the broker exam may be acquired in another state. Thus, a licensee moving to Illinois could take the broker examination immediately upon completion of the 90 hours of course work.

Illinois currently has out-of-state reciprocal licensing agreements with 11 states: Connecticut, Indiana, Iowa, Kansas, Kentucky, Minnesota, Missouri, Nebraska, North Dakota, Oklahoma, and South Dakota. Although the procedures and requirements to become licensed in any of these states are similar to the requirements for an out-of-state broker or salesperson to become licensed in Illinois, there are variances.

In order for an out-of-state *broker* to become licensed as a nonresident in Illinois, he or she must: (1) hold a license in the home state; (2) have been actively engaged in business in the home state for not less than two years immediately preceding the date of his or her Illinois application; (3) provide certification from the home state licensing authority that he or she has an active license, is in good standing, with no outstanding complaints; (4) appoint the Director of the Illinois Department of Professional Regulation as his or her agent for service of summons and other legal notices; (5) sign a statement agreeing to comply with all of the applicable state laws and rules governing the Illinois real estate practice; and (6) pay all of the customary licensure fees (original license fee, renewal fee, etc.).

Under similar circumstances, an out-of-state *salesperson* may also receive an Illinois license. In the case of a salesperson, he or she must: (1) have an active salesperson's license in his or her home state; (2) reside in the same state as the sponsoring broker—who must hold an Illinois license; (3) appoint the Director of the Illinois Department of Professional Regulation as his or her agent for service of summons and other legal notices; (4) sign a statement agreeing to comply with all of the applicable state laws and rules governing the Illinois real estate practice; and (5) pay all of the customary licensure fees (original license fee, renewal fee, etc.).

True reciprocity may never be achieved nationwide; however, based on the position taken by the National Association of Real Estate License Law Officials (NARELLO) in 1990, we may expect true reciprocity to become a reality between states with similar socioeconomic and geographic characteristics. For obvious reasons, the political forces in the "sunshine states" will resist the efforts to open their doors to the practitioner originally licensed elsewhere.

FIG 1-4

AGREEMENT

AGREEMENT made this _____ day of _____, 19____, between _____, with a principal place of business located at _____ ("Broker"), and _____, residing at _____ ("Associate").

WITNESSETH:

WHEREAS, Broker is licensed under the laws of the State of Illinois to engage in business as a real estate broker; and

WHEREAS, Associate is licensed by the State of Illinois to engage in the real estate business; and

WHEREAS, it is believed to be in the best interests of Broker and Associate to enter into this Agreement;

NOW, THEREFORE, in consideration of the premises and the mutual covenants hereinafter contained, the parties hereto do hereby agree as follows:

1. Broker is engaged in business as a real estate Broker. The Associate's listing and/or sale of real estate under this Agreement will be supervised by Broker or a member of Broker's management, and policies and procedures set forth by Broker with respect to such listing and sale must be adhered to by Associate.

2. Associate agrees:
   (a) to comply with the Policy and Procedures Manual prepared by Broker, a copy of which has been made available to Associate and the contents of which may be amended, supplemented or changed from time to time by Broker in his or her sole discretion upon 30 days written notice;
   (b) to use the name of Broker in conformity with all applicable standards for such use as heretofore or hereafter developed by Broker; and
   (c) to conform to and abide by all Codes of Ethics that are binding on or applicable to real estate brokers and salespersons operating in the State of Illinois, including, but not limited to, local real estate boards, multiple listing services and any and all local, state and national real estate associations.

3. Broker agrees to make available to Associate all current real estate listings except those that Broker may find expedient to place exclusively in the temporary possession of some other person (including Broker) and agrees to assist Associate by advice, suggestion and reasonable cooperation. Broker maintains and has available for Associate's use, a training program consisting of an orientation to real estate sales.

4. Broker agrees that Associate may share with other associates all of the office facilities. Broker agrees to furnish sufficient desks and telephones to permit Associate to conduct his or her business and perform his or her obligations pursuant to this Agreement. In addition, Broker shall supply such real estate sales contracts, listing agreements, prospect cards and other documents as are made available to other associates. However:
   (a) Associate may not be assigned any specific space, desk, telephone or other equipment, all of which are made available for common use;
   (b) Associate may not enjoy unlimited, unrestricted or unauthorized use of advertising cards, signs, decals, logos or other items bearing the name of Broker, all of which are subject to the use restrictions referred to in paragraph 2 above unless otherwise agreed to in writing by Broker in connection with the sale, listing for sale or lease of real estate;
   (c) Associate shall protect the property of Broker while being used with consent and return any such property or items upon request by Broker.

5. Broker will offer advice and assistance on any sales transaction and will use his or her best efforts to provide leads on real estate prospects and real estate listings to Associate. Any leads obtained by Broker may be accepted or rejected by Associate in his or her sole discretion.

6. Associate shall determine his or her own hours of work (quantity and schedule), time off, and vacations. Associate is not required to work any specified number of hours per week. All floor time or floor duty schedules and office hours will be established monthly on a voluntary basis. Associate shall work diligently and use his or her best efforts to sell or lease, as the case may be, any and all real estate currently and hereafter listed with Broker during the term of this Agreement, to solicit additional listings and customers for Broker and otherwise promote the business of serving the public in real estate transactions. Associate agrees to conduct his or her business and regulate his or her habits so as to maintain and increase the goodwill and reputation of Broker. All listings obtained by Associate during the term of this Agreement shall be and remain the property of Broker, and Associate shall forfeit any listings and/or listing fees with respect to properties not under contract at the time of Associate's departure, and Associate shall have no right to, or claim against, any listing and/or listing fees with respect to properties not under contract at the time of Associate's departure.

7. Associate shall pay all expenses incurred by him or her in connection with the sale or lease of any real estate listed with Broker, including, but not limited to, transportation, gasoline, automobile, telephone, and entertainment, excepting only those office expenses paid by Broker.

8. Associate shall pay any multiple listing fees, license fees, dues and other charges due or to become due to any local, state or national multiple listing service, real estate board or licensing authority. Associate represents that he or she is now duly licensed as a real estate broker or salesperson under the laws of the State of Illinois and that he or she will at his or her own expense maintain such license in good standing during the term of this Agreement.

9. Associate will not be treated as an employee with respect to the services provided pursuant to this Agreement for federal tax or other purposes. Associate's compensation hereunder shall be commissions earned on property sold or listed by him or her. No commission shall be deemed to be earned by Associate until such time as the title to the property sold passes from the seller to the buyer and commissions are received by Broker.

FIG 1-5

When such commissions are collected by Broker, they shall be promptly divided between Broker and Associate in the proportion to which each is entitled. Payment shall be made to Associate in the gross amount of commissions due, without withholding for Federal, State or local income taxes unless Broker is required by applicable law to withhold. Broker shall not be responsible for the payment of any F.I.C.A., F.U.T.A. or other similar charges with respect to Associate and Associate agrees to pay all self-employment and other taxes, including income taxes and estimates thereof, as shall be required by the Internal Revenue Code of 1954, as amended, and the laws, rules and regulations of any other governmental entity having jurisdiction over Associate. Broker may elect to maintain worker's compensation insurance with respect to Associate, it being understood that Broker would be doing so for the sole benefit of Broker.

10. An agreed-upon commission shall be charged for any service performed hereunder and Broker shall advise Associate of any special contract relating to any particular transaction to be undertaken by Associate. When Associate shall perform any service hereunder whereby a commission is earned, the commission shall, when collected, be divided between Broker and Associate in accordance with the latest applicable compensation program and schedule of commissions from time to time applicable and in effect as relates to particular transactions.

11. Broker shall not be liable to Associate for any expenses incurred by Associate, for any of Associate's acts, nor shall Associate be liable to Broker for office help or expense, Associate shall have no authority to bind Broker by any act, promise or representation, unless specifically authorized in a particular transaction. Nevertheless, expenses for attorney's fees, costs, revenue stamps, title abstracts and the like which must by reason of some necessity, be paid from the commission, or are incurred in the collection of, or the attempt to collect, or in an effort to retain, any commission, shall be paid by the parties in the same proportion as provided for herein in the division of the commissions. Suits for commissions shall, as required by law, be maintained only in the name of the Broker, and Associate shall be construed to be a subagent only with respect to the clients and customers for whom services shall be performed, and shall otherwise be deemed to be an "independent contractor," and not a servant, employee, partner or joint venturer of Broker.

12. Broker shall not be required to give any draws, or other advances, against future commissions to Associate.

13. During the term of this Agreement, Associate agrees to maintain Automobile Liability Insurance with minimum limits of $100,000/$300,000 covering bodily injury and property damage. Associate shall request that Broker be named as an additional insured or, alternatively, that Broker be given 30 days' notice of cancellation of such coverage.

14. Associate shall not, after the termination of this Agreement, use to his or her own advantage, or the advantage of any other person or corporation, any information gained for or from the files or business of Broker. Associate shall not, during the term of this Agreement and for a period of six (6) months following the termination hereof, directly or indirectly, solicit the listing of any real estate or property listed by Broker during the term of this Agreement. Associate further agrees that for a period of six months after termination of this Agreement, Associate will not directly or indirectly solicit or otherwise attempt in any manner to induce any sales associate or employee of Broker to terminate his or her affiliation or employment.

Upon termination of this Agreement, Associate shall deliver to or advise Broker in writing of any offer received, requested to be submitted or otherwise communicated to Associate with respect to any real estate or property listed with Broker or another broker which had not prior to such termination been delivered, submitted or otherwise communicated in writing to Broker. It is understood and agreed that upon termination of this Agreement, Broker retains as its separate property all financial interest to which it, as the broker or co-broker, is otherwise entitled pursuant to any such offer.

Referrals assigned to Associate by Broker are the property of Broker, and shall be returned to Broker, together with all documents and other instruments relating thereto, upon termination of this Agreement.

15. This Agreement is personal to Associate and neither it nor any of the rights or duties hereunder may be assigned, mortgaged, sublicensed or otherwise encumbered by Associate, by operation of law or otherwise, nor may Associate give up any control over the subject matter of this license. Rights not herein specifically granted to Associate are reserved by Broker and may be used by Broker without limitation. Broker shall have the right to assign this Agreement.

16. This Agreement and the association created hereby shall continue until terminated:
    (a) by either party at any time on fourteen days' advance written notice given to the other party; or
    (b) by Broker immediately upon delivery of notice to Associate that Associate has failed to comply with any of the terms or conditions of this Agreement.

In the event of such termination, the rights of the parties to any commission which accrued prior to the date of termination shall not be affected by reason of such termination. In addition, immediately upon termination of this Agreement, Associate shall return to Broker all files, training materials, booklets, publications and other literature belonging to or bearing the name of Broker. The obligations of the parties hereto shall survive termination of this Agreement.

17. This Agreement, together with the policies and manuals referred to herein, represents the entire agreement between Broker and Associate. This Agreement may not be changed orally but only in writing executed by both parties hereto. This Agreement shall be governed by and construed in accordance with the laws of the State of Illinois.

IN WITNESS WHEREOF, the parties hereto have hereunto set their hands and seals on the day and year first above written.

Signed, Sealed and Delivered in the presence of: NAME OF BROKER

_____   By: _____

_____   _____
                                                                                                        ASSOCIATE

CORPORATIONS

The License Act permits corporations to hold licenses. In order to be issued a corporate license, every corporate officer who actively participates in the real estate business must hold a valid broker's license, and every salesperson for the corporation must hold either a broker's or salesperson's license. No salesperson or group of salespersons may hold more than a 49% interest in the corporation, and each year the corporation must report to the Department the name of any individual holding more than 10% of the corporation's outstanding shares of stock.

PARTNERSHIPS

Similar to the corporate rules, a partnership (general or limited) may receive a broker's license. In the case of the partnership, all *general* partners must be licensed brokers. As with the corporate license, the following additional requirements must be met: (1) all salespersons for the partnership must be licensed salespersons or brokers; (2) no more than 49% of the partnership may be controlled by a salesperson or group of salespersons; and (3) annual reporting to the Department of persons holding more than a 10% interest in the partnership is required.

Both corporations and partnerships must fill out the same application form and, in addition to the form, they must submit to the Department several additional items. Rule 1450.30 sets forth these items as follows:

> *(a) Persons who desire to practice real estate in this State in the form of a partnership or corporation, shall, in accordance with Section 3 of the Act, file an application with the Department, on forms provided by the Department, together with the following:*
>
> *(1) If an assumed name is to be used, a copy of the assumed name certificate;*
>
> *(2) A Federal Employer Identification Number (FEIN). If a FEIN has not been issued, a photocopy of the FEIN application.*
>
> *(3) A properly completed consent to examine and audit special accounts form;*
>
> *(4) A properly completed real estate corporation/partnership information form;*
>
> *(5) The fee required by Section 15 of the Act.*
>
> *(b) All requirements for a license to practice as a corporation or partnership shall be met within 1 year of the date of the original application or the application shall be denied and the fee forfeited. Thereafter, to be considered for licensure, such applicant shall file a new application and fee.*
>
> *(c) Corporations, in addition to the above, shall submit the following:*
>
> *(1) The name of the corporation and its registered address, a list of all officers, and the license number for each officer who is licensed as a real estate broker;*
>
> *(2) A copy of the Articles of Incorporation bearing the seal of the office, in the jurisdiction in which the Corporation is organized, whose duty it is to register corporations under the laws of that jurisdiction. If it is a foreign corporation, a copy of the certificate of authority to transact business in this State is also required; and*
>
> *(3) All unlicensed officers shall submit with the corporation application affidavits of non-participation. Licensed salespersons cannot be officers of the corporation even if they submit an affidavit of non-participation.*
>
> *(d) Partnerships, in addition to the above, shall submit the following:*
>
> *(1) An application containing the name of the partnership and its business address and the names of all general partners, and the license number of each general partner;*
>
> *(2) An affidavit stating that the partnership has been legally formed.*
>
> *(e) Limited Partnerships, in addition to the above, shall submit the following:*
>
> *(1) A letter of authority from the Secretary of State's Limited Partnership Department; and*
>
> *(2) A listing of all limited partners and their license numbers.*

INOPERATIVE LICENSE

Only persons holding valid pocket or sponsor cards are entitled to engage in any manner as a real estate agent. Upon termination of association with a broker, the licensee's license becomes inoperative—and until a new sponsoring broker is secured, the practice of real estate is unlawful. "Inoperative license" status replaced "inactive" status, which was similar.

WHAT'S AHEAD?

We've dusted off our crystal ball. Looking into the glass, we see the following as the most likely major licensing changes by the end of the century:

Seller property disclosure—The question here is not if, but when.
Home inspection licensing—This will probably accompany seller property disclosure.
Separate property management licensing—The current exemption may be removed and a new license classification added.
Real estate auctioneer licensing—This has been on the horizon for more than ten years.
Prelicensing and/or postlicensing education upgrades—There's more to know than what can be taught in 30 hours.
A whole new License Act—Eventually, cutting and pasting new legislation into an existing act becomes impractical, and a totally new and rewritten act follows.
Degrandfathering continuing education—This may come as the result of litigation.
Agency legislation—Common law and court decisions are not keeping pace with an agent's need to know what the law is.

HELP??

The following addresses and phone numbers are provided in case your office Rolodex hasn't been updated recently.

Illinois Department of Professional Regulation
320 West Washington
Springfield, Illinois 62758
Telephone: 217-785-0800
Fax: 217-524-0142

State of Illinois Center
100 West Randolph, Suite 9-300
Chicago, Illinois 60601
Telephone: 312-814-4500

License Application Information and Forms
Telephone: 217-782-8556

License Renewal Information
Telephone: 217-782-0458

License Examination
Telephone: 1-800-274-0404
By dialing this number you will be in direct contact with Assessment Systems, Inc. (ASI) in Pennsylvania. ASI has contracted with the State of Illinois to administer the real estate license exam. This number can be used to register for exams and to obtain other related information. ASI's phones are open until 8:00 p.m. EST, and they are easiest to reach during the early morning and late afternoon.

CASES TO JUDGE

1. Proceedings were brought by the Department of Registration and Education to enjoin the defendant from engaging in certain practices without securing a real estate broker's license. The Department's complaint alleged that the defendant was engaged in the business of buying and selling real estate without a valid certification as a broker. The defendant engaged in the business of obtaining certificates of purchase from tax sales issued pursuant to the requirements of the Revenue Act. The certificates were generally bought from individuals or entities who had previously bid at tax sales. Thereafter, defendant would sell a certificate to a third party, surrender a certificate if a redemption was made, take no action in relation to a certificate thereby abandoning the investment, or implement legal proceedings to transfer a certificate into an order directing the issuance of a tax deed which ultimately led to acquisition of title. If the latter course of action was followed, the real estate was then either sold or held for investment.

   Is a certificate of purchase for delinquent real estate taxes an interest in real estate for purposes of the Real Estate License Act? [*People ex rel. Department of Registration And Education v. D.R.G., Inc.*, 62 Ill.2d 401, 342 N.E.2d 380 (1976)]

2. Plaintiffs sought recovery of a 3½% commission for the management of a 92-unit apartment complex. The plaintiffs did not have real estate licenses and claimed they were exempt from licensing because they were the owners of the property. The defendants contend that although at one time the plaintiffs were the owners of the property by virtue of their having entered into an installment sale of the real estate to defendants, they no longer were "owners or lessors" such as would exempt them from the licensing requirements.

   How should the court rule on the issue of whether or not a contract seller is exempt from the License Act when he manages property on behalf of the contract purchaser? [*Brandenberry Park East Apartments v. Zale*, 63 Ill.App.3d 253, 379 N.E.2d 674, 19 Ill.Dec. 802 (1978)]

3. In October 1974, plaintiff George H. White was a real estate broker and Fred W. Owens was a real estate salesperson. At that time, Owens's certificate of registration as a salesperson was in the possession of another broker by whom he was then employed. On October 25, 1974, the defendant seller of a parcel of real estate agreed to pay Owens a brokerage commission of 6 percent of the sales price. Owens's certificate of registration as a salesperson was transferred to plaintiff White on December 1, 1974. On January 3, 1977, the real estate was sold; however, the seller refused to pay the brokerage commission claiming that since Owens did not register to sell real estate as plaintiff's employee until December 1, 1974, the seller was not obligated to pay the agreed-upon commission.

   Under the above circumstances, should a commission be awarded? [*White v. Chicago Title & Trust Co.*, 99 Ill.App.3d 323, 425 N.E.2d 1017, 54 Ill.Dec. 800 (1981)]

4. Plaintiff, a corporation, sought to recover a real estate broker's commission for procuring a buyer on the sale of commercial property. Defendant attempted to avoid liability for the commission on the ground that an employee of the plaintiff, a Mr. Hickman, actively participated in the brokerage business of the plaintiff corporation although he was not licensed to act as a real estate broker. Hickman was responsible for assembling, assimilating, and correlating diverse financial and accounting information about petroleum clients. The material that he collected was incorporated in a brochure that the corporation originated and distributed. Hickman's contacts with defendants were necessary only for the purposes of acquiring financial information. The testimony indicated that much of Hickman's time spent with defendants was actually spent in consultation with their accountant.

   Did Hickman's unlicensed activities in connection with the sale of the real estate fall within the statutory definition of the term *broker* such that the court should deny a commission? [*Federated Petroleum Services, Inc. v. Daniels*, 56 Ill.App.2d 236, 205 N.E.2d 741 (1965)]

5. The plaintiff, a videotape service, claimed that a broker owed them a 1.2 percent commission on the sale of a farm in accordance with their agreement. The broker defended the suit on the basis that the plaintiff performed real estate brokerage services requiring a license, and since the videotape company was not licensed, their agreement was void.

   Similar to a multiple listing service agreement, the plaintiff offered a service to broker members whereby each member submitted listings of nonresidential property listed by members at a price of over $50,000. Once a listing was received by a member broker and sent to the association, the association's personnel would videotape the property, take an aerial view of the property, and pursuant to the membership agreement, each member was supplied with a videotape player and with the tapes of listed property as they became available. The member broker thus was free to use these videotapes to effect a sale of the property.

Are such services required to be performed by a licensed broker? [*Sunny Ridge Realty and Insurance, Inc. v. Williamson*, 74 Ill.App.3d 481, 393 N.E.2d 23, 30 Ill.Dec. 368 (1979)]

10-QUESTION DIAGNOSTIC QUIZ

1. Which of the following funds are NOT created by the License Act?
   A. Real Estate License Administration Fund
   B. Real Estate Research and Education Fund
   C. Real Estate Recovery Fund
   D. Real Estate Broker and Salesperson Fund

2. Of the nine members of the Real Estate Administration and Disciplinary Board, how many must be licensed brokers or salespersons?
   A. 3
   B. 4
   C. 5
   D. 6

3. An owner is selling his home. Four people have offered their assistance for a fee; however, three of the people may NOT do so unless they have a real estate license (broker's or salesperson's). Which person would NOT need a license?
   A. The next-door neighbor, who agrees to show the home during the week while the owner is at work.
   B. The owner's brother, who agrees to mass-market the property
   C. The owner's mother, who agrees to take messages while the owner is on vacation
   D. The owner's sister, who agrees to canvass the neighborhood for prospects and/or leads

4. Marcy Goldring works for E.Z. Realty. Since she doesn't have a real estate license, which of the following services is she prohibited from rendering to her employer?
   A. Serving as an auctioneer at real estate auctions conducted by her employer
   B. Drafting letters for the company president
   C. Going on "caravans" of recently listed property
   D. Staffing a sales booth at the annual county fair

5. In order for an Indiana broker to receive an Illinois out-of-state broker's license, the broker need NOT:
   A. have been an active broker in his of her home state for at least two years.
   B. take the Illinois broker exam.
   C. provide proof of his or her Indiana licensure and good standing.
   D. appoint the Director of the Department as his or her agent for service of summons and other notices.

6. Real estate, for purposes of the License Act, does NOT include:
   A. leasehold interests.
   B. easements.
   C. land outside Illinois.
   D. trade fixtures.

7. Which of the following documents must be sent to the Department within two days of the termination of an association between the broker and a salesperson?
   A. Pocket card
   B. Sponsor card
   C. Original license
   D. Photocopy of the license

8. Upon the termination of an association between a broker and a sponsored salesperson, the salesperson's license is:
   A. inoperative.
   B. inactive.
   C. incinerated.
   D. incompetent.

9. Which of the following officials is in charge of the day-to-day activities of the Real Estate Unit of the Department of Professional Regulation?
   A. Governor
   B. Director
   C. Commissioner
   D. Real Estate Administration and Disciplinary Board

10. All of the following are true with respect to a pocket card EXCEPT:
    A. When engaged in a licensed activity, the licensee must carry it at all times.
    B. It permits the licensee to engage in business while the licensee's sponsor card and license are being printed.
    C. It identifies the sponsoring broker.
    D. It provides evidence of the licensee's authority to engage in the real estate business.

CHAPTER 2

CONTRACTUAL REGULATIONS
(LET'S MAKE A DEAL)

○ CHAPTER OVERVIEW
Contracts are the hub of the real estate wheel. Surprisingly, however, they are not heavily regulated by license laws and rules. Loss of a commission, though, may be the least of a licensee's concerns in the event of an infraction of these contractual rules and regulations. A detailed look at the *Quinlan Tyson* case and a discussion of "safe fax" are also provided.

○ LEARNING OBJECTIVES
After completing your study of this chapter, you should be able to:
1) Recognize contractual situations giving rise to infractions of the License Act and resulting discipline.
2) Differentiate between advice that is permissible to convey to a client/customer and advice that may only be given by one who is licensed to practice law.
3) Understand the limitations imposed upon the real estate practitioner by the *Quinlan Tyson* case.
4) Enumerate the minimum requirements of a written listing contract.
5) Recognize the customary provisions of a sponsor (employment) agreement.
6) Explain the minimum requirements of a sponsor (employment) agreement.
7) Understand the drawbacks of facsimile (fax) negotiations/contracts.
8) Enumerate the requirements of written listing agreements.

○ 5 CASES TO JUDGE

○ 10-QUESTION DIAGNOSTIC QUIZ

CHAPTER 2

CONTRACTUAL REGULATIONS
(LET'S MAKE A DEAL)

9. OTHER TERMS AND CONDITIONS: This contract incorporates the Terms and Conditions set forth above, on the reverse side and the Riders signed by the parties and attached hereto numbered   401, 407, 412, 417, fax . THE PRINTED MATTER OF THIS CONTRACT HAS BEEN PREPARED UNDER THE SUPERVISION OF THE DUPAGE ASSOCIATION OF REALTORS® AND THE DUPAGE COUNTY BAR ASSOCIATION. THE PARTIES ARE CAUTIONED THAT THIS IS A LEGALLY BINDING CONTRACT AND TO SEEK LEGAL COUNSEL. ALL BROKERS INVOLVED IN THIS TRANSACTION HAVE AN AGENCY RELATIONSHIP WITH THE SELLER(S).

The foregoing paragraph appeared in a DuPage Board of REALTORS® preprinted form contract that was recently submitted to one of the authors of this text. The blank space containing the rider numbers had been filled in by the selling salesperson. As expected, rider 401 was a financing contingency, rider 407 a buyer's existing home sale contingency, 412 a home-inspection contingency, and 417 an interest-bearing earnest money account authorization. But what about fax? Was this a new DuPage rider? A hurried phone call to Robert Dougherty of the DuPage Board disclosed that the fax rider was not an approved form and that he knew of no boards that had adopted a fax provision or rider. Temporarily, this was the end of the story.

Two months later, while in the process of preparing this publication, we contacted the managing broker of the office that had prepared the contract to inquire as to the identity of the author of the rider. That conversation indicated why this chapter and continuing education are so important to the public and to the professional.

In a nutshell, several if not many real estate firms in DuPage County and elsewhere have been begging their Boards for a facsimile rider or facsimile paragraph. Since such a form may be months or years away from approval, these firms have adopted whatever fax rider they felt seemed to be the best of those that were "floating around." Neither the broker we spoke with nor anyone on her staff had had the form reviewed by an attorney, and she confessed that she had no idea as to the adequacy or inadequacy of the rider adopted. She knew that she and her staff were violating the *Quinlan Tyson* decision on a daily basis, and half apologetically and half defensively she suggested that they had deemed it necessary to adopt a fax rider to efficiently carry on their practice. Besides, many other firms were doing it.

On a daily basis you have to choose to either obey the rules and regulations relating to your practice or risk a tainted reputation and/or financial loss. Let's make a deal that the courts will enforce and that won't jeopardize our professional standing. This chapter will quickly take you through the provisions of the License Act and Rules that relate to your day-to-day contracts, and then it will focus on *Quinlan Tyson* and so-called safe fax techniques.

INTRODUCTION

Contracts and contract law are an integral part of every businessperson's day. From the simplest transaction, such as getting a haircut, to the most complex corporate merger, the contract is the hub of the business wheel. It should come as no surprise, then, that the License Act and Rules govern some of the licensee's most important contracts, which are the listing contract, employment contract, and sales contract. Surprisingly, the degree of control exerted by the license laws over an agent's contracts is relatively slight.

We will approach the regulation of contracts in chronological order as they would affect the career of a newly licensed salesperson, which would be as follows:

Employment Agreement—This is the first contract a salesperson must have before he or she may even claim to be in the real estate business.
Listing Contract—This is the contract that creates the salesperson's inventory.
Sales Contract—A majority of salespeople earn a living putting this contract together.
Miscellaneous—There are several miscellaneous restrictions of which a licensee must be aware. They relate to blank spaces, delivery of copies of contracts, and alterations.

EMPLOYMENT (SPONSOR) AGREEMENTS

Most employment situations do not require a written agreement. The parties orally come to an understanding as to wages, job description, benefits, etc., and proceed to perform the contract. Why then should the relationship be different in the real estate profession? The rationale for requiring written agreements in real estate is not dissimilar to the reasons we have for the statute of frauds. The public's interest is protected by the apprentice system whereby a salesperson conducts business under the supervision of a more experienced and presumably more knowledgeable broker. The statute of frauds was enacted to prevent fraud through perjured testimony relating to an oral contract. The legislature has concluded that the terms and conditions of the broker/sales associate relationship is of vital interest to the protection of the public and should be in writing to prevent fraud through perjured testimony.

For example, a salesperson has produced a buyer for a property that will bring in a $100,000 commission. The broker fires the salesperson, collects the commission, and then falsely testifies in court that he and the sales associate had agreed that no commission would be earned or paid after termination of their relationship. The other partners likewise perjure themselves by corroborating the false testimony.

The requirement of the written agreement also provides evidence of the broker's and salesperson's compliance with other rules and regulations relating to the issuance of sponsor cards, payment of commissions, and responsibility for the salesperson's actions. Rule 1450.60 sets forth the requirements for an employment contract and is relatively straightforward. All brokers who employ the services of another broker or salesperson must have an agreement that:
- is written;
- is dated;
- is signed by both parties; and
- sets forth the duties, compensation, and supervisory details surrounding their association.

In the event an associate is hired to manage an office, the agreement must so indicate and additionally set forth the address of the branch office, where a copy of the signed employment agreement must be kept and made available for inspection.

FIG 2-1   CHECKLIST FOR EMPLOYMENT (SPONSOR) AGREEMENT

PRELIMINARY MATTERS

- **Recitals**—most important contracts start out with a series of "whereas" clauses setting forth considerations leading to the agreement, such as the desire to associate with each other, and other matters, such as proper licensure.
- **Date and Parties**—mandated by Rule 1450.60.
- **Term of Agreement**—the agreement may be for an indefinite term, for a one-year term, or for any other period the parties agree to.
- **Independent Contractor Status**—from the broker's perspective this is a critically important provision, because the broker generally wants to make certain that the IRS views the sales associate as an independent contractor rather than an employee. A managing broker would not customarily be an independent contractor.
- **Mediation**—intraoffice disputes are often submitted to a committee set up for such purposes.

BROKER'S UNDERTAKINGS

- **Representations and Warranties**—here the broker generally blows his or her own horn about the broker's reputation for honesty, etc.
- **Office Services**—provisions are normally inserted providing the associate with access to all of the firm's equipment, stationery, and office facilities subject to reasonable limitations.
- **Compliance with Laws and Ethics**—the broker undertakes to comply with all local, state, and national laws and the ethics of professional organizations and associations.
- **Commission Payments**—a very important topic to the associate is the subject of when commissions are earned, payable, and at what rate. Often the commission splits are set forth in a separate document.

SALES ASSOCIATE'S UNDERTAKINGS

- **Soliciting Sales, Listings, and Management**—the stock provisions relating to sales, listings, and leasing are summarized in a job description.
- **Expenses**—other than the office services provided by the broker, typically the sales associate is responsible for everything else.
- **Liability Insurance**—the associate agrees to secure such insurance, with specified limits, naming the broker as an additional insured.
- **Compliance with Laws and Ethics**—the associate undertakes to comply with all local, state, and national laws and the ethics of professional organizations and associations.

- **Restrictions on Activities After Termination**—any type of covenant not to compete can be disastrous to the associate but extremely and unfairly beneficial to the broker—WATCH OUT!

TERMINATION

- **With Cause**—the relationship is typically terminated immediately if either party has just cause.
- **Without Cause**—the relationship is normally terminable upon advance written notice of a specified number of days.
- **Effects on Commissions and Listings**—critically important to both parties and a clause to be either read or prepared with great care.

BOILERPLATE PROVISIONS

- **Notices**—sets forth the manner of and an address for mailing notices.
- **Changes**—generally requires that any amendment must be in writing and signed.
- **Law Applicable**—Illinois law should control.
- **Validity**—if one paragraph is invalid, the rest of the contract will not be affected.
- **Heirs and Assigns**—the benefits will pass to the respective party's heirs or estate.
- **Nonassignable**—the contract may be assigned by the broker but not by the associate.
- **Trademark and Name**—brokers holding franchises will set forth the rules and regulations regarding the use of the name/mark.
- **Signatures**—the document must be signed by both parties.
- **Extensions**—to avoid tax and regulatory problems, automatic extensions on a month-to-month basis are common.

ADDITIONAL CONSIDERATIONS

Provisions addressing the following items are important, but more often than not they are left out of the contract and covered in a separate document, such as an office policies and procedures manual.

- **Training**
- **Continuing Education**
- **Floor Time**
- **MLS Membership**
- **Advertising**
- **Agent-Owned Sales/Listings**
- **Errors & Omissions**—(Malpractice Insurance)

There is no such thing as a standard, uniform, approved, or otherwise customarily used employment agreement. The form is prepared by the broker and as a general rule will contain provisions favoring the firm and should be negotiated where possible and necessary to effect a fair and equitable arrangement.

Figure 2-1 contains a checklist of the items normally covered in an employment agreement. A brief summary of the typical arrangement follows each item. Since presumably every participant in a continuing education program has entered into one or more employment agreements, the checklist of customarily covered topics is offered primarily for the few readers who may have overlooked the requirements of a written agreement or who may be reading this publication for purposes other than continuing their real estate education.

LISTING AGREEMENTS

Prior to the adoption of new rules, open listings could be oral agreements, but all exclusive listings (exclusive right to sell and exclusive agency) were required to be in writing and conform to other requirements set forth in the rules. The rules that became effective in July 1991 no longer require any listing agreement to be written. If, however, a listing is reduced to writing, Rule 1450.70 requires that the agreement set forth:
- the list price
- the agreed basis (percentage) or amount of commission
- the time the commission is payable
- the duration of the agreement
- the names of the parties (broker and seller)
- an identification of listed property (address, location, or legal description)
- the signature of the parties
- a provision indicating that the amount of commission or time of payment may not be altered unless the alteration is made in writing and signed by the parties
- a provision clearly stating that it is illegal for either the owner or broker to refuse to display or sell to any person because of his or her race, color, religion, national origin, sex, handicap, or familial status

The Act and Rules also include the following provisions:
- A *written* listing must have a specific termination date and, except for "protection periods," may not contain an automatic extension clause. A listing that violates this restriction is void and a commission will not be awarded by a court.
- If a listing agreement for a residential property of four units or less provides for a protection period subsequent to its termination date, the agreement must provide that no commission or fee will be due and owing if, during the protection period, a valid written listing agreement is entered into with another licensed broker.
- If the terms of the listing agreement are such that seller may not receive the earnest money deposit, in the event of a purchaser's default, a statement to this effect shall appear in the listing agreement, and in letters larger than those generally used in the listing agreement.

PURCHASE AND SALE AGREEMENTS

Other than restrictions placed on a licensee under the *Quinlan Tyson* court decision (discussed at length below), the only provisions of the License Act and Rules that relate directly to sales contracts are Rules 1450.70(c) and 1450.80(d). They simply state:

> *No licensee shall use Sale Contract forms that change previously agreed commission payment terms unless seller and listing agent agree to such changes in a written*

memorandum separate from the Sale Contract. Any such Sale Contract forms may state that a commission is to be paid to a named licensee pursuant to a separate agreement.

and

All forms used by licensees intended to become binding real estate contracts shall clearly state this in the heading in large bold print. No licensee shall use a form designated Offer to Purchase when it is intended that such form be a binding real estate contract.

CONTRACTUAL MISCELLANY

Rule 1450.80 contains a number of requirements that relate to written contracts in general. These may be summarized as follows:

- **Blank spaces**—contracts or other documents relating to a real estate transaction must not contain any blank spaces to be filled in after signing or initialing.
- **Alterations**—no addition to, deletion from, or alteration of any signed contract or other document relating to a real estate transaction without the written, telefax, or telegraphic consent or direction from all signatories. No licensee shall process any contract or other document that has been altered after being signed, unless each addition, deletion, or alteration is signed or initialed by all signatories at the time of such addition, deletion, or alteration.
- **Delivery of copies**—a true copy of the original or corrected contract or other document relating to a real estate transaction shall be hand-delivered or mailed within 24 hours of the time of signing or initialing such original or correction to the person signing or initialing any such contract or other document.

THE *QUINLAN TYSON* CASE

At what point does the practice of real estate become the practice of law? Courts and legislative bodies have wrestled with this issue for years and are expected to continue the quest for an exact long-lasting answer for years to come. In Illinois, the *Quinlan Tyson* decision is critically important to the real estate professional, but it hasn't forever settled the related issues. In the 1966 case of *Chicago Bar Association et al. v. Quinlan and Tyson, Inc.*, 34 Ill.2d 116 (1966), the Illinois Supreme Court found that real estate licensees could lawfully complete preprinted forms in general use in the area of the broker's practice but that only lawyers were entitled to prepare additional clauses and conveyancing documents.

At the time of the Quinlan Tyson circuit court hearing, 23 salespersons and three brokers were employed by the firm. The Chicago Bar Association complained that Quinlan Tyson permitted its staff to fill out preprinted contracts, to draft revisions to the preprinted contract, to draft contracts for which a preprinted form was not available, and to prepare deeds, bills of sale, closing statements, and such other documents as were required to consummate a given transaction.

The circuit court ruled that all the conduct in the complaints—except for the filling in of blanks in a customarily used preprinted form contract—constituted the practice of law, and accordingly, it enjoined the further unlawful practice of law. The appellate court disagreed with the part of the circuit court's decision that permitted the filling in of blanks on customarily used preprinted contracts, but it affirmed the trial court's decision on the other specified practices.

THE STUDY OF CASE DECISIONS

The Supreme Court's opinion, including the strong dissenting opinion by Justice Underwood (Figures 2-2 and 2-3) should be studied and understood by all licensees. It is reprinted on the following two pages. Prior to studying the case, however, the following excerpt from Professor Karl Llewellyn's *The Bramble Bush* will be helpful in acquainting the novice with the study of case law:

> *The first thing to do with an opinion, then, is read it. The next thing is to get clear the actual decision, the judgment rendered. Who won, the plaintiff or defendant? And watch your step here. You are after in first instance the plaintiff and defendant below, in the trial court. In order to follow through what happened you must therefore first know the outcome below; else you do not see what was appealed from, nor by whom. You now follow through in order to see exactly what further judgment has been rendered on appeal. The stage is then cleared of form—although of course you do not yet know all that these forms mean, that they imply. You can turn now to what you want peculiarly to know. Given the actual judgments below and above as your indispensable framework—what has the case decided, and what can you derive from it as to what will be decided later?*
>
> *You will be looking, in the opinion, or in the preliminary matter plus the opinion, for the following: a statement of the facts the court assumes; a statement of the precise way the question has come before the court—which includes what the plaintiff wanted below, and what the defendant did about it, the judgment below, and what the trial court did that is complained of; then the outcome on appeal, the judgment; and, finally the reasons this court gives for doing what it did. This does not look so bad. But it is much worse than it looks.*
>
> *For all our cases are decided, all our opinions are written, all our predictions, all our arguments are made, on certain four assumptions. They are the first presuppositions of our study. They must be rutted into you till you can juggle with them standing on your head and in your sleep.*
> *1. The court must decide the dispute that is before it. It cannot refuse because the job is hard, or dubious, or dangerous.*
> *2. The court can decide only the particular dispute which is before it. When it speaks to that question it speaks ex cathedra, with authority, with finality, with an almost magic power. When it speaks to the question before it, it announces law, and if what it announces is new, it legislates, it makes the law. But when it speaks to any other question at all, it says mere words, which no man needs to follow. Are such words worthless? They are not. We know them as judicial dicta; when they are wholly off the point at issue we call them obiter dicta—words dropped along the road, wayside remarks. Yet even wayside remarks shed light on the remarker. They must be very useful in the future to him, or to us. But he will not feel bound to them, as to his ex cathedra utterance. They came not hallowed by a Delphic frenzy. He may be slow to change them; but not so slow as in the other case.*
> *3. The court can decide the particular dispute only according to a general rule which covers a whole class of like disputes. Our legal theory does not admit of single decisions standing on their own. If judges are free, are indeed forced, to decide new cases for which there is no rule, they must at least make a new rule as they decide. So far, good. But how wide, or how narrow, is the general rule in this particular case? That is a troublesome matter. The practice of our case-law, however, is I think fairly stated thus: it pays to be suspicious of general rules which look too wide; it pays to go slow in feeling certain that a wide rule has been laid down at all, or that, if seemingly laid down, it will be followed. For there is a fourth accepted canon:*
> *4. Everything, everything, everything, big or small, a judge may say in an opinion, is to be read with primary reference to the particular dispute, the particular question before him. You are not to think that the words mean what they might if they stood alone. You are to have your eye on the case in hand, and to learn how to interpret all that has been said merely as a reason for deciding that case that way.*

BROKER LAWYER ACCORD

Subsequent to the *Quinlan Tyson* decision, the Illinois Association of Real Estate Boards, the Chicago Real Estate Board, the Chicago Bar Association, and the Illinois State Bar Association entered into an agreement known as

FIG 2-2

34 Ill.2d 116
The CHICAGO BAR ASSOCIATION et al.,
Appellees,
v.
QUINLAN AND TYSON, INC., Appellant.
No. 39131.
Supreme Court of Illinois.
January 25, 1966
As Modified on Denial of Rehearing
March 23, 1966

PER CURIAM:

The Chicago Bar Association filed a complaint in the circuit court of Cook County to enjoin a real-estate brokerage firm, Quinlan and Tyson, Inc., from engaging in the unauthorized practice of law. After a lengthy hearing before a master of chancery it was found that the activities in question, performed in connection with negotiating purchases and sales of real estate for customers, constitute the practice of law. A decree was entered as prayed, except that the defendant was permitted to fill in the blanks of customary offer forms and contract forms as a necessary incident to its business. Upon review in the appellate court that part of the decree was reversed which allowed the filling in of forms, the court holding that none of the challenged services could be performed by persons not licensed to practice law. (*Chicago Bar Association v. Quinlan and Tyson*, 53 Ill.App.2d 388, 203 N.E.2d 131.) We have granted leave to appeal. The Illinois State Bar Association, the Chicago Real Estate Board and others have appeared and filed briefs as *amici curiae*.

The defendant is a corporation employing some fifty or sixty persons of which three are licensed real-estate brokers and twenty-three are licensed real-estate salesmen. In conducting its business defendant prepares offers to purchase real estate, draws contracts of purchase and sale, prepares deeds and other instruments necessary to clear or transfer title, and supervises the closing of the transaction. No separate fee is charged for these services, the defendant's compensation consisting solely of brokerage commissions.

The documents ordinarily used—consisting of the contract of sale, the deed, bill of sale for personalty, escrow agreement, application for a mortgage and affidavits waiving possible objections to title—come in standardized forms which defendant's brokers, real-estate salesmen and office personnel fill out for the parties involved. The forms are completed by inserting pertinent factual information and by deleting or striking out portions which do not apply. The forms themselves have been drawn or composed by lawyers.

Defendant contends such services do not amount to the practice of law because their performance by real-estate men has become an established custom and no harm is shown to have resulted. It is argued that they are a necessary incident of the real-estate business and that the filling in of these forms is a simple matter, for which ordinary business intelligence is sufficient. Relied upon also is the assertion that no compensation is charged for the service. Cited and discussed, State by State, are decisions from other jurisdictions tending to support the position taken by the defendant.

We have considered the authorities referred to but find it unnecessary to discuss them at length. The question is not one of first impression in this State. It was settled by our decision in *People ex rel. Illinois State Bar Association v. Schafer*, 404 Ill. 45, 87 N.E.2d 773, where a licensed real-estate broker was held in contempt of court for preparing contracts, deeds, notes and mortgages in transactions for which he received a broker's commission. This court found unacceptable the contention that the drawing of such instrument was proper because done in connection with his real-estate business. Rejected also was the argument which considers those acts to be more or less mechanical and routine, requiring no legal knowledge or skill. We pointed out (at p. 54, 87 N.E.2d at p. 777) that "Those who prepare instruments which affect titles to real estate have many points to consider. A transaction which at first seems simple may upon investigation be found to be quite involved. One who merely fills in certain blanks when other pertinent information should be elicited and considered is rendering little service but is acting in a manner calculated to produce trouble."

Except for the matter of filling in blanks on the customary preliminary contract-of-sale form, which we shall hereinafter discuss, we agree with the appellate court that the *Schafer* case is not distinguishable from the case at bar. The fact that other kinds of unauthorized practice were also involved in that case does not affect the holding. Nor are we convinced from defendant's arguments that this authority should be overruled. It is not decisive that defendant is compensated only by its commission, making no special charge for the services in question; nor is it relevant that the services are customarily provided by real-estate men and that no identifiable harm is proved to have ensued. As the appellate court pointed out, it is the character of the acts themselves that determines the issue. If by their nature they require a lawyer's training for their proper performance it does not matter that there may have been a widespread disregard of the requirement or that considerations of business expediency would be better served by a different rule.

We think, however, that in one respect the prohibition in the appellate court's opinion is too broad. In the *Schafer* case this court did not in so many words discuss the preliminary or earnest money contract form, nor did we specifically condemn the mere filling in of the blanks on such forms. The decree of the trial court in the case at bar, permitting real-estate brokers to fill in the blanks of whatever form of such contract is customarily used in the community and to make appropriate deletions from such contract to conform to the facts, is approved. In the usual situation where the broker is employed to find a purchaser he performs this service when he produces a prospect ready, willing and able to buy upon the terms proposed by the seller. (See *Fox v. Ryan*, 240 Ill. 391, 88 N.E. 974.) The execution of an offer or preliminary contract is an evidencing or recording of this service in bringing together the buyer and seller. It coincides with the job the broker was employed to perform and which he is licensed to perform, and in practice it marks the point at which he becomes entitled to his commission. It seems reasonable therefore that he be authorized to draft this offer or preliminary contract, where this involves merely the filling in of blank forms. *Keys Co. v. Dade County Bar Ass'n* (Fla.1950), 46 So.2d 605.

In *Gustafson v. V. C. Taylor & Sons*, 138 Ohio St. 392, 35 N.E.2d 435, a real-estate broker followed the practice of filling in the blanks of a printed "offer to purchase" form which, like those involved in the case at bar, had been prepared by a regularly admitted attorney-at-law. In a suit to enjoin this as unauthorized practice of law the court held that where the broker did nothing more than fill in simple factual material such as the date, price, name of the purchaser, location of the property, date of giving possession and duration of the offer he was not engaging in the practice of law. It was pointed out that such services require no more than ordinary business intelligence and do not require the skill peculiar to one trained and experienced in the law. The *Gustafson* case was cited and fully states in the opinion of this court in the *Schafer* case, where we proceeded to say that if a particular service performed by the broker "requires legal skill or knowledge, or more than ordinary business intelligence, it constitutes the practice of law" but that "when filling in blanks as directed he may not by that simple act be practicing law, * * *." We think, therefore, that the broker may properly fill in the usual form of earnest money contract or offer to

FIG 2-3

purchase where this involves merely the supplying of simple factual data.

But when the broker has secured the signatures on the usual form of preliminary contract or offer to purchase, completed by the insertion of necessary factual data, he has fully performed his obligation as broker. The drawing or filling in of blanks on deeds, mortgages and other legal instruments subsequently executed requires the peculiar skill of a lawyer and constitutes the practice of law. Such instruments are often muniments of title and become matters of permanent record. They are not ordinarily executed and delivered until after title has been examined and approved by the attorney for the purchaser. Their preparation is not incidental to the performance of brokerage services but falls outside the scope of the broker's function. *Commonwealth v. Jones & Robins*, 186 Va. 30, 41 S.E.2d 720; *Washington State Bar Ass'n v. Washington Ass'n of Realtors*, 41 Wash.2d 697, 251 P.2d 619.

The defendant and the real-estate board *amici* argue that all the forms in question are so standardized that only ordinary business intelligence is required to complete them. If the question were merely one of skill in filling out forms the argument would be persuasive. But more is involved than this simple operation and the question cannot realistically be viewed in such isolation. The legal problems involved often depend upon the context in which the instrument is placed, and only a lawyer's training gives assurance that they will be identified or pointed out. The mere completion of a form can readily be done by a stenographer. But it requires a lawyer's advice to determine whether it will accomplish the desired result under all the circumstances. As this court emphasized in the *Schafer* case, 404 Ill. at p. 52, 87 N.E.2d at p. 777 quoting from a Missouri decision: "'Any one who wants to pay the price may purchase a set of form books and read and copy them. He may use them in his own business if he so desires. But when he advises others for a consideration, that this or that is the law, or that this form or that is the proper form to be used in a certain transaction, then he is doing all that a lawyer does when a client seeks his advice'."

Drafting and attending to the execution of instruments relating to real-estate titles are within the practice of law, and neither corporations nor any other persons unlicensed to practice the profession may engage therein. (*People ex rel. Illinois State Bar Association v. People Stock Yards State Bank*, 344 Ill. 462, 176 N.E. 901.) Nor does the fact that standardized forms are usually employed make these services an incident of the real-estate broker business. Many aspects of law practice are conducted through the use of forms, and not all of the matters handled require extensive investigation of the law. But by his training the lawyer is equipped to recognize when this is and when it is not the case. Neither counsel nor *amici* have suggested any practicable way in which an exception to the general rule can be made where only the use of forms is involved, or where the transaction is a "simple" one. Mere simplicity cannot be the basis for drawing boundaries to the practice of a profession. A pharmacist, for example, might be competent to prescribe for many of the simpler ailments, but it takes a medical background to recognize when the ailment is simple. Protection of the public requires that only licensed physicians may prescribe or treat for any ailment, regardless of complexity or simplicity. And protection of the public requires a similar approach when the practice of law is involved.

The judgment of the appellate court is affirmed except insofar as it reversed in part the judgment of the circuit court. In that respect it is reversed. The decree of the circuit court is affirmed.

Appellate court affirmed in part and reversed in part; circuit court affirmed.

UNDERWOOD, Justice (dissenting):

In resolving the very difficult questions presented in this case this court has compromised the differing positions of the parties in a result with which I cannot agree. Most of the reasons compelling my dissent are adequately treated in the well considered opinion of the appellate court (53 Ill.App.2d 388, 203 N.E.2d 131), and it would add little for me to restate them here. There is, however, one undiscussed facet of the many serious questions requiring informed consideration by the parties to every real-estate transaction before a contract is signed.

Increasingly apparent in recent years is the fact that every real-estate purchase and sale involves far-reaching tax consequences of a character partially or wholly unknown to the ordinary buyer and seller. As to such property the dollar amount of estate, inheritance and income tax liabilities of the parties will be determined largely by the manner in which the transaction is consummated. The year in which it occurs, the manner in which title is taken, whether it is a cash or installment sale or an exchange of properties will all substantially affect tax liability, not only of the parties but of their estates and heirs. As a result, such tax obligations may be increased, diminished or completely eliminated, depending on the decisions made by the parties as to the terms of their contract.

The opinion of this court permits real estate brokers to prepare contracts for the purchase and sale of real estate by "filling the blanks" in, and making "appropriate deletions" from form contracts customarily used in the community and to secure the signatures of the parties thereon. It prohibits explanation by the brokers of the provisions of the contract and bars them from preparing any other documents subsequent to the contract. Actually, the contract between the parties is the fundamental instrument in a real-estate transaction and determines their future rights and obligations. It seems to me somewhat anomalous to permit the broker to prepare the controlling agreement but not those which it controls. Be that as it may, the practical result of this decision will be a binding contract executed by the parties without informed consideration of the serious questions involved except in those instances where the buyer or seller is aware of the inherent hazards and consults his attorney before signing the contract.

The desired objective here is neither the preservation of business for lawyers nor commissions for brokers—it is the protection of the public. In my opinion this is best accomplished by entrusting the preparation of real-estate contracts to those trained to recognize the substantial questions involved and competent to advise the parties regarding what, in many instances, is the most important investment they will ever make.

For these reasons, as well as those set forth in the appellate court opinion, the judgment of that court should be affirmed.

the Broker Lawyer Accord. The Accord endeavored to spell out in more detail the rules of lawyers and brokers in real estate transactions, to round off the jagged edges of the lawyer/broker relationship, and to provide a mechanism for the resolution of questions and disputes.

Due to a threatened antitrust suit by the federal government, the Accord was abolished in 1983. During the Accord's brief existence, the relationship between the two professions improved dramatically. Although not precedents for future court decisions, the opinions issued and decisions rendered by the Accord's committee (two members from each organization) are useful to consider and may carry some weight in future court decisions.

The committee found the following practices not within the province of a broker:
- Completion and use of individualized forms of contracts or riders
- Completion of land contracts (articles of agreement for warranty deed/installment contracts)
- Obtaining signatures to a contract that one of the parties' attorneys had expressly disapproved
- Preparing closing statements
- Conducting closings
- Offering advice as to the effect of closing documents
- Preparation of forms under the direction of a lawyer or for a lawyer's approval

THE *HOMESTEAD* CASE

There have been several appellate level cases since the *Quinlan Tyson* decision; however, none of these cases provides further direction as to the questions left unanswered. Although not appealed (perhaps judiciously so), a circuit court case of statewide notoriety was decided in Cook County, in a 1977 case entitled *South Suburban Bar Association v. Homestead Realty*. Similar to Quinlan Tyson, Homestead Realty used contract-to-purchase forms published by two title companies. The forms had large blank spaces which the firm's employees took advantage of by filling in deal-specific provisions. Additionally, the salespeople, besides dissuading customers from seeking legal representation, prepared closing statements and conducted closings. The court issued an injunction prohibiting the firm and its employees from advising against legal representation, filling in large blank spaces in preprinted contracts, preparing closing statements, transmitting title clearance documents, and giving opinions relating to the legal significance of any documents. Perhaps of most significance, it defined the permitted extent of filling in blanks as "factual data in spaces provided for between two words..."

Issues that neither the courts nor the Accord committee addressed were: what was a form customarily in use in a community and from where may that form originate? We don't pretend to have the answers; however, with the abandonment of the Accord came a bevy of ad hoc local bar/REALTOR® committees that meet on a regular basis to prepare revisions to the "local board's contract." As these preprinted contracts mushroom with riders and optional "check-off" provisions, we come closer and closer to another *Quinlan Tyson* donnybrook that neither profession should want to risk. The risk of another Supreme Court case is that gray may become black or white.

BLACK, WHITE, OR GRAY?

Sister states have handled cases similar to *Quinlan Tyson* in one of three ways. For discussion purposes, we'll call them black, white, and gray. In the black states, brokers are effectively barred from preparing any forms whatsoever that will become binding upon the parties and are, of course, not permitted to prepare any conveyancing documents. In the sister states we shall call white, the broker is permitted to prepare any and all forms necessary to fully consummate a transaction—including deeds, closing statements, and the like. In the gray states, there is some sharing of responsibility.

Because of a Supreme Court case in Arizona effectively barring brokers from preparing any contracts, the real estate profession was successful in having a constitutional amendment and legislation passed that effectively shut the door on an Arizona attorney's residential real estate practice. In other states, brokers are standing in line at lawyers' doors waiting for their contracts to be drafted. Illinois has a shade of gray that was working just fine when the "customarily preprinted" contracts were only two legal-sized preprinted pages of reasonable-sized type. The four-page multiple-choice contract that we now see in many areas of the state is a disaster in the making unless we wake up and provide a solution before nine gray-haired justices in black robes concur with the dissenting justice in *Quinlan Tyson* and decide that you can't give a form book to a 21-year-old with 30 hours of prelicensing education and expect no harm to the public when he or she improperly fills in paragraphs or riders numbered 892 and 1096.

The Supreme Court did not envision that, for the sake of peace and harmony, the legal and real estate professions would take advantage of its decision—and, more importantly, the consumer—by stretching its permissive authority to the extent now evident. The solutions for the avoidance of another major collision between these two professions are suggested below.

Will the fact that bar and REALTOR® groups have put these complicated form books (contracts) together favorably impress the Supreme Court? We think not. The monkey see, monkey do defense was already addressed by the Supreme Court in that portion of the *Quinlan Tyson* decision where it is stated: "It does not matter that there may have been a widespread disregard of the requirement or that considerations of business expediency would be better served by a different rule."

Several years ago, one of the best-selling nonfiction books was *The Peter Principle*. The theory of the book is that each of us rises to a level of incompetency. This idea has practical application to the subject matter under consideration. There are some brokers who could far outdistance most attorneys in putting together a contract for the sale of a 25-story office building. Yet those same brokers, when purchasing for their own account, recognize the need for greater competency and secure the services of a competent attorney.

After 30 hours of prelicense education and a training program of uncertain duration, a new licensee is authorized to fill in the blanks in a contract for the sale of real estate that will probably be sold for a sum in excess of $100,000. In many communities along Chicago's North Shore, such as Highland Park, sales prices in excess of $1,000,000 are commonplace.

Most lawyers don't like the attorney review contingency, and most real estate agents don't either, especially the ones who have the skill and knowledge to recognize precisely when and where to seek the assistance or recommend the assistance of legal counsel. The difficulty with today's multipaged contract, however, is that the less experienced, skillful and knowledgeable practitioners don't know at what point they have reached their level of incompetency such that their completion of a contract will be detrimental to the public.

We, your authors, like gray. We have seen a marked improvement in the interprofessional relationship since 1966 and submit that lawyers and real estate professionals should work together *professionally*. Members of both professions must recognize their limitations, not individually but as a whole.

WHO VIOLATES *QUINLAN TYSON?*
We have yet to find a licensee who has not violated the restrictions placed on a real estate licensee by the court's decisions, especially if one strictly construes the various holdings, dissenting opinions, *dicta* and *obiter dicta*. For instance, early on in all standard preprinted contracts is a provision for the insertion of the amount of earnest money the buyer will deposit. The licensee who claims never to have explained the consequences of filling in this "blank space between two words" is fibbing. Rarely will a first-time buyer know all there is to know about earnest money deposits and will probably ask a question or two such as, "If I don't get financing, will I get my earnest money back?" We know of no real estate agent who would correctly respond to such a question with, "I would suggest that you speak with an attorney because I am not permitted to explain the contract to you." A proper and complete answer to such a question would take the licensee well into the realm of practicing law. A lawyer might spend several minutes explaining the necessity of being punctual in making the loan application(s),

the duty to notify the seller of his or her inability to procure financing, the possibility that the seller will not authorize the release of the earnest money, and the further possibility that the broker will convert the deposit. The buyer should also be advised that the legal costs (attorney's fees and court costs) incurred in a lawsuit seeking a refund may exceed the amount of the recovery.

When buyers ask, "If I don't get financing, will I get my earnest money back?" and when agents respond simply, "Yes, you will," they are not only violating the law, but also exposing themselves to lawsuits from buyers seeking the recovery of their earnest money, attorneys' fees, and possibly other damages (emotional—punitive) that may exceed the deposit by several times. Will the fact that every agent does a little explaining of the offer protect you? It will protect you about as well as it protected Quinlan Tyson, Homestead Realty, and all the other licensees who have been sued for malpractice. NO!

Old habits and common practices are hard to change, yet the practice of law by real estate licensees could be easily avoided through the distribution to consumers of Board booklets that explain the applicable Board form, explain the licensee's inability to advise a customer/client, and suggest that the early intervention of an attorney—before the offer is prepared—is far superior to his or her entry onto the scene after the damage is done.

AVOIDING BLACK OR WHITE

Only the Supreme Court can define what is and is not the practice of law. It must render decisions on a case-by-case basis. Only then may it legislate. The real estate profession may be regulated by legislation and administrative rules, and we suggest that for the sake of gray, consideration be given to the following possible solutions for keeping the peace:
- Supporting one state-approved form that, based on the minimum educational requirements for a real estate professional, can be competently completed
- Mandatory education in the use of the state-mandated form
- A rule requiring each managing broker to "sign off" on a contract before its submission
- Expanded prelicensing education requirements
- The distribution of a consumer booklet explaining the preprinted contract

The cynic may say that the Supreme Court's rulings are not protective of the public but of the legal profession's best interests. If so, do we want to chance our shade of gray, keeping in mind that the "customary contract" has quadrupled in size since *Quinlan Tyson*, whereas competence for entry into the real estate profession remains virtually unchanged?

The *Quinlan Tyson* decision and the issues addressed and left unanswered will undoubtedly be a continuing part of your continuing education for years to come. Hopefully, the trend of peaceful coexistence will continue. It will not continue, however, unless the professionals who are members of the ad hoc revision committees of real estate and lawyer boards recognize the *minimum* qualifications of the persons authorized to fill in the blanks and the dangers posed by further expansion of the customary form.

SAFE FAX

"Let's do lunch" has been replaced in corporate America by "fax it to me." In less than a decade, the facsimile machine has, in the eyes of most, become a necessity. Yet few if any businesses are making full use of this technology because of legal questions lawyers are quick to point out but somewhat slow to answer. The acronym C.Y.A. explains the delay in the fax machine's total acceptance.

Until such time as the major questions are addressed by several courts, appropriate contractual provisions are necessary to insure that one's reliance on a faxed document is justified. Ironically, as will be seen, if you don't rely on the fax, a risk will also be taken, i.e., we may be between a rock and a hard spot for years to come as these issues are sorted out. Meanwhile, our files will take up twice as much storage area as we save the fax, the transmission reports, and the "plain paper with ink" copy that may or may not be *the* original.

The two main issues that are delaying our wholesale acceptance of faxed transmissions are:
- **Statute of Frauds**—does the fax transmission comply with the statute of frauds?
- **Best Evidence Rule**—if litigation results, which document(s) will be admitted into evidence as "the original contract" or best evidence?

As of this writing, the only appellate level court case that sheds considerable light on the subject is a Canadian case from British Columbia. The court addressed these issues in holding that a faxed proxy was valid and enforceable.

STATUTE OF FRAUDS

In 1677, the English adopted a statute entitled "An Act for the Prevention of Frauds and Perjuries." Section 4 of the Act provided in pertinent part:

> *...no action shall be brought...upon any contract or sale of lands, tenements, or hereditaments, or any interest in or concerning them; ...unless the agreement upon which such action shall be brought, or some memorandum or note thereof, shall be in writing, and signed by the party to be charged therewith, or some other person therein to by him lawfully authorized.*

The Act is now known simply as the Statute of Frauds. Illinois as well as all other states, except Louisiana, have adopted statutes of frauds, many of which are virtually identical to the 1677 English Act.

The purpose of the Statute of Frauds was to prevent fraud that would be perpetrated on a defendant and the courts through perjured testimony. By requiring important contracts to be in writing and signed, perjured testimony (oftentimes bought and paid for) could not be used to prove a fraudulent oral contract. The writing and signature thus became indispensable to the proof of an agreement to sell real estate.

Illinois's Statute of Frauds can be found in Chapter 15 of the Illinois Revised Statutes. Section 2 of the Act provides:

> *No action shall be brought to charge any person upon any contract for the sale of lands, tenements or hereditaments or any interest in or concerning them, for a longer term than one year, unless such contract or some memorandum or note thereof shall be in writing, and signed by the party to be charged therewith, or some other person thereunto by him lawfully authorized in writing, signed by such party. This section shall not apply to sales for the enforcement of a judgment for the payment of money or sales by any officer or person pursuant to a judgment or order of any court in this State.*

It is doubtful that our courts will be called upon to rule whether a fax is a writing because they have already ruled that such things as telegrams, telexes, and Mailgrams are writings for purposes of the Statute of Frauds. The main issue expected to arise (and which has arisen already in a handful of cases in other states) is whether or not a faxed transmittal contains a signature.

A signature is not necessarily writing one's name. In its earliest state, a signature merely was a mark one adopted to show the source or authenticity of a writing, drawing, or other tangible object. Long before the origination of language as we know it, early humans were signing the art work in their caves. Because of illiteracy, infirmity, or choice, modern humans do not *write* their names as a signature. Evidence of this fact is regularly seen on a doctor's prescription for medicine. The pharmacist, accustomed to a doctor's hieroglyphics, does not send the customer back to the doctor for a readable written name.

The following excerpt should not only supply the answer to whether a signed fax is or will be acceptable in Illinois but should also provide support for the recommended fax paragraph offered below. In the case of *Witt v. Panek*, 408 Ill. 328, 97 N.E.2d 283 (1951), the Illinois Supreme Court stated:

> *There seems to be no dispute but what a grantor may, in some circumstances, execute a valid deed by signing his mark, or by having his hand guided when signing, or by directing a third party to affix his signature in his presence. In such cases the disposing capacity and the act of mind which are essential and efficient ingredients of the deed are the grantor's, who merely uses the hand of another, instead of his own, to do the physical act of making a written sign. (16 Am.Jur. 492, par. 95.) Language of similar purport was used by this court in* Kerr v. Russell, *69 Ill. 666. It is appellants' contention, however, that the deed here is a complete forgery, and not signed by Michael Witt, aided or unaided. In determining whether an attacking party has adduced proof sufficient to establish that the signature on a deed was in fact forged, the rule is that the record of conveyance and the certificate of acknowledgement can be overcome only by proof which is clear, convincing and satisfactory, and by disinterested witnesses.* Koepke v. Schumacher, *406 Ill. 93, 92 N.E.2d 152;* Finley v. Felter, *403 Ill. 372, 86 N.E.2d 188. The proof of forgery in the present case is limited to the opinions of the handwriting expert, and to the notary's repudiation of his official seal and act. While we find no case of a similar nature wherein the testimony of professional handwriting analysts has been considered, we have held that the opinion that a signature was a forgery, expressed by nonexperts familiar with a grantor's signature, is not sufficient to overcome a certificate of acknowledgement and prove forgery.*

The last portion of the court's decision suggests (in several writers' opinions, including ours) a foolproof method of assuring that an important contract is accepted by the courts: Have the document notarized before transmission.

Besides the unusual signatures mentioned above, the courts have accepted the following types of signatures:
- stamps
- typewritten
- engraved
- photographed
- a signature cut from one instrument and pasted on to another
- lithography
- bar codes

Whatever means or design one chooses to employ to represent himself or herself will probably be accepted by the courts.

Therefore, if a buyer signs an offer with a provision such as "I, [signature] John Doe, do hereby intentionally adopt as and for my signature the facsimile of my signature as produced by the facsimile machine receiving this document," there is little question that the issue of whether the document has been signed will be resolved in favor of the enforceability of the contract. Having the document notarized is extra protection, which, for the time being, wouldn't hurt.

BEST EVIDENCE RULE

In order to have a document, such as a lease or real estate contract, accepted by a court as evidence of the parties' agreement, the rules of evidence require the "best evidence." In the case of a contract, the best evidence is the original contract.

For example, a landlord is suing a tenant for his failure to properly account for and pay the appropriate percentage rent. The court will require production of the original signed lease. As noted above, depending on the manner in which the deal was made, the fax may be the original or the original may be the document whereon the pen and ink signature appears. In any event, until such time as the courts iron out the wrinkles in this area of the law and unless the parties agree otherwise, BOTH documents should be retained for their evidentiary value.

The best evidence rule also provides for less than best evidence (secondary evidence). If the original document, the best evidence, has been lost, stolen, or destroyed, the courts will accept secondary proof, such as photocopies or carbon copies. There is no question that the courts will permit the introduction of fax copies if the original is not available and providing the other requirements for its admission are likewise met (in legal parlors that is called laying the foundation), the discussion of which is not important for our purposes here but is most relevant to your office policies and practices.

When you transmit a signed offer across town and you receive a call back that the offer is accepted, what have you got? You may have a totally unenforceable contract, because your client's signature on the faxed document is not a "signature"—or you may have a contract that is only enforceable against your client because the other side has not signed the document. If the contract is enforceable, who has the original? The courts may say that the document with the manual signature is the original, or the contract received by facsimile is the original, or both are originals. Nevertheless, by simply faxing the document across town, you may have obligated your client to a deal that the other side may avoid. Several days later, if you receive an offer that is better than the first deal, what do you do if the faxed offer has not been returned or has been faxed back with signatures—but the contract with manual signatures is still in the mail? Your client may or may not be able to cancel the first deal.

If all this sounds confusing, how do you suppose it will be entangled in the event of litigation? We're as clueless as you are; however, we have a solution. The first solution is the least complicated but nullifies the major benefit of the telecommunications technology, which is the ease and speed with which one can make a deal. The easiest solution is to insert a paragraph on all fax cover sheets that recites:

> *The facsimile transmission that follows is not a binding offer, counteroffer, or contract. Only a document with the manually affixed signatures of the parties is intended to be and become a binding instrument, and neither party to a faxed transmission is justified in relying upon a faxed instrument.*

The use of this language in the cover sheet or stamped in or on the contract itself will assure that both sides should not rely on a facsimile. Therefore, if a better offer arrives before the "original" contract with manual signatures, the parties are free to act with full knowledge of their liabilities and responsibilities.

On the other hand, if the parties do want to do business over the phone, a fax rider or paragraph addressing the parties' intentions will, if properly drafted, undoubtedly be accepted and enforced by the courts. Such a rider appears in Figure 2-4. Each paragraph is designed to overcome a potential issue that might be raised as to the validity and enforceability of a faxed deal. The purposes behind each paragraph are as follows:

FIG 2-4

FACSIMILE RIDER

Attached to and made a part of Real Estate Purchase and Sale Agreement between _____ _____, as Seller, and _____ as Purchaser, for the premises commonly known as _____, _____ County, Illinois.

The parties hereto are desirous of facilitating the expeditious negotiation of a binding and enforceable contract for the purchase and sale of the real estate described above, and to that end agree that the parties' best interests will be served by the facsimile transmission of offers, counteroffers, and acceptances. In consideration of the foregoing, the parties hereto agree as follows:

A. Statute of Frauds - The document of which this Rider is a part and/or its several counterparts is a "writing" within the meaning and purview of Chapter 59 Illinois Revised Statutes paragraph 2 and the parties do therefore agree not to raise and do hereby waive such issue as a defense to the enforcement of the within contract.

B. Facsimile Signatures - The parties hereto intentionally adopt as and for their signatures including initials, the impression of their signatures electronically produced by a receiving facsimile machine. Further, the parties agree not to raise an issue as to the validity of a facsimile signature as a defense to the enforcement of the within contract and do hereby waive such issue.

C. Best Evidence - In the event this offer, counteroffer, or contract as the case may be, is offered into evidence, the original document for such purposes is the document(s) bearing the electronically produced signatures of the parties, the document electronically transmitted, and/or a true, accurate and correct photocopy of the aforedescribed documents.

D. Notary - To further authenticate the signatures of the parties, prior to transmitting an offer, counteroffer, or acceptance, the transmitting party's signature may be notarized in the space provided below.

E. Counterparts - The contract of which this Rider is a part may be executed in one or more counterparts, each of which is deemed to be an original hereof, and all of which shall together constitute one and the same instrument.

F. Notice - In addition to the methods of providing notice set forth in the main body of the document to which this Rider is appended, notice may be given by facsimile transmission to the parties' respective designated fax numbers set forth below.

G. Performance Documents - Any documents salient to either party's performance including but not limited to title commitments, surveys, payoff letters, insurance certificates, leases, and other similar documents required *prior* to the closing may be faxed; however, the originals thereof and all transfer documents including but not limited to deeds, bills of sale, affidavits of title, real estate transfer tax declarations, and alta statements shall not be deemed originals but shall be submitted in their customary and conventional form at the time of closing.

H. Conformance - Upon the request of either party, the parties hereto shall manually affix their signatures in the conventional manner to a duplicate copy of this document. In such event, such duplicate shall be and become a duplicate original contract.

I. Waiver Limitations - Nothing hereinabove contained shall be deemed to prevent a party from raising a defense as to the inducement for one's signature or any and all other defenses available to a party whose signature is affixed in a conventional manner. The intent and purpose of this Rider is to circumvent the purely technical issues peculiar to facsimile transmissions and the telecommunications technology and to enable the parties to rely upon the validity of any document transmitted or received in accordance with the above and foregoing provisions.

Buyer fax number: _____   Seller fax number: _____

Buyer(s)'s signature(s) and notarization   Seller(s)'s signature(s) and notarization

_____   _____

_____   _____

Buyer(s)'s signature(s) subscribed and sworn to before me   Seller(s)'s signatures subscribed and sworn to before me

this _____ day of _____, 19____.   this _____ day of _____, 19____.

_____   _____
                Notary Public   Notary Public

© 1992 Clarke R. Marquis. Reprinted with permission.

Prologue—The prologue clearly identifies that it is the intent of the parties to consummate a deal through facsimile transmissions.

Paragraph A—This paragraph removes from consideration the remote possibility that a claim will be made that a fax is not a writing.

Paragraph B—This paragraph clearly indicates that the parties' signatures are intended to be the facsimile reproductions made by the receiving facsimile device.

Paragraph C—In the event of litigation, several originals are available for purposes of producing evidence of the parties' deal.

Paragraph D—The authenticity of a signature is immeasurably aided by having the transmission document notarized. The solemnity of occasions calling for notarization also strengthens support for the parties' intentions. Note that the language used is "may," and therefore, if deemed necessary, the word "shall" could be substituted, thus mandating the notarization of any facsimile.

Paragraph E—This paragraph is advisable in case the preprinted contract to which the rider is attached lacks such a provision.

Paragraph F—The selling broker's fax number *should not* be designated as the buyer's fax number unless the selling broker is the *buyer's agent*. Otherwise, this paragraph should be self-explanatory.

Paragraphs G, H, and I—These paragraphs may avoid occasional difficulties; admittedly, however, they may be overkill.

Although your local Boards may not adopt a facsimile provision, the exhibited rider with minor alterations can be used for other purposes that are not precluded by the court's decision in the *Quinlan Tyson* case. It may adapted for use in transactions to which the broker/salesperson is a party, such as in a listing or management agreement. For example, your client is a thousand miles away. Mailing delays may cost you and your client a week or more of exposure to a hot market. Through slight revisions to the fax rider, you can take that listing this morning and have the planned open house this evening.

FINAL FAX

The primary purpose of the foregoing discussion is preventative medicine. Very few businesspeople have considered the ramifications of faxed documents because there have been so few lawsuits that discuss the related issues. Therefore, we blindly go about our business without the foggiest notion as to how to maximize our use of the fax machine, and at the same time, how to minimize our potential exposure to liability.

Those Boards that take the lead in adopting a clear-cut fax provision (either for it or against it) will assure that the parties represented know the effects of their fax transmittals. Without a fax provision one may have the displeasure of being the expensive test case in the trial and appellate courts.

REFERENCES, PLEASE??

Rather than field hundreds of phone calls for references, we offer the following list of authorities along with a short synopsis as to their scope and usefulness.

The Law of Electronic Commerce—EDI, Fax and E' Mail, Benjamin Wright, Little, Brown & Company, ISBN #0-31695632-5—over 400 pages of text and cases and the best, if not the only, comprehensive guide to electronic communications. One full chapter is devoted to fax law and offers checklists for office practices and other forms for use in maximizing the technology.

"Electronic Contracts: Are They Enforceable Under Article 2 of the UCC?" Gregory Johnson, *Software Law Journal*, Volume IV, pp. 247-269 (1991)—a comprehensive study with legal authorities supporting the use of EDI (a technology similar to fax) for use in transactions covered by the Uniform Commercial Code.

"Fax Pacts," Benjamin Wright, *Network World*, February 3, 1990, p. 69—summary of legal considerations, case decisions, and suggestions on fax usage.

Real Estate Law Report, Vol. 1, No. 1, Fall 1991, Sonnenschein, Nath, & Rosenthal, Attorneys At Law, Chicago, Illinois—concise summary of legal considerations in fax transmissions.

Bazak International v. Mast Industries, 73 N.Y.2d 113, 535 N.E.2d 633, 538 NYS2d 503 (1989)—a New York court case where faxed purchase orders were in dispute.

People v. Snyder, 181 Mich.App. 768, 449 N.W.2d 703 (1989)—an excellent case in support of faxed documents wherein a faxed search warrant was approved by a Michigan Appellate Court.

Calabrese v. Springer Personnel of New York, 141 Misc.2d 566, 534 NYS2d 83 (1988)—a New York court decision that upheld the service of court notices by fax.

Hessenthaler v. Farzin, 564 A2d 990 (1989)—a thorough discussion of the different forms a signature may take under the Statute of Frauds.

American Insurance Company v. First National Bank In St. Louis, 409 F2d 1387 (1969)—a leading case supporting the reliance on a photostatic copy of a document.

Beatty v. First Exploration Fund, 25 BCLR2d 377 (1988)—this is the British Columbian case referred to above that continues to be the most thorough discussion of facsimile law.

CASES TO JUDGE

1. Disciplinary proceedings were brought against an attorney for aiding in the unauthorized practice of law, which was an infraction of the Attorney's Code of Professional Responsibility. The attorney signed taxation valuation complaints that were either blank or not inspected, and transmitted complaints to a nonlawyer under circumstances where the attorney knew that the complaints would be filled out by the nonlawyer, filed with the county board of tax appeals, and that a nonlawyer would appear for the purposes of a hearing.

   Can a nonlawyer prepare and file real estate tax valuation complaints and appear before a county board of appeals for a hearing on such complaints? [*In Re Jiro Yamaguchi, Attorney, Respondent*, 118 Ill.2d 417, 515 N.E.2d 1235 (1987)]

2. James A. Floyd, an employee of the Cook County Housing Authority, a municipal corporation, filled in a preprinted form issued by the Circuit Court of Cook County and filed the complaint with the court. Following is the form that Floyd completed. (The words Floyd inserted appear in italics, with the balance of the words being the preprinted form.)

   "Complaint
   The plaintiff__ claim__ as follows:
   1. The plaintiff *is* entitled to the possession of the following described premises in the
      City of *Evanston, Illinois*.
      A dwelling consisting of Five (5) rooms with bath.
   2. The defendant *is* unlawfully withhold*ing* possession thereof from the plaintiff__. The plaintiff__ claim*s* possession of the property.
      s/ *James A. Floyd*
         Agent ~~Attorney~~ for plaintiff
   Address and telephone *1314 Wentworth Ave.—Chicago Heights, Illinois—757-7640*
   I, *James A. Floyd*, on oath state that I am the *Agent for* plaintiff in the above entitled action. The allegations in this complaint are true.
      s/*James A. Floyd*
   Signed and sworn to before me
   May 10, 1982
   s/ *Margaret T. Stoner*
      Notary Public"

   Did Floyd's action constitute the unauthorized practice of law? [*Housing Authority of Cook County v. Tonsul*, 115 Ill.App.3d 739, 450 N.E.2d 1248, 71 Ill.Dec. 369 (1983)]

36 Chapter 2 Contractual Regulations

3. Albert Wolfenberger, a real estate broker, received a jury award in the amount of $33,982 as a brokerage commission for his efforts to sell George Madison's 170-acre farm. The defendant, Madison, claimed on appeal that the real estate broker, as the seller's agent, owed seller a fiduciary duty to disclose all material facts that might affect the transaction, and that such duty was not honored in that the broker failed to inform the seller of the tax advantages of trading, rather than selling, his farm.

   Should the broker have disclosed such information, or is such information and advice prohibited by the *Quinlan Tyson* decision? [*Albert Wolfenberger v. George A. Madison et al.*, 43 Ill.App.3d 813, 357 N.E.2d 656 (1976)]

4. An insurance adjuster prepared and explained a release of claims to the victim of an automobile collision. The victim signed the release and settlement check with the understanding that he was only releasing the negligent driver and his insurance company from property damage claims and that the victim could still pursue his claim for personal injuries. The release was in fact a full and complete release of all claims.

   One of the issues in the court proceedings was whether the adjuster had practiced law by preparing a release of claims and offering advice on the legal consequences of signing the check and release.

   Did the adjuster violate *Quinlan Tyson*? [*Alvin P. Herman et al. v. Prudence Mutual Casualty Company et al.*, 41 Ill.2d 468 (1969)]

5. On January 30, Frederick Bliesener entered into a lease option arrangement and deposited $3,000 with the defendant, Baird & Warner. At the time the agreement was made, the listing agent for Baird & Warner knew that the lessor/seller was delinquent in his mortgage payments but did not disclose this fact to the lessee/buyer. In fact, a foreclosure suit had been filed three days prior to the signing of the lease/option; however, there was conflicting evidence as to whether the listing agent knew that suit had been filed.

   The lease/option was to commence on April 1; however, on March 7 the buyer decided to back out of the deal. Since the $3,000 deposit was given to the lessor/seller pursuant to the terms of the lease as advance rent, the buyer filed a lawsuit against the seller and the seller's broker, Baird & Warner, seeking a return of his $3,000 deposit. The trial court awarded a $3,000 judgment against Baird & Warner on the theory that they had failed to disclose the mortgage delinquency.

   On appeal, should the appellate court hold that the salesperson has a duty to disclose the fact that the seller was delinquent in his mortgage payments? [*Frederick W. Bliesener v. Baird & Warner*, 88 Ill.App.2d 383, (1967)]

10-QUESTION DIAGNOSTIC QUIZ

1. Which of the following are most likely to have violated *Quinlan Tyson*?
   A. Salesperson Wilson, who adds the following sentence to his independent contractor/sponsor agreement: "Salesperson Wilson shall be entitled to a commission on any listings sold by sponsoring broker subsequent to the termination of this agreement."
   B. Broker Thomas, who adds the following provision to the MLS Board's standard listing agreement: "Broker shall be entitled to a $1,000 bonus if the property is sold prior to October 1."
   C. Broker Davidson, who fills in the sentence, "Closing shall be on _____, 19___" with "the earlier of the 30th day following buyer's receipt of a written mortgage commitment, March 1, 1992, or sellers' closing on their new home."
   D. Salesperson Alverez, who obliterates (strikes out/deletes) the following provision in an offer: "A broker's commission shall be paid by seller to, or as directed by, the listing broker at the time of closing in accordance with seller's listing agreement."

2. A written listing agreement must contain each of the following, EXCEPT:
   A. a minimum selling price.
   B. a fixed term.
   C. the names and signatures of the parties.
   D. a description of the property.

3. An employment contract between a salesperson and a sponsoring broker must:
   A. contain a stated automatic expiration date.
   B. set forth all company policies and procedures.
   C. be dated.
   D. set forth a provision relating to the illegality of certain discriminatory housing practices.

4. In the event a broker/salesperson contract is terminated:
   A. the broker is prohibited from paying a commission earned prior to the termination directly to the salesperson.
   B. the salesperson is entitled to all earned commissions and commissions subsequently earned by the broker from the subsequent sale of the salesperson's listings.
   C. the salesperson may either terminate or take his or her listings to the new sponsoring broker.
   D. the contract, if specified, will control the salesperson's entitlement to further commissions.

5. Which of the following statements by a real estate licensee would most likely violate the *Quinlan Tyson* prohibitions?
   A. "I have no idea what a tenancy by the entirety says."
   B. "Paragraph 2 states, 'This contract is contingent upon purchaser obtaining a firm commitment for a purchase money mortgage loan in an amount of not less than $40,000.'"
   C. "I own my home as a joint tenant; however, I can't suggest which form of ownership will be the best for you."
   D. "You can't change the warranty deed provision to quit claim because the warranty deed is better and it's in the preprinted contract."

6. A real estate licensee:
   A. may use preprinted *offer to purchase* forms.
   B. should not give a buyer/offeror a copy of an offer until it is accepted.
   C. has 48 hours within which to provide copies of an accepted offer to each of the parties.
   D. may alter a document if the parties fax their permission.

7. Under *Quinlan Tyson*, which of the following may a real estate licensee do?
   A. Fill in the blank spaces on a preprinted installment note
   B. Provide testimony in court as to the value of purchased property
   C. Explain the benefits of a Starker (1031) exchange of investment real estate
   D. Advise a party that legal representation in a simple real estate deal is unnecessary

8. Which of the following is not one of the three major issues related to contracting via facsimile?
   A. Whether a fax is a *writing* within the meaning of the Statute of Frauds
   B. Whether a facsimile signature will satisfy the Statute of Frauds
   C. Which document(s) is an original under the best evidence rule
   D. Whether oral promises will be permitted by the parole evidence rule

9. The major problem with using the fax machine in securing a binding contract is:
   A. lack of judicial acceptance.
   B. uncertainty as to receipt of the document.
   C. the tendency of fax copies to fade over time.
   D. defective transmissions/receptions are commonplace.

10. The Rules for the Administration of the Real Estate License Act require that:
    A. all contracts for the sale of real estate must be in writing.
    B. sale contracts must contain the signatures of both parties to the transaction.
    C. listing agreements must set forth the legal description of the real estate.
    D. no contract may contain any blanks for the licensee to fill in after the parties have signed.

CHAPTER 3

OFFICE AND ADVERTISING REGULATIONS
(GOTCHA!)

○ **CHAPTER OVERVIEW**
Advertising is the lifeblood of all professional salespeople. In advertising real estate, the consumer's most important investment, the licensee must be knowledgeable about marketing restrictions, which are covered in this chapter. Chapter 3 also provides a primer in the legal aspects of office administration. Branch offices, assumed names, and the responsibility for the activities of non-licensees are just a few of the administrative details covered here.

○ **LEARNING OBJECTIVES**
After completing your study of this chapter, you should be able to:
1) Identify the types of information/services unlicensed office personnel may and may not provide.
2) Explain two restrictions relating to the selection of an office site.
3) Summarize the requirements in opening a branch office.
4) Establish office policies and practices for the maintenance of records.
5) List at least five different License Law infractions involving advertising.
6) Appreciate the need for a careful preview and postreview of advertising copy.
7) Enumerate the requirements for advertising a licensee's own real estate.
8) Identify ads that violate the License Act and/or Rules.
9) List the steps required to lawfully transact business under an assumed name.

○ **5 CASES TO JUDGE**

○ **10-QUESTION DIAGNOSTIC QUIZ**

CHAPTER 3

OFFICE AND ADVERTISING REGULATIONS
(GOTCHA!)

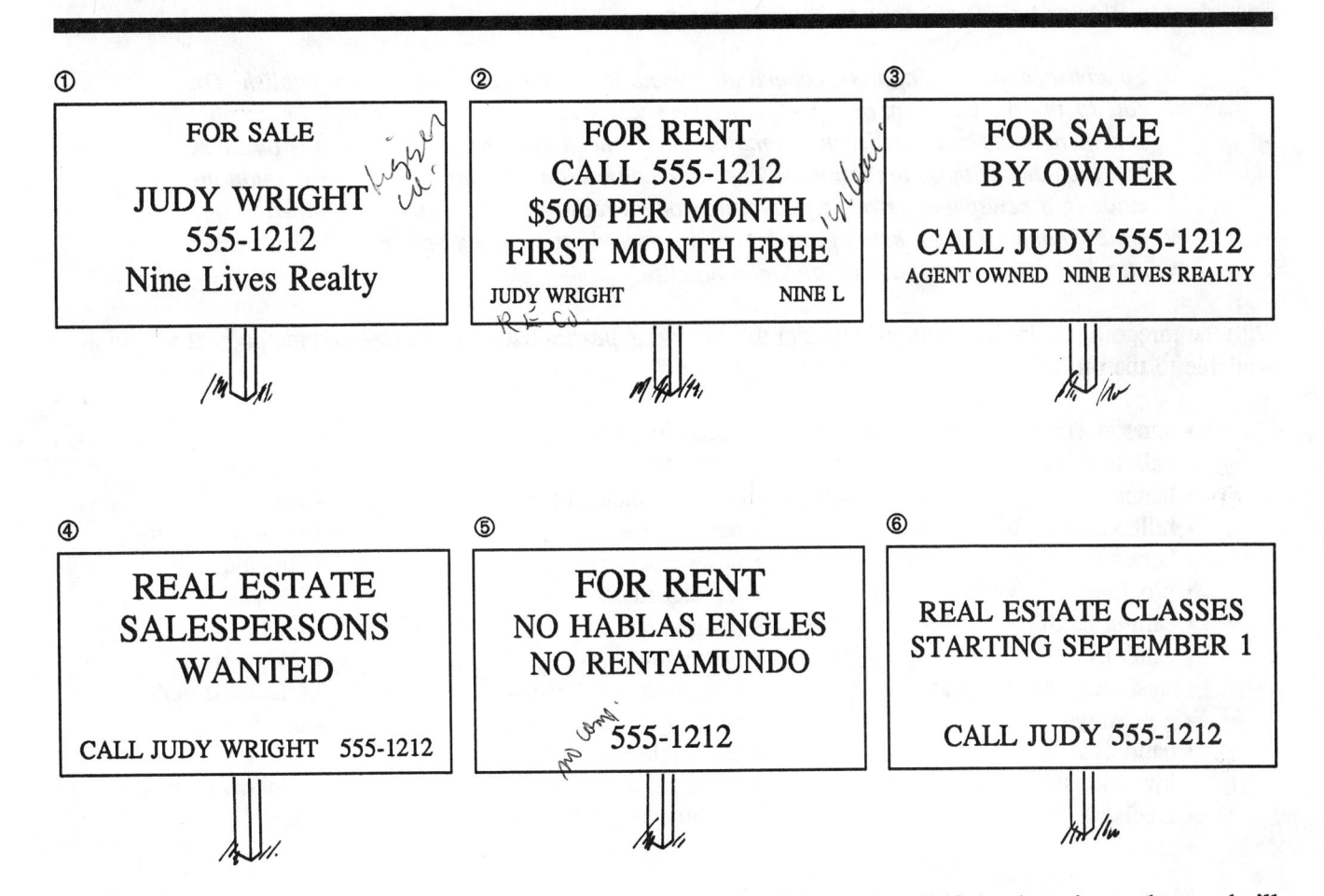

① FOR SALE
JUDY WRIGHT
555-1212
Nine Lives Realty

② FOR RENT
CALL 555-1212
$500 PER MONTH
FIRST MONTH FREE
JUDY WRIGHT   NINE L

③ FOR SALE
BY OWNER
CALL JUDY 555-1212
AGENT OWNED   NINE LIVES REALTY

④ REAL ESTATE
SALESPERSONS
WANTED
CALL JUDY WRIGHT 555-1212

⑤ FOR RENT
NO HABLAS ENGLES
NO RENTAMUNDO
555-1212

⑥ REAL ESTATE CLASSES
STARTING SEPTEMBER 1
CALL JUDY 555-1212

Judy's last name is obviously a misnomer; it should have been "Wrong." And if she doesn't watch out, she'll need nine real estate lives—because each of the signs pictured above is an infraction of the License Act and/or Rules. For the most part, licensees committing advertising and business infractions don't do so with evil motives; rather, the infractions happen through ignorance. If you're having difficulty recognizing the problems associated with the various signs, your continuing education should pay for itself in this one chapter, because there is no other area in which a licensee is so exposed to the wrath of an enemy than in advertising. You're a sitting duck for an adversary to cry "Gotcha!" when your illegal ad shows up in the morning paper. That enemy doesn't even need to disclose his or her identity, because your ad does all of the talking that's necessary.

ADVERTISING

It should come as no surprise that advertising is regulated by state license laws. One of the most important functions of the seller-broker and owner-property manager relationships is the professional's ability to market the property better than the owner. As with other License Law provisions, the intent of the General Assembly in enacting the license laws and in amending the acts is to protect the consumer.

Chapter 3 Office and Advertising Regulations

Set forth on the facing page are all of the sections of the License Act and Rules that directly relate to advertising. Several of these provisions are redundant and overlapping. To most agents the provisions are at best confusing and at worst incomprehensible. At the end of this section we offer a checklist of other considerations pertaining to real estate advertising of which the licensee should also be knowledgeable.

WHAT IS ADVERTISING?

This is not a joke, but a very important question—the correct answer to which all licensees must be cognizant. According to *Black's Law Dictionary*, to advertise means:

> *To advise, announce, apprise, command, give notice of, inform, make known, publish. On call to the public attention by any means whatsoever. Any oral, written, or graphic statement made by the seller in any manner in connection with the solicitation of business and includes, without limitation because of enumeration, statements and representations made in a newspaper or other publication or on radio or television or contained in any notice, handbill, sign, catalog, or letter, or printed on or contained in any tag or label attached to or accompanying any merchandise.*

With the foregoing definition in mind, consider the following *partial* list of the modes and methods of advertising available to the professional:

- announcements
- balloons
- banners
- billboards
- books
- brochures
- calling cards
- catalogs
- facsimile transmissions
- giveaways
- handbills
- invitations
- labels
- letters
- magazines
- magnets
- motor vehicle signs
- newsletters
- newspapers
- novelty items
- painted fences
- pamphlets
- postcards
- posters
- press releases
- programs
- public address systems
- publicity stunts
- radio ads
- skywriting
- stationery
- streamers
- TV ads
- tags
- telegrams
- telephone calls
- thank-yous
- tickets
- window signs
- yard signs

The Department was recently asked whether company name tags had to comply with all of the advertising regulations, as well as whether company "uniforms" were likewise covered. The Department responded in the negative; however, because shifts occur in the Department's policies and personnel, the answer could as easily have been in the affirmative.

In a nutshell, any device used for calling attention to one's product or services could be considered advertising. The rules outlined below apply not only to advertising listed property, but also to "help wanted" ads, school ads, career nights, and seminar ads.

A few years ago a licensed salesperson who had completed all of her broker's courses and who was scheduled to take the state exam was asked by a member of her church to purchase space in the church bulletin. She obliged by having her new business card displayed, which identified her as a "Broker." She had not used her new

LICENSE ACT

§18. Refusal to issue or renew license—Probation, suspension, revocation of license—Reprimand or penalty—Causes. The Department may refuse to issue or renew a license, may place on probation, suspend or revoke any license, or may reprimand or impose a civil penalty not to exceed $10,000 upon any licensee hereunder for any one or any combination of the following causes: . . .

(h) Where the licensee in performing or attempting to perform or pretending to perform any act as a broker or salesperson, or where such licensee, in handling his own property, whether held by deed, option, or otherwise, is found guilty of:

1. . . . untruthful advertising; . . .

3. . . . the making of false promises through . . . advertising . . .

4. Any misleading or untruthful advertising, or using any trade name or insignia of membership in any real estate organization of which the licensee is not a member; . . .

17. Displaying a "for rent" or "for sale" sign on any property without the written consent of an owner or his duly authorized agent, or advertising by any means that any property is for sale or for rent without the written consent of the owner or his authorized agent; . . .

20. Advertising any property for sale or advertising any transaction of any kind or character relating to the sale of property by whatsoever means, without clearly disclosing in or on such advertising one of the following: the name of the firm with which the licensee is associated, if a sole broker, evidence of the broker's occupation, or a name with respect to which the broker has complied with the requirements of "An Act in relation to the use of an assumed name in the conduct or transaction of business in this State," approved July 17, 1941, as amended, whether such advertising is done by the broker or by any salesperson or broker employed by the broker . . . .

27. Advertising or offering merchandise or services as free if any conditions or obligations necessary for receiving such merchandise or services are not disclosed in the same advertisement or offer. Such conditions or obligations include, but are not limited to, the requirement that the recipient attend a promotional activity or visit a real estate site. As used in this paragraph 27, "free" includes terms such as "award", "prize", "no charge", "free of charge", "without charge" and similar words or phrases which reasonably lead a person to believe that he may receive, or has been selected to receive, something of value, without any conditions or obligations on the part of the recipient; . . .

ADMINISTRATIVE RULES

§1450.50 Disclosure

(c) A licensee shall disclose, in writing, to all parties in that transaction his status as a licensee and any and all interest he or it does have or may have in the real estate constituting the subject matter thereof or in such transaction, directly or indirectly according to the following guidelines:

(1) On broker yard signs, no disclosure of ownership is necessary, however such ownership shall be indicated on any property data form and disclosed to people responding to the ad or the sign. The term "broker owned" or "agent owned" is sufficient disclosure.

(2) Only licensees holding inoperative licenses may advertise by owner. Inoperative licensees shall comply with the following if advertising by owner:

(A) On "By Owner" yard signs, inoperative licensees shall indicate "broker owned" or "agent owned". "By Owner" newspaper ads shall use the term "broker owned" or "agent owned".

(B) If an operative licensee runs an ad, for the purpose of purchasing real estate, he shall disclose in that ad that he is a licensee.

§1450.90 Advertising

(a) Except for inoperative licensees selling their own property, the broker's business name (which in the case of a franchise shall include the franchise affiliation as well as the individual firm) shall be displayed in all real estate advertisement, including but not limited to newspapers as defined by Section 4(14) of the Act.

(b) No blind advertisements may be used by any licensee regarding the sale or lease of real estate, including his own, or regarding real estate activities or the hiring of all licensees under the Act.

(c) No advertising is to be fraudulent, deceptive, inherently misleading, or proven to be misleading in practice. It is considered misleading or untruthful if, when taken as a whole, there is a distinct and reasonable possibility that it will be misunderstood or will deceive the ordinary purchaser, seller, renter, or owner. Advertising shall contain all information necessary to communicate accurately. The form of communication shall be designed to communicate the information contained therein to the public in a direct and readily comprehensible manner.

(d) A sponsored licensee cannot advertise under his own name. All advertising shall be under the direct supervision of the employing broker and in the name of the employer.

(e) No licensee shall list his name under the heading or title "Real Estate" in the telephone directory or otherwise advertise in his own name to the general public through any media of advertising as being in the real estate business without listing the business name of the broker with whom he is affiliated. Printed information relating to the licensee and his name cannot be larger in size than that pertaining to the broker's business name.

business cards, but she decided that since the publication date was after her scheduled state exam there would be no problem. We think you know the rest of the story: She failed the exam, the church bulletin was printed, and a competing church lady complained to the Department. The last we knew, the salesperson and her broker were scheduled to attend an informal disciplinary conference. Since her ad was untrue, we assume that she was given a small fine and a reprimand. We assume further that her competitor took great pleasure in spreading the news throughout the congregation.

STRICT LIABILITY

Laws that establish civil, criminal, and administrative penalties generally define the degree of culpability for infractions and/or set forth defenses to claimed violations. In other situations, where the General Assembly has failed to establish defenses or a mental state, the courts have "legislated" defenses that they deem fair and equitable. For example, there are no legislative defenses to a traffic charge of speeding. Generally, if you are caught speeding, it makes no difference if you knew it (your speedometer was broken) or whether you intended to speed (you weren't paying attention). With the exception of a few very carefully worded and narrow judicially created exceptions, you are strictly liable for exceeding the speed limit.

The License Act and Rules in the area of advertising are like speeding offenses; there are no legislative defenses. Most of the disciplinary cases involving advertising irregularities are in the nature of clear-cut technical violations, e.g., blind ads, salesperson ads that do not include the name of the sponsoring broker, and other prohibited types of advertising as will be discussed below. Illinois has never had an appellate court case that explains the scope of these prohibitions. Since the courts have historically taken a hands-off approach to disciplinary proceedings, and since nationwide there is a dearth of advertising cases, we can only speculate that the courts will *not* legislate defenses and that strict liability will be the rule. With this hands-off concept in mind, we now turn to the various advertising (speeding) infractions.

TRUE OR FALSE?

All ads must be truthful. If you advertise a two-story, four-bedroom, two-and-a-half bath, two-car attached garage, Colonial home, and the home is in fact exactly as represented, your ad is truthful. If, however, any of the listed amenities are incorrect, then your ad is untruthful and you have violated the License Law. It does not matter that your secretary typed "four bedrooms" when you told her "three," that the owner told you the wrong lot dimensions, or that the ad was placed prior to an increase in the listing price. You are a professional, and, similar to a physician who accidently leaves a sponge behind in closing a patient at the conclusion of surgery, you may be held strictly accountable for your mistake.

Considering all of the various types of advertising and the quantity of information processed in our industry on a daily basis, it's easy to make a mistake. How many times have you found inaccuracies in listing sheets? Probably hundreds, if not thousands, of times. Data cards/listing sheets are advertising, and the information should be thoroughly checked before distribution.

We repeat, under the License Act you are strictly accountable for advertising that is untrue. An honest mistake, a typographical error, or misinformation from your principal are not defenses against your being disciplined. An honest mistake may mitigate your discipline, and an ad retraction may lessen the penalty, but you must be prepared for discipline in the event of an advertising error.

FALSE PROMISES

Promises are representations as to future events. In advertising, they are made much less frequently than statements of existing or past facts. If, however, you advertise a promise in an ad, it must be truthful. The

following is a list of several promises that a licensee might make in advertising; any of them, if untrue, could subject the licensee to a disciplinary complaint:
- "Owner will assist in financing"
- "Potential for in-law or office arrangement"
- "Financing available"
- "We will sell your home in less than 90 days"
- "Tenants will be given the first choice to purchase"
- "Next year this home's value will increase 20 percent"
- "Property may be converted to a two-flat"
- "Commercial zoning permitted"

MISLEADING ADVERTISING

One of the most perplexing prohibitions in the License Act is against misleading advertising. A truthful ad made with no intent to deceive nor with actual knowledge of its tendency to deceive may nevertheless be the subject of a disciplinary complaint if, when taken as a whole, "there is a distinct and reasonable possibility that it will be misunderstood or will deceive the *ordinary* purchaser, seller, renter, or owner" [emphasis added]. Just who is this ordinary person, and will the ad be "taken as a whole"?

Clarke R. Marquis, one of the authors of this text, recently received a warning letter from the Department complaining that a *book* he had authored entitled *State of Illinois Real Estate License Act, Rules, and Forms*, might be misleading. The book contains the Real Estate License Act of 1983, the Rules for the Administration of the Real Estate License Act of 1983, the most commonly needed state forms, and several handy reference charts.

Complimentary copies of the book were *given* to each member of the Disciplinary Board, the Director of the Department, the Commissioner of Real Estate, and to the Illinois Association of REALTORS®, and it is assumed that one of these complimentary copies was the seed for the issuance of the warning letter. We don't get it, and we are clueless as to what an *ordinary* person would misunderstand about a book or how he or she could possibly be deceived.

Although he would not divulge the source of the complaint, the Department's attorney, who wrote the warning letter, theorized that someone might be deceived into thinking that the book was approved, authorized, or published by the State of Illinois. In retrospect, we suppose that if the complainant never opened the book, that he or she might conclude from the cover that the contents were authored by the State of Illinois. Not only is and was that the furthest thing from the author's mind, but what evil or harm can befall the ordinary consumer who opens the book and is immediately presented with a notice, a clear preface, and an order blank that clearly indicate the book was a private publication and not an official state publication? We leave it to you, the reader, to untangle the thought process of the *ordinary* person. More important, we hope you appreciate the fact that an enemy may be deceived by or misunderstand his or her own shadow.

PUFFERY

Puffing is a time-honored and permissible form of advertising. "Great view," "super neighborhood," "best location," "gourmet kitchen," "tastefully decorated," and the like fall within the realm of permitted subjective statements of opinion and should never cause a problem—unless, of course, there is no kitchen. Puffing usually includes a degree of exaggeration. "Easy," "perfect," "amazing," "prime," "wonderful," "excellent," and other such terms have generally been considered acceptable forms of advertising.

On the other hand, if a home of ordinary construction was billed as "energy efficient," an expectation might be created that the home has superior insulation, weather stripping, or cost-saving mechanical devices. Therefore, such advertising might be construed as untrue or misleading or both.

Chapter 3 Office and Advertising Regulations

When does puffing become untrue and/or misleading? According to the comedian Gallagher, a substantial segment of the population is drawn to any sign that says "on sale." Put a ridiculous price tag on something and then announce, "Prices slashed 50%!" and the bargain hunters come out in droves. Not only do they come out, but they buy large quantities of merchandise at only reasonable prices. Is there a "distinct and reasonable possibility" that these ads will be misunderstood or will deceive the "ordinary" purchaser? We suggest that the correct answer to our query depends on the *ordinary* person or persons selected as judges—and that it could go either way.

In the chart below are several statements.
1. Which of the statements on the left, if untrue, should be considered puffing?
2. Without reference to the accompanying notes on the right, which statements are misleading?
3. With the accompanying notes, which statements are still misleading?

STATEMENT	NOTE
Owner-assisted financing available	The owner will speak to the bank president on your behalf.
Low down payment	$500 is a low down payment, but not necessarily for a lot being sold for $1,000.
New construction	The home has never been occupied, but it has been on the market for three years.
No offer too low	This doesn't mean any offer will be accepted.
Price reduced 25%	The home is still 25% overpriced.
Lake view property	With binoculars, you can see the lake from the second-floor bedrooms.
Equestrian's delight	There's a bridle path in the front yard, but subdivision regulations prohibit horses.
Free color TV with each purchase	You get a choice of a red, green, or blue black-and-white TV.
Free travel alarm with each showing	You receive a plastic-coated reusable note to give to the hotel desk clerk for a wake-up call.
Old World craftsmanship	A good carpenter did the trim work.
Public transportation available	There's a bus stop two miles to the east.
List with a superstar	The salesperson hasn't yet made his first deal.
Close to all schools	The closest school is 1½ miles away and the farthest is 5 miles away.

Based on a straw poll of students, we wouldn't want our careers hanging in the balance if we were defending any of the above ads.

TRADEMARK VIOLATIONS
Trade/service marks and names may not be used by a licensee unless authorized by the holder of the mark or name. Consumers (and far too great a number of licensees) think that REALTOR® is a synonym for "real estate agent," and that any licensed real estate agent may use the term in his or her practice. REALTOR® is a service name registered to the National Association of REALTORS®, and only an agent's affiliation with NAR will enable the agent to use the name and related mark. Nonmembers are routinely disciplined for the unauthorized use of the name and mark. Likewise, a licensee may not use the name or logo of a real estate franchise unless authorized by the applicable organization.

WRITTEN CONSENT
By virtue of a recent change in the Rules, *all* listing agreements may be oral contracts; however, any advertising done under either an oral or written listing agreement may only be accomplished with the written consent of the owner or authorized agent. Removing "for sale" or "for rent" signs promptly from sold or rented properties is an important consideration here, because the agent's authority to advertise comes to an end upon the transfer of ownership. Many practitioners, either through laziness or design, leave their signs on sold property as long as they can, thus subjecting themselves to a disciplinary complaint from the new owners, who want the sign out of their yard.

BROKERAGE DISCLOSURE
All ads must disclose the name of the brokerage firm. Besides the sponsoring broker's responsibility for supervising an agent's advertising, *all* advertising done by a salesperson must be done under the broker's name. Salesperson advertising must also set forth the sponsoring broker's name in a type size equal to or larger than that of the salesperson's name. For example, the business card pictured to the left (below) violates this provision, because the salesperson's name is in larger type than the firm's name. The card on the right displays the same information properly.

GARFIELD T. KATT, Broker 1 East Main Street Hometown, Illinois 708/555-0555 Business 708/555-1563 Fax 708/555-6784 Residence NINE LIVES REALTY	**NINE LIVES REALTY** 1 East Main Street Hometown, Illinois 708/555-0555 Business 708/555-1563 Fax 708/555-6784 Residence GARFIELD T. KATT, Broker

FREE ADVERTISING
Any licensee planning to give away merchandise, offer free services, or participate in any giveaway program should carefully study all of the provisions for advertising in the License Act and Rules. Particular attention should be paid to Section 18(h)(27), which requires that the promotional material or advertising disclose any conditions attached to the receipt of the merchandise, services, or other prizes to be awarded.

LICENSEES AS "BY OWNER"
Operative licensees are prohibited from advertising "by owner" when selling their own property. If a licensee does advertise the sale or purchase of owned property, he or she must disclose his or her company's name in all ads. The licensees may, if they wish, use their home telephone numbers; however, any yard signs employed must be those of the sponsoring broker. The operative licensee must disclose his or her status as an active Illinois real

estate licensee to any individuals who respond to signs or ads. The licensee also must disclose any and all interest he or she has in the property, either directly or indirectly. The disclosure must be made in writing on property data forms (listing sheets, MLS sheets, or the "remarks" section of computer printouts). It is advisable that a licensee include a paragraph in any sales contract or written lease to confirm the fact that this ownership disclosure was given to the other party prior to signing the contract. For purposes of making the necessary disclosure, a simple notation, such as "agent owned" or "broker owned," is sufficient.

Inoperative licensees (licensees who do not have an active license) may advertise "by owner." On "by owner" yard signs, inoperative licensees must indicate "broker owned" or "agent owned." All other advertising done by an inoperative licensee requires disclosure in the ad that the advertiser is a real estate licensee. As with the operative licensee, the terms *broker owned* or *agent owned* are sufficient disclosures.

OTHER ADVERTISING RESTRICTIONS

The licensee should become familiar with advertising restrictions placed on the licensee through other legislation. Time and space limitations preclude any meaningful discussion of these restrictions; however, the following is a brief listing and description of the most important areas of concern.

Fair Housing Laws — Federal, state, and local fair housing laws and ordinances prohibit discriminatory advertising based on race, color, creed, national origin, sex, familial status, physical and/or mental handicaps/diseases, and (in some instances) sexual preference. An adjudication of a licensee's having violated these laws will ordinarily result in severe penalties under the License Act.

Sign Ordinances — Many municipalities have restricted the use of both office and yard signs. A violation of a local ordinance of this type could be prosecuted under the "unworthiness or incompetency" subsections of Section 18 of the License Act (see Chapter 5).

Truth in Lending Act — Advertising by a licensee of financial terms may be subject to the extensive and rather complicated provisions of Regulation Z. A licensee should be thoroughly familiar with this legislation prior to the publication of any ads that include terms of available financing.

OFFICE ADMINISTRATION

The opening or management of a real estate office should be undertaken only with the assistance of competent professionals (accountant and attorney); however, these professionals may not be fully versed in the License Act and Rules. Therefore, this section will highlight those areas of the License Act and Rules that must be considered independently by the broker and/or brought to the attention of the professionals the broker employs. The information contained is not meant to be a substitute for competent advice; it is simply a checklist of important considerations. Several of the items are developed more fully elsewhere in this publication.

ASSUMED NAME

Every year several licensees are disciplined for violating Section 1450.140 of the Rules, which prohibits a licensee from using a business name (assumed name) different from his or her given name unless the licensee complies with the Illinois Assumed Business Name Act *and* provides proof of compliance to the Department within 30 days of registering an assumed name. Although the typical discipline for noncompliance is a modest fine and a reprimand, there is no reason why a licensee should ever be disciplined for such a violation.

Section 1 of the Assumed Business Name Act sets forth the filing requirements as follows:

> *No person or persons shall conduct or transact business in this State under an assumed name, or under any designation, name or style, corporate or otherwise, other than the real name or names of the individual or individuals conducting or transacting such business, unless such person or persons shall file in the office of the County Clerk of the County in which such person or persons conduct or transact or intend to conduct or transact such business, a certificate setting forth the name under which the business is, or is to be, conducted or transacted, and the true or real full name or names of the person or persons owning, conducting or transacting the same, with the post office address or addresses of such person or persons and every address where such business is, or is to be, conducted or transacted in the county. The certificate shall be executed and duly acknowledged by the person or persons so conducting or intending to conduct the business.*
>
> *Notice of the filing of such certificate shall be published in a newspaper of general circulation published within the county in which the certificate is filed. Such notice shall be published once a week for 3 consecutive weeks. The first publication shall be within 15 days after the certificate is filed in the office of the County Clerk. Proof of publication shall be filed with the County Clerk within 50 days from the date of filing the certificate. Upon receiving proof of publication, the clerk shall issue a receipt to the person filing such certificate but no additional charge shall be assessed by the clerk for giving such receipt. Unless proof of publication is made to the clerk, the certificate of registration of the assumed name is void.*

Compliance with the Assumed Business Name Act and the License Act is a relatively simple four-step process:
- Step 1: Fill out an assumed name certificate. No special form is necessary; however, the certificate must set forth the business name to be assumed, the actual names and addresses of the owners of the business, and the addresses where the business will be conducted (see Figure 3-1).
- Step 2: The signed and notarized certificate must be filed with the County Clerk of the county in which the business is located. When the certificate is filed, the Clerk will prepare a publication notice similar to the one that appears in Figure 3-2.
- Step 3: The signed publication notice should be taken to a local newspaper and published once a week for three consecutive weeks.
- Step 4: After the third publication, the newspaper publisher will issue a certificate of publication, which must be filed with the Clerk, who will then issue a document evidencing compliance with the Assumed Name Act. A certified copy of the Clerk's certificate should be obtained by the licensee and (along with a cover letter) mailed to the Department by certified mail, return receipt requested.

Once the return receipt from the Department is received, it should be stapled to the transmittal letter and retained with the broker's other business records. The total cost of compliance should not exceed $100, whereas the cost of noncompliance is typically a fine of $250 and a reprimand.

OFFICE LOCATION
The only considerations under the License Act as to the selection of an office location are that it not be located in a retail establishment unless the space is separate and apart from the retail business and that the site selected must also permit the display of a sign of "adequate size and visibility to be seen from the exterior of the premises." The impact of these restrictions is of little consequence to most professionals, but of some importance to the self-employed broker who operates out of his or her home.

FIG 3-1

ASSUMED BUSINESS NAME CERTIFICATE

In accordance with the Illinois Assumed Business Name Act, the undersigned hereby certifies to the following:

1. The name under which the business is, or is to be, conducted or transacted:
_____

2. The true or real full name or names of the person or persons owning, conducting, or transacting the same, with the post office address or addresses of such person or persons is:

NAME	ADDRESS
_____	_____
_____	_____

3. Each address where such business is, or is to be, conducted or transacted in the county is:

No. & Street   City   State   Zip Code

4. The type of business to be transacted under said assumed name: <u>A general real estate brokerage business</u>

_____
_____

State of Illinois   )
) SS
County of _____   )

The foregoing certificate was acknowledged before me this _____ day of _____, 19___, by _____.

_____ Notary Public
My commission expires: _____

FIG 3-2

**LEGAL NOTICE
ASSUMED NAME
PUBLICATION NOTICE**

Public Notice is hereby given that on March 13, 1992, a certificate was filed in the office of the County Clerk of Jackson County, Illinois, setting forth the names and addresses of all persons owning, conducting and transacting the business known as Nine Lives Realty located at 1968 Saluki Circle, Carbondale, Illinois 62901.

Dated March 13, 1992.

/s/   *County Clerk*
Jackson County Clerk

Most municipalities permit home occupations but restrict such callings to businesses that can be conducted without a sign. If a licensee places a sign of adequate size and visibility on his or her home, the city may force its removal and even fine the violator. If a Department investigator drives by the home and can't see that the broker's business is located there, the broker may be fined and disciplined by the Department. If faced with this dilemma, the licensee should, of course, comply with both requirements and either move the office to a location that permits a sign, or abandon the independent practice of real estate.

BRANCH OFFICES

A broker may open additional offices provided an application for such purposes is made with the Department. The application requires:
- the name of the firm
- the license number of the firm
- the business structure (sole proprietorship, corporation, partnership)
- the main address of the firm
- the name of the proposed branch office, which must be the same or similar to the main office (e.g., John Doe Realty and John Doe Realty North)
- the address of the proposed branch office
- the name and license number of the managing broker
- the payment of a $20 fee
- that a Consent to Audit Special Account form must accompany the application, even though the branch office may elect not to have a separate special account

The branch office may not open until a branch office license is issued. Once the branch office license is received, the managing broker must issue sponsor cards to associates and send the hard copy of the sponsor cards to the

Department along with the associates' original licenses, which are removed from the walls of the main office. The employment contracts of any transferred associates should be transported to the branch office, and branch office files maintained for such purposes.

In the event the branch manager dies or his or her employment is otherwise terminated, the branch office must technically cease operations until another branch manager is secured. However, the Act does allow for the continued operation of the office, provided an application is made to the Department within ten days of the branch manager's termination of employment. The application must state the name and license number of the broker who will oversee the branch office operations during the interim period. Unless extended, the authorization to continue operations will only permit the business to continue for 30 days.

It is important to point out that the *figurehead* branch manager is in nearly as much jeopardy as the figurehead owner/broker who lends his or her license to a salesperson or group of salespersons for purposes of operating a real estate business. The branch manager who fails to manage and supervise his or her staff is likely to be disciplined if he or she fails to recognize and remedy the unlawful, incompetent, and/or unethical practices of branch office associates and nonlicensed personnel.

NONLICENSED EMPLOYEES

Telephone conversations similar to the following are heard daily in offices that adhere to proper training practices for nonlicensed employees.

Receptionist: "Good morning, XYZ Realty."
Prospect: "May I speak with Mary?"
Receptionist: "I'm sorry, she's not in. May I take a message?"
Prospect: "Can you tell me how much the house on Fourth Street is listed for?"
Receptionist: "I'm sorry, I don't have that information—could I have Mary call you?"
Prospect: "Is it still available?"
Receptionist: "I really don't know—could I give you to a sales associate?"
Prospect: "No, but could you arrange to have Mary meet us for a showing?"
Receptionist: "I'm sorry, but Mary would have to make those arrangements."
Prospect: "Well....could you photocopy the listing sheet so that we could pick it up later this morning?"
Receptionist: "I'll ask Mary when she returns."
Prospect: "What? Do you have to ask Mary for everything?"
Receptionist: "Sir, I'm as frustrated as you are, and next month I hope to have a real estate license so I may be of further assistance to Mary and everyone else in the office. Unfortunately, if I gave you any of the information you wanted, I and my firm would be violating the law. About the only thing I can do is answer the phone, take messages, take dictation, type, make coffee, run errands, and perform other tasks that don't involve direct client contact. Everything I write, do, or say must be strictly supervised by a salesperson or a broker. I can take a message, and I can give you a message; I can draft a letter to you, but it must be mailed under Mary's signature. I can type up your contract, but Mary must review it before you see it. I may put a 'for sale' sign in your yard and a lock box on your house, but Mary will be there telling me when and where. I may design and create an ad for your property; draft the transmittal letter, check, and instructions for publication; and deliver the letter—but it won't leave this office until Mary sees it, signs it, and tells me to deliver it. I can fill out an exclusive agency, open, or exclusive right-to-sell listing agreement, go through the MLS records and pick out comps, prepare CMAs, render a value opinion, and do an estimate of the net proceeds of a sale at various list prices—but Mary will be the only one to see it and discuss it with me. There's a lot I can do for Mary, but very little I can do for you. Do you get the drift?"
Prospect: "You do all these things, but you can't give me a listing price?"
Receptionist: "You got it."

Prospect: "What can you give me?"
Receptionist: "Coffee, the time of day, a message, a letter from Mary, a place to sit and wait for Mary, Mary's card, and information as to when Mary will return—that's about it."
Prospect: "Well, any firm with a receptionist as bright, competent, and ethical as yours is the kind I want to do business with. Will you please have Mary call me?"
Receptionist: "Yes I will, and thank you for the compliment."
Prospect: "You're welcome, and oh, by the way, in all my 30 years as an investigator for the Illinois Department of Professional Regulation, I don't think I've ever talked with such a well-trained employee."
Receptionist: "(Gulp).....i..i..is it okay for me to sit at an open house and hand out literature as long as I don't talk about the house? Mary said I could."
Prospect: "This is one of the few areas where, for the public's benefit, we have relaxed our rules. Obviously, a successful salesperson can't be at ten different open houses on a weekend. Therefore, Mary is right, and from what I've heard just now, I'm sure she has told you that your role is not to 'market the property or Mary's services' but, like a security officer, keep an eye on the house and its contents."
Receptionist: "Whew, I feel better now."
Prospect: "Any other questions?"
Receptionist: "Would you take my license exam for me?"
Prospect: [*Check off the response you prefer*]
[ ] "Every man has his price."
[ ] "And you even have a sense of humor!"

CHECKLIST OF OTHER CONSIDERATIONS

The following is a checklist of other administrative considerations (they are discussed more fully elsewhere in this publication).

- **Agency Disclosure Forms**—brokers must maintain these forms for a period of five years. See Chapters 5 and 8 for a complete discussion.
- **Licenses and Sponsor Cards**—The issuance and proper display of licenses, along with timely notification to the Department, are all discussed in Chapter 1.
- **Bookkeeping**—This critical area of concern is fully developed in Chapter 4.
- **Type of Business Organization**—Chapter 1 sets forth the requirements for becoming licensed as a corporation or partnership.
- **Employment Agreements**—Prior to being issued a sponsor card, each employee must sign a written employment agreement, the contents of which are discussed in Chapters 1 and 2.
- **Listing/Sales Contracts**—A broker will want to adopt both listing and sale contract forms for use in his or her business. The requirements for these contracts are discussed in Chapter 2.

WHAT'S WRONG WITH JUDY'S SIGNS?

In case you haven't figured out by now why Judy's signs, which appeared at the beginning of this chapter, violate the License Act and/or Rules for the Administration of the License Act, we offer the following explanations:

Sign 1: Judy's name is displayed in a type size larger than her broker's.
Sign 2: Could someone rent the unit for only two months? Probably not. Therefore, the ad is undoubtedly misleading.

Sign 3: Operative licensees may *not* advertise property by owner according to Rule 1450.50(c)(2). Also, as the first sign, Judy's name is displayed in type larger than her broker's.

Sign 4: The sponsoring broker's name must appear in all advertising, including "help wanted" signs and ads.

Sign 5: This ad, which translates as "If you can't speak English, you can't rent here," is obviously impermissible, because it is discriminatory. Also, the broker's name must appear in all advertising.

Sign 6: As in the fifth sign, the sponsoring broker's name must appear in all advertising. Additionally, if the real estate classes will be conducted by a real estate school, the name of the school must be inserted in the broker's advertising.

CASES TO JUDGE

1. The defendant, a chiropractor, was charged with having violated the advertising regulations governing individuals licensed under the Medical Practice Act. The Supreme Court ruled that the advertising restrictions were unconstitutional; however, the defendant was also charged with engaging in dishonorable, unethical, or unprofessional conduct of a character likely to deceive, defraud, or harm the public. One of the several ads that the defendant had run appears below.

The Department suspended the defendant's chiropractic license for 90 days, and the circuit court reversed the decision on the basis of the unconstitutional breadth of the statute.

Should the Supreme Court have ruled that the defendant's ad was likely to deceive, defraud, or harm the public? *Talsky v. Department of Registration and Education*, 68 Ill.2d 579, 370 N.E.2d 173, 12 Ill.Dec. 550 (1977)]

2. Dollar-A-Day Car Rentals was sued by the Federal Trade Commission (FTC). The FTC claimed that the company's name was deceptive in that a consumer might conclude that the company offered car rentals for a daily rate of one dollar. The company defended its name on the basis that the consumer was capable of finding out the rental rates by simply asking.

Is the name of the company misleading? [*Resort Car Rental System, Inc. v. FTC*, 518 F2d 962 (1975)]

3. "Wonder Bread builds strong bodies 12 ways" ran the ad, which many readers may remember. The Federal Trade Commission filed a complaint claiming deceptive advertising in that all breads had the same vitamins and minerals. The FTC said the ad, although truthful, was misleading because a person might conclude that other breads were inferior to Wonder Bread.

Is the ad misleading? [*FTC v. Hunt-Wesson Foods*, (citation unavailable)]

4. *Reader's Digest* published an article generally critical of cigarettes reporting that, according to its tests, there were no major differences in the levels of tar and nicotine among the leading brands tested. The lowest levels of tar and nicotine, however, were found to be in a brand manufactured by Lorillard. Lorillard subsequently ran ads stating that the *Reader's Digest* study had found their cigarettes to be the lowest in tar and nicotine. The ad did not mention that the survey was critical of all tobacco products; nor did it mention that *Reader's Digest* had concluded that the differences were insignificant. The FTC claimed that selectively using the information—even though it was totally truthful—was deceptive.

Should the ad be halted? [*P. Lorillard Co. v. FTC*, 186 F2d 52 (1950)]

5. "Reserve cooling power" was an advertised quality of the Fedders Corporation air-conditioning units. Contrary to its advertising, Fedders had no proof that its equipment was unique. The FTC issued a cease and desist order against the company, which was appealed to the courts.

Was Fedders' advertising misleading? [*Fedders Corp. v. FTC*, 529 F2d 1398 (1976)]

10-QUESTION DIAGNOSTIC QUIZ

1. If a branch manager dies:
   A. the manager of the main office is automatically in charge of the branch office.
   B. the branch office may not, under any circumstances, continue operations until a replacement is hired.
   C. the branch office may, under certain circumstances, be allowed to continue operations for up to 30 days.
   D. the branch office associates' licenses are automatically transferred to the main office.

2. Which of the following activities may be performed by unlicensed office personnel?
   A. Providing price quotations to prospective purchasers
   B. Conducting home canvasing for listings
   C. Repairing leaky faucets in the office
   D. Providing a client with an MLS book of available homes

3. If a broker does business under an assumed name, all of the following statements are correct EXCEPT:
   A. The broker is violating state law.
   B. The broker is using a name in his or her business other than or in addition to his or her given name.
   C. The broker must file an assumed name certificate with the county.
   D. The broker must notify the Department of his or her assumed name.

4. Compliance with the Assumed Name Act is NOT:
   A. easy.
   B. beneficial to the public.
   C. necessary unless you assume a name for business purposes that is different from your given name.
   D. required if the name assumed is an acronym of the given name, e.g., "John Doe, a/k/a J. D. Realty."

5. In order to discipline a licensee under the License Act for an untruthful ad, the State must prove that the ad was false and that it was done:
   A. intentionally.
   B. knowingly.
   C. negligently.
   D. None of the above

6. A broker wishing to open a branch office must:
   A. make application to the Secretary of State.
   B. certify the broker's capacity to properly manage and supervise both offices.
   C. go out on a limb.
   D. hire a broker to manage the office.

7. Which of the following, if performed by a licensee, would NOT be a violation of the License Act and/or Rules?
   A. Permitting a nonlicensed employee to solicit listings
   B. Advertising a one-acre lot as containing "1.1 acres"
   C. Doing business out of a home office
   D. Advertising storage space for rent without including the name of the sponsoring broker

8. Which of the following advertising statements would be most likely to "deceive the ordinary" consumer?
   A. "We get results."
   B. "Our listings sell faster."
   C. "We slam-dunk the competition."
   D. "We guarantee the highest prices available for your home."

9. A branch office license may not be issued unless:
   A. a licensed broker is hired to manage the office.
   B. the name of the office is identical to the main office.
   C. the office has a special account for escrow monies.
   D. the office is incorporated.

10. In dealing with his or her own real estate, an operative salesperson:
    A. may advertise "by owner."
    B. may place his or her broker's sign in the yard.
    C. may not indicate "agent owned" in advertising the property.
    D. may not list the real estate with a competitor of the salesperson's broker.

CHAPTER 4

ESCROW
(KNOCK, KNOCK—WHO'S THERE?)

○ CHAPTER OVERVIEW
As the custodian of funds belonging to others, a broker is governed by stringent rules and regulations regarding the handling of and accounting for such deposits. This chapter fully covers these requirements. It also provides a primer in the actual practice of escrow account bookkeeping, so that you won't be afraid if the answer to "Knock, knock—who's there?" is, "An auditor from the Illinois Department of Professional Regulation."

○ LEARNING OBJECTIVES
By the time you have finished studying this chapter, you should be able to:
1) Define "escrow monies," "journal," "ledger," and "reconciliation."
2) Describe and illustrate the use of a journal and a ledger.
3) Enumerate the time requirements for the deposit and disbursement of earnest monies, the reconciliation of monthly bank statements, the retention of reconciliation worksheets, and notifying the Illinois Department of Professional Regulation of changes in banking information.
4) Describe under what circumstances an escrow deposit may bear interest.
5) Give an overview of the creation and operation of an acceptable escrow account bookkeeping system.
6) Detail the circumstances under which disputed earnest monies may be disbursed.
7) Explain how escrow deposits must be handled when one of the parties to a transaction is a real estate licensee.
8) Enumerate the circumstances requiring the filing of a Consent to Examine and Audit Special Accounts form with the Department.

○ 5 CASES TO JUDGE

○ 10-QUESTION DIAGNOSTIC QUIZ

CHAPTER 4

ESCROW
(KNOCK, KNOCK—WHO'S THERE?)

There's a knock at your door, and lo and behold, you find yourself face to face with an auditor from the Illinois Department of Professional Regulation, who produces identification and announces that he is here to perform a random audit of your escrow accounts. Your escrow account is a shambles and has been ever since your bookkeeper left six months ago. You are about to be disciplined.

As will again be noted in Chapter 6, roughly 25 percent of all disciplinary action taken by the Illinois Department of Professional Regulation against a licensee comes as the result of the improper handling of monies belonging to clients/customers. The most severe penalties are assessed against licensees found guilty of converting a client's funds; and the least harshly penalized misconduct typically relates to poor bookkeeping practices that could easily have been avoided through a little effort. The purpose of this chapter is to assure that all licensees know what is expected, so that consumers' monies and your license are protected.

To help put things into perspective, consider this: If your bank only credited your account with a deposit whenever it got around to it, would you continue doing business with that bank? If your bank took your checking account monies and on a regular basis let its employees borrow from your account, would you be pleased? What if a teller took your cash deposit, lost it at the racetrack, and then wrote you a note saying he or she would get the money back to you—but it would take a few days?

These ludicrous examples are meant to underscore the fact that you should view yourself and how you handle funds belonging to others in much the same manner as you view a bank. The funds you handle may represent a couple's entire life savings. In view of this fact, the Department has high expectations for a licensee's handling of clients' and customers' monies.

PRELIMINARY CONSIDERATIONS

Several subsections of Section 18 of the Real Estate License Act mention or directly govern the licensee's handling of money or property belonging to others; however, Section 1450.40 of the Rules sets forth extensive rules for the handling of *escrow monies*, which are defined in Section 4 of the Act as:

> *all monies, promissory notes or any other type or manner of legal tender or financial consideration deposited with any person for the benefit of the parties to the transaction. Escrow monies include, but are not limited to, earnest monies and security deposits, except those security deposits in which the person holding the security deposit is also the sole owner of the property being leased and for which the security deposit is being held.*

Owner/brokers, managing brokers, and any staff or outside bookkeeping personnel would be well advised to closely examine Section 18(h)(9) and (10) of the Act as well as Section 1450.40 of the Rules for the Administration of the License Act.

NEED FOR SPECIAL ACCOUNT

Since each application for or renewal of a broker's, corporate, partnership, limited partnership, or branch office license must be accompanied by a Consent to Audit Special Account form, brokers oftentimes erroneously conclude that they must have an escrow account. Special accounts are not mandatory unless a broker will be holding monies belonging to others. Although salespersons are not expressly prohibited from holding monies belonging to others, they do not establish special (escrow) accounts.

DEPOSITORY AND ACCOUNT DECISIONS

FDIC Insurance. Once a decision is reached as to the necessity for a special account, the broker's next consideration will be the selection of a depository. Since deposits must be made promptly (by the next business day), brokers will want to maintain an escrow account at a convenient banking institution, one in close proximity to the office. The institution selected must be federally insured; therefore, certain credit unions may not qualify as an acceptable depository.

Monthly Statements. Most banks provide monthly bank statements; however, some institutions provide statements less frequently. Since the Rules require that you reconcile your accounts within ten days of your receipt of the "monthly bank statement," the Rules imply that you must select a depository that provides monthly statements.

Minimum/Maximum Deposit. To open an account, depositories normally require a minimum deposit. Oftentimes minimum deposits and monthly service charges will be waived by the depository if the bank official is made aware of the fact that the account is for escrow purposes. In the alternative, rather than letting automatic bank charges deplete your account to the point where an escrow check is bounced for insufficient funds, you may want to maintain a minimum balance and avoid service charges. As a final alternative, rather than maintaining a minimum balance, you may be able to direct the depository to charge the monthly service charge to another account maintained at the depository. Regardless of the option chosen, Section 1450.40(f) of the Rules provides:

> *Commingling Prohibited. Each broker shall deposit only funds received in connection with any real estate transaction in a special account designated as a special account and shall not deposit personal funds in a special account, except a broker may deposit from his own personal funds, and keep in any special account, an amount sufficient to avoid incurring service charges relating to the special account. The sum shall be specifically documented as being for service charges and the broker shall have proof available that the amount of his own funds in the special account does not exceed the minimum amount required by the depository to maintain the account without incurring service charges.*

Checks and Deposit Tickets. No particular form of check or deposit ticket is mandated by the Rules; therefore, the choice of such items is up to the broker and/or his or her accountant/bookkeeper. Due to many banks' custom of not returning deposit tickets with the month-end statement, a self-duplicating form of deposit ticket is advisable. To simplify your bookkeeping practices, follow the KISS (keep it simple, stupid) rule.

Check Register. Since the check register selected may serve as your "journal" (discussed below), you may wish to choose a register that serves both purposes.

Account Signatories. There are no restrictions as to who must or must not be a signatory on a special account, i.e., an authorized salesperson or an unlicensed office worker may be permitted to sign on the account. Therefore, logic and an accountant's advice may be your guide. Due to the notice requirements relating to changing signatories, you may wish to keep the number of authorized signatories to a minimum.

56 Chapter 4 Escrow

CONSENT TO AUDIT

Reproduced in Figure 4-1 is a Consent to Examine and Audit Special Accounts form. This form must be completed and sent to the Department within ten (10) days of opening a special account. The use of this form is more fully discussed in the following section.

FIG 4-1

IMPORTANT NOTICE: Completion of this form is necessary to accomplish the statutory purpose outlined in Chapter 111 of the Illinois Revised Statutes. Disclosure of this information is REQUIRED. Failure to provide any information could result in discipline as outlined in paragraph 5818 of Chapter 111. This form has been approved by the Forms Management Center.

RETURN COMPLETED FORM TO:

DEPARTMENT OF PROFESSIONAL REGULATION
POST OFFICE BOX 7086
SPRINGFIELD, ILLINOIS 62791

CONSENT TO EXAMINE AND AUDIT SPECIAL ACCOUNTS

☐ I have special account(s) and authorize the Department to examine same. (Complete A and B of this form.)
☐ I do not maintain special account(s) and do not hold money belonging to others. (Complete only Part A of this form.)

PART A

1. NAME OF INDIVIDUAL BROKER, PARTNERSHIP, CORPORATION, OR ASSOCIATION	2. LICENSE NUMBER

3. BUSINESS ADDRESS

PART B - DEPOSITORY IN WHICH REAL ESTATE SPECIAL ACCOUNT(S) ARE MAINTAINED

1. NAME OF BANK OR SAVINGS AND LOAN ASSOCIATION	2. CITY	3. ACCOUNTS TO BE INCLUDED a. ☐ All Special Accounts at This Depository b. ☐ Accounts Listed Below

4. SPECIFIC SPECIAL ACCOUNTS TO BE EXAMINED AND AUDITED (Only if 3b is checked)

Title(s) of Special Account(s)	Identifying Number(s) Required by IRS (FEIN or Social Security Number)	Account number

5. LIST THOSE PERSONS AUTHORIZED TO WITHDRAW FUNDS FROM ABOVE-NAMED SPECIAL ACCOUNT(S)

Name	Title	Broker or Salesperson No. (If Applicable)

I hereby authorize the above-named bank or savings and loan association to allow at any time a duly authorized representative of the Department to examine and audit the above-named special accounts.

Executed at: _____ By: _____
Officer or Partner Duly Authorized to Grant Above Consent

Date: _____ Title: _____

CERTIFICATION OF DEPOSITORY

The undersigned, a duly authorized official of the _____ of _____
Name of Depository   City

in behalf of said depository, does hereby certify that the above does maintain real estate special account(s) as set forth above and agrees that the depository will allow a duly authorized representative of the Department of Professional Regulation to examine and audit the above-named special account(s) upon demand.

SEAL OF DEPOSITORY

By: _____

Title: _____ Date: _____

A separate consent to audit form is required for each depository in which you maintain special account(s). Copy this form as needed.
IL486-1258 6/89 (RE)

INTEREST-BEARING ACCOUNTS

A broker may not maintain an interest-bearing special account unless *all parties* to a particular transaction direct *in writing* that the deposit be made in an interest-bearing account and specify who will be entitled to the interest earned on the deposit.

OPERATIONAL RULES

Depending on the volume of business and the size of particular transactions, there is a great deal of support for maintaining more than one special account at different financial institutions. The troubles of the thrift industry should heighten awareness of the fact that each *depositor* of a bank is insured by the FDIC to the extent of only $100,000. In the case of custodial accounts, each client/customer of the broker is deemed a depositor; therefore, the insurance afforded a special account is $100,000 per client/customer up to a maximum of $10,000,000 per institution. If a broker foresees the possibility of the total balance of a special account exceeding $100,000, additional special accounts should be considered in order to avoid the possibility that a portion of the deposit will be lost in the event of the insolvency of the depository. Remember, each depositor (not each account) is insured only to the extent of $100,000; therefore, if a client also maintains a sizable account at the same institution as the broker, the total protection for the client in that institution is $100,000.

BANKING CHANGES AND CONSENT TO AUDIT

A new consent to audit must be transmitted to the Department if: (1) a new account is opened; (2) a change of depository is accomplished; (3) an additional person is authorized to sign on the account; (4) an individual is removed as a signatory on the account; or (5) a change is accomplished in the method of doing business (name change or the creation/dissolution of a partnership, limited partnership, or corporation). Failure to timely file the consent form is deemed an endangerment of the public interest and sufficient cause for discipline under Section 18(h)(12) of the Act. Although it's not a requirement of the Rules to do so, good business sense dictates that any time an authorized signatory terminates his or her employment, an immediate cancellation of that person's authority to sign checks or withdraw funds from the special account should be documented in the bank's records and a new consent form should be completed and transmitted to the State.

DISPUTES OVER DEPOSITS

Defaults or breach of contract often lead to disputes over the entitlement to money escrowed with a broker. Less often, an escrow deposit is made and the depositor dies or disappears. In each case, the broker holding the funds must continue to act as the custodian until: (1) the parties provide the broker with a written direction as to the disbursement of the deposit; (2) a court order is entered directing the disbursement; or (3) the funds are turned over to the Illinois Department of Financial Institutions. Little known, apparently, are the provisions set forth in Section 1450.40(c)(2) of the Rules, which states:

> *In the event of a dispute over the return of escrow monies a broker is authorized to withdraw from his special account such amounts as may be provided for by contract and which are necessary to reimburse the broker for the handling of the escrow monies, including the participation in or filing of any civil action to determine the appropriate disposition of the monies, or to pay any commissions or fees authorized by subsection (i) below. This subsection applies to interpleader action only.*

We have yet to see a preprinted contract that incorporates and thus takes advantage of this beneficial provision of the Rules. An interpleader action is a lawsuit the broker may bring to resolve the dispute over the escrowed funds. Such litigation would have to be financed solely by the broker, who would have no ability to recoup his or her attorney's fees—unless the agreement (e.g., purchase and sale agreement) under which the deposit was made reflects the broker's authority to defray such expenses from the deposit.

LICENSEE AS A PARTY

A question that licensees oftentimes direct to the Department is: "If I am a party to a sale or lease, what must I do with the earnest money deposits?" The Rules and Department policies provide the following answers:

1. If the licensee is the seller or buyer, earnest money must be held in a special account on which the licensee *is not* a signatory;
2. If the licensee is a *sole* owner of leased property, security deposits need not be escrowed;
3. If the licensee is one of the owners of leased property, security deposits must be held in a special account on which the licensee is not a signatory.

Licensees are obligated to transact their own affairs in the same manner and are subject to the same rules as in their professional dealings. When licensees sell their own property they must handle earnest money in the same manner as they would if they were the agent, i.e., they must not commingle money or property of another with their own. In fact, the Department has taken the position that if a licensee is a party to the transaction, the earnest money must be held by a third party and not merely deposited in the broker's own special account.

A licensee, then, is placed in a worse position than most sellers/landlords in that if a buyer or a tenant defaults on a deal with a nonlicensee, the nonlicensee has immediate access to the deposited funds (assuming an FSBO). The licensee, however, must face the burden of suing the defaulting party to recover the deposits. With these inequities perhaps in mind, the Department has adopted new rules that permit the avoidance of this situation if a tenant provides the licensee with a knowledgeable waiver of the requirement that security deposits be held in a special account. The waiver requirements are set forth below. Additionally, if the licensee/landlord is the sole owner of the property being leased, the security deposits are not within the definition of escrow monies and a waiver under such circumstances is unnecessary. A waiver is not permissible for earnest money deposits.

PROPERTY MANAGEMENT

Mention should be made that property managers and others licensed under the Act are required to place all escrow monies collected on behalf of owners pursuant to a property management arrangement into a special account. However, this requirement may be waived by a tenant as long as the waiver is in writing. If the waiver is included in the lease agreement, the waiver must appear in bold print.

BANKING TIME REQUIREMENTS

The following is a summary of activities that must be performed by a licensee within a specific time frame. All licensees should be cognizant of these requirements.

1. All funds accepted by a broker on behalf of others must be placed in the broker's special account no later than the NEXT BUSINESS DAY.
2. If a broker does not maintain a special account at a branch office, the managing broker must deliver or mail special account funds received at the branch office to the broker's main office not later than the NEXT BUSINESS DAY.
3. Funds received at the main office from a branch office must be deposited in the broker's special account upon receipt of same, not later than the NEXT BUSINESS DAY.
4. Commissions and/or fees earned by a broker must be withdrawn by the broker from funds deposited in a special account no earlier than the day the transaction is consummated or terminated and not later than the NEXT BUSINESS DAY.
5. After the receipt of monthly statements, each special account maintained by such broker must be reconciled within TEN DAYS.
6. Upon changing the method of doing business, account number, location, or permitted signatories to a special account, the broker must notify the Department within TEN DAYS.
7. The worksheets for each reconciliation of a broker's special account must be kept for at least THREE YEARS.

BOOKKEEPING SYSTEM

Rule 1450.40 requires the broker to follow generally accepted accounting practices in the handling of his or her trust or escrow account(s). The Rules further set forth the requirements for minimum compliance. As mentioned above, Section 1450.40 should be reviewed in its entirety; however, there are three major requirements. They are the maintenance of a JOURNAL and a LEDGER and the monthly RECONCILIATION of escrow or special account(s). Subparagraph (f) of Section 1450.40 sets forth these requirements as follows:

> *f. Bookkeeping System. Each broker shall maintain, in his office or place of business, a bookkeeping system in accordance with sound accounting practices, and without limiting the foregoing, such system shall consist of at least the following:*
>
> *1) A record book, called a journal, for each special account. Such journal shall show the chronological sequence in which funds are received and disbursed by the broker.*
>
> > *A. For funds received, such journal shall include the date, the name of the party who delivers such funds to the broker, the name of the person on whose behalf such funds are delivered to the broker, and the amount of such funds so delivered.*
> >
> > *B. For fund disbursements, such journal shall include the date, the payee, the check number, and amount disbursed.*

> The journal is nothing more than an expanded checkbook register. The only difference between a checkbook register and the journal required by the license Rules are that deposits and disbursements must be referenced to a particular deal and purpose. See Figure 4-2 for an illustration of a blank page of a journal.

> > *C. A running balance shall be shown after each entry (receipt or disbursement).*

> Of importance also is the maintenance of a running balance. In other words, although it may be acceptable for an individual to only periodically strike a balance in a personal checking account, this practice is not permitted in the handling of an escrow account. A balance *must* be entered after every deposit and/or disbursement.

> *2) A ledger or a record book which shall show the receipt and the disbursement of such funds as same affect a single particular transaction as between buyer and seller, or landlord and tenant, or the respective parties to any other relationship. Such ledger shall include the names of both parties to a transaction, the amount of such funds received by such broker and the date of such receipt. Such ledger shall show, in connection with the disbursement of such funds, the date thereof, the payee, the check number and the amount disbursed. Such ledger shall segregate one transaction from another transaction. There shall be a separate ledger or separate section of each ledger, as the broker shall select, for each of the various kinds of real estate transactions.*

60 Chapter 4 Escrow

FIG 4-2

Date	Disbursement To/Received From	Check #	Description of Disbursement/Receipt	Property/Matter	Credits	Debits	Balance

Journal for Escrow Account #00-00-0

A ledger is a loose-leaf book of accounts. The ledger a broker uses may be a loose-leaf notebook, or in the alternative, a card file with three-by-five index cards for each account (deal). Regardless of the form the ledger takes, each loose-leaf page or index card will be "posted" with the information from each journal entry. See Figure 4-3 for an illustration of a blank ledger page/card.

3) Each broker shall reconcile within ten days after receipt of the monthly bank statement, each special account maintained by such broker except where there has been no transactional activity during the previous month. Such reconciliation shall include a written work sheet comparing the balances as shown, the bank or savings and loan association statement, the journal and the ledger, respectively, in order to insure agreement between the special account and the journal and the ledger entries with respect to such special account. Each such reconciliation shall be kept for at least three years from the last day of the month covered by such reconciliation.

The required monthly reconciliation differs from the reconciliation of a personal checking account only in the respect that the reconciled bank statement must agree with the journal (check register) balance *and* the ledger balance (total balance of all account/deal balances).

Chapter 4 Escrow   61

BOOKKEEPING ILLUSTRATION

The following bookkeeping illustration should help licensees with little or no bookkeeping experience understand the Department's minimum bookkeeping expectations as to a licensee's handling of escrow account(s).

Richard (Dick) H. Bettner passed his state broker's exam on October 22, 1991, and decided to open his own office under the assumed name My Realty Company. He notified the Department of his assumed name; sent in his sponsor card and application for a broker's license; had the phones and office equipment installed in his new office; and on November 1, 1991, opened his doors for business.

Since Dick's only phone call all morning long was a call from his elderly mother, who asked that he stop by after work to show her how to operate the controls on the VCR he had given her the previous Christmas, he decided at lunchtime to go to the bank to set up his trust account and to the office supply store to pick up some ledger cards, a journal, and a metal file box to hold his ledger cards. During his lunch hour, he opened up his special account and put $5 in the account as an initial deposit. When he returned to the office, he sat down and looked over the blank journal and ledger cards, which looked like the forms that appear in Figures 4-2 and 4-3.

After looking over the journal and ledger cards, Broker Bettner made the first entry into his journal, showing the $5 deposit he made to open the account. His banker agreed to waive monthly service charges and to charge Dick's business account with any check-printing charges. Dick also filled out a ledger card. The completed journal and ledger card entries are illustrated in Figures 4-4 and 4-5.

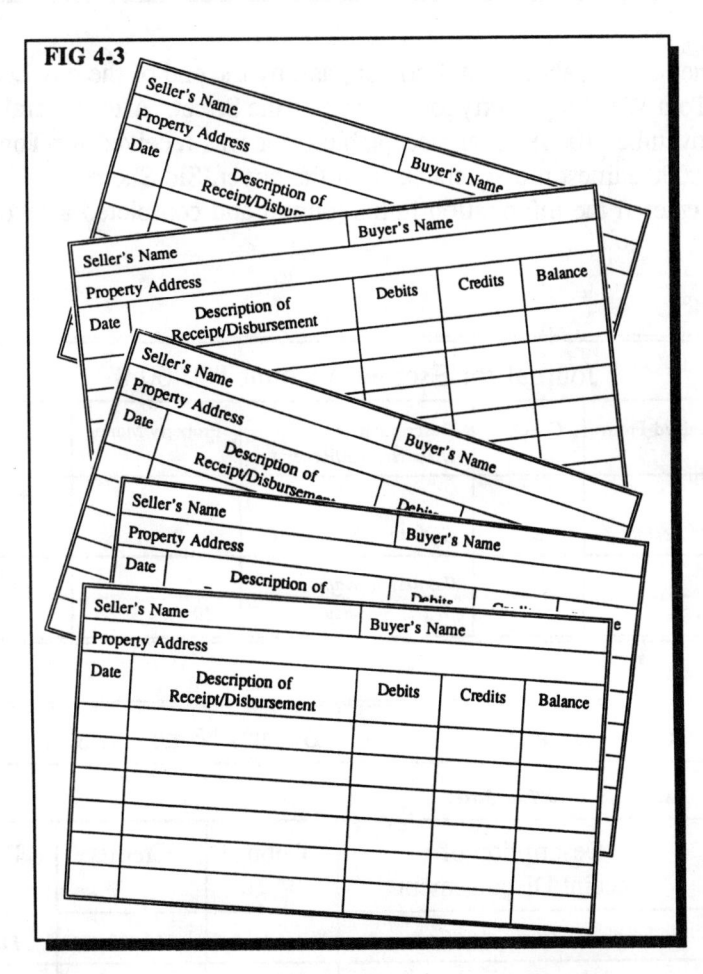

FIG 4-3

FIG 4-4

Journal for Escrow Account #00-00-0

Date 1991	Disbursement To/Received From	Check #	Description of Disbursement/Receipt	Property/Matter	Debits	Credits	Balance
11/01	Received from Richard Bettner		Cash to open account			$5.00	$5.00

FIG 4-5

Seller's Name *Dick Bettner*		Buyer's Name *N/A*		
Property Address *N/A*				
Date 1991	Description of Receipt/Disbursement	Debits	Credits	Balance
11/01	Deposit to open account		$5.00	$5.00

Fortunately, the phone started to ring about midafternoon, and by the end of the day Dick had sold his first house and had taken a listing on Tom Watts's property located at 10 Pine Street. After several productive days of selling and listing property, on November 10, 1991, an acceptable offer was received for Tom Watts's property, which was accompanied by a $10,000 earnest money check from the buyer, Sid Shore. Dick deposited the check in his special account. Then he entered the information in his journal and completed a second ledger card as follows (Figures 4-6 and 4-7):

FIG 4-6

Journal for Escrow Account #00-00-0

Date 1991	Disbursement To/Received From	Check #	Description of Disbursement/Receipt	Property/Matter	Debits	Credits	Balance
11/01	Received from Richard Bettner		Cash to open account			$5.00	$5.00
11/10	Received from Sid Shore		Earnest money; Watts property	10 Pine Street		$10,000.00	$10,005.00

FIG 4-7

Seller's Name *Tom Watts*		Buyer's Name *Sid Shore*		
Property Address *10 Pine Street*				
Date 1991	Description of Receipt/Disbursement	Debits	Credits	Balance
11/10	Received from Sid Shore		$10,000.00	$10,000.00

Chapter 4 Escrow 63

Over the next couple of weeks, Dick's escrow account and ledger further memorialized the following transactions:

DATE TRANSACTION
11-14 $5,000 earnest money check was received from Al Wade for Barbara Lee's property located at 1921 Elm Street.
11-20 Fran Foster deposits $500 as a security deposit for Edna Bank's rental home at 1121 First Avenue.
11-21 An offer for the home located at 351 South 4th Street is accepted by Jim Bell.
11-22 Marilyn Taylor's earnest money check of $3,000 for the Bell property is received.
11-23 John Firth deposits $10,000 as earnest money for the purchase of Freida Sheet's property at 821 Indiana Court.
11-27 The Watts sale to Shore is closed and Dick pays himself his first commission of $9,000 and disburses the remainder to Tom Watts.
12-01 Dick receives his bank statement, showing a November 30 account balance of $19,505.00.

All checks that Dick had issued to the date the statement was received were returned paid by his bank, with the exception of check #102, which had been issued to Tom Watts. All of Dick's deposits were credited to his account. Dick took out all of his open ledger cards, his journal, and a reconciliation worksheet, and proceeded to reconcile his journal balance, ledger balances, and bank statement. Depicted in Figures 4-8 and 4-9 are the properly completed components of a minimally acceptable bookkeeping system for an escrow account.

FIG 4-8 — Journal for Escrow Account #00-00-0

Date 1991	Disbursement To/Received From	Check #	Description of Disbursement/Receipt	Property/Matter	Debits	Credits	Balance
11/01	Received from Richard Bettner		Cash to open account			5.00	5.00
11/10	Received from Sid Shore		Earnest money; Watts property	10 Pine Street		10,000.00	10,005.00
11/14	Received from Al Wade		Earnest money; Lee property	1921 Elm St.		5,000.00	15,005.00
11/20	Received from Fran Foster		Security deposit; Banks property	1121 1st Ave.		500.00	15,505.00
11/22	Received from Marilyn Taylor		Earnest money; Bell property	351 So. 4th		3,000.00	18,505.00
11/23	Received from John Firth		Earnest money; Sheets property	821 Indiana Court		10,000.00	28,505.00
11/27	Paid to Richard Bettner	101	Commission; Watts sale	10 Pine Street	9,000.00		19,505.00
11/27	Paid to Tom Watts	102	Overage; Watts sale	10 Pine Street	1,000.00		18,505.00

64 Chapter 4 Escrow

FIG 4-9

Seller's Name	Dick Bettner	Buyer's Name	N/A		
Property Address	N/A				
Date 1991	Description of Receipt/Disbursement	Debits	Credits	Balance	
11/01	Deposit to open account		5.00	5.00	

Seller's Name	Tom Watts	Buyer's Name	Sid Shore		
Property Address	10 Pine Street				
Date 1991	Description of Receipt/Disbursement	Debits	Credits	Balance	
11/10	Received from Sid Shore		10,000.00	10,000.00	
11/27	Paid to Dick Bettner (Check #101)	9,000.00		1,000.00	
11/27	Paid to Tom Watts (Check #102)	1,000.00		-0-	

Seller's Name	Barbara Lee	Buyer's Name	Al Wade		
Property Address	1921 Elm Street				
Date 1991	Description of Receipt/Disbursement	Debits	Credits	Balance	
11/14	Received from Al Wade		5,000.00	5,000.00	

Seller's Name	Edna Banks	Buyer's Name	Fran Foster		
Property Address	1121 First Avenue				
Date 1991	Description of Receipt/Disbursement	Debits	Credits	Balance	
11/20	Received from Fran Foster		500.00	500.00	

Seller's Name	Jim Bell	Buyer's Name	Marilyn Taylor		
Property Address	351 South 4th Street				
Date 1991	Description of Receipt/Disbursement	Debits	Credits	Balance	
11/22	Received from Marilyn Taylor		3,000.00	3,000.00	

Seller's Name	Freida Sheets	Buyer's Name	John Firth		
Property Address	821 Indiana Court				
Date 1991	Description of Receipt/Disbursement	Debits	Credits	Balance	
11/23	Received from John Firth		10,000.00	10,000.00	

RECONCILIATION WORKSHEET

DATE STATEMENT RECEIVED: 12/01/91
DATE OF RECONCILIATION: 12/01/91

1. Balance shown on Bank Statement $19,505.00
2. ADD Deposits (if any) not yet credited to Account $ —
3. SUBTOTAL $19,505.00
4. Checks issued but not yet charged to Account

   No. 102 $1,000.00   No. ____ $ ____
   No. ____ $ ____   No. ____ $ ____
   No. ____ $ ____   No. ____ $ ____
   No. ____ $ ____   No. ____ $ ____

   TOTAL of Checks Outstanding $1,000.00

5. BALANCE after subtracting Line 4 from Line 3 $18,505.00

   (BALANCE must agree with Journal and Ledger Balances)

   JOURNAL BALANCE $18,505.00

   LEDGER BALANCE $18,505.00
   Open Accounts
     Bettner $5.00
     Lee $5,000.00
     Banks $500.00
     Bell $3,000.00
     Sheets $10,000.00

MISCELLANEOUS CONSIDERATIONS

BOOKKEEPING FOR INTEREST-BEARING ACCOUNTS

An interest-bearing account set up for a particular deal is an additional escrow account for which a ledger, journal, reconciliation, and consent to audit are technically required by a strict interpretation of the Act and Rules. The best way of handling this type of escrow monies, however, and one that is approved by the Department, is to establish a special journal and section of your ledger to handle such accounts. The journal and ledger sheet/card for a particular transaction would reflect the same information as if the account were non-interest-bearing.

ACCOUNTING FOR BOUNCED CHECKS/OTHER SERVICE CHARGES

Due to the relatively sizable amount of earnest money checks, occasionally the buyer's check will reach his or her account prior to the availability of the funds from the covering deposit. In such cases, the broker's bank will return the check to the broker along with a debit memo that may include a service charge. For example, a $500 check may arrive in the mail along with a debit memo for $510. Besides immediately notifying the buyer and the broker's principal, the broker should enter the debit memo into the journal as a disbursement of $510, deposit $10 from the broker's own funds to cover the service charge, and post the applicable ledger card with a $500 debit. The $10 service charge is a cost of doing business and *should not* result in the broker's posting a negative balance in the ledger. The embarrassed buyer may and should write separate checks to cover the returned item: One check should be written to replace the bounced item, and a second check for $10 to cover the broker's expense.

Similarly, if a cashier's check, wire transfer, or other bank charge is incurred in conjunction with servicing an account, the service charge should be handled "outside" the journal and ledger. The broker should pay for such fees with cash or with a business check and be reimbursed from the business or operating account.

DELAYED CLOSINGS

Checks that must be paid out of a special account at the time of a closing are normally cut the day of (or, in the case of larger firms, several days before) the closing. There is nothing wrong with such a practice so long as the checks are not delivered and negotiated prior to the actual closing. In the event a deal is simply delayed, there is no need to void the checks and credit the amount back to the journal and ledger. If, however, a deal is terminated or indefinitely delayed, then the checks should be voided and the appropriate bookkeeping entries made in the journal and ledger.

BOOKKEEPING EXERCISE

The simplicity of the required bookkeeping practices may perhaps only be appreciated through practice. Therefore, we have supplied you with a bookkeeping exercise to help you become comfortable with the process. The exercise should take only a few minutes.

Based on the information that follows, fill out a journal, ledger, and reconciliation worksheet. The necessary forms for this exercise may be found in Figures 4-10 and 4-11.

Broker Joanna Hoshaw opens Her Realty Company and, during the first month of operation, must record and reconcile her special account based on the following transactions:

66 Chapter 4 Escrow

DATE	TRANSACTION
05-01-92	Joanna deposits $100 in her special account and receives a letter from the vice president of her bank verifying the fact that $100 is the minimum deposit Ms. Hoshaw must make in the escrow account to avoid incurring monthly service charges.
05-05-92	William Smith deposits $1,000 as earnest money for the purchase of Martha Jones's property, which Joanna has listed and which is located at 100 East Main.
05-25-92	ABC Realty delivers $1,500 in cash for M. Brown, who has contracted to purchase Joanna's listing at 10 North Cedar. The property is owned by Russ Newberg.
05-27-92	At the closing on the sale of 100 East Main, Joanna writes a $1,000 check (#101) to Martha Jones, which represents the earnest monies on deposit.
05-28-92	Joanna writes three checks, numbered 102 through 104, in conjunction with the Newberg closing. Check #102 was made payable to Her Realty Company, representing the $750 commission Joanna earned on the sale of 10 North Cedar. Check #103 was payable to the seller, Newberg, in the amount of $500, and the final check, #104, was issued to the County Collector in the amount of $250 for the 1991 taxes on the property.
06-02-92	Joanna receives her bank statement showing a balance on hand of $1,600. The only check that had cleared her bank was check #101.

FIG 4-10   Journal for Escrow Account #00-00-0

Date 1992	Disbursement To/Received From	Check #	Description of Disbursement/Receipt	Property/Matter	Debits	Credits	Balance

FIG 4-11

Seller's Name		Buyer's Name		
Property Address				
Date	Description of Receipt/Disbursement	Debits	Credits	Balance

Seller's Name		Buyer's Name		
Property Address				
Date	Description of Receipt/Disbursement	Debits	Credits	Balance

Seller's Name		Buyer's Name		
Property Address				
Date	Description of Receipt/Disbursement	Debits	Credits	Balance

RECONCILIATION WORKSHEET

DATE STATEMENT RECEIVED: _____
DATE OF RECONCILIATION: _____

1. Balance shown on Bank Statement .... $ _____

2. ADD Deposits (if any) not yet credited to Account .... $ _____

3. SUBTOTAL .... $ _____

4. Checks issued but not yet charged to Account

   No. ____ $ _____   No. ____ $ _____

   No. ____ $ _____   No. ____ $ _____

   No. ____ $ _____   No. ____ $ _____

   No. ____ $ _____   No. ____ $ _____

   TOTAL of Checks Outstanding .... $ _____

5. BALANCE after subtracting Line 4 from Line 3 .... $ _____

   (BALANCE must agree with Journal and Ledger Balances)

   JOURNAL BALANCE .... $ _____

   LEDGER BALANCE .... $ _____

CASES TO JUDGE

1. Betty Buyer submitted a written complaint to the Department seeking its assistance in securing a refund of a $1,500 earnest money deposit she had made in connection with a contract to purchase a HUD-acquired property. As a result of Betty's complaint, an investigation ensued concerning: the salesperson with whom Betty was working, Sue Salesperson; Sue's sponsoring broker, John's Realty, Inc., a corporation solely owned by John Broker; and the managing broker of John's Realty, Inc., Elaine Broker, John Broker's wife.

On August 10, 1988, Betty bid on a HUD-owned property located in Island Lake, Illinois. At the time she signed the offer, she deposited a $1,500 check with Sue Salesperson. The bid required a $2,000 deposit and Betty promised to bring in the additional $500 if the offer was accepted. Sue Salesperson signed the HUD offer to purchase, certifying that John's Realty, Inc. had received $2,000 in earnest money, and placed the $1,500 check in the brokerage firm's safe. On August 13, HUD rejected Betty's offer.

On August 15, Betty asked Sue Salesperson to put in a bid on another HUD-owned property, this one being located in Lake Villa. The offer was submitted, again showing a $2,000 deposit. This bid was accepted, and a closing was set for October 19, 1988. For a variety of reasons (allegedly Betty's need for an operation, her pregnancy, her inability to obtain financing, and her father's failure to make a promised gift), Betty was unable to close the transaction, and in accordance with the contract, HUD declared a forfeiture of the earnest money and demanded that the brokerage firm surrender the earnest money on deposit within five days. HUD's demand letter concluded with the statement, "Failure to remit the earnest money deposit as instructed will result in denial of participation in the HUD sales program."

In accordance with HUD's demand, on November 2 Elaine Broker removed Betty's $1,500 check from the office safe and purchased a $2,000 cashier's check payable to HUD with Betty's $1,500 and $500 of the brokerage firm's own monies. (Betty never brought in the promised $500 in additional earnest money; rather than lose the firm's ability to continue doing HUD transactions, Elaine provided the additional funds from the firm's operating account.) In response to Betty's demand for a return of her earnest money, Sue Salesperson wrote Betty the following (*unedited*) letter:

Dear Betty,
The first house you bid on was August 10, 1988, it was 3312 Eastway, Island Lake, Ill. for $35,001.00. You brought in $1500 and said you'd bring in the rest-$500 later, but never did. On August 15, 1988, you bid on 37439 Antonio, Lake Villa for $36,540.00 from the extended list you found in newspapers. You had plenty of time to know how much money you needed to close the house. I'm sorry your dad didn't follow through with his promises. If by chance you should get your $1500 back from the $2000 we had to send in, we will expect our $500 back also. We will be checking HUD to see if you do get the money back.
Sincerely, Sue Salesperson

HUD refused to refund any portion of the earnest money.

What action should the Department have taken, and against whom? [*Illinois Department of Professional Regulation v. Licensee*, Case #89-5747 (1989)]

2. The following (*unedited*) complaint was made to the Department:
Dear Sirs:
I'm writing to you because of a problem I'm having with a Real Estate broker for he released earnst money without my approval. On Aug. 27, 1988 I wrote to Foolish Realty stating not to release the earnst money and send me a copy of the real estate contract. On Aug. 31, 1988 Foolish Realty Acknowledged my letter. On Oct. 13, 1988 I came to an agreement with the attorney for purchaser on splitting the earnst money. On Oct. 14, 1988 the purchaser's attorney sends me another letter stating our agreement is null and void due to Foolish Realty released the earnst money. I never gave the broker permission to release the earnst money, I'm very disappointed in Foolish Realty's professional ethics for said broker broke his fiduciary responsibility. I hope your office can do something so this will not happen again.
Thank You

The Department's investigation revealed that Foolish Realty was a partnership owned by I. M. Foolish and Ny Eve, the managing broker. The investigation further confirmed that the managing broker had, in fact, refunded the buyer's earnest money without the consent of all parties to the transaction.

In defense of the charges, I. M. Foolish and Ny Eve established through their records, correspondence, and/or testimony that:

    1. They both closely examined the Real Estate License Act and could not determine what they should do in a case where the parties refused to agree to the disposition of the earnest money;

    2. The firm's attorney, Eve N. Dummer, had advised them that they had no legal right to withhold the earnest money from the buyer; and

3. The buyer's attorney had, both orally and in letter form, threatened legal action if the earnest money was not refunded, stating in his last correspondence, "There is no legal reason to further delay the return of the earnest money deposit in this matter. The Contract between the buyer and seller has been declared null and void and therefore, by its terms, the earnest money should rightfully be returned to my client."

Under these circumstances, should either of the licensees be disciplined? [*Illinois Department of Professional Regulation v. Licensee*, Case #89-2041 (1989)]

3. An attorney representing the buyer of an apartment building in Chicago notified the Department that a lawsuit had been filed seeking a refund of his client's $12,200 earnest money deposit. The notice further indicated that a claim might possibly be made against the Real Estate Recovery Fund if, as alleged in the complaint, the broker had converted the buyer's earnest money.

Upon receipt of the notice, an auditor was dispatched by the Department to determine whether the broker did or did not in fact have the earnest monies properly deposited in a special account. The auditor's report indicated that the $12,200 was, *at the time of his audit* (April 28, 1989), properly on deposit in the broker's escrow account; however, the deposit was not made until April 18, 1989, almost nine months after the buyer's earnest money check had been issued and deposited in the *seller's* personal account. The source of funds for the broker's deposit on April 18, 1989, was a check written on the seller's business account. Otherwise, the auditor noted that the broker's escrow account and bookkeeping records were in balance and fully complied with the Department's rules and regulations.

What action against the licensee would, in your opinion, be justified for the broker's conduct in permitting her client access to the earnest money? How would your opinion differ if the client had not remitted the earnest money to the broker? [*Illinois Department of Professional Regulation v. Licensee*, Case #89-1851 (1989)]

4. In 1954, Mr. and Mrs. Thomas Coleman, Jr., as purchasers, entered into an agreement with Mr. and Mrs. Henry Cooper, as sellers, for the sale and purchase of certain real estate in Chicago. Henry B. Huff was the real estate broker in the transaction. The Colemans deposited $1,300 with Huff as earnest money, $200 of which he turned over to the sellers. Before the sale was consummated, Henry Cooper died. His wife refused to go through with the transaction and returned the $200 to the Colemans. The broker, however, refused to return to the Colemans the $1,100 earnest money that he retained in his possession.

The Colemans then filed a complaint with the Department, and after an informal hearing on January 6, 1956, the real estate supervisor of the Department advised Huff that he should return the deposit of $1,100 to the Colemans. Huff refused to return the deposit and represented that he would file a civil suit against the Colemans and Mrs. Cooper to establish his right to a commission. Thereafter, Huff filed suit in the Municipal Court of Chicago against the Colemans and Mrs. Cooper, wherein he claimed the $1,100 as broker's commission. In the municipal court suit, the Colemans counterclaimed for the return of the deposit of $1,100. The complaint before the Department was continued generally pending the outcome of the civil suit.

On October 6, 1959, the municipal court dismissed Huff's complaint and rendered judgment for the Colemans on their counterclaim in the sum of $1,100 plus interest and costs. Huff did not appeal the municipal court judgment.

Thereafter the hearings upon the complaint before the Department were resumed. The Disciplinary Commission found that the broker had neglected, failed, and refused to return the earnest money deposit of $1,100 with or without interest to the Colemans, although repeatedly requested to do so, and further found that he had neglected, failed, and refused to divulge the disposition made by him of such deposit. On the basis of these facts, the committee found that the plaintiff had violated certain specific provisions of the act relating to real estate brokers.

What action should the Department have taken? [*Huff v. Department of Registration and Education*, 24 Ill.2d 140, 180 N.E. 460 (1962)]

5. As the result of an audit, licensees John P. Shermerhorn (a broker) and J. P. Shermerhorn & Company (the Company) were charged with having commingled escrow monies. Gilbert Lynn, chief audit supervisor for the Department, audited the books of the Company and discovered that $75,000 had been withdrawn from the Company's property-management account and placed in a commercial paper investment in the name of J. P. Shermerhorn & Company. The Company offered property-management services to its customers and maintained a management account wherein monies collected in the course of rendering those services were deposited and held in trust. Lynn's audit further revealed that by taking funds from its property-management account and investing them in commercial paper in the Company's name, the Company had earned approximately $33,000 in interest from 1980 through 1983. Plaintiffs deposited the interest so earned into the Company's operating account and credited it as interest income; the commercial paper investment was recorded as cash in its property-management account.

Assuming that the court rejected the licensee's claims that their client had consented to the arrangement, what would be the appropriate disposition of this case? [*J. P. Shermerhorn v. Department of Registration and Education*, 185 Ill.App.3d 883, 542 N.E.2d 42, 134 Ill.Dec. 42 (1989)]

10-QUESTION DIAGNOSTIC QUIZ

1. A security deposit delivered with a signed lease to a broker managing an apartment building must be deposited in the broker's special account:
   A. immediately.
   B. within 48 hours.
   C. not later than the next business day following the receipt of the funds.
   D. not later than the third business day following the receipt of the lease.

2. Which of the following funds should NOT be placed in a broker's special account?
   A. Land contract collections for a client
   B. Commission payments
   C. Earnest monies
   D. Rental collections

3. A broker's records of receipts on client accounts must contain all of the following EXCEPT the:
   A. name of the person delivering the funds.
   B. date such funds are received.
   C. name of the person on whose behalf such funds are delivered to the broker.
   D. employee/independent contractor responsible for procuring such funds.

4. For funds disbursed by a broker, the broker's bank records must contain the date of the:
   A. contract.
   B. closing.
   C. disbursement.
   D. listing.

5. Which of the following brokers has violated the Real Estate License Act relative to the handling of earnest monies?
   A. Broker Fred, whose special account is maintained at a federal savings and loan association
   B. Broker Mary, who, at the written direction of the seller, places the earnest money deposit in an interest-bearing special account maintained solely for that client's transactions
   C. Broker Fran, who disburses her commission check out of the escrow account the same day as the closing
   D. Broker Harry, who, with the written direction of the parties to a transaction, places earnest monies in an interest-bearing account but neglects to have the parties designate the name of the depository

6. A broker must do which of the following:
   A. Provide the Illinois Department of Professional Regulation with the name of each depository where his or her business accounts are maintained
   B. Provide the Illinois Department of Professional Regulation with the names of all persons authorized by him or her to withdraw funds on deposit from a special account
   C. Notify the Department of Professional Regulation if his or her bank changes its name
   D. Maintain a sufficient special account balance to avoid incurring monthly bank charges

7. A broker may deposit his or her own personal funds in a special account so long as the funds do not exceed:
   A. one and one-half times his or her average daily balance.
   B. $50.
   C. $100.
   D. the minimum amount required by the depository to avoid incurring monthly service charges.

8. The minimum acceptable bookkeeping/banking practices for the handling of a broker's special account must include:
   A. regular audits by a state-licensed auditor or accountant.
   B. a journal and a ledger.
   C. overdraft protection.
   D. fidelity insurance.

9. All except one of the following statements are true. Which statement is FALSE?
   A. A broker may employ a sophisticated bookkeeping system that utilizes electronic data-processing equipment.
   B. A broker must retain all accounting and bookkeeping records for a period of no less than three years.
   C. A broker may not under any circumstances deposit earnest monies in an interest-bearing account.
   D. A broker may, under certain circumstances, retain earnest monies forfeited by a defaulting buyer in payment of the broker's fees.

10. If earnest monies are received by a branch office, such funds must be deposited:
    A. in the main office's special account, since branch office special accounts are not permissible in Illinois.
    B. in the branch office's special account (if such an account is maintained), not later than the next business day.
    C. in a special account (branch or main office) not later than the third business day.
    D. not later than the third business day following the branch office's receipt of the funds.

CHAPTER 5

THOU SHALT NOT
(§18 OF THE ACT)

○ CHAPTER OVERVIEW
Like driving a car without knowing what a red light means, practicing real estate without knowing the rules of the road is dangerous to both the driver (licensee) and pedestrian (consumer). In real estate, however, just one blown stoplight can cost you your driving privileges. Chapter 5 will assure that you know the most important rules of the road.

○ LEARNING OBJECTIVES
By the time you have finished studying this chapter, you should be able to:
1) Enumerate at least 30 different causes for the disciplining of licensees.
2) Recognize and assist in remediating conduct of others that violates the License Act and/or Rules.
3) Conform your own conduct and the conduct of others for whom you are responsible, if any, to the mandates of the License Act and Rules.
4) List the penalties leviable under the Act.
5) Differentiate between violations that subject the offender to criminal penalties and those that carry civil penalties.
6) Appreciate the full scope of each prohibited activity.
7) Avoid conduct in your personal affairs that may jeopardize your professional standing.
8) More fully appreciate the rationale for conduct prohibited by the License Act and Rules to the end that compliance becomes less burdensome.

○ 5 CASES TO JUDGE

○ 10-QUESTION DIAGNOSTIC QUIZ

CHAPTER 5

THOU SHALT NOT
(§18 OF THE ACT)

Albert M. Suguitan, Illinois's Commissioner of Real Estate, was recently interviewed by a newspaper reporter in connection with disciplinary proceedings against a well-known real estate broker. A transcript of their conversation follows. (The names of the other parties have been changed to protect their identities.)

Reporter: "What brought Garfield T. Katt's disciplinary infraction to your attention, Mr. Suguitan?"
Suguitan: "We received a five-page letter from Ms. Gloria Goofy. The letter was written in crayon on construction paper and was somewhat difficult to read. In a nutshell, the letter alleged that Mr. Katt and/or his firm, Nine Lives Realty: (1) made a substantial misrepresentation; (2) failed to disclose a material defect; and (3) mishandled her escrow monies—all of which, if true, are serious violations of the License Act."
Reporter: "What did you do after you got the letter?"
Suguitan: "As with any complaint, we immediately assigned the file to an investigator to follow up. Since a portion of the complaint related to improper bookkeeping, we immediately dispatched an auditor to Mr. Katt's office to conduct an unannounced audit of Nines Lives' books and records. Mr. Katt was extremely cooperative with the auditor, and because of the impeccable condition of his records and bookkeeping practices, the audit was completed in less than half a day. The auditor reported that the only mistake he could find was the failure to promptly send in a consent to audit form for two new special accounts that had been opened the month prior to the audit. When asked about the consents, Mr. Katt produced the forms, which were on his desk and ready for mailing to the Department. Since the accounts had been open for 45 days and the rules require mailing within ten days, the auditor was required to note this technical violation in his report. This technical violation might have been ignored, except for the fact that we had this pending investigation."
Reporter: "How long did your investigation of Mr. Katt take?"
Suguitan: "Six months."
Reporter: "Why did it take so long—did Katt obstruct the investigation?"
Suguitan: "No, quite the contrary; Mr. Katt was most gracious and cooperative. The problem with the investigation was in substantiating Goofy's complaint of misrepresentation and failure to disclose."
Reporter: "What was the basis for the other two charges?"
Suguitan: "Well...I hope you'll appreciate that this is off the record."
Reporter: "Sure."
Suguitan: "Well, it seems Ms. Goofy, poor soul, has a long history of mental disturbances. She's been hearing voices since she was ten, and her complaint that Mr. Katt had failed to disclose a material defect was related to her belief that the house was haunted by ghosts. We checked with several previous owners of the home, who confirmed our initial impression that Ms. Goofy continues to suffer from some form of mental illness. Ms. Goofy's other complaint was misrepresentation. Once we were able to piece together her complaint, it seems she objected to buying the home for $2,000 under the $102,000 listing price. She reasoned that if she could buy something for $100,000, an asking price of $102,000 was a misrepresentation."
Reporter: "So Goofy was just plain goofy?"
Suguitan: "Those are your words, not mine."
Reporter: "Why, then, was Mr. Katt disciplined?"

Chapter 5 Thou Shalt Not   73

HOMETOWN CHRONICLE

50¢   Jones County's Community Newspaper Since 1881   Tuesday, January 14, 1992

Local Real Estate Broker Disciplined by State Licensing Authorities

Garfield T. Katt, a broker with Nine Lives Realty, was recently fined and disciplined by the Illinois Department of Professional Regulation and could also face criminal charges for his conduct. The action taken yesterday ends a six-month-long investigation into Mr. Katt's professional conduct. According to the Illinois Commissioner of Real Estate, Albert Suguitan, Mr. Katt has exhausted his appeals of the decision of the Illinois Real Estate Administration and Disciplinary Commission, and the fine levied by the Department and disciplinary action taken against Mr. Katt's license stand. Although Nine Lives Realty officials were not available for comment, the action taken by the Department came as the result of a complaint filed by one of Nine Lives' clients, Gloria Goofy. Goofy charged in her complaint to the Department that Mr. Katt had misrepresented the value of a home, failed to disclose material defects in the home, and mishandled her earnest monies. Although Mr. Katt was exonerated of two of the charges, an audit conducted by the Chief Auditor of the Department's Real Estate Investigations Unit regarding Mr. Katt's handling of the financial records of Nine Lives Realty provided the basis for the disciplinary action taken.

Visibly upset with the decision of the Board, Mr. Katt was unable to comment on his future with Nine Lives Realty. When contacted by phone, Ms. Goofy expressed relief that "the awful nightmare was over" and that she could return to her normal activities.

SCHOOL OVERFLOW IS TOUGHEST ON PARENTS

As local growth jams our classrooms, many children will grow up without learning the concept of a 'neighborhood' school. For some new west-side residents, learning their third-graders will be bused across town to school may be the biggest adjustment to moving.

Area growth continues to add students to our classrooms. However, there is no more room in a number of classes, such as the third-grade classrooms at North Avenue School.

No more third-graders can enroll at North Avenue School this year, even if they move in down the street.

Robert and Dannette Pegg's family moved in December to the Town Square subdivision. One of the first things they

Please see **PARENTS** page 8

MEETING SHEDS NO LIGHT ON BALL DIAMOND ISSUE

A joint meeting between the Hometown Community Park and the Hometown School Board Monday night failed to provide an answer on whether a lighted softball diamond belongs on the Fedder property.

Controversy about the park district's offer to pay for the lights on the school district's land erupted last month when school board members questioned the fiscal responsibility of making improvements to property earmarked as a future building site.

School Board member John Menze said he is the one representative from the school board that agreed to spend nearly $2 million for the 75 acres of land north of the Hometown High School on Dunpast Road.

"The thing that disturbs me, more than anything else, is I'm not too comfortable that I understand where the school district is going with that property," Menze said.

Menze said he is afraid that if the property is allowed to be developed into lighted baseball diamonds, the school district may draw community criticism when the time comes to build on the site.

"If this isn't going to impact us building a high school or junior high, then I don't have a problem with is," Menze said.

The park district has agreed to pay the $30,000 cost of lighting one of the softball diamonds on the Fedder property in return for the right to hold summer league games there.

Park Board President Debra Massey said the proposal is a fiscally responsible move for both taxing bodies. High school sports teams could take advantage of the lights during the school year, while the park district will save the money it would have spent acquiring a similar piece of land.

"We are not trying to paint you into a corner as the bad buy or say you are

Please see **LIGHT** page 3

Suguitan: "Quite frankly, I don't know. I wasn't part of the administration and disciplinary board's deliberations. I wish all of our licensees were as virtuous as Mr. Katt."
Reporter: "Could it be the fact that Gloria is the sister of a high-ranking Illinois politician?"
Suguitan: "I really don't know—but it's a shame that Mr. Katt's sterling reputation and record were tarnished for such an insignificant and technical error."
Reporter: "What discipline did Mr. Katt receive?"
Suguitan: "He was fined $25 and reprimanded. To put his discipline in perspective, if Mr. Katt had been charged with a traffic violation, the offense and penalty would be on the same level as an overtime parking charge."
Reporter: "Isn't it true that Mr. Katt could also be criminally charged for violating the License Act?"
Suguitan: "Yes, he could be, but the chances of that happening in this instance are a trillion to one."
Reporter: "I think that's it—thank you."
Suguitan: "You're welcome. Good-bye."
Reporter: "Good-bye."

Perhaps it was a slow news day in Hometown—or perhaps some other evil motive prompted the published story. Regardless, the printed article, as seen on the preceding page, IS NOT libelous. Every word of the article is truthful, and truth is a complete defense against libel charges.

Truth is oftentimes stranger than fiction. The foregoing, however, is pure fiction. We can authoritatively state, though, that similar albeit less dramatic cases have arisen. What a local newspaper does with a disciplinary report and what they choose to report and don't report is freedom of the press. Our purpose here is not to scare the bejeebees out of you, but to assure that to the best of our ability, given limited time and space, you the licensee do not suffer a similar fate. What you don't know or overlook can be financially, psychologically, and emotionally disastrous.

INTRODUCTION

The bulk of the activities for which discipline may be imposed are found in Section 18 of the Real Estate License Act. Not only may the Department discipline a licensee, but with a few exceptions, a licensee may also be criminally prosecuted for violations of the Act.

CIVIL PENALTIES
An Illinois licensee found guilty of an infraction of the License Act may receive one or a combination of the following disciplines:
- a fine of up to $10,000
- license revocation
- license suspension
- probation
- reprimand
- refusal to issue or renew a license

The Department issues a monthly news release listing the names, addresses, professions, and a brief description of the infraction and discipline taken against all professionals licensed and regulated through the Department. Most local and regional newspapers are on the Department's mailing list, and the newspapers regularly report the discipline of a local professional. Therefore, besides the actual discipline, most disciplined licensees also find that their errors and omissions are reported in their local newspapers and, occasionally, in radio and television broadcasts.

CRIMINAL PENALTIES

Although most infractions of the License Act *could* be criminally prosecuted, criminal proceedings are rarely instituted against licensees. The License Act provides that ALL violations of the License Act may be criminally prosecuted EXCEPT a violation of Section 18(h)(4), which prohibits a licensee from "any misleading or untruthful advertising, or using any trade name or insignia of membership in any real estate organization of which the licensee is not a member." The chart below sets forth the potential criminal penalties for violating the License Act.

MISDEMEANORS AND FELONIES BY INDIVIDUALS		
Infraction	Fines of: and/or	Imprisonment for:
Practicing real estate without a valid license First offense: Class A misdemeanor	not over $1,000	up to 1 year
Practicing real estate without a valid license Subsequent offense(s): Class 4 felony	not over $10,000	1 to 3 years
Violation of all other sections First offense: Class C misdemeanor	not over $500	not over 30 days
Violation of all other sections Subsequent offense(s): Class A misdemeanor	not over $1,000	up to 1 year
BUSINESS OFFENSES BY CORPORATIONS OR PARTNERSHIPS		
Practicing real estate without a valid license First offense	not over $10,000	———
Practicing real estate without a valid license Subsequent offense(s)	$10,000 - $25,000	———
Violation of all other sections First offense	not over $2,000	———
Violation of all other sections Subsequent offense(s)	$2,000 - $5,000	———

SECTION 18 VIOLATIONS

The remainder of this chapter will address each of the disciplinary infractions set forth in Section 18 of the Act. In italics following each topical heading will be the actual statutory provision. The statutory provision will then be discussed to the end that you appreciate the rationale and/or the application of each infraction. As you will see, Section 18 is not quite as straightforward as the Talmud or Ten Commandments, from which we stole this chapter's title.

OBTAINING LICENSE UNLAWFULLY

§18(a) Where the applicant or licensee has, by false or fraudulent representation, obtained or sought to obtain a license.

All applicants for a real estate license are asked the following questions at the beginning of the license exam:
1. Are you a high school graduate or have you received a GED?
2. Have you ever been convicted of any criminal offense in any state or in federal court (other than minor traffic violations)?
3. Do you now suffer from, have you ever suffered from, have you been diagnosed as having, or have you ever been treated for any disease or condition which is generally regarded by the medical community as chronic, i.e., (1) mental or emotional disease or condition; (2) alcohol or other substance abuse; or (3) physical disease or condition that could interfere with your ability to practice your profession?
4. Have you been denied a professional license or permit or the privilege of taking an examination, or have you ever had a professional license or permit disciplined in any way by any licensing authority in Illinois or elsewhere?
5. Have you ever been discharged other than honorably from the armed services or from a city, county, state, or federal position?
6. Are you a U.S. citizen OR a lawfully admitted alien of the United States?

In responding to the foregoing questions, many candidates have outright lied and others have, without malice of forethought, edited their backgrounds to avoid the hassle of having to document and explain a 30-year-old felony drug conviction for the possession of a quantity of marijuana that today would be a petty offense. Unfortunately, the hassle of documenting such an item is far less burdensome, less embarrassing, and less costly than having to explain the conviction after the matter is brought to the attention of the Disciplinary Board. One hundred percent honesty is the best policy in regard to an applicant's response to the foregoing questions.

In addition to the above questions, to which all license candidates must respond, broker candidates must submit a VE-RE form wherein they certify, "I was sponsored and supervised in the active practice of real estate for the time period indicated (one year out of the immediately preceding three years)." The VE-RE form is signed by both the broker applicant and the applicant's sponsoring broker, and details the applicant's real estate experience.

A frequently asked question is, "What is the 'active' practice of real estate such as will permit me to qualify for a broker's license?" The terms are not defined in the License Act or the Rules, and an inquiry to the Department will not provide guidance. If you and your broker sign the VE-RE form and it is later determined by the Department that you were not active, both you and your broker are subject to discipline. If you are in doubt as to whether you or a sponsored salesperson fit into the "active" status, the VE-RE form should reflect your uncertainty with a clear statement to this effect along with an accompanying statement as to the extent of the applicant's activity.

CRIMINAL CONVICTIONS

§18(b) Where the applicant or licensee has been convicted of any crime, an essential element of which is dishonesty or fraud or larceny, embezzlement, obtaining money, property or credit by false pretenses or by means of a confidence game, has been convicted in this or another state of a crime which is a felony under the laws of this State or has been convicted of a felony in a federal court.

A *criminal conviction* is the first requirement under Section 18(b). Crimes are offenses the legislature defines as such and include not only your typical offenses of robbery, murder, battery, and the like, but also such activities as practicing real estate without a license, sniffing glue, child neglect, and even fraternity/sorority hazing if bodily injury results. The number of crimes one can commit in Illinois is mind-boggling. Fortunately, only certain crimes are covered by this section of the License Act. Conviction means a final judgment on a verdict or finding of guilty, a plea of guilty, or a plea of no contest. Court supervisions, pardoned convictions, and successful appeals (reversals) *are not* convictions.

Under Illinois law, there are basically two classifications of crimes: misdemeanors (less serious) and felonies (most serious). For example, murder, rape, certain batteries, manslaughter, and many drug offenses are felonies, and if committed by a licensee, they are grounds for discipline under Subsection 18(b) of the License Act.

To be disciplined for a misdemeanor conviction, an essential element of the crime must be dishonesty, fraud, larceny, embezzlement, or obtaining money, property or credit by false pretenses or by means of a confidence game. This portion of the subsection is complicated enough to spend several pages defining and describing; however, the term *dishonesty* is an essential element of each of the specified forms of conduct, and therefore we will simply reflect on the meaning of that term alone.

As defined by any dictionary, dishonesty is the disposition to lie, cheat, steal, or defraud. Therefore, any misdemeanor that involves lying, cheating, stealing, or fraud may subject the licensee to discipline under this section.

Common offenses that are dishonesty misdemeanors would be writing bad checks, switching price tags, fraud, shoplifting, and theft. Misdemeanors such as simple battery, indecent exposure, driving while intoxicated, trespass, and adultery would not be cause for the discipline of a licensee under this section; however, as will be noted later, such acts may form the basis for disciplinary action under the "catchall" provisions of Subsections 18(h)(12) and/or (16), which are discussed below.

MENTAL DISABILITY

§18(c) Where the applicant or licensee has been adjudged to be a person under legal disability or subject to involuntary admission or to meet the standard for judicial admissions as provided in the Mental Health and Developmental Disabilities Code, as now or hereafter amended.

Probably the least of such a person's worries is the loss of a real estate license. We will permit this subsection to stand on its own with no further discussion.

OFFICES IN RETAIL ESTABLISHMENTS

§18(d) Where the licensee performs or attempts to perform any act as a broker or salesperson in a retail sales establishment, from an office, desk or space that is not separated from the main retail business by a separate and distinct area within such establishment.

Few professions, if any, are free of the influence of politics. The real estate profession is certainly not one of them, and this subsection simply removes a perceived competitive edge that many of the larger real estate firms and retailers might pursue unless outlawed. Consider the convenience of buying shoes, a wrench, and a new home all in the same store. A blue-light special in the commercial office building department is what every consumer wants and what apparently has concerned some politically well-connected real estate firms.

We certainly would look forward to the convenience of parking in the Woodfield Mall parking lot, hiking three blocks to the entrance, through women's apparel, down the escalator to the first floor, through the kitchen and bath shops to the real estate counter. We may be mistaken, but we don't perceive the need for this anticompetitive measure, which, if tested in the courts, might very well be declared unconstitutional. Whoever sponsored this legislation didn't understand that the industry's bywords ("location, location, location") don't mean putting your real estate office between women's apparel and boys' wear. Regardless, until the rule is successfully challenged in our courts, the practitioner should be careful to not hand out any business cards or otherwise conduct business in a retail store unless the practitioner has his or her own separate and distinct space.

DISCIPLINARY ACTION OUTSIDE ILLINOIS

§18(e) Discipline by another state, the District of Columbia, territory, or foreign nation of a licensee if at least one of the grounds for that discipline is the same as or the equivalent of one of the grounds for discipline set forth in this Act.

It is not unusual for a broker or salesperson to be licensed in more than one state. This is especially true of licensees in communities proximate to state borders. Licensees with multistate licensure should be mindful of the fact that the license laws of most states contain similar provisions. A violation and discipline in one state may have multistate repercussions.

PRACTICING REAL ESTATE WHILE UNLICENSED/INOPERATIVE

§18(f) Where the applicant or licensee has engaged in real estate activity without a license, or after the licensee's license was expired, or while the license was inoperative.

As fully covered in Chapter 1, a licensee is permitted to act as a licensee only when in possession of a valid sponsor card or pocket card and current license. During periods between sponsoring brokers, while a license is in the status of nonrenewed, or during a suspension, the licensee's practice of real estate is unlawful. This means that during such periods, the licensee may not:

- sell, exchange, purchase, rent, or lease real estate;
- offer to sell, exchange, purchase, rent, or lease real estate;
- negotiate, offer, attempt or agree to negotiate the sale, exchange, purchase, rental, or leasing of real estate;
- list, offer, attempt or agree to list real estate for sale, lease, or exchange;
- buy, sell, offer to buy or sell, or otherwise deal in options on real estate or improvements thereon;
- collect, offer, attempt or agree to collect rent for the use of real estate;
- advertise or represent himself or herself as being engaged in the business of buying, selling, exchanging, renting, or leasing real estate; or
- assist or direct in procuring prospects, intended to result in the sale, exchange, lease, or rental of real estate.

CHEATING ON LICENSE EXAM

§18(g) Where the applicant or licensee attempts to subvert or cheat on the Real Estate License Exam, or aids and abets an applicant to subvert or cheat on the Real Estate License Exam administered pursuant to this Act.

Over the last several years, prelicensing real estate schools, instructors, licensees, and license candidates have been disciplined for alleged infractions relating to the state-administered license exams. None of those disciplined appealed their cases; although until 1990, when Section 18(g) was added to the License Act, there was no clear authority for the discipline levied.

To fully appreciate the scope of this newly enacted subsection, attention must be given to the words *subvert* and *aids and abets*. Most everyone can appreciate the remainder of this violation. Using cheat-sheets (ponies, crib sheets), talking to others, looking at the exams of others, and so on, are the typical and well-known methods of cheating.

Several years ago a prelicensing school instructed its students to memorize one particular question from the exam and then provide the school with that question, which was then transcribed and, along with questions submitted by others, put into a booklet of questions for other student's preexam review. Individual instructors, schools, and school directors have pursued similar courses and, when caught, have conceded to their discipline, which has ranged from heavy fines and probation to license suspension.

The above illustrations are examples of "subverting" the license exam. Subvert means to destroy; by providing students (aiding and abetting) with actual exam questions, the effectiveness of the exam is destroyed. If a school or instructor simply collected questions to make sure that none of their material was being used by the testing agency (which would be a copyright infringement), then Section 18(g) would not be violated; but, by giving students the actual questions, the school/instructor is aiding and abetting the student in destroying the effectiveness of the exam.

PERSONAL AND/OR PROFESSIONAL INFRACTIONS

> *§18(h) Where the licensee in performing or attempting to perform or pretending to perform any act as a broker or salesperson, or where such licensee, in handling his own property, whether held by deed, option, or otherwise, is found guilty of:...*

The foregoing language should be read as if preceding each of the 30 infractions that follow. It is important that a licensee recognize that his or her obligation to comply with the License Act and Rules is not limited to business dealings. The Act and Rules must be adhered to even in the handling of a licensee's own property.

MISREPRESENTATION

> *§18(h)(1) Making any substantial misrepresentation, or untruthful advertising;*

Misrepresentation may be committed under four different formats, all of which are prohibited under this subsection. The four formats are: (1) intentional misrepresentation by commission; (2) intentional misrepresentation by omission; (3) negligent misrepresentation by commission; and (4) negligent misrepresentation by omission.

Before outlining the different types of misrepresentation, it is important for us to note that fraud is more than misrepresentation. Fraud requires (in addition to one of the four forms of misrepresentation) reasonable reliance on the misrepresentation and damages occasioned by that reliance.

For example, a broker who knows that a property is infested with termites tells the buyer that the home is pest-free and shows the buyer a forged termite inspection report as "proof." (The broker has committed an intentional misrepresentation by commission, and he or she is subject to discipline.) The buyer, however, gets his or her own report showing severe termite infestation and structural damage and cancels the deal. Since the buyer did not rely on the misrepresentation and suffered no damages, there is no fraud.

Intentional misrepresentation by commission is the most common form of misrepresentation. Here the licensee intentionally makes a knowingly false statement or representation. For example, the licensee says, "This house is pest-free" when he or she knows the house is infested with critters. Or: "The furnace is in excellent condition," when the broker knows the furnace is pumping dangerous levels of carbon monoxide into the home. Or: "The basement is watertight," when the broker knows an inch or more of rain floods the basement on a regular basis. Or: "The neighborhood is as quiet and peaceful as I've ever seen," when in fact 20 members of a notorious motorcycle gang live next door.

In the case of an intentional misrepresentation by omission, a broker had a duty to say something, but he or she intentionally did not mention the condition. In each of the above situations (except the last one), a broker who fails to bring the defects to the buyer's attention is as guilty of misrepresentation as the broker who affirmatively made the misrepresentation.

Using the same four examples, a broker who doesn't know one way or the other what the conditions are, but nevertheless makes the same representation, is guilty of negligent misrepresentation by commission. Thus, this broker is also guilty of violating the rule.

A broker who actually knows nothing and says nothing—but has reason to suspect a problem and does nothing—is guilty of negligent misrepresentation by omission.

The misrepresentation must be *substantial*, which is not defined in the License Act or Rules but is generally defined by the courts as important or material. If you were the buyer in the four illustrated cases, you'd have little doubt as to the importance and materiality of the matters misrepresented. The fine line between substantial and insubstantial or material and immaterial is beyond the scope of this particular chapter. Good judgment and common sense should provide most of your answers as to what is material and substantial.

Weird court decisions in sister states have brought on many questions as to the licensee's obligation to disclose ghost reports, murders, suicides, and other unseemly events having no bearing on the quality, fitness, or value of a particular property. Rule 1450.50(d) specifically protects the licensee from disciplinary proceedings for the failure to disclose such information.

Untruthful advertising is the second prong of this subsection, and fortunately, it requires little explanation. If an ad is true, licensees have no problem. If, on the other hand, an ad is untruthful, then the ad is a lie and the licensee is subject to discipline. A multitude of untruths could be envisioned; however, the following are but a sampling of the types of ads for which discipline has been levied against licensees. The ads read:

- "Must sell to settle estate"—when, in fact, no estate whatsoever was involved
- "Owner transferred, must sell quickly"—when, in fact, the transferee's employer had taken over the home
- "List with a Re/Max Superstar"—when, in fact, the advertising broker had never been employed by or associated with Re/Max
- "Nine percent owner financing available"—when, in fact, the owner could not under any circumstances provide financing
- "3,000 square-foot colonial home . . . only $110,000"—when, in fact, the home had only 2,000 square feet
- "Ten acres of prime commercially zoned farm land"—when, in fact, the farm land was zoned farm land and probably would not be given commercial zoning
- "Fully assumable VA mortgage"—when, in fact, the existing loan was a conventional loan with a due-on-sale clause

FALSE PROMISES
§18(h)(2) *Making any false promises of a character likely to influence, persuade, or induce;*

What types of false promises would be likely to influence, persuade, or induce? An impatient seller might be persuaded by a licensee's promise that the property will sell quickly. A buyer may be induced by a broker's promise that the value of property will increase dramatically within a short period of time. A promise that you'll "get a property rezoned if it's listed" with you might persuade a buyer. These are but a sampling of promises, which, if false, are likely to violate this subsection. This subsection is rarely cited in disciplinary proceedings, due in part to the overlapping prohibitions of subparagraphs (h)(1), (2), and (3), and due further and perhaps more importantly to the basic difference between misrepresentations and promises. Representations (true or false) are statements relating to the present and past conditions or facts, whereas promises look to the future. Promises of future conditions or events are made much less frequently than statements of present or past facts or conditions.

MISREPRESENTATIONS BY OTHERS

§18(h)(3) Pursuing a continued and flagrant course of misrepresentation or the making of false promises through agents, salespersons or advertising or otherwise;

In light of subparagraph 18(h)(1), the first part of this infraction (continued and flagrant course of misrepresentation) seems to be of little relevance or assistance in protecting the public. We are hard-pressed to conceive of a continued and flagrant (shocking) course of misrepresentation that wouldn't fall into the straightforward prohibition of "substantial misrepresentation" as is set forth in subparagraph 18(h)(1).

The second portion of this subparagraph, "...the making of false promises through agents, salespersons or advertising or otherwise," also appears to be redundant of Section 18(h)(2). This subsection, however, does not require "likely to influence, persuade, or induce," and therefore, it prohibits any false promise whatsoever, regardless of its persuasiveness. Like the preceding subsection, this subsection is rarely cited in support of disciplinary action.

MISLEADING ADVERTISING

§18(h)(4) Any misleading or untruthful advertising, or using any trade name or insignia of membership in any real estate organization of which the licensee is not a member;

According to Section 1450.90(c) of the Rules, advertising is misleading "if, when taken as a whole, there is a distinct and reasonable possibility that it will be misunderstood or will deceive the ordinary purchaser, seller, renter, or owner. Advertising shall contain all information necessary to communicate accurately. The form of communication shall be designed to communicate the information contained therein to the public in a direct and readily comprehensible manner."

Also prohibited by this subsection is the use of any trade name (e.g., Century 21, Realty World, Prudential Preferred, etc.) or insignia (trademark or service mark) of any real estate organization of which the licensee is not a member. Thus, a broker may not refer to himself or herself as a REALTOR® unless the broker is in fact a member of a local board that belongs to a state association that is a member of the National Association of REALTORS®. The registered mark may not be used in advertising, on calling cards, or on stationery and the like unless the broker is in fact a member of NAR. Likewise, the unlicensed/unauthorized use of a national franchise mark would also subject a licensee to discipline.

DUAL AGENCY

§18(h)(5) Acting for more than one party in a transaction without providing written notice to all parties for whom the licensee acts;

Even after disclosing one's position as a dual agent, the licensee is in the precarious position of faithfully serving two masters with competing interests. Why such an arrangement is permitted at all is a mystery, and although it's permissible, it is ill-advised except in the rarest of situations. See Chapter 8 for a more detailed discussion of dual agency.

DUAL EMPLOYMENT

§18(h)(6) Representing or attempting to represent a broker other than the employer;

Under Illinois's and most other states' licensing laws, a salesperson may be employed by only one sponsoring broker at a time. A licensee with a broker's license may be self-employed *or* employed by another broker; however, not both. It is the job of the sponsoring broker to supervise the activities of those brokers and salespeople he or she employs. This function/obligation would be difficult at best were licensees able to work for several employers. How can you supervise someone who, at any given moment, may be working for another broker? The answer, of course, is you can't. Therefore, to protect the public, each licensee must answer to only one superior. In the event the superior fails to supervise an associate's activities, both parties may be disciplined.

MISHANDLING OF PROPERTY OR DOCUMENTS

§18(h)(7) Failure to account for or to remit any moneys or documents coming into their possession which belong to others;

An obvious intent of this section is to penalize the licensee who converts and is incapable of repaying earnest money or other funds of which the licensee becomes the custodian. Less obvious are the other types of conduct this section was also designed to require, such as: accounting for rents and security deposits, mortgage payments, installment contract payments, and other monetary payments; providing receipts for purchases under property-management arrangements and leases; and surrendering upon request documents such as title policies, deeds, surveys, and financial declarations.

BOOKKEEPING

§18(h)(8) Failure to maintain and deposit in a special account, separate and apart from personal and other business accounts, all escrow monies belonging to others entrusted to a licensee while acting as a real estate broker, escrow agent, or temporary custodian of the funds of others, or failure to maintain all escrow monies on deposit in such account until the transactions are consummated or terminated, except to the extent that such monies, or any part thereof, shall be disbursed prior to the consummation or termination in accordance with the written direction of the principals to the transaction or their duly authorized agents. Such account shall be non-interest-bearing, unless the character of the deposit is such that payment of interest thereon is otherwise required by law or unless the principals to the transaction specifically require, in writing, that the deposit be placed in an interest-bearing account;

Twenty-five percent of the disciplinary actions taken by the board relate to a licensee's mishandling of a client's funds. See Chapter 4 for a full discussion of this very important subsection.

COOPERATION WITH DEPARTMENT

§18(h)(9) Failure to make available to the Department's real estate enforcement personnel during normal business hours all escrow records and related documents maintained in connection with the practice of real estate;

The element of surprise is as important to a Department auditor as it is to a police officer executing a search warrant. This provision gives the Department a necessary tool to effectively investigate allegations of improper conduct.

COPIES OF DOCUMENTS

§18(h)(10) Failing to furnish copies upon request of all documents relating to a real estate transaction to all parties executing them;

Although this rule is not often violated, it should be noted that the parties to a transaction are entitled to have a copy of any document that they have signed. Motives an unscrupulous broker might have in delaying or refusing delivery of a copy of a signed document include: (a) the broker forged or made an unpermitted revision to a document; (b) the broker is covering up a misrepresentation (such as, "Yes, the seller has signed the contract," when, in fact, the seller hasn't); (c) the broker is afraid of losing the deal if the party looks over the document carefully; (d) the broker has added or deleted information in a credit application, rental application, financial statement, listing agreement, etc.; or (e) the broker has lost or misplaced the document.

PAYMENTS FOR UNLICENSED SERVICES

§18(h)(11) Paying a commission or valuable consideration to any person for acts or services performed in violation of this Act;

Only licensed brokers and salespersons are permitted to practice real estate, and in turn, be paid for such services. The public benefits from such licensing in that entry into the profession is limited to those the legislature feels pose no threat to the consumer. Convicted felons, incompetents, illiterates, and so on are effectively barred from the profession. If an unlicensed person could practice and be paid for services, then the entire system and Act would be subverted.

UNWORTHINESS OR INCOMPETENCE

§18(h)(12) Having demonstrated unworthiness or incompetency to act as a broker or salesperson in such manner as to endanger the interest of the public;

Amazingly enough, this particular subsection has brought about litigation in more than one state, although on its face, the provisions seem to be a catchall with extremely imprecise boundaries. What type of conduct could possibly be prohibited here that isn't covered elsewhere more succinctly? Two areas of particular concern to the Department have been discrimination and rental-finding services. This concern led to the adoption of two Rules (1450.100 and 1450.170), which specifically state that a licensee who violates the rules relating to rental-finding services or who is found to have unlawfully discriminated "shall be deemed to have demonstrated unworthiness or incompetence as a broker."

In addition to the adopted rules, the Department has used this subparagraph along with subparagraph 18(h)(16) to penalize conduct that couldn't be pigeonholed elsewhere. Unworthiness or incompetence could include a plethora of activities ranging from gross negligence to violations of equal employment rights. This is similar to shopping for a dress or a piece of artwork: although you can't describe exactly what you're looking for, you'll know it when you see it.

COMMINGLING

§18(h)(13) Commingling the money or property of others with his own;

Commingling is a mixing together such that identification of the ownership of a particular item is impossible because of the identical nature of the items. Typically, a broker guilty of commingling has placed escrow monies into his or her business operating or personal account. This subsection is developed more fully in Chapter 4.

Note that this subsection also prohibits the commingling of property. Although this rarely happens, an escrow deposit may be made in some form other than legal tender (money). Bearer bonds, endorsed stock certificates, motor vehicle titles, and even farm products have been used as earnest money, security deposits, rental payments, etc. Section 18(h)(13) thus requires that these items, like money, must not be commingled.

TEMPORARY EMPLOYMENT

§18(h)(14) Employing any person on a purely temporary or single deal basis as a means of evading the law regarding payment of commission to non-licensees on some contemplated transactions;

This section prohibits the exact same conduct as is prohibited by Subsection (h)(11), but it closes a loophole some licensees might be prone to use to evade the law. Section 6 of the License Act permits an unlicensed employee of an owner of property to market and sell the employer's property. Therefore, a property owner or broker marketing his or her own property could put a nonlicensee on the payroll and evade the licensing requirements. Or a broker could temporarily employ an individual as a receptionist at, say, $1,000 per day in return for the referral of customers or assistance in the sale of property.

OFFICES MANAGED BY SALESPERSONS

§18(h)(15) Permitting the use of his license as a broker to enable a salesperson or unlicensed person to operate a real estate business without actual participation therein and control thereof by the broker;

This rule enforces the minimum standards for the operation of a real estate brokerage by prohibiting licensed brokers from "lending" their licenses to salespeople while the broker pursues other vocations or retirement. For example, both authors of this book are licensed brokers who are pursuing other vocations. It would be easy and tempting to "lend" our licenses to our children, relatives, friends, or others for the purpose of running a real estate office. We wouldn't have the time for or interest in overseeing the operation of the brokerage firm and would simply be figureheads who, from time to time, would sign required documents (such as sponsor cards and employment agreements) and perform similar ministerial functions.

At the foundation of the apprentice system of licensing in Illinois is the concept that it protects the consumer by requiring an experienced broker to supervise, train, and guide salespeople. Lending a broker's license to a salesperson contravenes not only the public's best interests, but also the interests of the firm and those employed by the firm.

How inactive may a broker be without violating this mandate? Each case must be examined on its own facts. A one-salesperson office requires far less attention than a 30-person firm. Facts such as to whom the day-to-day questions are addressed; who writes the checks, makes the deposits, runs staff meetings, and orders furniture, furnishings, office supplies, and equipment; and the number of hours the managing broker spends in the office, etc. are all elements tending to prove or disprove an alleged infraction.

DISHONEST DEALING

§18(h)(16) Any other conduct, whether of the same or a different character from that specified in this Section which constitutes dishonest dealing;

This subsection is the second of the catchall prohibitions. It simply prohibits dishonest dealing and, like Subsection 18(h)(12) (unworthiness or incompetency), it has very imprecise boundaries. Until recently, when Rule 1450.100 was adopted, this subsection was oftentimes used against a licensee practicing racial discrimination. Its use in curtailing discrimination was approved by our courts. In the only remaining disciplinary action not relating to discrimination where Subsection 18(h)(16) was considered by our courts, the Department's decision was reversed.

Dishonest means to lie, cheat, or defraud; untrustworthiness; and a lack of integrity. *Dealing* means a transaction in the course of trade or business.

The Department has in the past used this subsection as a weapon to extract consent orders from licensees whose conduct didn't clearly fit into other subsections. Some examples are: (a) several real estate instructors and schools that endeavored to collect and then distribute state exam questions were charged under this subsection prior to recent changes in the License Act which now provide a straightforward prohibition; (b) situations where it appeared that licensees took advantage of clients'/customers' senility, ignorance, illiteracy, and other physical, mental, or psychological infirmities; (c) transactions totally unrelated to real estate, such as where a licensee rolls back the odometer on his or her automobile and then sells it in its altered state; and (d) such other conduct that ought to result in discipline but for which there appeared to be either insurmountable defenses or, as stated above, no other subsection was more precisely on point.

ADVERTISING WITHOUT CONSENT

§18(h)(17) Displaying a "for rent" or "for sale" sign on any property without the written consent of an owner or his duly authorized agent, or advertising by any means that any property is for sale or for rent without the written consent of the owner or his authorized agent;

This subsection was principally enacted to halt a previously widespread practice of brokers placing their own signs on any property that had an existing "for sale" sign on the property. There are a number of reasons sellers don't want signs erected. Businesses oftentimes fear that customers who see a "for sale" sign may assume financial difficulties or the intent to go out of business; homeowners fear that the signs will attract nosey neighbors or criminal elements; and municipal sign ordinances sometimes prohibit the posting of "for sale" signs. The erection of a sign thus is an item to be negotiated between the parties.

Also, in the past, some licensees erected signs on properties that were not even for sale. The broker's motives were to expose his or her firm to the public, secure buyers for other property, secure listings for other property, and even secure a listing for the property on which the broker's sign was erected by deterring other firms from seeking the listing. Lastly, many firms are slow to remove their signs following a closing or the termination of a listing, and this subsection provides a remedy for this practice as well. Once title has been transferred to a new owner, a real estate agent's authority relating to a sign has expired.

TIMELY PRODUCTION OF INFORMATION

§18(h)(18) Failing to provide information requested by the Department, within 30 days of the request, either as the result of a formal or informal complaint to the Department or as a result of a random audit conducted by the Department, which would indicate a violation of this Act;

In order to complete an audit or investigate a complaint against the licensee, it is oftentimes necessary to secure documents possessed solely by the investigated licensee. Occasionally the licensee will be the only source for evidence that will support his or her discipline. Therefore, if a licensee, by delay, fails to cooperate in an investigation, he or she may nevertheless be prosecuted under this section. The resulting discipline under this subsection can be more severe than the discipline levied for the charge under investigation. In a recent case, a broker was fined $1,000 and his license suspended for his failure to provide a copy of a particular ad he had run that was under investigation. Once the information was surrendered and the fine paid, his license was reinstated and the charges dismissed, because the advertising complaint was found to be without merit.

VIOLATION OF ACTS OR RULES

§18(h)(19) Disregarding or violating any provision of this Act, or the published rules or regulations promulgated by the Department to enforce this Act, or aiding or abetting any individual, partnership or corporation in disregarding any provision of this Act, or the published rules or regulations promulgated by the Department to enforce this Act;

This violation should alert all licensees to the need for continuing education, especially the mandatory six hours that cover the subject areas most often forming the basis for disciplinary action. All the training manuals, inspirational tapes, amortization tables, MLS books, and the like are worthless if you lose your license. Much of the License Act and Rules is covered in the main text of this book; however, you should continue your education by reviewing the entire Act and Rules.

BLIND ADS

§18(h)(20) Advertising any property for sale or advertising any transaction of any kind or character relating to the sale of property by whatsoever means, without clearly

disclosing in or on such advertising one of the following: the name of the firm with which the licensee is associated, if a sole broker, evidence of the broker's occupation, or a name with respect to which the broker has complied with the requirements of "An Act in relation to the use of an assumed name in the conduct or transaction of business in this State," approved July 17, 1941, as amended, whether such advertising is done by the broker or by any salesperson or broker employed by the broker.

All ads placed by a licensee must comply with this requirement and its related rules. See Chapter 3 for a more thorough discussion of the advertising requirements of the Act and Rules.

GUARANTEED SALES PLANS

§18(h)(21) "Offering guaranteed sales plans" as defined in subparagraph (A) except to the extent hereinafter set forth:

(A) A "guaranteed sales plan" is any real estate purchase or sales plan whereby a broker enters into a conditional or unconditional written contract with a seller by the terms of which a broker agrees to purchase a property of the seller within a specified period of time at a specific price in the event the property is not sold in accordance with the terms of a listing contract between the broker and the seller or on other terms acceptable to the seller;

(B) A broker offering a "guaranteed sales plan" shall provide the details and conditions of such plan in writing to the party to whom the plan is offered;

(C) A broker offering a "guaranteed sales plan" shall provide to the party to whom the plan is offered, evidence of sufficient financial resources to satisfy the commitment to purchase undertaken by the broker in the plan;

(D) Any broker offering a "guaranteed sales plan" shall undertake to market the property of the seller subject to the plan in the same manner in which the broker would market any other property, unless such agreement with the seller provides otherwise;

(E) Any broker who fails to perform on a "guaranteed sales plan" in strict accordance with its terms shall be subject to all the penalties provided in this Act for violations thereof, and, in addition, shall be subject to a civil penalty payable to the party injured by the default in an amount of up to $10,000.

Due to the infrequency of the use of this type of program and the lack of any recent violations coming to our attention, we will simply note that any broker who plans to institute such a program should carefully review this section to assure compliance.

FAIR HOUSING AND ILLINOIS HUMAN RIGHTS ACT

§18(h)(22) Influencing or attempting to influence, by any words or acts a prospective seller, purchaser, occupant, landlord or tenant of real estate, in connection with viewing, buying or leasing of real estate, so as to promote, or tend to promote, the continuance or maintenance of racially and religiously segregated housing, or so as to retard, obstruct or discourage racially integrated housing on or in any street, block, neighborhood or community;

§18(h)(23) Engaging in any act which constitutes a violation of Section 3-102, 3-103, 3-104 or 3-105 of the Illinois Human Rights Act, whether or not a complaint has been filed with or adjudicated by the Human Rights Commission;

As the overview to Chapter 7 observes, "Our children and our children's children deserve to live in a nation free from undeserved bias and discrimination." Hopefully, some day a large proportion of licensees will wonder what precipitated the enactment of these provisions. Unfortunately, if the number of disciplinary complaints and lawsuits are reliable indicators, achieving the goal of eradicating discrimination may be many decades, if not centuries, away.

Note that Subsection 18(h)(22) prohibits *only* racial and religious discrimination. However, Subsection 18(h)(23) incorporates the Illinois Human Rights Act into the License Act; therefore, it is imperative that licensees become as familiar with the Illinois Human Rights Act as they are (or should be) with the License Act and Rules. Fair housing and the Illinois Human Rights Act will be covered in detail in Chapter 7; however, Figure 5-1 summarizes the prohibited discriminatory practices most salient to the real estate professional.

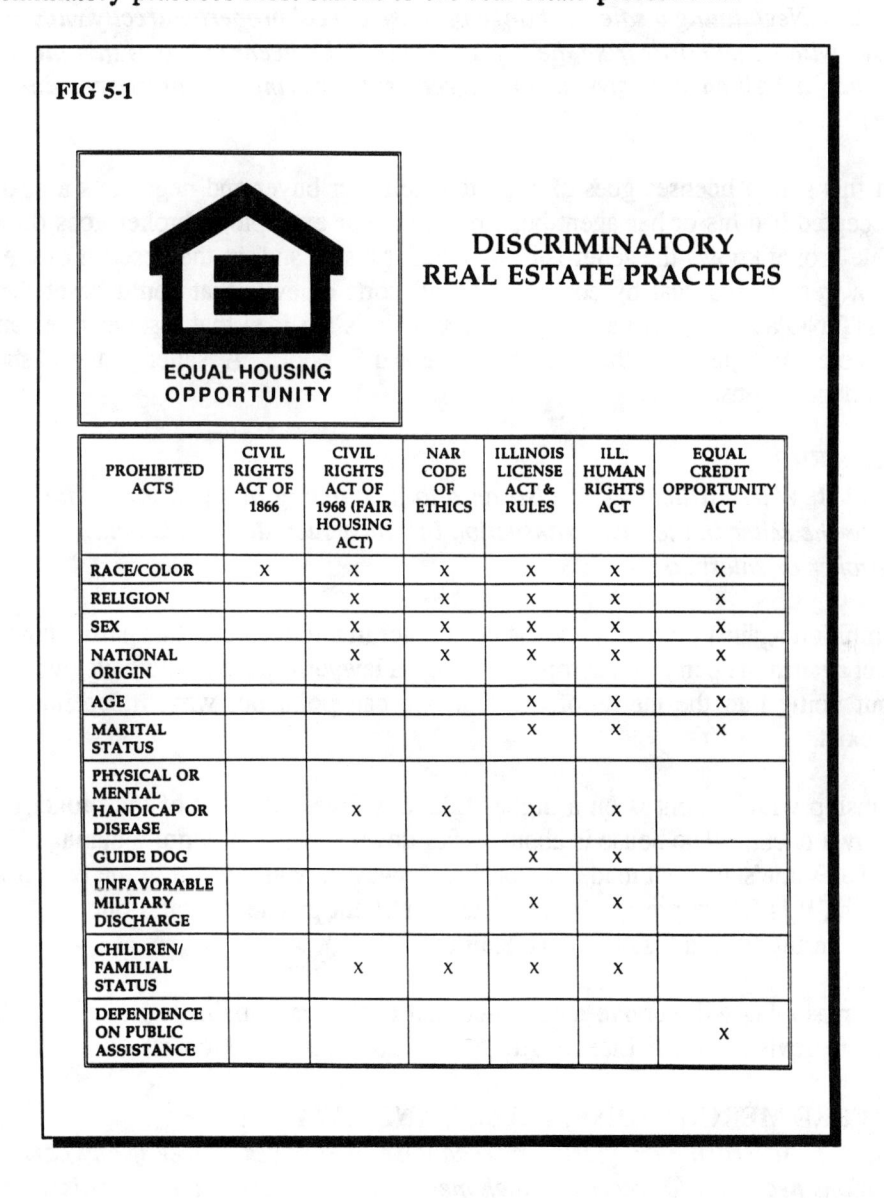

FIG 5-1

DISCRIMINATORY REAL ESTATE PRACTICES

PROHIBITED ACTS	CIVIL RIGHTS ACT OF 1866	CIVIL RIGHTS ACT OF 1968 (FAIR HOUSING ACT)	NAR CODE OF ETHICS	ILLINOIS LICENSE ACT & RULES	ILL. HUMAN RIGHTS ACT	EQUAL CREDIT OPPORTUNITY ACT
RACE/COLOR	X	X	X	X	X	X
RELIGION		X	X	X	X	X
SEX		X	X	X	X	X
NATIONAL ORIGIN		X	X	X	X	X
AGE				X	X	X
MARITAL STATUS				X	X	X
PHYSICAL OR MENTAL HANDICAP OR DISEASE		X	X	X	X	
GUIDE DOG				X	X	
UNFAVORABLE MILITARY DISCHARGE				X	X	
CHILDREN/ FAMILIAL STATUS		X	X	X	X	
DEPENDENCE ON PUBLIC ASSISTANCE						X

CONTRACT RAIDING

§18(h)(24) Inducing any party to a contract of sale or listing agreement to break such a contract of sale or listing agreement for the purpose of substituting, in lieu thereof, a new contract for sale or listing agreement with a third party;

Contract raiding is obviously evil—legally, morally, and ethically. State laws have been enacted throughout the country to curtail this predatory practice.

A violation of Subsection 18(h)(24) typically involves the licensee inducing a buyer or seller to breach or break an existing contract to purchase or sell in order for the licensee to earn a commission by producing (in the case of a seller) another buyer at perhaps a better price, or (in the case of a buyer) a nicer home at the same or a lesser price. If the licensee is successful in inducing the breach, all of the original parties are or may be injured. The original broker(s) has potentially lost his or her commission(s), the licensee's client may be sued for breach of contract, and the other party may have suffered damages as the result of the default.

UNAUTHORIZED CONTRACTUAL NEGOTIATIONS

> *§18(h)(25) Negotiating a sale, exchange or lease of real property directly with an owner or lessor without authority from the listing broker if the licensee knows that the owner or lessor has a written exclusive listing agreement covering the property with another broker;*

In an infraction of this sort, a licensee goes directly to a seller or buyer and negotiates a deal the buyer or seller would not have accepted had his or her agent been present. For example, a broker goes directly to the seller of some property. The broker knows the seller is desperate for a sale and, in the absence of the seller's agent, cuts himself or herself a tremendous deal by conjuring up all sorts of evils that could beset the seller if the seller doesn't sell "RIGHT NOW!" Sometimes lost in the shuffle is the idea that a seller hires an agent to negotiate the best deal possible—not just put the listing in the MLS pool. A seller's agent should be present to counterbalance the negotiations.

ATTORNEY BROKERS

> *§18(h)(26) Where a licensee is also an attorney, acting as the attorney for either the buyer or the seller in the same transaction in which such licensee is acting or has acted as a broker or salesperson;*

Similar to the prohibition against placing a real estate counter in a retail store, this particular restriction was borne of politics to protect against the perceived competitive edge a lawyer/broker would have over most other real estate licensees. Without going into the merits of the fear, we can point out why, independent of politics, such a restriction should exist.

A lawyer's relationship with a client is on a higher fiduciary level than that of the broker/client. For example, if a lawyer is told by a client, "The house is about to fall down because of termite damage," the lawyer may not reveal the secret. The same statement made to a broker, however, would result in the broker's having to disclose the defect. Therefore, it is fair to presume that the lawyer/client privilege would outweigh the lawyer's duty as a broker to disclose, resulting in a loss to the consumer.

Whether the above reasoning will survive a constitutional challenge remains to be seen. Ultimately, we would expect this particular provision of the License Act to be challenged in the courts.

ADVERTISING FREE MERCHANDISE, PRIZES, AND AWARDS

> *§18(h)(27) Advertising or offering merchandise or services as free if any conditions or obligations necessary for receiving such merchandise or services are not disclosed in the same advertisement or offer. Such conditions or obligations include, but are not limited to, the requirement that the recipient attend a promotional activity or visit a real estate site. As used in this paragraph 27, "free" includes terms such as "award", "prize", "no charge", "free of charge", "without charge" and similar words or phrases which*

reasonably lead a person to believe that he may receive, or has been selected to receive, something of value, without any conditions or obligations on the part of the recipient;

This section may have been enacted as a knee-jerk response to its predecessor section, which was declared unconstitutional. This section restricts the advertising of free merchandise and is perhaps duplicitous of Section 18(h)(3) (misleading/untruthful ads). In the case of *Coldwell Banker v. Illinois Department of Registration and Education*, the Illinois Supreme Court declared the following section of the License Act unconstitutional:

Using prizes, money, free gifts or other valuable consideration as inducements to (1) secure customers to purchase, rent or lease property when the awarding of such prizes, money, free gifts or other valuable consideration is conditioned upon the purchase, rental or lease, or (2) secure clients to list properties with registrant;

The current law, subject to Section 18(h)(11), permits giveaway ads as long as any conditions for receipt of the gifts are clearly spelled out in the ad.

TIME-SHARE VIOLATIONS
§18(h)(28) Disregarding or violating any provision of the Illinois Real Estate Time-Share Act, enacted by the 84th General Assembly, or the published rules or regulations promulgated by the Department to enforce that Act.

Time and space limitations preclude any meaningful discussion of this violation. The Illinois Real Estate Time-Share Act may be found in Chapter 30, paragraph 701 et.seq. of the Illinois Revised Statutes, and copies of the Rules for the Administration of the Illinois Real Estate Time-Share Act may be obtained from the Department. Any licensee who deals on a regular basis with this rather new form of property ownership should obtain and study copies of both the Act and the Rules.

VIOLATION OF DISCIPLINARY ORDERS
§18(h)(29) A finding that the licensee has violated the terms of the disciplinary order issued by the Department.

Obviously, if a licensee's license is suspended, practicing real estate during his or her suspension would violate this provision. Sometimes a license is issued, renewed, or placed on probation conditioned on such things as the licensee's attending AA meetings, obtaining drug or alcohol abuse treatment or counseling, paying a fine or restitution, etc. This section then provides the Department with the necessary enforcement capabilities.

PAYMENTS TO COOPERATING SALESPERSONS
§18(h)(30) Paying fees or commissions directly to a licensee employed by another broker.

Even with the permission of a sponsoring broker, a licensee must never pay a fee or commission directly to a licensee employed by another. Although it would be permissible to draw a check payable to the other licensee's employee and deliver the check to the sponsoring broker for later delivery to the employee, there would rarely be justifiable reason to risk the appearance of an impropriety. If such a situation were to arise, the payor licensee should be sure to document the transaction, e.g., by obtaining a receipt from the sponsoring broker's office showing delivery of the check to the broker. This section does not prohibit a sponsoring broker from paying fees or commissions to terminated licensees for services rendered prior to termination.

OTHER SELECTED DISCIPLINARY VIOLATIONS

FAILURE TO PAY TAXES
§18.1 The Department may refuse to issue or renew, or may suspend the license of any person who fails to file a return, or to pay the tax, penalty or interest shown in a filed return, or to pay any final assessment of tax, penalty or interest, as required by any tax Act administered by the Illinois Department of Revenue, until such times as the requirements of any such tax Act are satisfied.

As the cliché goes, two things in life are certain—death and taxes. Collection personnel from the Illinois Department of Revenue are well trained in securing the prompt payment of delinquent taxes from Illinois professionals, such as doctors, lawyers, dentists, and real estate licensees. All licensed Illinois businesses and professions are subject to having their licenses suspended for failure to pay their Illinois taxes. Note that the only covered taxes are those administered by the Illinois Department of Revenue, which include, among others, income, sales, use, and motor-fuel taxes. Not covered are federal taxes, local taxes, and real estate taxes.

AGENCY DISCLOSURE
§18.2 Persons licensed under this Act shall disclose in writing to prospective buyers the existence of any agency relationship between the licensee and the seller, or shall disclose in writing to sellers, or their agent, the existence of an agency relationship between the licensee and a prospective buyer at a time and in a manner consistent with regulations established by the Department.

This subsection, along with Rule 1450.55, is discussed in detail in Chapter 8. Figure 5-2 is a handy reference chart that may assist the reader in becoming more comfortable with this relatively new license requirement.

UNPAID STUDENT LOANS
Many of the professions licensed in Illinois require extensive educational requirements, which were and are financed by state guaranteed student loans. A large number of students receiving Illinois licenses as doctors, nurses, lawyers, etc. have defaulted on their loans, leaving the state holding the bag as a guarantor. As with the income taxes, the state has discovered an excellent way of collecting from the loan recipients—suspending their licenses until the loan is repaid or satisfactory repayment arrangements have been made.

Although few if any prelicensing real estate educations are funded with guaranteed loans, the state's collection sleuths found that there were licensees in all professions who owed the state monies for student loans on which they had defaulted. Therefore, if you took out a student loan to pay for a nursing degree and several years after abandoning that pursuit and the loan payments you decide to apply for a real estate license, you should be prepared to cough up the defaulted loan balance.

CHILD SUPPORT DELINQUENCY
Effective January 1, 1992, all licensing agencies in Illinois became subject to the provisions of Public Act 87-412, which amended Chapter 127, paragraph 1016(c) of the Illinois Revised Statutes (Illinois Administrative Procedure Act) and which provides in pertinent part as follows:

FIG 5-2

AGENCY DISCLOSURE QUICK REFERENCE CHART

	If you are a **SELLER'S AGENT**	If you are a **BUYER'S AGENT**	If you are a **DUAL AGENT**
To whom must disclosure be made?	Prospective buyer	Seller/Seller's Agent	All parties
When must disclosure be made?	At the time of "**first significant contact**"	At the time of "**first significant contact**"	At the time of or before the creation of the dual agency
What is "**first significant contact**"?	The earlier of: A) the beginning of the showing of property (other than an open house); or B) preparation of offer to purchase; or C) prequalification of a prospective buyer or similar request for specific financial information	The first contact with seller or seller's agent on behalf of one or more prospective buyers concerning a property's: (a) availability; (b) price; (c) condition; or (d) showing instructions.	Not applicable
How must the disclosure be made?	In writing	In writing. (If first significant contact is by phone, then orally and followed up in writing.)	In writing and signed by all parties
How may the disclosure be delivered?	In person, by mail, fax, or similar means	In person, by mail, fax or similar means	By whatever means will produce a signed writing prior to the creation of the dual agency
Must the disclosure be signed by anyone?	No	No	Yes, by all parties
Must the disclosure be dated?	Yes	Yes	No
Must a copy of the disclosure be retained, and if so, for what period of time?	Yes, for 5 years	Yes, for 5 years	Yes, for 10 years
What transactions, if any, are exempt?	1. Lease or rental transactions, unless there is an option to purchase 2. Referrals, when the referring Licensee has no significant contact with the buyer or seller	1. Lease or rental transactions, unless there is an option to purchase 2. Referrals, when the referring Licensee has no significant contact with the buyer or seller	None

Each agency shall require the licensee to certify on the renewal application form, under penalty of perjury, that he or she is not more than 30 days delinquent in complying with a child support order. Every renewal application shall state that failure to so certify may result in a denial of the renewal, and that making a false statement may subject the licensee to contempt of court. The agency shall notify each licensee who acknowledges a delinquency or who, contrary to his or her certification, is found to be delinquent, that the agency intends to take disciplinary action. Accordingly, the agency shall provide written notice of the facts or conduct upon which the agency will rely to support its proposed action and the licensee shall be given an opportunity for hearing in accordance with the provisions of the Act concerning contested cases. Any delinquency in complying with a child support order can be remedied by arranging for payment of past due and current support. Upon a final finding of delinquency, the agency shall revoke or refuse to renew the license.

Therefore, all future renewal applications as well as initial applications for licensure will require licensees to verify under oath that they are not more than 30 days delinquent in their child support obligations. Although the quoted legislation does not specifically provide for the suspension of licenses between renewals, Subsections 18(h)(12) and/or (16) of the License Act might form the basis for interim discipline.

CONCLUSION

Knowing what is expected of a licensee is only part of continuing education. Conforming one's conduct to these requirements is the second part. In the preparation of this publication, we asked a licensee to write a couple of paragraphs as to the effects of being a party to disciplinary proceedings and the resulting fine and probation. What follows IS NOT fiction but the real-life reaction of a very nice, competent, and honest licensee, who, like Mr. Katt in the fictionalized introduction to this chapter, had an impeccable reputation bruised and contused by disciplinary proceedings.

In my attempt to assist people, I offended someone. An anonymous negative letter to the Department brought about an investigation that ended one year later with the tarnishment of a perfect, unblemished career that had survived better than 15 years.

Although I was able to continue selling, my license was placed on probation and I received a sizable fine, in addition to personal attorney's fees. But the penalties didn't end there. . . .

The nightmare began with my entire career being scrutinized and dissected by the investigation team attempting to find any minute flaw that could be sued in the present litigation. I relived my entire career, wondering if I may have committed some infraction that could come back "to bite me." Sleepless nights became a norm. People approached me and told me they'd been interviewed and asked, "What did you do?" My nerves were stretched to the breaking point. I was constantly defending myself or attempting to be as matter-of-fact about the situation as possible.

This process went on for almost a year. Finally came my opportunity to explain my side. Every word I uttered was challenged and questioned or misinterpreted. After the hearing, another eternity began of sleepless nights waiting for the Board's decision. Finally, the recommendation—probation and a fine.

But it wasn't over; not by a long shot. My case was written up in the newspapers for my family and friends to see, causing additional embarrassment to both me and my loved ones. The mental stress was more than you can believe. And what about my employment? People looked at me as if I had committed a heinous crime. I felt like I was constantly being watched.

And that's only the beginning. The long-term ramifications are inconceivable. My firm had to show that they had "clean hands," so I was discharged from the position I had filled successfully for several years. Add to this the loss of wages, referral business, etc., [and] the fact that my peers looked at me strangely. Other firms did not want me on their staff with such a stigma attached . . . and of course, I was prohibited from doing the work I excelled at doing.

While we, in the real estate business, are always concerned with the bottom line, let me put some hard numbers to this unbelievable experience. As this disciplinary action took place several years prior to this writing, I would estimate to date, excluding fines levied by the Board, this transaction has cost me in excess of $100,000. This would reflect lost wages and personal business.

I learned a great deal from this costly experience. Given the opportunity of doing things differently, I surely would. My lesson was extremely expensive to me and to my family, from both a monetary and professional basis. Hopefully, others will learn and benefit from this scenario. Don't think it can't happen to you. I thought that, too. Unfortunately, it happened, and the price I paid was astronomical!!

CASES TO JUDGE

1. Two transactions forming the basis for disciplinary proceedings against David Moy's salesperson's license occurred at a time when Moy was between real estate jobs. Moy had been employed by Ideal Realty. In December 1975, he notified Ideal Realty that he was terminating his employment. Moy then made arrangements to go to work for another broker, Kaplan Realty. However, because Kaplan Realty failed to promptly file Moy's change of employment application with the Department, it was not dated until February 20, 1976.

   While his change of employment application was being prepared by Kaplan Realty, Moy told the company that he was working on two transactions: one involved his sister and her husband, and the other involved one of his teaching colleagues. The owner of Kaplan Realty told Moy he was not interested in either deal.

   Walter H. Djokie, a lawyer and licensed real estate broker, testified at the administrative hearing that he was approached by another lawyer who was representing Moy's sister and brother-in-law as purchasers of real estate. Djokie testified that the lawyer advised him that Moy had asked the lawyer to close the transaction, and that it required a broker.

   Djokie then met with Moy, who told Djokie that his brother-in-law was purchasing the property in question and that he had left his employment with Ideal Realty. He asked Djokie to act as the broker in the deal. Djokie agreed, provided Moy indemnified him against any claims that might be made by any other broker for a commission. When Djokie received the brokerage commission of $5,280, he retained $230 and paid the balance to Moy.

   Within a few days the other lawyer and Moy spoke to Djokie about a transaction in which a fellow teacher of Moy's was the purchaser. This transaction was handled in the same manner, with Djokie identified as the broker. In this deal, Djokie retained $190 and paid the balance of the $4,100 commission to Moy.

   Moy acknowledged that he never asked Djokie to be his sponsoring broker even though Djokie was identified as the broker in both contracts.

   The complaint filed by the Department seeking the revocation of Moy's salesperson's license charged that Moy represented or attempted to represent a real estate broker other than the employer and demonstrated unworthiness or incompetency to act as a real estate broker or salesperson in such manner as to safeguard the interest of the public.

   Do you agree that Moy's license should be revoked? [*Moy v. State Department of Registration and Education*, 85 Ill.App.3d 27, 406 N.E.2d 191, 40 Ill.Dec. 490 (1980)]

2. Petra Peteris and his wife, Ona, owners of a property in Chicago, called broker Charles Norville asking him to sell it for them. They signed an exclusive listing contract for a 90-day period at a price of "$15,000 net to owner plus or minus prorations." Thereafter in the printed portion it recited: "* * * or any less sum which I shall agree to accept, and to pay you the usual commission as established by the Chicago Real Estate Board, on such sale price * * *."

   About a week later Norville's salesperson found a buyer for $15,500. A printed form of purchase contract was signed by the purchasers in triplicate. It provided for Norville's broker's commission "as agreed" and related that it had to be signed within four days. The salesperson then took the three counterparts of the contract to Peteris and obtained his signature upon all three. Norville had told the salesperson to try for a 6 percent commission. She wrote on one of the copies in longhand below the signatures, the words: "We agree to pay Norville Real Estate 6 percent commission as per Chicago Real Estate Board," and Peteris signed below the quoted phrase. The following morning Mrs. Peteris, who had been away working when her husband signed, added her signature to the three copies of the contract and also signed her name below the clause on the one copy. This signed copy was retained by the salesperson, and one of the other copies was given to the sellers.

Norville retained from the down payment 6 percent of the sales price, or $930. Peteris and his wife objected, stating that he was only entitled to $500, the excess over their net figure of $15,000. The sellers then filed a complaint against Norville with the Department.

Did Norville's actions in renegotiating his listing contract constitute dishonest dealings and/or demonstrate unworthiness and incompetence to act as a real estate broker within the meaning of the license act? [*Norville v. Department of Registration and Education*, 27 Ill.2d 111, 187 N.E.2d 702 (1963)]

3. Defendant James Fletcher, a real estate broker, appealed from a judgment requiring him to pay a real estate commission in the sum of $1,260 to the plaintiff, Jean Murray, for property sold by her after she left his employ. On April 1, 1978, while working for Fletcher as a salesperson, Murray obtained a listing of real property located at 9933 Katwin Court, Peoria, Illinois. The listing was for a 120-day period. In May or June, 1978, Murray terminated her employment with Fletcher and began working for Lincoln National Realty. On July 18, 1978, while working for Lincoln, Murray sold the Katwin Court property, and Fletcher divided the commission with Lincoln after deducting a small sum for the multiple listing fee. Lincoln received $2,513.60, one half of which Lincoln paid to Murray. Murray asserted her claim against Fletcher for one half of the commission retained by him. When Fletcher refused to pay, Murray filed suit.

Fletcher claimed in the appeal that even though his agreement with Murray provides for a commission payment, he is not permitted by the License Act to pay a commission to a salesperson not employed by him.

Should the appellate court affirm or reverse the lower court's ruling? [*Murray v. Fletcher*, 93 Ill.App.3d 289, 417 N.E.2d 195, 48 Ill.Dec. 793 (1981)]

4. The Department issued a complaint against Benjamin A. Rasky, a broker, setting forth a number of outrageous conditions (rats, roaches, peeling paint, broken plaster, leaky malfunctioning plumbing, etc.) existing in certain apartment buildings owned and operated by him which were in violation of the Municipal Code of Chicago and endangered the health and safety of the inhabitants. The complaint asked that Rasky's real estate broker's license be suspended or revoked.

Should Rasky be disciplined for "unworthiness"? [*Rasky v. Department of Registration and Education*, 87 Ill.App.3d, 580 410 N.E.2d 69, 43 Ill.Dec. 69 (1980)]

5. Ronald R. Coles was charged with having violated the License Act in that he had been convicted of two counts of the offense of "Interference with commerce by threats or violence," a felony, in the United States District Court. At the time of the alleged crimes, Coles was president of the Lake County Board and as such, was the liquor commissioner of Lake County. The two counts on which Coles was found guilty alleged that, while serving as liquor commissioner, he extorted $500 from one liquor applicant and $300 from another applicant. Coles was sentenced to serve three years of probation. As a partial defense to the disciplinary proceedings, Coles claimed that because his conviction in federal court was totally unrelated to his real estate practice, he should not be disciplined.

Under these circumstances, may the Department discipline the licensee, and if so, to what extent? [*Coles v. Department of Registration and Education*, 59 Ill.App.3d 1046, 376 N.E.2d 269, 17 Ill.Dec. 270 (1978)]

10-QUESTION DIAGNOSTIC QUIZ

1. Which of the following acts would most likely jeopardize the licensee's status as a licensed real estate salesperson?
   A. If he had memorized several of the most difficult state exam questions, and after the exam, wrote them down on paper for his own review in case he failed the exam
   B. If she is convicted of simple assault (a misdemeanor)
   C. If he is convicted of passing bad checks (a misdemeanor)
   D. If she voluntarily commits himself to a drug or alcohol rehabilitation center

2. All of the following acts could subject the broker to disciplinary action EXCEPT:
   A. Broker opens a satellite office at a counter in a large department store.
   B. To generate traffic for a client's home, broker falsely advertises that the home has three bathrooms as opposed to the actual one bathroom, but he points out this fact when he shows the home.
   C. Broker promises a prospective client to sell her home for $100,000 although the broker knows that it will not sell for anywhere near that amount.
   D. Broker permits her salespeople to regularly advertise free merchandise for attending open houses.

3. A broker refused to refund a buyer's earnest money because he didn't know whether the offer had been accepted or rejected by the seller. Under such circumstances, if the buyer complained of the broker's conduct, the State of Illinois would probably:
   A. revoke the broker's license.
   B. suspend the broker's license.
   C. censure the broker.
   D. do nothing.

4. For which of the following acts would a broker NOT be subject to discipline?
   A. If a broker pays a referral fee directly to a salesperson who regularly refers business to the broker but whom the broker does not sponsor
   B. If a broker employs an unlicensed telemarketing firm to solicit listings by phone for the brokerage firm
   C. If a broker installs "for sale" signs on properties listed with competing firms
   D. If a broker neglects to place a large cash earnest money deposit in his or her escrow account until the day after the buyer's offer is accepted, which is two weeks after the earnest money deposit was made

5. Which of the following actions, if performed by a licensee, would most likely result in the licensee's discipline?
   A. The failure to discover and divulge that a client's water softener was inoperative
   B. The disclosure of a defect in a client's plumbing system
   C. The licensee's conviction for misdemeanor theft
   D. The failure to divulge that the most recent occupant of an apartment had been murdered while sleeping in the bedroom

6. A broker places an ad in the local newspaper that states: "Free color TV to the first 100 visitors to Newborn Estates." Which of the following circumstances would be least likely to affect the broker's licensure?
   A. The televisions were red, white, and blue, but the pictures on the televisions were black and white.
   B. The broker gives away only 50 televisions and tells the remaining visitors they're too late.
   C. The televisions are much smaller than they appear to be in the ad.
   D. The televisions are a cheap, bottom-of-the-line model.

7. Joe Baker complained to the state that his broker should be disciplined. For which of the following acts, if proven, should Joe Baker's broker be disciplined?
   A. Permitting Joe to accept an offer on his home that was $10,000 under the list price
   B. Telling the purchasers of the property that the basement leaked occasionally
   C. Telling Joe that the purchasers were married when in fact they were only engaged
   D. Falsely telling the purchasers that as soon as Joe moved out of the neighborhood, the property could be sold for at least $10,000 more than the listed price

8. Which of the following licensee behaviors would probably violate the provisions of the License Act relating to "unworthiness" or "incompetency"?
   A. Taking a net listing
   B. Truthfully telling a client that the licensee has a customer who will make a super offer for the home but that the licensee won't put the deal together unless his or her commission is increased
   C. Placing his or her "for sale" signs on every corner lot in town
   D. Refusing to take a listing at a commission less than 15 percent

9. Attorney Johnson is also licensed as a real estate broker. Under such circumstances, Johnson MAY NOT:
   A. when acting as a broker, prepare his own riders for attachment to clients' real estate contracts.
   B. manage a branch real estate office.
   C. provide free homebuyer seminars.
   D. act as the attorney for the seller of the home he has listed and sold.

10. Pete Smiley gave his broker: $2,500 as earnest money, a credit report, a financial declaration, and a certified copy of his divorce decree. The seller accepted Pete's offer but refused to close the deal. Pete demands the return of his earnest monies and documents, but the seller has directed the broker to withhold the items until the buyer signs a release. The broker should:
   A. honor her client's directions.
   B. return all of the items.
   √C. return the documents but continue to hold on to the $2,500 earnest money.
   D. under the facts and circumstances, do whatever she feels is ethical.

STUDENT NOTES

CHAPTER 6

DISCIPLINARY PROCEDURES AND HEARINGS
(OOPS, PARDON MY BLOOPER)

○ **CHAPTER OVERVIEW**
What happens when you run a red light? This chapter fully explains how to handle traffic court (or in some instances, felony court) when and if the real estate rules of the road are violated.

○ **LEARNING OBJECTIVES**
By the time you have finished studying this chapter, you should be able to:
1) Define a consent order.
2) Summarize the disciplinary process.
3) Identify conduct determined to be the most reprehensible by the Department.
4) Differentiate between an informal conference and a disciplinary hearing.
5) Recognize situations calling for the licensee's retention of legal counsel.
6) State the ramifications of failing to respond to a notice of hearing.
7) Appreciate the significance of avoiding conduct that might result in a disciplinary complaint.
8) Enumerate and discuss the five steps in a formal disciplinary hearing.
9) Define "clear and convincing" as it relates to the Department's burden of proof in disciplinary matters.

○ **5 CASES TO JUDGE**

○ **10-QUESTION DIAGNOSTIC QUIZ**

CHAPTER 6

DISCIPLINARY PROCEDURES AND HEARINGS
(OOPS, PARDON MY BLOOPER)

FIG 6-1

NOTICE OF INFORMAL CONFERENCE

May 1, 1992

Mr. Garfield T. Katt
1 East Main Street
Hometown, Illinois

Dear Mr. Katt:

It has come to our attention that your practice of real estate may be in violation of the laws of the State of Illinois.

You are hereby required to appear at the office of the Department of Professional Regulation, 100 West Randolph Street, Suite 9-300, Chicago, Illinois 60601, on June 15, 1992, at 9:30 a.m. to offer information and speak on behalf of yourself.

Kindly cooperate by your prompt attendance. Failure to provide the information requested may result in suspension of your license based upon a violation of the Illinois Real Estate License Act of 1983, Illinois Revised Statutes, Chapter 111, Section 18(e)(17), which is quoted as follows:

Failing to provide information requested by the Department, within 30 days of the request, either as the result of a formal or informal complaint to the Department or as a result of a random audit conducted by the Department, which would indicate a violation of this Act;

Should you require further information, please contact us at 312/917-4500.

DEPARTMENT OF PROFESSIONAL
REGULATION of the State of Illinois

DIRECTOR

By:/s/ *Agent of Director*
Director of Statewide Enforcement

FIG 6-2

STATE OF ILLINOIS
DEPARTMENT OF PROFESSIONAL REGULATION

DEPARTMENT OF PROFESSIONAL REGULATION)
of the State of Illinois, Complainant) 92-0000
GARFIELD T. KATT,)
License No. 75-000000, Respondent)

NOTICE OF PRELIMINARY HEARING

TO: GARFIELD T. KATT
1 East Main Street
Hometown, Illinois

PLEASE TAKE NOTICE that on June 15, 1992, at 10:00 A.M., you are directed to appear before the Real Estate Administration And Disciplinary Board of the Department of Professional Regulation of the State of Illinois located at 100 West Randolph Street, Suite 9-300, Chicago, Illinois, 60601, at which time a hearing date will be set. You are requested to then and there present any and all routine motions you may wish to have heard regarding the charges contained in the attached Complaint. Any motions presented on the above date should be served on the Prosecution Division of the Department of Professional Regulation, at 100 West Randolph Street, Suite 9-300, Chicago, Illinois, 60601, at least three (3) business days in advance of the scheduled meeting.

Your appearance on the scheduled date is mandatory and failure to so appear may result in the selection of a hearing date in your absence, unless a continuance has been secured in advance of the meeting. Your appearance may be made personally or through counsel. CORPORATIONS must be represented by counsel.

It is required that you file a VERIFIED ANSWER to the attached Complaint with the Department of Professional Regulation within 20 days of the date of service.

RULES OF PRACTICE IN ADMINISTRATIVE HEARINGS IN THE DEPARTMENT OF PROFESSIONAL REGULATION AND BEFORE COMMITTEES OR BOARDS OF SAID DEPARTMENT are available upon request.

DEPARTMENT OF PROFESSIONAL
REGULATION, of the State of Illinois
By:/s/ *Attorney*
Its attorney

Attorney for the Department
of Professional Regulation of the State of Illinois
100 West Randolph Street, Suite 9-300, Chicago, Illinois 60601
312/917-4541

If you receive either of the exhibited letters in the morning mail, it's not going to be a nice day. Regardless of your guilt or innocence, your stomach will do flip-flops, your body will tremble, and your hands will shake. There is always a cost incurred in becoming a party to disciplinary proceedings. It may be lost time and, therefore, money, or it may be emotional, psychological, and/or physical stress and trauma. In the worst-case scenario, the cost will be the revocation of your license, a $10,000 fine, and the attendant humiliation, lost income, job loss, etc.

Even if you win your case, you're a loser. What do you suppose your competitors, acquaintances, and others will think and say behind your back if an investigator from the Illinois Department of Professional Regulation presents his or her card and credentials and proceeds to discuss YOU with them?

If you haven't already done so, you may wish to read the conclusion in Chapter 5 for an account of how being disciplined affected one particular licensee. After you read the licensee's brief story, we hope you will return to this page with a renewed interest in this chapter. Only someone with a sociopath's (aggressively antisocial) personality is impervious to the rigors of the disciplinary process. There's nothing humorous about a disciplinary blooper, and with few exceptions, your oops won't be pardoned.

INTRODUCTION

Approximately 1,500 real estate–related complaints are registered annually with the Department. Of these, nearly one half are either frivolous or founded upon ignorance of the Department's main purpose, which is protecting the public. Consumers whose earnest monies are either being withheld or not remitted upon a declaration of forfeiture are one of the most common sources of these unfounded complaints. The consumers don't understand why an earnest money deposit they feel rightfully entitled to receive should not be immediately surrendered. They don't believe the other party's written consent is necessary. The Department also is not a collection agency for salespersons' and cooperating brokers' unpaid commissions, which are the subject of other unfounded complaints that are routinely dismissed.

Regardless, the Department must give each complaint its attention, and this chapter will fully explain how the various complaints may be handled. The process and procedures will be discussed in some detail to the end that the reader will develop an understanding of the system.

ADVERSARY SYSTEM

At the outset, it is important for the student to fully understand and appreciate that the disciplinary proceedings are adversarial in nature. Our entire judicial system is based on the adversary system for settling disputes, and the disciplinary process should be viewed in this respect from its very beginning to end. In this type of system, the parties initiate and conduct the litigation. As the theory goes, only an investigation and presentation of evidence by opponents who are both motivated by self-interest will produce the true and correct picture for the judge, jury, or other ultimate arbiter of the dispute.

In the case of disciplinary proceedings, you the licensee are under investigation, and although you won't receive a Miranda warning, you must understand that anything you say may be used against you. An investigator or attorney from the Department is a potential adversary, whose job is to assure that if a violation has occurred, you are disciplined. Conversely, if an infraction has not been committed, the Department personnel are not adversaries but simply fact finders who will be happy to return to their office with a recommendation that the charges be dismissed. Should you elect to speak with an investigator or a Department attorney or attend an informal conference or a formal hearing without the assistance of an attorney, you should make sure that you understand and appreciate the adversarial nature of the proceedings and that your self-interest and the interests of the Department may be diametrically opposed.

Has anyone ever been incarcerated for a crime they didn't commit? Of course they have. Many of those wrongful convictions were the result of incompetent representation or no representation whatsoever. Likewise, there are licensees whose conduct was wrongfully disciplined due to a lack of competent representation. What you say may extricate you from one charge but assure your discipline under another, i.e., "out of the frying pan and into the fire." For example, let's imagine an investigator is investigating your conduct in having placed a misleading ad. In the course of your interview, you mention that the ad was designed to appeal to a particular Caucasian age group. The end result is that not only are you charged with misleading advertising, but you may also face charges of discrimination. Even if you are innocent of both charges, an enormous cost may have been compounded because of an inadvertent comment.

COMPLAINTS

Most disciplinary complaints are initiated by the general public. The complaints come from buyers, sellers, tenants, competitors, employees, attorneys, title companies, and just about anyone involved in the real estate business. Even anonymous complaints from who-knows-where (ex-spouse, sibling, neighbor ??) are investigated. Regardless of the source of the complaint, a file is created, a number is assigned to it, the complaint is time stamped, and it is given to an investigator for further action.

Section 17 of the License Act mandates that the Director of the Department hire one full-time Chief of Real Estate Investigations. Additionally, one full-time investigator and one full-time auditor must be hired for every 15,000 licensees. With nearly 80,000 brokers and salespersons in the state, the Department has an investigatorial staff of 11 including the Chief. With 1,500 complaints coming in on an annual basis, it should be apparent that the Department is neither financially nor physically capable of initiating large numbers of investigations and disciplinary proceedings on its own.

If the allegations of a complaint pertain to an activity and/or licensee that doesn't fall under the Department's jurisdiction, an investigation may be conducted and then, if appropriate, referred to either the Attorney General, the State's Attorney's office, or an appropriate state agency. For example, if a complaint arises against an alleged broker who is not in fact licensed, an investigation may be conducted, and upon conclusion of the investigation, the matter would be referred to the State's Attorney's office in the county where the infraction took place. The alleged broker could then be prosecuted for practicing real estate without a license.

The License Act defines the types of behavior that may result in discipline. The principal grounds for which the Department may deny a license or discipline a licensee are set forth in Chapter 5; however, any violation of the License Act or Rules may be cause for discipline.

INVESTIGATIONS

When a complaint is received by the Department, the *Complaint Review Committee* "logs" it into the system. The Complaint Review Committee is an informal committee of two Board members, the Commissioner, the Chief of Real Estate Investigations, and a Department attorney, who periodically review investigations and render decisions as to their disposition. Once a number and investigator are assigned to the case, the investigation usually begins with a computer check of the involved licensee(s). This check will provide the investigator with the licensee's license number, license status, and information regarding previous complaints. A thorough interview of the complainant follows. Generally, the licensee under investigation is contacted next for his or her response to the allegations.

There may be additional interviews and the collection of relevant documents. When the investigator feels he or she has a clear picture of the complaint, the investigator may contact a member of the Real Estate Administration and Disciplinary Board(s) for guidance on the matter under investigation. As noted above, approximately one half of the complaints filed annually involve no violation of the Act or Rules, and at this point these cases are closed after being reviewed by the Complaint Review Committee.

If it appears that there may have been a violation of the Act or Rules, the investigation continues. Due to the variety of charges possible under the Act and the number of individuals who may be involved in the process, there is no real structure to an investigation. Some investigations are virtually open-and-shut cases, and others take considerable time, effort, and skill to fully develop. For example, a blind ad placed by a licensee is typically of the open-and-shut variety. Conversely, a case of misrepresentation may take longer to document.

Once an investigation has reached the stage where the case is ready to be prosecuted, a determination will be made as to whether further action should proceed formally or informally. Factors such as the seriousness of the violation, likelihood of success, disciplinary record of the licensee, and the licensee's demeanor during the investigation are just a few of the many considerations.

On occasion, the Department will investigate a case that results in the discovery of an infraction so minute that further action is not deemed appropriate, and the licensee is simply warned that future similar conduct will be just cause for further action. For example, under the Rules, a consent to audit must be mailed to the Department within ten days of the opening of an escrow account. If the notification was not mailed for 11 days, the Department might not even bother wasting postage on a warning letter. If, on the other hand, the consent was delayed for 15 days, the Department might elect to send out an *administrative warning letter* (see Figure 6-3) rather than prosecute the infraction. If the consent was delayed for 20 days, a *cease and desist letter* might be the chosen manner of terminating the case. A cease and desist letter is simply a more aggressive approach to a perhaps clear technical error. A cease and desist letter appears in Figure 6-4.

FIG 6-3

Mr. Garfield T. Katt
1 East Main Street
Hometown, Illinois

May 1, 1992

RE: Administrative Warning Letter
    License #75-000000

Dear Mr. Katt:

Please be advised that the Department has concluded its investigation into the above matter. After careful review of the facts, the Department at this time has decided not to initiate formal charges for failure to submit to the Department a consent to audit special accounts within 10 days of opening such an account which may be a violation of the Real Estate License Act of 1983. Illinois Revised Statutes (1989), Chapter 111, paragraph(s) 5818(h)12 and 19. However, should such conduct reoccur or persist, the Department will reinstate these allegations, as well as any additional ones.

                Sincerely,
                /s/ Chief
                Chief of Business Prosecutions

FIG 6-4

Mr. Garfield T. Katt
1 East Main Street
Hometown, Illinois

May 1, 1992

RE: Cease and Desist Letter
    License #75-000000

Dear Mr. Katt:

Please be advised that the Department has concluded its investigation into the above matter. After careful review of the facts, the Department at this time has decided not to initiate formal charges for failure to submit to the Department a consent to audit special accounts within 10 days of opening such an account which may be a violation of the Real Estate License Act of 1983. Illinois Revised Statutes (1989) Chapter 111, paragraph(s) 5818(h) 12 and 19. You are hereby ordered to cease and desist from further such conduct; however, should such conduct reoccur or persist, the Department will reinstate these allegations, as well as any additional ones.

                Sincerely,
                /s/ Chief
                Chief of Business Prosecutions

Note that in the previous discussion we used a lot of "mights," "mays," "coulds," etc. The size of the Department staff, the philosophy of the supervisory personnel, and the licensee's past disciplinary history are all considerations; therefore, the reader should not conclude that technical rule violations will not be prosecuted. They are! The purpose of the foregoing discussion is to merely acquaint you with the administrative handling of some of the less serious offenses. These letters may also be used where the conclusion is reached that there's probably a violation but the Department doesn't feel that they have the ability to prove the infraction. More succinctly, there are no rules or regulations that may be taken lightly. The only safe harbor from disciplinary proceedings is 100 percent compliance with the Act and Rules.

PROSECUTION

Quite often, the whole disciplinary process will take place over the phone, such as when the licensee has committed a very technical and insignificant violation. Department staff may telephone a salesperson who has placed a newspaper ad that discloses all of the necessary information but in which the salesperson's name was in larger type than the sponsoring broker's name—a violation of the Rules for the Administration of the License Act. An attorney from the Department might call the licensee and, after confirming that the salesperson ran the ad and that the published ad was just as the salesperson placed it (no mistakes), might offer to settle the case for a discipline consisting of a $50 fine and a reprimand. If the licensee agrees, the necessary paperwork (consent order, as discussed below) would be typed, mailed to the licensee, and the licensee would sign and return the paperwork for processing.

As one would expect, serious infractions are at the top and purely technical, minor infractions at the bottom of the investigator's/auditor's prioritized list. These same factors are also considered in determining the method of investigation and course of disciplinary procedure.

INFORMAL HEARING

If the Department concludes that an informal conference is appropriate, the first notice (illustrated at the beginning of this chapter in Figure 6-1) is mailed to the involved licensee(s). The notice seems friendly enough, and oftentimes the licensee will choose to attend the conference without benefit of counsel and without the foggiest notion as to what the conference is all about. This may be the biggest mistake of the licensee's professional life.

Department hearings are held in either Springfield or Chicago. An imaginary line drawn through Peoria determines the site selection for a particular hearing. All licensees north of the line will have their cases heard in Chicago, and those south of the line in Springfield. Although it depends on the volume of cases and the availability of Board members, informal conferences are usually scheduled once a month in Springfield, and two or three times a month in Chicago. Formal hearings are generally a monthly event and are combined with the Board's monthly administrative meetings.

Both the formal and informal conferences are conducted in rather Spartan-like conference rooms, i.e., the furniture (folding tables, folding chairs) and furnishings (painted walls, a clock, and the absence of wall hangings) are very unlike the posh surroundings of a typical court room. The atmosphere is more like a civic committee meeting than a critically important hearing.

At this informal conference will typically be the licensee, an investigator/auditor, an attorney for the Illinois Department of Professional Regulation, and a member of the Disciplinary Board. This seems like an awfully ominous chit-chat to the uninitiated. The twofold purpose of the conference is to further investigate the matter and, if possible, to dispose of the case either by dismissal or by a *consent order* whereby the licensee consents to the discipline agreed upon (negotiated) by the parties. Although you closed $8,000,000 in deals in 1991, your negotiating techniques may be lost in this unfamiliar territory. You don't know whether you did or did not violate the License Act—if you did, what your infraction justifies in the way of discipline. You panic and agree to a consent order that you later learn was not a very good deal.

Fortunately, the consent order is not prepared and signed the day of the conference. Rather, the order is drafted and mailed to the licensee for his or her signature. If, after having the order reviewed by an attorney, the licensee wants to back out of the deal, the licensee may. Occasionally, a deal may be renegotiated at this point, but more often, unless the order is signed and returned to the Department within 30 days, the case will proceed to a formal complaint and hearing.

At the conclusion of the conference, one of several resolutions is possible. The case may be closed, a consent order may be negotiated, or the case may be referred for formal prosecution. A sample consent order for Garfield T. Katt appears in Figures 6-5 and 6-6. Note that the consent order must be signed by a member of the Board. The signature of the Board member constitutes a recommendation to the Director that the agreed-upon resolution be accepted.

> **FIG 6-5**
>
> STATE OF ILLINOIS
> DEPARTMENT OF PROFESSIONAL REGULATION
>
> DEPARTMENT OF PROFESSIONAL REGULATION)
> of the State of Illinois, Complainant) 92-0000
> GARFIELD T. KATT,)
> License No. 75-000000, Respondent)
>
> CONSENT ORDER
>
> The Department of Professional Regulation by one of its attorneys, and GARFIELD T. KATT, Respondent, hereby agree to the following:
>
> STIPULATION
>
> GARFIELD T. KATT is licensed as Real Estate Broker in the State of Illinois, holding license No. 75-000000. At all times material to the matter set forth in this Consent Order, the Department of Professional Regulation of the State of Illinois had jurisdiction over the subject matter and parties herein.
>
> Information has come to the attention of the Department that Respondent failed to notify the Department of the opening of a special account and failed to submit a Consent To Audit for such account within ten (10) days.
>
> Such action by Respondent, if proven to be true, would constitute grounds for suspending or revoking Respondent's license as a Real Estate Broker, on the authority of Illinois Revised Statutes (1989), Chapter 111, paragraph 5818(h)(19)
>
> As a result of the foregoing allegations, the Department held an Informal Conference at the offices of the Department, 100 West Randolph Street, Suite 9-300, Chicago, Illinois, on June 14, 1992. Respondent appeared in person on that date. Present were a member of the Real Estate Administration and Disciplinary Board of the State of Illinois, and an attorney for the Department. Respondent admitted to the allegations.
>
> Respondent has been advised of the right to have the pending allegations reduced to written charges, the right to a hearing, the right to contest any charges brought, and the right to administrative review of any order resulting from a hearing. Respondent knowingly waives each of these rights, as well as waiving any right to administrative review of this Consent Order.

> **FIG 6-6**
>
> Respondent and the Department have agreed, in order to resolve this matter, that GARFIELD T. KATT be permitted to enter into a Consent Order with the Department, providing for the imposition of disciplinary measures which are fair and equitable in the circumstances and which are consistent with the best interests of the people of the State of Illinois.
>
> CONDITIONS
>
> WHEREFORE, the Department, through its attorney, and GARFIELD T. KATT, agree:
>
> A. The Real Estate Broker's license of GARFIELD T. KATT, License No. 75-000000, shall be reprimanded.
>
> B. Respondent shall pay a Twenty-Five Dollar ($25.00) fine payable to the Real Estate Recovery Fund.
>
> C. Any violation by Respondent of the terms and conditions of this Consent Order shall be grounds for the Department to immediately file a Complaint to revoke the Respondent's license to practice as a Real Estate Broker in the State of Illinois.
>
> D. This Consent Order shall become effective immediately after it is approved by the Director of the Department.
>
> DEPARTMENT OF PROFESSIONAL REGULATION
> 07/14/92   /s/ *Attorney*
> DATE   Its attorney
>   Attorney for the Department
> 07/07/92   /s/ *Garfield T. Katt*
> DATE   Garfield T. Katt
>   Respondent
> 07/20/92   /s/ *Member*
> DATE   Member, Real Estate Administration and
>   Disciplinary Board
>
> The foregoing Consent Order is approved in full.
> DATED THIS 18th day of August, 1992.
>   DEPARTMENT OF PROFESSIONAL REGULATION
>   /s/ *Director*
>   Director

FORMAL HEARING

If an informal conference fails to resolve the complaint or if an informal conference is not held, the next step is a formal complaint and hearing. This process very closely resembles civil litigation, whereby a formal complaint is filed, the parties "discover" what information and witnesses the other side intends to present at the hearing, and both sides otherwise prepare their cases, witnesses, and evidence for presentation.

Central to our legal system is the concept of *due process*. Due process is applicable to disciplinary proceedings and requires that procedural safeguards be adhered to throughout the hearing process. Although many cases have interpreted the term, the fundamental safeguards of due process are: 1) the licensee must be notified of the charges placed against him or her; 2) the licensee must be able to understand the nature and scope of the charges placed against him or her; 3) the licensee must be afforded the opportunity of defending against the charges; and 4) a decision on the charges must be made by an impartial arbiter. If due process is not afforded a licensee being charged with a violation of the Act or Rules and if a judicial review of the decision is undertaken, the Department's decision will be reversed.

Periodically, disciplined licensees claim that their discipline was politically motivated and/or that the Board was prejudiced against them. Although most Board members would automatically excuse themselves if they felt they could not be fair and impartial, if a licensee truly believes that the Board or a member thereof is biased or prejudiced against him or her, the licensee may and should seek relief prior to the formal hearing. The courts will not consider such an issue on appeal unless it was first addressed prior to the formal hearing.

The processes and procedures of the hearing are governed by the Administrative Procedure Act (Chapter 127 Ill.Rev.Stat. par. 1004(a)(1)), the Rules for the Administration of the Rules of Practice in Administrative Hearings (68 Admin. Code Sect. 1110 et seq.), and Section 20 of the License Act. In order to become totally familiar with the hearing process, one needs to review all three of these laws and rules. Our purpose here, however, is to apprise the reader of the basic protections and procedures, which can be chronologically divided into the following steps:

Step 1: filing of formal complaint and notice of preliminary hearing
Step 2: preliminary hearing
Step 3: status hearing
Step 4: prehearing conference
Step 5: formal evidentiary hearing

STEP 1: FORMAL COMPLAINT AND NOTICE OF PRELIMINARY HEARING

After an investigation is completed, a summary is prepared by the investigative unit and delivered to the prosecutions unit of the Department. The prosecutions unit is composed of lawyers who will, upon acceptance of the prosecution, draft a *formal complaint* and, along with a *notice of preliminary hearing*, mail the complaint to the licensee. The notice advises the licensee that an answer must be filed within 20 days. An example of a notice of preliminary hearing is the second document reproduced at the beginning of this chapter (Figure 6-2). Failure to *answer* the formal complaint results in a *default*, which means that a recommendation for discipline may be made solely on the basis of the Department's evidence, without any testimony or evidence from the licensee. An answer is simply an admission or denial of each allegation set forth in the complaint and can be prepared quickly by an attorney. Unless the licensee plans on representing himself or herself, the licensee should not delay retaining counsel, because the attorney selected should not be hired on the morning of the 19th day and be expected to draft an answer and messenger the document to the Department before the close of business. A formal complaint for Garfield T. Katt's violation of the License Act and Garfield's answer are illustrated in Figures 6-7 and 6-8.

STEP 2: PRELIMINARY HEARING

The preliminary hearing may be the first time that the parties actually meet face to face. At this time a "hearing officer" sets up a hearing schedule, which includes times for filing motions, exchanging information, status hearing, prehearing conference, and final hearing date. The preliminary hearings are normally very brief and perfunctory, similar to asking for a continuance the first time a traffic ticket is scheduled.

Discovery is the aptly named part of litigation where each side has the opportunity of discovering what the other side has in the way of witnesses, documents, and other evidence. The Perry Mason-style surprise witness is a rarity in real life because the discovery process requires both sides to disclose these surprises well in advance of a hearing.

Section 1110.130 of the Rules of Practice in Administrative Hearings permits the following discovery:
1. The names and addresses of all witnesses
2. Copies of any documents that may be offered as evidence
3. A description of any other evidence that may be offered
4. Any evidence that tends to support the licensee's position or call into question the credibility of any Department witness
5. Copies of any investigative reports summarizing an investigator's interview with the licensee
6. Any additional discovery agreed upon by the parties

In civil litigation, the discovery process goes on for years as the attorneys "depose" everyone on the face of the earth who was awake on the night of a minor fender bender. Depose means to take a deposition, which is simply a question-and-answer session that is recorded by a court stenographer. A witness or party to an event is placed under oath and asked questions as to what they saw, heard, etc. Unless both parties to a disciplinary proceeding agree, depositions are not generally available, and this absence has both a positive and negative impact on disciplinary proceedings. The positive effect is the reduction of expense and the lessening of delays in setting hearing dates. The negatives are that a witness with crucial testimony may refuse to talk with a party or with the party's representatives (attorney/investigators), and then at the time of the hearing, might provide surprise testimony that may or may not be truthful.

FIG 6-7

STATE OF ILLINOIS
DEPARTMENT OF PROFESSIONAL REGULATION

DEPARTMENT OF PROFESSIONAL REGULATION)
of the State of Illinois, Complainant) 92-0000
GARFIELD T. KATT,)
License No. 75-000000, Respondent)

COMPLAINT

Now comes the DEPARTMENT OF PROFESSIONAL REGULATION of the State of Illinois, by its Attorney, and as its COMPLAINT against GARFIELD T. KATT, Respondent, complains as follows:

1. GARFIELD T. KATT is presently the holder of a Certificate Of Registration as a Real Estate Broker in the State of Illinois, License No. 75-000000, issued by the Department Of Professional Regulation of the State of Illinois, and at all relevant times mentioned herein was in active status.

2. The Department Of Professional Regulation of the State of Illinois has jurisdiction over the Respondent and the subject matter at all relevant times mentioned herein.

3. That Respondent, as holder of a Certificate Of Registration in the State of Illinois, authorized the Department Of Professional Regulation to examine and audit any and all escrow accounts utilized by him in connection with his real estate business. 68 Illinois Administrative Code, Section 1450.40.

4. That pursuant to the above statutory provision, the Department Of Professional Regulation examined and audited Respondent's records.

5. That the Department Of Professional Regulation, after receiving bank records and other data, determined that a Consent To Audit had not been submitted to the Department although a special account had been opened for over ten (10) days in violation of Illinois Revised Statutes (1989), Chapter 111, paragraph 5818(h)(19) and 68 Illinois Administrative Code, Section 1450.40.

6. The foregoing acts and/or omissions are grounds for revocation or suspension of a Certificate Of Registration pursuant to Illinois Revised Statutes (1989), Chapter 111, paragraph 5818(h)(19).

WHEREFORE, based on the foregoing allegations, the DEPARTMENT OF PROFESSIONAL REGULATION of the State of Illinois, its Attorney, prays that the Real Estate Broker license of Respondent be suspended, revoked, or otherwise disciplined.

DEPARTMENT OF PROFESSIONAL REGULATION
By:/s/ *Attorney*
Attorney for the Department
Attorney for the Department of Professional Regulation of the State of Illinois
100 West Randolph Street, Suite 9-300, Chicago, Illinois 60601
312/814-4623

FIG 6-8

STATE OF ILLINOIS
DEPARTMENT OF PROFESSIONAL REGULATION

DEPARTMENT OF PROFESSIONAL REGULATION)
of the State of Illinois, Complainant) 92-0000
GARFIELD T. KATT,)
License No. 75-000000, Respondent)

ANSWER

Now comes the Respondent, GARFIELD T. KATT, by and through his attorney, Clarke R. Marquis, and for his answer to the complaint filed herein by the Complainant, DEPARTMENT OF PROFESSIONAL REGULATION OF THE STATE OF ILLINOIS, alleges and states as follows:

1. Respondent admits the allegations contained in paragraph 1 of the Department's complaint.

2. Respondent admits the allegations contained in paragraph 2 of the Department's complaint.

3. Respondent admits the allegations contained in paragraph 3 of the Department's complaint.

4. Respondent admits the allegations contained in paragraph 4 of the Department's complaint.

5. Respondent denies the allegations contained in paragraph 5 of the Department's complaint.

6. Respondent denies the allegations contained in paragraph 6 of the Department's complaint.

WHEREFORE, Respondent, GARFIELD T. KATT, prays that the DEPARTMENT OF PROFESSIONAL REGULATION's complaint be dismissed.

GARFIELD T. KATT
By:/s/ *Clarke R. Marquis*
Clarke R. Marquis, his attorney

Clarke R. Marquis
P.O. Box 168
St. Charles, Illinois 60174
708/377-1500

As those familiar with the civil legal process will also note, interrogatories are also not provided for under the discovery rules. Interrogatories are similar to depositions except they are written questions that a party submits to his or her opponent and that must be answered within a certain time period. The absence of both interrogatories and depositions speeds up the process but also makes preparation for a hearing more difficult unless each side's witnesses voluntarily talk with the opposing party's attorneys.

The discovery process will generally start at the conclusion of the preliminary hearing with an exchange of information. Discovery in most cases is cut off 30 days prior to the hearing.

STEP 3: STATUS HEARING

A status hearing is generally set at the time of the preliminary hearing for the purpose of reporting the progress of the case to the hearing officer. The progress of discovery is reported, as well as the date when the parties expect that their investigation and discovery will be complete. If a settlement is to be reached prior to a formal hearing, a status hearing is usually the time for negotiations to have been completed. This hearing will not require the licensee's attendance and, like the preliminary hearing, is generally quite brief and routine.

STEP 4: PREHEARING CONFERENCE

After the status hearing, the case is set for a prehearing conference that normally precedes the actual hearing by a couple of weeks. The prehearing conference is designed to expedite or even avoid an actual hearing. By the time of the prehearing conference, both sides should know the strengths and weaknesses of their respective cases. If the parties are still unable to negotiate a satisfactory compromise, the prehearing may nevertheless be used to negotiate issues that will make the hearing proceed more smoothly or quickly, such as the limitation of issues and witnesses and the exclusion or admission of certain evidence or testimony. Once a hearing is scheduled, barring events of major significance (illness, death of an attorney, etc.), the hearing may be expected to proceed. Last-minute continuances are not routinely granted.

STEP 5: FORMAL EVIDENTIARY HEARING

A hearing officer, who is an attorney and an employee of the Department, conducts the formal hearing. The hearing officer conducts the hearing in a manner similar to that of a judge in that the hearing officer makes certain that the procedural rules have been abided by, rules on the admissibility of evidence, and is present at all times during the hearing. Occasionally the Commissioner or another member of the Board will act as the hearing officer.

Usually several Board members are present for the formal hearing. Since the hearings are open to the public, there may also be several spectators and occasionally a newspaper reporter. Although a quorum of the Board (five members) is necessary for the full resolution of a hearing, the hearing may proceed without a quorum. In the event a quorum is not present, the Board's decision will be delayed until a sufficient number of members have had the opportunity to review the transcript of the hearing and a quorum of the Board is assembled for deliberations and a decision.

The actual conduct of the hearing, virtually identical to an ordinary civil trial, is structured as follows:
1. The Department's attorney makes an opening statement, which is then followed by the licensee's opening statement.
2. The Department calls its witnesses and presents its evidence.
3. The licensee calls his or her witnesses and presents his or her evidence.
4. The Department may call additional witnesses to rebut the testimony of the licensee's witnesses and evidence.
5. The Department makes a closing statement followed by the licensee's closing statement, which the Department then has the ability to rebut and may include a request for specific disciplinary action.

The Department has the burden of proving its case. The degree to which it must prove the infraction is by "clear and convincing" evidence. The burden in criminal cases is "beyond a reasonable doubt," whereas in the case of most civil litigation, the burden is "a preponderance of the evidence." So what is clear and convincing?

According to most Illinois cases, clear and convincing is "proof that should leave no reasonable doubt in the mind of the trier of the facts concerning the truth of the matters in issue." Since a criminal case must be proven beyond a reasonable doubt, one may conclude that the two standards are in reality no different. Regardless, the standard of proof in disciplinary proceedings is much greater than the civil standard of a preponderance of the evidence, which is scarcely greater than a 50/50 proposition.

During the presentation of witnesses and evidence, the Board and hearing officer may ask questions. This is an important part of the hearing process and the one feature that is most different from civil and criminal proceedings tried before a jury. Members of a jury are not permitted to ask a witness questions. The professional expertise of Board members enables them to clarify testimony that the attorneys may not have thought was important but which the Board member knows has been of some importance in previous deliberations. The questioning by Board members may be of significant assistance to a licensee or, in appropriate cases, it may be detrimental.

108   Chapter 6   Disciplinary Procedures and Hearings

The Board members are not adversaries. They are highly respected professionals who view their positions on the Board as an honor and, more importantly, a privilege. The privilege is to be of further service to the profession by discharging their duties fairly and impartially. In judging the conduct of their peers, the members of the Board have "been in the trenches" and know the ins and outs and the ups and downs of real estate practice and use this experience in judging the conduct of their colleagues. In a nutshell, one only needs to view the Board or a member of the Board as an adversary if one is, in fact, guilty of an infraction. The Board could have been the author of the following quote from a speech by Abraham Lincoln:

> *I am not bound to win, but I am bound to be true. I am not bound to succeed, but I am bound to live up to what light I have. I must stand with anybody that stands right: stand with him while he is right and part from him when he goes wrong.*

If you are right, the Board and its members will stand with you; but if you go wrong, they will part from you.

THE BOARD DECISION

In most cases, the Board will render its decision later that day. Similar to the jury process, the Board goes into a closed meeting for purposes of their deliberations. Most often, the Board is capable of reaching a decision rather quickly, because they are "professional" jurors. They hear cases on a regular basis, they are familiar with the business and the law to be applied, and they know how they have voted in previous cases of a similar nature. Therefore, they can quickly focus on the main issues, if any, left unresolved by the hearing.

Occasionally, such as when a quorum is absent, there will not be an immediate decision. In these instances, the court stenographer will transcribe the testimony, and the transcript (along with the evidence) will be reviewed by all the members of the Board, who will then make a decision.

In the Board's deliberations, they first generally determine what facts they believe to be true and what facts they do not. Once factual findings are made, the members will decide whether the facts constitute a violation of the License Act or Rules and, if so, what type of recommendation should be made to the Director regarding the licensee's discipline. Once a decision has been reached, findings of fact, conclusions of law, and a recommendation to the Director are prepared for the members to review. Upon the final approval by the members consisting of at least a majority of the Board, the findings, conclusions, and proposed recommendations are mailed to the licensee, who then has 20 days within which to file a request for a rehearing or reconsideration. Figures 6-9, 6-10, and 6-11 illustrate the findings, conclusions, and recommendations and 20-day notice.

If the licensee fails to request a rehearing within 20 days and the Director subsequently agrees with the Board's decision, the Director will sign the final order effectuating the recommendation. Should the Director disagree, he or she may grant the request for a rehearing and return it to the Board for a rehearing. Upon notice of the Director's final order, a licensee has 35 days within which to appeal the agency's decision. Figures 6-12 and 6-13 illustrate the notice of final order and the Department's final order.

APPEALS

If a licensee is dissatisfied with the final decision of the Director, the decision may be appealed. The first step in the appeals process is to file a lawsuit in the circuit court. The lawsuit, as noted, must be filed within 35 days of the Director's notice of final order. The lawsuit will NOT result in a trial; instead, a judge will review the proceedings (complaint, motions, transcript of the witnesses' testimony, exhibits, etc.) and the applicable law and, after hearing sometimes extensive oral arguments from the parties' attorneys, will either affirm or reverse the Department's order. The courts may not freely reconsider the testimony but may reach a contrary conclusion only if the evidence and testimony is "against the manifest weight of the evidence." Of course, the legal issues are

Chapter 6 Disciplinary Procedures and Hearings 109

FIG 6-9

STATE OF ILLINOIS
DEPARTMENT OF PROFESSIONAL REGULATION

DEPARTMENT OF PROFESSIONAL REGULATION	)	
of the State of Illinois, Complainant	)	92-0000
GARFIELD T. KATT,	)	
License No. 75-000000, Respondent	)	

FINDINGS OF FACT, CONCLUSION OF LAW
AND RECOMMENDATION TO THE DIRECTOR

Now comes the Real Estate Administration and Disciplinary Board of the Department of Professional Regulation of the State of Illinois and, after conducting a hearing in this matter, a majority of its members hereby makes the following Findings of Fact, Conclusion of Law and Recommendation to the Director: FINDINGS OF FACT

1. That GARFIELD T. KATT, Respondent, is now a duly registered Real Estate Broker in the State of Illinois, having been issued a Certificate of Registration, License No. 75-000000 by the Department of Professional Regulation. Respondent's license is in active status.
2. That the Department filed a Complaint against the Respondent and sent notice of said Complaint to the Respondent by certified and regular mail on May 15, 1992.
3. That a hearing on the Complaint was held on September 5, 1992, at the Department's office in Chicago, 100 West Randolph Street, Suite 9-300, Chicago, Illinois 60601. A quorum of the Real Estate Administration and Disciplinary Board was present and listened to evidence presented on that date, as evidenced by their signatures below.
4. That the Department was represented at the hearing by one of its attorneys.
5. That Respondent failed to answer or appear after the Department made sufficient attempts to inform him of the charges and of the hearing date.

FIG 6-10

6. That after the presentation of all evidence and arguments, the Board deliberated and made its Findings of Fact, Conclusions of Law and Recommendation to the Director.
7. A Department audit of GARFIELD T. KATT's records revealed that he had failed to submit a Consent To Audit to the Department within ten (10) days of his having opened a special account contrary to and in violation of 68 Illinois Administrative Code, Section 1450.40

CONCLUSIONS OF LAW

1. That the Real Estate Administration and Disciplinary Board of the Department of Professional Regulation of the State of Illinois has jurisdiction over the subject matter and of the parties in this case.
2. That Respondent, GARFIELD T. KATT, License No. 75-000000 has violated Illinois Revised Statutes (1989), Chapter 111, paragraphs 5818(h)(19) and Title 68, Section 1450.40 of the Illinois Administrative Code.

RECOMMENDATION

The Real Estate Administration and Disciplinary Board of the Department of Professional Regulation of the State of Illinois, after making the above Findings of Fact and Conclusions of Law, recommends to the Director of the Department of Professional Regulation, that the Certificate of Registration, License No. 75-000000, of GARFIELD T. KATT be Indefinitely Suspended and a civil penalty of $10,000 be imposed.

DATED this 8th day of October, 1992.

/s/ Commissioner	/s/ Member
Commissioner	Member
/s/ Member	/s/ Member
Member	Member
/s/ Member	/s/ Member
Member	Member

FIG 6-11

STATE OF ILLINOIS
DEPARTMENT OF PROFESSIONAL REGULATION

DEPARTMENT OF PROFESSIONAL REGULATION	)	
of the State of Illinois, Complainant	)	92-0000
GARFIELD T. KATT,	)	
License No. 75-000000, Respondent	)	

20 DAY NOTICE

TO: GARFIELD T. KATT
1 East Main Street
Hometown, Illinois

PLEASE TAKE NOTICE that the Real Estate Administration and Disciplinary Board of the Department of Professional Regulation of the State of Illinois, after hearing and considering evidence presented in the above case, has recommended indefinite suspension of your license to carry on the practice of Real Estate Brokerage in the State of Illinois. A copy of the Real Estate Administration and Disciplinary Board's Findings of Fact, Conclusion of Law and Recommendation are attached hereto.

YOU ARE HEREBY NOTIFIED that you have 20 days from the date this Notice is mailed to present to this Department your written Motion for a Rehearing. Said Motion shall specify the particular grounds for a Rehearing.

The Director of this Department may grant oral argument on this Motion if he deems it necessary for a clearer understanding of the issues presented.

DEPARTMENT OF PROFESSIONAL REGULATION
By:/s/ Attorney
Attorney for the Department

Attorney for the Department of Professional Regulation of the State of Illinois
100 West Randolph Street, Suite 9-300, Chicago, Illinois 60601
312/814-4623

FIG 6-12

STATE OF ILLINOIS
DEPARTMENT OF PROFESSIONAL REGULATION

DEPARTMENT OF PROFESSIONAL REGULATION	)	
of the State of Illinois, Complainant	)	92-0000
GARFIELD T. KATT,	)	
License No. 75-000000, Respondent	)	

NOTICE

TO: GARFIELD T. KATT
1 East Main Street
Hometown, Illinois

PLEASE TAKE NOTICE that the Director of the Department of Professional Regulation did sign the attached Order.

YOU ARE FURTHER NOTIFIED that you have a right to judicial review of all final administrative decisions of this Department, pursuant to the provisions of the "ADMINISTRATIVE REVIEW ACT", approved May 8, 1945, and all amendments and modifications thereof, and the rules adopted pursuant thereto.

The Order of the Director of the Department of Professional Regulation will be implemented as of the date of the Order unless the Order states otherwise.

DEPARTMENT OF PROFESSIONAL REGULATION
of the State of Illinois
By:/s/ Clerk
Clerk of the Department

All inquiries should be directed to the Prosecution Unit 312/814-4477

FIG 6-13

STATE OF ILLINOIS
DEPARTMENT OF PROFESSIONAL REGULATION

DEPARTMENT OF PROFESSIONAL REGULATION of the State of Illinois,	Complainant)	) 92-0000
GARFIELD T. KATT, License No. 75-000000,	Respondent	))

<u>ORDER</u>

This matter having come before the Real Estate Administration and Disciplinary Board of the Department of Professional Regulation of the State of Illinois, and the Real Estate Administration and Disciplinary Board, having made certain Findings of Fact, Conclusions of Law, and a Recommendation to the Director of the Department; and the Department having complied with all required notices; and the time allowed for filing of a Motion for Rehearing before the Director of the Department having now passed;

NOW THEREFORE, I, as the DIRECTOR OF THE DEPARTMENT OF PROFESSIONAL REGULATION of the State of Illinois, do hereby adopt the Findings of Fact, Conclusions of Law, and Recommendation of the Real Estate Administration and Disciplinary Board in this matter.

IT IS THEREFORE ORDERED that the Certificate of Registration, License No. 75-000000, heretofore issued to GARFIELD T. KATT, to carry on the practice of Real Estate Brokerage in the State of Illinois, is indefinitely suspended and a fine of Ten Thousand ($10,000.00) Dollars shall be imposed.

DATED this 11th day of November, 1992.
DEPARTMENT OF PROFESSIONAL
REGULATION of the State of Illinois
/s/ *Director*
Director

fully within the judge's jurisdiction. Chapter 110, paragraph 3-101 et seq. of the Illinois Revised Statutes (1989) governs the review procedures.

During the process of the appeal, the Department's order is stayed, meaning that the fine and discipline are "on hold" until the conclusion of all appeals. Therefore, the licensee may continue practicing real estate until his or her appeals are fully and finally determined by the courts.

After the circuit court hears the case and renders a decision, the case may be appealed further to our appellate courts (Appellate and Supreme). Similar to the circuit court proceedings, the appellate courts will review the record and the parties' "brief" (a misnomer for a quite lengthy booklet setting forth written arguments as to why the circuit court's opinion was right or wrong), and, if requested and desirable, oral arguments will be heard. Eventually the Illinois Supreme Court may render its decision.

Unless federal law or constitutional issues are involved, the appeal process will end at the Illinois Supreme Court level, since the Supreme Courts of the various states are the supreme arbiters of their states' laws. If, however, federal law was incorrectly interpreted and applied or if constitutional issues are involved, the case may be appealed further; however, due to its rarity, such an appeal merits no further discussion here.

Once the final order is issued and further avenues of appeal are unavailable, the Department's discipline will become immediately effective. As noted above, however, until the final decision is rendered, the licensee may continue the practice of real estate.

RESTORATION OF LICENSE

Thus far we have centered our attention on the disciplinary process from the Department's perspective as a prosecutor. Mention should, however, be made that many of the foregoing procedures apply equally but in reverse to the situation where a revoked or indefinitely suspended licensee seeks a return or reinstatement of a license. That is, if a previously licensed individual is desirous of the restoration of his or her license, he or she must file a petition with the Department and the Department will notify the licensee of the hearing date where the licensee may present witnesses and evidence of the licensee's rehabilitation and worthiness to be reinstated.

In the restoration process, the licensee has the burden of proof; however, the licensee's burden is based on a "preponderance of the evidence" test rather than the Department's test of clear and convincing. As noted earlier, the preponderance of the evidence test is slightly more than a 50/50 proposition.

DURATION OF THE PROCEEDINGS

Disciplinary proceedings follow no set time schedule. The gravity of the offense, the complexity of the issues, and other considerations too numerous to mention all affect the duration of disciplinary proceedings. Listed in the following table are actual time schedules for four randomly selected disciplinary proceedings.

	CASE 1	CASE 2	CASE 3	CASE 4
DATE COMPLAINT RECEIVED	02/01/89	04/24/89	03/24/89	06/09/89
SOURCE	Attorney	Buyer	Buyer	Employee
ALLEGED INFRACTION	Escrow violation	Escrow violation	Escrow violation	Escrow violation/ conversion
INVESTIGATOR ASSIGNED	03/06/89	04/24/89	03/28/89	06/12/89
INVESTIGATION BEGAN	04/28/89	04/28/89	04/05/89	06/21/89
INVESTIGATION COMPLETED	05/08/89	05/01/89	05/01/89	
NOTICE OF INFORMAL HEARING	05/19/89	05/17/89	06/12/89	01/09/90*
INFORMAL HEARING HELD	06/16/89	06/14/89	07/13/89	03/14/90*
CONSENT ORDER SIGNED BY ALL PARTIES	08/17/89	07/19/89	09/20/89	02/14/91
CONSENT SIGNED BY DIRECTOR	09/22/89	08/18/89	10/27/89	06/26/91
NOTICE OF ORDER	09/25/89	08/30/89	10/27/89	06/26/91
TOTAL TIME ELAPSED	234 days	114 days	213 days	747 days
DISCIPLINE TAKEN	$500 fine & 2 years probation	$1000 fine & 1 year probation	$100 fine & reprimand	$10,000 fine & indefinite suspension

* An informal hearing conference was not held. These dates represent the dates of the notice of complaint and preliminary hearing.

FREQUENCY OF VARIOUS VIOLATIONS

The Department recently completed a study of the frequency of infractions relating to the various prohibited activities. The study focused on a 15-month period and also undertook to study the uniformity of disciplines for similar violations. The study divided the various infractions into the following categories. Preceding each category is the percent of violations falling within each.

- **(30%) Improper Business Practices**—improper supervision, corporate and partnership licensing, and contractual infractions
- **(25%) Deception/Willful Intent**—misrepresentation, false statements, substance abuse, student loan defaults, and felonies
- **(25%) Escrow Account/Financial Violations**—commingling, conversion, and bookkeeping irregularities
- **(12%) Advertising in Violation of the Act and Rules**
- **(8%) Technical Violations**—failure to adhere to the various time requirements for the filing of notices and documents with the Department

Of the 204 cases studied, 42 resulted in suspensions or revocations. Twenty-five of the suspensions were escrow violations, leading the author of the study to conclude, "Although the Department appears to be lenient in most matters, financial, escrow, tax and drug violations resulted in harsher penalties, either (1) probations with stringent conditions or (2) suspension or revocation." During the period studied, over $150,000 was assessed in fines, and during the same period, $74,000 was collected. A breakdown of the various infractions and disciplines is offered in the following table.

Chapter 6 Disciplinary Procedures and Hearings

INFRACTION	NO.	ADMONISHMENTS REPRIMANDS	PROBATIONS	SUSPENSIONS REVOCATIONS
FINANCIAL	(27)	9	11	7
ESCROWS	(27)	6	10	11
ADS	(25)	20	3	2
FELONIES	(19)	0	12	7
IMPROPER SUPERVISION	(14)	11	3	0
CORPORATE LICENSES	(12)	10	2	0
CONTRACTS	(11)	11	0	0
MISREPRESENTATIONS	(10)	8	2	0
NON-OPERATIVE/ NON-RENEW STATUS	(10)	7	1	2 STAYED
OTHER VIOLATIONS	(10)	3	0	7
DISCLOSURE	(7)	4	3	0
FALSE STATEMENTS	(6)	2	3	1
TAXES	(5)	0	1	4
BRANCH OFFICE	(4)	3	1	0
SUBSTANCE ABUSE/DRUGS	(4)	0	2	2
NO MANAGING BROKER	(3)	1	2	0
FAIR HOUSING VIOLATION	(3)	0	2	1
STUDENT LOAN DEFAULTS	(3)	0	3	0
TRADEMARK VIOLATIONS	(2)	1	1	0
LICENSE TRANSFERRALS	(1)	1	0	0
ALTERCATION/PHYSICAL CONTACT	(1)	0	1	0
TOTALS	204	97	63	42

REAL ESTATE RECOVERY FUND

Many early license laws required as a condition to the issuance of a license that an applicant post a surety bond payable to any person aggrieved by the applicant's dishonest real estate activities. Most states have abandoned bonding in favor of state-operated recovery funds.

Illinois has a Real Estate Recovery Fund that, under certain conditions, may be used to provide compensation for the acts of a licensee. Sections 23 through 30 of the License Act and Rule 1450.200 govern the administration of the fund. The fund is financed solely through $10 deposits made by all new licensees as well as by licensees renewing expired licenses.

To recover any monies from the recovery fund the victim must have suffered a financial loss as a result of an:
> *act, representation, transaction or conduct of a duly licensed broker, salesperson or unlicensed employee, which is in violation of this act or the regulations promulgated pursuant thereto, or which constitutes embezzlement of money or property or results in money or property being unlawfully obtained from any person by false pretenses, artifice, trickery, or forgery or by reason of any fraud, misrepresentation, discrimination or deceit by or on the part of such licensee or the unlicensed employee of any such broker, and which results in a loss of actual cash money as opposed to losses in market value, may recover.*

Anyone having a potential claim against the fund should carefully read the provisions of the Act and Rules, because very strict procedural rules must be followed. The following is a list of some important conditions, exceptions, and limitations on recovery:
1. The maximum recovery by any one individual is $10,000 plus court costs and attorney's fees of up to 15 percent of the recovery.
2. The maximum sum of money the fund will pay out for the acts of any one licensee is $50,000 plus court costs and attorney's fees of up to 15 percent of the recovery.
3. The claimant must sue the licensee and be awarded damages.
4. The loss must be actual cash losses and not pain and suffering, emotional loss, or loss in market value.
5. The claimant must sue the licensee within two years of the act and, within seven days of filing suit, notify the Department that a claim may be made against the recovery fund.
6. After a judgment is entered in the favor of the claimant and against the licensee, the claimant must notify the Department within 30 days and make reasonable efforts to secure payment from the licensee.
7. A court order must be secured directing payment from the fund.

Recovery from the fund is not available:
1. if the broker or salesperson was unlicensed;
2. if the broker or salesperson was not acting in his or her licensed capacity, i.e., if the broker or salesperson was dealing with his or her own property;
3. for interest on the judgment; and
4. for claims relating to the Time-Share Act or the Land Sales Act of 1989.

In the event a claim is paid by the Recovery Fund, the involved licensee's license will be automatically revoked. Restoration of the license will not be considered until the Fund is reimbursed for its payment. Bankruptcy will not excuse the licensee from this requirement for the restoration of his or her license.

CASES TO JUDGE

1. The buyer of a parcel of real estate sued the seller and the broker for a return of his earnest money. Subsequently, the buyer recovered a $10,000 judgment against the broker and proceeded to enforce the judgment. Three thousand fifty dollars of the award was collected; however, the broker declared bankruptcy and was discharged from his debts, including the $6,950 balance of the judgment. The buyer then filed a notice and motion seeking recovery of the balance of the judgment from the Recovery Fund. Over the objections of the State of Illinois, the trial court entered judgment against the State of Illinois and the State appealed the award on the basis that the buyer had failed to notify the State at the time the lawsuit was filed. The buyer claimed that at the time the suit was filed, there was no reason to believe that the claim would not be paid by the broker once it was established that the buyer was entitled to a return of the deposit. If the State's position was correct, all lawsuits relating to one's entitlement to the earnest money would necessarily result in the State being notified of any and all such lawsuits.

   Should the appellate court have affirmed the trial court's decision, or should it be necessary to notify the State every time an earnest money dispute is litigated? [*Toufexis v. Hughes*, 137 Ill.App.3d 882, 485 N.E.2d 569, 92 Ill.Dec. 758 (1985)]

2. The licenses of two individual brokers and the corporate license of the brokers' employer were suspended for violating the Act and Rules relating to racial discrimination. The evidence clearly supported the discipline against the individuals; however, the only evidence elicited at the hearing regarding the employer's conduct was testimony indicating that the employer had forbidden its employees from engaging in racial discrimination and required each employee to sign an agreement to adhere to fair housing laws. The employer also displayed equal housing posters in each of its offices. The issue on appeal was whether an employer's license may, under the proven facts, be suspended.

   Should the appellate court have affirmed or reversed the Department's decision? [*McKey v. Poague, Inc.*, 63 Ill.App.3d 142, 379 N.E.2d 1198, 20 Ill.Dec. 130 (1978)]

3. A physician appealed an order of the Department revoking his medical license. One of the issues on appeal was whether a quorum was necessary at the time of the Departmental hearing. At the time of the hearing, only one of the seven members of the Medical Disciplinary Board was present during the actual hearing, although six members of the Board read the transcript of the hearing, were present for the deliberations, and were signatories to the findings of fact, conclusions of law, and recommendations to the Director.

   Does due process require that a quorum be present for a hearing? [*Bruns v. Department of Registration and Education of the State of Illinois*, 59 Ill.App.3d 872, 376 N.E.2d 82, 17 Ill.Dec. 189 (1978)]

4. Two salespersons and their sponsoring broker appealed the Department's order revoking their licenses for engaging in deceptive business practices. All three licensees appealed their discipline on the basis that the Department did not have the authority to act upon the recommendation of less than a majority of the Board's members. The Circuit Court of Cook County ruled that the Department did not have the authority and the Department appealed. At the time of the hearing, there were seven (now nine) voting members of the Disciplinary Board, and only three of which—along with the Commissioner—were present and signatories to the findings, conclusions, and recommendations to the Director.

   Should the Director be permitted to act without a majority of the Board members' recommendations? [*Olson v. Dept. of Registration and Education*, 63 Ill.App.3d 166, 379 N.E.2d 802, 19 Ill.Dec. 930 (1978)]

5. On February 9, 1975, a white tester went to the office of Twin City Realty pretending to be interested in a home in the $30,000 to $35,000 price range in the Berwyn area. He was given a listing book with 30 or 40 listings, of which 11 were in Cicero, which at the time was occupied exclusively by Caucasians. The tester talked with two salespeople in the same office as the defendant but did not talk with the defendant. Thirteen days later, a black tester went to the defendant's office and told the defendant he was interested in a home in the $45,000 price range near the intersection of Cermak and Cicero. The defendant indicated that there were no homes available that met the tester's requirements, and the defendant suggested a Maywood home priced at $25,000. On this evidence, the Board concluded that the defendant had committed a violation of the License Act by not making a home available on account of racial discrimination. On appeal, the defendant claimed that there was no testimony whatsoever (and there wasn't) that any of the homes were still available on February 22.

   Did the Department prove its case? Discuss "clear and convincing" in light of a hot market versus a cold market. [*Strickland v. Dept. of Registration and Education*, 60 Ill.App.3d 1, 376 N.E.2d 255, 17 Ill.Dec. 256 (1978)]

10-QUESTION DIAGNOSTIC QUIZ

1. A consent order:
   A. permits the Department to examine a licensee's escrow account.
   B. terminates a disciplinary case by agreement of both parties.
   C. provides for discovery of the opposing party's witnesses.
   D. must be agreed to by the Governor.

2. A notice of informal conference:
   A. requires the attendance of a licensee.
   B. may not, even in the licensee's absence, without the licensee's consent, result in discipline.
   C. must set forth a full statement of the facts and alleged infractions.
   D. must be hand-delivered by a Department investigator.

3. A formal complaint:
   A. is always made for commingling.
   B. is an itemized statement of the charges against the licensee.
   C. is signed by the Director of the Department.
   D. requires that the licensee attend an informal conference.

4. The most frequent source of complaints against a licensee is/are:
   A. lawyers.
   B. competitors.
   C. the general public.
   D. Department investigators.

5. Of the following types of infractions, the LEAST frequent would be:
   A. improper business practices.
   B. improper financial practices.
   C. deceptive/willful intent infractions.
   D. advertising violations.

6. If a person is found guilty of a drug-related misdemeanor and the Department is made aware of the conviction, the Department will probably:
   A. revoke the person's license, if the person is a licensee.
   B. refuse to issue a license, if the person is a license applicant.
   C. discipline the employer licensee, if the person is an unlicensed employee of a licensee.
   D. impose some form of discipline, if the person is a licensee.

7. The Director of the Department:
   A. may not order that a disciplinary case be reheard.
   B. may revoke a licensee's license without a hearing if the licensee's conduct is of serious and grave danger to the public.
   C. may discipline a licensee prior to the receipt of the disciplinary board's recommendation.
   D. may discipline or refuse to discipline a licensee regardless of the disciplinary board's contrary recommendations.

8. During an appeal of the disciplinary proceeding, the licensee's license status is:
   A. inoperative.
   B. valid.
   C. valid, but on probation.
   D. determined by the Department.

9. The Recovery Fund:
   A. will pay up to $50,000 to an individual claimant.
   B. will not honor a claim made more than two years after the occurrence.
   C. was established to aid licensees recovering from qualifying illnesses.
   D. was established as a petty cash fund to be depleted in an emergency by the Governor.

10. During a disciplinary hearing, the licensee is entitled to all of the following EXCEPT:
    A. the services of an attorney.
    B. cross-examination of witnesses.
    C. the services of a Department investigator.
    D. the issuance of subpoenas.

CHAPTER 7

FAIR HOUSING
(TESTING, TESTING, 1-2-3)

○ **CHAPTER OVERVIEW**
Our children and our children's children deserve to live in a nation free from undeserved bias and discrimination. Until such time as each of us voluntarily affords equal treatment to others, we must at least conform our conduct to the mandates of the law. Chapter 7 provides a foundation for our continuing knowledge and appreciation of both federal and state fair housing laws.

○ **LEARNING OBJECTIVES**
By the time you have finished studying this chapter, you should be able to:
1) Describe the important provisions of several specific instances of fair housing legislation: the Civil Rights Act of 1866, the Civil Rights Act of 1969, and the Civil Rights Act of 1991.
2) Understand the Americans with Disabilities Act with regard to employment, public accommodations, transportation, and telecommunications and how the act affects Americans with physical and mental disabilities.
3) Describe the important provisions in the Illinois Human Rights Act and how it differs from the federal acts with regard to the number of protected classes.
4) Discuss the specific sections of the Illinois Real Estate License Act that relate to fair housing practices and the conduct expected of Illinois real estate brokers and salespeople.
5) Identify which local municipalities currently have fair housing laws.
6) Explain the illegal discriminatory practices of blockbusting and racial steering and their impact on the daily activities of the real estate practitioner.
7) Explain the Illinois Real Estate Solicitation Act and how it applies to the daily practice of real estate professionals.
8) Itemize the ways in which real estate professionals might conduct themselves to protect themselves from allegations of illegal discriminatory practices.
9) Enumerate and explain the activities in which a real estate office might engage to protect itself from allegations of illegal discriminatory practice.
10) Discuss the legal and practical fair housing aspects a real estate office must consider when printing or publishing advertisements and promotions for real property sales or leases.

○ **5 CASES TO JUDGE**

○ **10-QUESTION DIAGNOSTIC QUIZ**

CHAPTER 7

FAIR HOUSING
(TESTING, TESTING, 1-2-3)

A REALTOR® should never be instrumental in introducing into a neighborhood . . . members of any race or nationality or any individual whose presence would be clearly detrimental to property values in that neighborhood.
—National Association of REALTORS®
Code of Ethics, 1950

The REALTOR® shall not be a party to any plan or agreement to discriminate against a person or persons on the basis of race, color, sex, handicap, familial status, or national origin.
—National Association of REALTORS®
Code of Ethics, 1992

One of the most sensitive, important, and critical issues facing the real estate industry is that of fair and open housing for all home seekers in the United States. A HUD study published in 1991 reported an incidence of discrimination against African-Americans and Hispanics nationally of 55 percent. In the Chicago area this figure was 45 percent.

Through the 1940s racial segregation was either mandated or maintained through the use of zoning requirements, restrictive covenants, and/or lending underwriting criteria. The notion of separate but equal remained a predominant legal principle through the mid-1950s. And while housing discrimination was made illegal by the late 1960s, old customs die hard; discriminatory policies and practices of government and real estate and real estate-related industries continued to foster segregation.

No one group of individuals is more important to accomplishing our national goal of fair housing than real estate professionals. Whether engaged in residential or commercial brokerage, leasing, property management, development, lending, or auctioning, your understanding and abiding by the federal, state, and local laws affecting fair housing must become a top priority.

The penalties for noncompliance are severe—they include criminal penalties, civil penalties, and possible loss of licensure.

FEDERAL CIVIL RIGHTS ACTS

CIVIL RIGHTS ACT OF 1866
The efforts of the federal government to provide equal opportunity and access to housing began with the passage of the Civil Rights Act of 1866. Based on the Thirteenth Amendment to the U.S. Constitution (1865), this law prohibits discrimination based on race. The act stated, "All citizens of the United States have the same right in every state and territory as is enjoyed by white citizens thereof to inherit, purchase, lease, sell, hold, and convey real and personal property." The constitutionality of the law was upheld by the U.S. Supreme Court in the case of *Jones v. Alfred H. Mayer Company*, 392, U.S. 409 (1968). The importance of this decision is that it supports the 1866 Act and prohibits "all racial discrimination, private and as well as public, in the sale or rental of

housing." As a result of *Jones v. Mayer*, all discrimination based on race is illegal. There are no exceptions. This applies even to homeowners selling their property themselves.

In 1917, zoning laws that required block-by-block segregation were declared unconstitutional by the Supreme Court. In 1948, another case made it illegal to enforce racially restrictive covenants. In 1962 an executive order was issued guaranteeing equal housing opportunity in FHA- and VA-financed housing. And with the passage of the Civil Rights Act of 1964, discrimination in all federally funded public housing was prohibited.

CIVIL RIGHTS ACT OF 1968

Title VIII of the Civil Rights Act of 1968, amended in 1974 and again in 1988, known as the Federal Fair Housing Law, created a national fair housing policy throughout the United States. While that act applies specifically to selling or leasing residential properties (including single-family and multifamily housing, condos, and co-ops), it also applies to vacant land to be used for the development of residential dwellings, and it specifically precludes lending discrimination and discrimination in appraisals.

This Civil Rights Act of 1968 and its amendments make it illegal to discriminate against a number of protected classes. These include race, color, religion, sex, handicap (including physical and mental handicap, as well as diseases like AIDS, cancer, and alcoholism), familial status (families with children under 18), or national origin. The act does contain some exemptions, including single-family housing (one to four units), where real estate agents and advertising are not used, and permits housing exclusively for "older persons," as defined by law. The law—regarding nondiscrimination against families with children—also allows for the application of reasonable occupancy standards to protect against overcrowding.

Harassment of anyone exercising his or her fair housing rights is prohibited under the fair housing law. This provision includes the protection of real estate providers who are serving "protected class" persons. To accommodate disabled persons, landlords must allow physical modifications to enable accessibility, at the tenant's expense, and guide or support animals. As of March 1991, and thereafter, all new multifamily housing must be accessible to the disabled.

An aggrieved person may file a complaint within one year of the occurrence of the discriminatory action with the Secretary of the Department of Housing and Urban Development or within two years bring a civil action in federal court. Furthermore, the Department of Justice has authority to bring "Pattern or Practice" cases and to seek civil penalties of $50,000 for a first offense and $100,000 for subsequent offenses. In civil cases courts can award unlimited compensatory and punitive damages and attorney's fees and legal costs. The courts have typically interpreted fair housing law broadly, to further the goals of the law.

AMERICANS WITH DISABILITIES ACT

The Americans with Disabilities Act was enacted by Congress in July 1990. Its purpose is to bar discrimination against the 43 million Americans (1.5 million in Illinois) with physical and mental disabilities, including visual and hearing impairments. The ADA will affect real estate professionals in two ways—as employers and as business owners and practitioners. Under the law an employer may not discriminate against a qualified individual with a disability during the work life of the individual, including the benefits, terms, conditions, and privileges of employment. Additionally, employers will have to make "reasonable accommodations" to hire disabled people who can perform the "essential functions" of a job. For employers with 25 or more employees, these employment provisions will take effect July 26, 1992. For employers with 15 to 24 employees, the effective date is July 26, 1994. It is unclear how ADA will affect employers with less than 15 employees. However, all employers must adhere to the provisions of the Illinois fair housing acts as they apply to employment practices.

Title III of the act deals with the accessibility of public accommodations. This part of the act will have an impact on developers, building owners, property mangers, tenants, and those who represent them as agents. Virtually every type of commercial property—office, retail, and industrial—must remove existing architectural and communication barriers to the disabled, "where removal is readily achievable" and "easily accomplishable and able to be carried out without much difficulty or expense." Existing structures have until January 26, 1992, to comply. Any new building constructed after January 26, 1993, must be barrier-free (i.e., accessible).

Legal responsibility for making alterations under ADA will depend on who has the legal authority to make alterations, typically determined by the lease agreement between landlord and tenant. In most cases the landlord will be responsible for common areas. It should be noted that the new law does contain a provision that allows for up to $15,000 in tax credits to businesses to cover the costs of making establishments accessible. Accessibility applies to services as well as facilities.

The U.S. Department of Justice, Office of Americans with Disabilities has the authority to prosecute ADA violators—up to $50,000 for the first occurrence and $100,000 for each offense thereafter. Under the act individuals can sue for a court order requiring compliance, not for monetary compensation. In matters of employment, however, those with complaints may seek compensatory damages as well as compliance. The Justice Department is to use a "rule of reasonableness" in bringing suits.

The Illinois Chamber of Commerce and the Building Owners Management Association are preparing information and offering seminars on the act. Questions may also be addressed to the City of Chicago, Office of People with Disabilities. This office was established in 1991 as an information source for the ADA law and two other laws—The Illinois Environmental Barriers Act, which relates to accessibility, and the Chicago Human Rights Ordinance, which prohibits discrimination against the disabled.

For more information on ADA, call the U.S. Justice Department at 202-514-0301. Employment questions can be directed to the Equal Employment Opportunity Commission at 1801 L Street, NW, Washington, DC 20507 or call 800-669-EEOC.

FAIR LENDING
Discrimination in the financing of residential real estate is illegal under the federal fair housing law, including transactions to the secondary mortgage market and the servicing of loans. The law prohibits discrimination against individuals and communities (redlining), based on their protected class status.

FEDERAL EQUAL CREDIT OPPORTUNITY ACT
The Equal Credit Opportunity Act prohibits lenders and others who grant or arrange credit from discriminating on the basis of race, religion, national origin, sex, marital status, age (provided applicants are of legal age), or because the applicant receives public assistance. Real estate agents—considered to be issuers of credit—are covered by this act. In addition, lenders and other creditors must inform all rejected applicants, in writing within 30 days, of the principal reason for the credit denial. Credit applicants must be considered only by criteria based on income, net worth, job stability, and satisfactory credit rating. For more information, contact the Federal Trade Commission office in Chicago at 312-353-4023.

HOME MORTGAGE DISCLOSURE ACT OF 1975
Historically, many lenders and insurers employed a practice of redlining, refusing to make mortgage loans or issue insurance policies in areas or communities because of their racial composition. HMDA, which was passed in 1975, requires all banks and savings and loan associations with assets of more than $10 million to make annual reports by census tract on the number and dollar amount of mortgage loans the institution has made. The law

enables the detection of lending patterns that may constitute redlining. In 1989, Congress amended HMDA to require disclosure of data on loan applications and denials by race, sex, and income of applicants, and mortgage companies for the first time will have to report.

COMMUNITY REINVESTMENT ACT

The Community Reinvestment Act passed in 1977 requires that banks and savings and loan associations help to meet the credit needs of their local communities. It also provides community organizations the right to challenge bank acquisitions, closings, openings, and mergers, if it can be shown that the community reinvestment record of the institution is poor.

ILLINOIS CIVIL RIGHTS STATUTES

ILLINOIS HUMAN RIGHTS ACT

The Illinois Human Rights Act prohibits unlawful discrimination by an owner, broker, agent, salesperson, or any other person engaging in a real estate transaction. Unlawful discrimination means discrimination against a person because of his or her race, color, religion, national origin, ancestry, age, sex, marital status, physical or mental handicap, familial status (children under the age of 18), or unfavorable discharge from military service. As with the federal law, there are owner exceptions to this act, but none for brokers and salespersons. Complaints are filed with the Illinois Department of Human Rights and adjudicated by the Human Rights Commission.

ILLINOIS REAL ESTATE LICENSE ACT

The Illinois Real Estate License Act of 1983, as amended in 1989, contains important sections relating to prohibitions against discriminatory acts and the conduct of the real estate licensee:

> Section 18(h)22. *Influencing or attempting to influence, by words or acts a prospective seller, purchaser, occupant, landlord, or tenant of real estate, in connection with viewing, buying or leasing of real estate, so as to promote the continuance or maintenance of racially and religiously segregated housing, or so as to retard, obstruct, or discourage racially integrated housing on or in any street, block, neighborhood, or community.*

> Section 18(h)23. *Engaging in any act which constitutes a violation of Section 3-102, 3-103, 3-104, 3-105, of the Illinois Human Rights Act, whether or not a complaint has been filed with or adjudicated by the Illinois Human Rights Commission.*

> Section 18.3. *When there has been an adjudication in a civil or criminal proceeding that a licensee has illegally discriminated while engaged in any activity for which a license is required under this Act, the Department, upon the recommendation of the Board as to the extent of the suspension or revocation, shall suspend or revoke the license of the licensee in a timely manner, unless adjudication is in the appeal process. When there has been an order in an administrative proceeding that a licensee has illegally discriminated while engaged in any activity for which a license is required under the Act, the Department, upon recommendation of the Board as to the nature and extent of the discipline, shall take one or more of the disciplinary actions provided for in Section 18 in a timely manner, unless the administrative order is in the appeal process.*

The Illinois License Act is enforced by the Illinois Department of Professional Regulation, and penalties for violations can include a refusal to issue or renew a license, a reprimand, a revocation or suspension of a license, or a fine of up to $10,000.

The Rules for Administration of the License Act contain additional responsibilities and sanctions for the real estate licensee. Section 1450.100 prohibits licensees from entering into listing agreements or being involved with the disposition of any property where discriminatory practices are present. The prohibition is against discrimination based on race, color, creed, religion, national origin, sex, handicap, or familial status. Any judgment or conviction by a court of competent jurisdiction of violation of discrimination in housing—whether on a federal, state, or local level—will be deemed a demonstration of "unworthiness" or "incompetency" and may subject the licensee to license revocation, a refusal to issue or renew a license, or license suspension.

SOLICITATION REGULATION
The Discrimination in Sale of Real Estate Act (Anti-Solicitation Act, Illinois Revised Statutes, Chapter 38, Section 70-51) passed in 1967 makes it illegal to "panic peddle," to solicit for listings on the grounds of loss of value due to the presence of persons of a particular race, color, religion, national origin, ancestry, creed, handicap, or sex, or to distribute materials or make phone calls designed to induce homeowners to sell for these same reasons.

This law provides that homeowners may serve written notice on real estate firms that they do not want to be solicited. Oftentimes, local community organizations will gather affidavits from area residents stating that they specifically do not want to be solicited by real estate licensees. The community group then prepares a "Non-Solicitation List" or "Anti-Solicitation Book" and presents them to area real estate firms. Once the list of names has been served by certified or registered letter or in person to a real estate office, the office is prohibited from contacting homeowners on the list.

The Cook County State's Attorney's Office has indicated that no solicitation means no contact of any kind. Contact includes a free market analysis (or an offer of one); an offer to appraise, list, or sell property; even handing out business cards to anyone whose name appears on the list with which an office has been served during the "life span" or time period of the list—typically five years.

Check with your local State's Attorney's Office to make certain that if "antisolicitation neighborhoods" are present in your business or marketing area that you are aware of them. Any person violating this act shall be guilty of a misdemeanor on first offense, a felony on the second, and shall be reported by the clerk of the court to the Department of Professional Regulation, which shall revoke the license of the salesperson or broker.

HATE CRIMES
The State of Illinois has a hate crime law (Illinois Revised Statutes, Chapter 12, Section 12-7.1) that imposes penalties on those who commit certain crimes against people or their property because of race, color, creed, religion, ancestry, sexual orientation, physical or mental disability, or national origin. This law is enforced by the State's Attorney and/or by private civil action in circuit court.

LOCAL MUNICIPALITIES
A growing number of municipalities have enacted fair housing ordinances, some of which are "substantially equivalent" to the federal law. Many local laws cover protected classes different from the federal law. For instance, Chicago's Human Rights Ordinance extends coverage to sexual orientation, age, marital status, military discharge status, and lawful source of income.

PROFESSIONAL ORGANIZATIONS
Article 10 of the National Association of REALTORS® Code of Ethics requires that "The REALTOR® shall not be a party to any plan or agreement to discriminate against a person or persons on the basis of race, color, religion, sex, handicap, familial status, or national origin." REALTORS® and REALTOR® Associates who deny equal professional services to anyone are violating Article 10 and risk expulsion or fine from the local Association/Board of REALTORS®. Other real estate associations have similar prohibitions.

TYPES OF DISCRIMINATORY PRACTICES

The Federal Fair Housing Law prohibits the following acts when based on race, color, religion, sex, familial status, handicap, or national origin:
- To refuse to rent or sell
- To refuse to negotiate for a sale or rental
- To deny or otherwise make unavailable a dwelling
- To discriminate in the terms, conditions, or privileges of a sale or rental of a dwelling
- To indicate any preference, limitation, or discrimination in advertising
- To falsely represent that a dwelling is not available for inspection, sale, or rental
- To coerce, intimidate, threaten, or interfere in anyone's protected rights
- To engage in blockbusting (panic peddling)
- To deny membership or access to a multiple listing service
- To refuse to permit reasonable rental unit modifications by handicapped tenants

What follows are a list of areas of service where inconsistent, discriminatory treatment may occur:
- Arranging appointments and making call-backs
- Greeting customers who enter or call the office (acts of courtesy and hospitality)
- Information exchanged at an initial meeting to discuss needs
- Qualifying and financing information requested and given
- Personal information requested
- Availability, location, and quality of properties presented for consideration or shown
- Keeping appointments
- Follow-up
- Method of determining properties to show

In each of these areas, if customers are consistently treated differently on racial or other protected-class bases, illegal discrimination may be construed.

INTENT v. EFFECT

Under the Federal Fair Housing Law, a complainant does not necessarily have to prove that a real estate provider intended to discriminate in order to prevail. Actions that have the effect of unequal treatment can be found to be unlawful under the Federal Fair Housing Law.

Most cases rely on intentional discrimination claims—for instance, a real estate agent fails to provide information about particular listings because of a buyer's race. However, courts have consistently ruled against practices that have discriminatory effects, without requiring an intent to discriminate. And while the Federal Fair Housing Law itself does not provide direct guidance on this matter, a principal sponsor of the act stated, "It thus seems only fair, and is constitutional, that Congress should now pass a fair housing act to undo the effects of these past State and Federal unconstitutionally discriminatory actions." Furthermore, Congress, when it originally passed the Fair Housing Act in 1968, and again in 1988 when it amended the law, rejected efforts that would have required proof of an intent to discriminate.

Real estate professionals should review all marketing efforts—advertising, qualifying procedures, showing practices, and other office procedures—in light of this situation, to avoid practices that may have discriminatory effects.

BROKER/OWNER LIABILITY
Federal courts have consistently ruled that real estate salespeople are agents of the firm's owner or broker; therefore broker/owners are responsible—and hence, liable—for the acts of their agents under the fair housing law. Courts have specifically ruled that salespeople are not independent contractors—with respect to fair housing compliance—but rather, agents, and therefore broker/owners and their firms and/or corporations are liable.

In a 1991 decision, the broker of a firm in the City of Chicago was found liable in Federal District Court for the acts of his agents—who were engaging in racial steering—and was ordered to pay $91,000 in damages and $160,000 in attorney's fees and costs.

RACIAL STEERING
Steering is a common form of discrimination. Steering is defined as limiting or attempting to limit the choices of home seekers by words or conduct in connection with viewing, buying, renting, or occupying a dwelling so as to perpetuate segregation or to undermine or discourage integration.

An important characteristic of steering is that it is choice-limiting, focusing a customer's attention on some housing choices while excluding others, usually based on the racial characteristics of the customer or a neighborhood (though it may focus on some other protected-class issue, such as religion). The other important characteristic of unlawful steering is that it promotes segregation. For example, if, when working with a minority buyer, you were to select homes to show only in minority or integrated areas, this could be viewed as steering. Similarly, if, when showing a minority buyer a home in an integrated area, you were to say, "I'm sure you'll feel very comfortable in this neighborhood," such a statement may be construed as a steering. Likewise, if you were working with a white buyer and showed only white areas and made disparaging or discouraging remarks about minority or integrated areas, this would represent unlawful steering.

Federal court decisions have ruled that the Fair Housing Law prohibits the practice of steering. Furthermore, many local ordinances and the state license law specifically outlaw steering.

PANIC PEDDLING
Panic peddling is the illegal act whereby a person—for profit—induces a homeowner to enter into a real estate transaction by representing that a change in the neighborhood is occurring or may occur with respect to the race, sex, color, religion, national origin, handicap, or familial status of residents, which will result in lowered property values, a decline in the quality of the neighborhood or schools, or an increase in crime. This prohibited practice may occur in person, by phone, by mail, or through the distribution of literature. At least one court decision and current federal regulations indicate that uninvited real estate solicitations in areas of racial change, that convey to reasonable people the idea that homeowners should sell because of this change, may be found to represent panic peddling. Based on this practice, and legislation and judicial rulings, some communities or neighborhoods are protected by antisolicitation laws.

"FOR SALE" SIGNS
A number of municipalities have enacted ordinances regulating the use of "for sale" signs. In most cases, courts have struck down outright bans of signs as unconstitutional. However, the courts have held that where the presence of "for sale" signs may contribute to "sudden and wrenching change," they may be banned. Furthermore, courts have upheld the right of municipalities to regulate the time, manner, and placement of signs. Under some municipal ordinances, signs are to be removed within ten days after a contract has been signed on a particular piece of property.

RACIAL COMPOSITION QUESTIONS
Customer questions about racial composition of neighborhoods are dangerous for real estate salespeople. Comments by a salesperson about the racial makeup of an area can have a discriminatory—and therefore,

illegal—effect. If a buyer is discouraged from considering an area because of the salesperson providing this information, a charge of discriminatory behavior may be made.

Often this kind of information has been used to influence white buyers to avoid minority or racially diverse areas and to encourage black and other minority buyers to avoid areas that are essentially white. Therefore, for legal reasons, and because up-to-date information about racial composition is subject to change, a real estate salesperson should not volunteer information on the racial composition of areas and will do best to sell his or her product—houses—and the positive attributes of various communities.

Persistent questions about racial makeup should be referred to the city or village hall, to the planning departments of local government, or to a local fair housing group.

DISCRIMINATORY ADVERTISING

Under Section 804(c) of the Fair Housing Law, it is unlawful "to make, print or publish any notice, statement or advertisement, with respect to the sale or rental of a dwelling that indicates any preference, limitation or discrimination because of race, color, religion, sex, handicap, familial status or national origin, or an intention to make any such preference, limitation or discrimination."

Federal fair housing advertising regulations outline what to avoid when advertising, including:
   a) words or phrases that signal exclusiveness based on protected-class factors, e.g., adults only, singles, Irish enclave, located in St. Joseph's parish;
   b) selective use of advertising media that may have discriminatory effects, e.g., use of local papers that circulate only in white areas, when other media are available; or selection of particular zoned editions of newspapers;
   c) strategic placement of ads or promotional material that may have discriminatory effects, e.g., brochure distribution or billboard placement that limits access to individuals in a racially definable geographic area;
   d) selective use of the Equal Housing Opportunity slogan or logo or promotion of lending instruments (usually FHA) that signal availability to particular racial groups, e.g., using the logo or inviting FHA only when advertising in minority or integrated areas but not predominantly white areas;
   e) selective use of human models, e.g., consistently depicting models of only one race. Typically this has taken the form of using only white models in real estate ads. When models are used in ads, they should reasonably depict majority and minority groups in the metropolitan population.

Federal guidelines state, "All advertising of residential real estate...should contain an equal housing opportunity logo, statement or slogan..." Requirements apply to all forms of advertising, including print ads, electronic media, and other promotional material. Newspapers, by law, should place at the heading of classified real estate sections a "Publisher's Notice" indicating that all housing advertised therein is covered by the Federal Fair Housing Law. State law also bans discriminatory advertising.

Federal regulations do recognize the legitimacy of affirmative marketing, advertising designed to reach groups not likely to seek housing in a particular market without special outreach. An example of this would be advertising a listing located in an essentially white area in an African-American-oriented publication.

Increasing attention is being given to problems of advertising content and placement. Several complaints have been brought in various areas around the country, including the Chicago area. These complaints have often resulted in substantial judgments or settlements, ranging from $15,000 to $450,000. Real estate advertisers, ad agencies, and media outlets have all been responsible and are potentially liable in these cases.

Refer to Chapter 3, Office and Advertising Regulations, for more information on advertising and how it relates to fair housing issues.

HARASSMENT

Incidents of harassment of real estate licensees, buyers, sellers, renters, or others—when related to race, color, religion, sex, national origin, disability, or the presence of children—are illegal under federal law. Criminal and civil action can result from such harassment. In a number of cases courts have held that in the context of housing discrimination, sexual harassment is an activity that is proscribed by law. In one case the court ruled that sexual harassment can occur by either creating a pervasively "offensive environment" or by "conditioning a tenancy, or continued tenancy, on sexual consideration." HUD and the Justice Department have a responsibility to investigate cases of harassment prohibited under federal laws.

The State of Illinois has a hate crime law that imposes severe penalties on those who commit criminal assault, trespass, or damage to real or personal property because of race, color, creed, religion, ancestry, sexual orientation, physical or mental disability, or national origin. Furthermore, parents and guardians of minors are liable for damages under the terms of this law. Criminal provisions of the law are enforced by the State's Attorneys; civil provisions are enforced through private civil action.

In one such case in Illinois, a jury awarded $1.8 million to victims of anti-Semitism. In another case, $475,000 was awarded to an African-American victim of a racial attack. In 1991, an Illinois Appeals Court upheld the sentencing of a man to 18 years for a racially motivated firebombing.

Local law-enforcement groups and the local State's Attorney's office should be notified of incidents of racial or ethnic harassment.

PROTECTING YOURSELF FROM DISCRIMINATION CHARGES

EDUCATION

The license requirement mandating continuing education indicates recognition by the State of Illinois and real estate trade organizations that there is a need for regular reviews and updates for real estate professionals in key areas, including fair housing, to best assure professionalism and consumer protection. Several local real estate groups have required new and existing member training in the area of fair housing for several years. All brokers and agents should attend equal housing opportunity training classes on a periodic basis, to insure that all customers and clients are served on an equal basis. Effective training will utilize a variety of teaching formats, including lectures, audiovisuals, role plays, resource handouts, and quizzes.

Fair housing law is constantly evolving through court decisions, and brokers and agents will do well to review and keep up to date on recent developments. High-quality fair housing educational materials are available from various real estate trade groups—including the National Association of REALTORS®—and fair housing organizations. Fair housing should be a regular topic at sales meetings.

Broker/owners should keep a record of all sales agents who have attended educational programs that include fair housing as a topic, including the program sponsor and the date of attendance. Employee agreements or independent contractor contracts should specify that the said employee/independent contractor "Acknowledges and will abide by the policy of the firm to comply strictly with the letter and spirit of the fair housing laws to provide equal professional service to all persons regardless of their race, color, religion, sex, handicap, familial status, national origin, or other protected-class status, as provided under federal, state, and local fair and open housing laws and understands that any violation shall constitute cause for immediate termination of the agreement." This provision should be a separate affidavit, signed, notarized, and retained with the company records.

OFFICE POLICY AND PROCEDURES

To establish the right atmosphere for agents, for the general public, and for "protected-class" home seekers, every real estate office should establish a clear and unequivocal policy statement of support for fair housing and equal opportunity. Such a statement should make clear the company's goal to provide equal professional service, to help each potential buyer find the most suitable housing for his or her needs on a nondiscriminatory, affirmative basis, and to observe the letter and spirit of fair housing laws.

Companies would also do well to establish a comprehensive set of equal housing opportunity office procedures that will minimize the likelihood of fair housing violations.

If, within an office, each agent uses his or her individual manner of interviewing, qualifying, and following up with customers, and selecting and showing homes, there is a risk of perceived unequal service. Development and implementation of standards are particularly important to broker/owners who are, after all, responsible and liable for the acts of their agents. As part of this set of procedures, broker/owners should make clear to agents that these procedures are not recommendations, but rather requirements.

A procedures manual should outline company practices for handling situations where fair housing violations tend to occur. This includes the following areas: taking listings, qualifying buyers, providing equal professional service, selecting and showing properties, avoiding steering and panic peddling, responsible and legal use of solicitation and "for sale" signs, handling racial composition questions, appropriate advertising practices, and the reporting of harassment of customers, clients, or agents. The procedures manual should also outline the responsibilities of various staff and the corrective action that will be taken should discrimination by an agent be discovered.

What additional steps can be taken by an office to protect itself from discrimination?
1. If you are a REALTOR®, be a signatory to the Voluntary Affirmative Marketing Agreement (VAMA). This agreement is a joint agreement between the NAR and HUD defining responsibilities for solving minority and protected-class-person housing problems. For you to be a signatory member your local Board must be a participating party. In Illinois 94 percent of all Boards have signed the VAMA. Other real estate trade groups have negotiated similar VAMAs with HUD.
2. Use the fair housing logo (illustrated to the right) or slogan on letterhead, signs, business cards, advertising, listing agreements, sales contracts, leases, etc. The VAMA asks each signatory to include the official Equal Housing Opportunity logotype in all display and classified advertising that is six column inches or larger. Federal fair housing regulations state that all display ads should use a fair housing logo or statement.
3. Conspicuously display the current fair housing poster in your office or conference room. Contact your real estate board or HUD to get one. A copy of the poster appears in Figure 7-1.

FIG 7-1
U.S. Department of Housing and Urban Development

EQUAL HOUSING OPPORTUNITY

We Do Business in Accordance With the Federal Fair Housing Law
(The Fair Housing Amendments Act of 1988)

It is Illegal to Discriminate Against Any Person Because of Race, Color, Religion, Sex, Handicap, Familial Status, or National Origin

- In the sale or rental of housing or residential lots
- In advertising the sale or rental of housing
- In the financing of housing
- In the provision of real estate brokerage services
- In the appraisal of housing
- Blockbusting is also illegal

Anyone who feels he or she has been discriminated against may file a complaint of housing discrimination with the:

U.S. Department of Housing and Urban Development
Assistant Secretary for Fair Housing and Equal Opportunity
Washington, D.C. 20410

Previous editions are obsolete
form HUD-928.1 (3-89)

Several real estate associations in the Chicago area have now adopted comprehensive fair housing procedures manuals for use by member firms. Such manuals, and the steps they provide for—when put to use—serve as affirmative efforts by broker/owners to minimize the likelihood of fair housing violations and as a mitigating factor if legal action should occur.

EQUAL PROFESSIONAL SERVICE
The following is a summary of how real estate professionals should conduct themselves in order to avoid discriminatory practices:
1. Standardize procedures for qualifying customers, determining housing needs, and showing, renting, and/or selling housing.
2. Train all staff in fair housing laws and practices.
3. Maintain good records, utilizing an equal service report form.
4. Use an Equal Housing Opportunity logo or statement on all ads and promotional material.

5. Advise all sellers and buyers of fair housing laws and the responsibilities of brokers, buyers, and sellers. (Use listing agreements with provisions outlining the requirement that marketing practices conform with fair housing laws.)
6. Avoid marketing practices—when advertising, selecting, and showing homes—that have the effect of promoting racial segregation or retarding integration. Make available a range of properties to maximize choice and to avoid even unintentional steering.
7. Advertise consistent with federal rules and regulations.
8. Avoid all discussions of racial and ethnic composition that might have the effect of discouraging a prospective buyer from considering a particular area.
9. Refuse to facilitate real estate transactions where discriminatory conditions or terms are present, or where access is denied on the basis of race, color, religion, sex, national origin, familial status, or handicap.
10. Avoid statements or actions that indicate that the presence of persons of any particular race or color is in any way detrimental.

There are some rules of conduct that can help you in your everyday practice. Following are a few suggestions to help protect you from engaging in discriminatory practices:

Provide Housing Options and Let the Buyer Set the Limits. Never assume where a buyer might want to live. While offering to make available all listings within your market area, remember to let the purchaser make the choice of an area or neighborhood. You will not get into trouble under fair housing laws by expanding housing options.

Assure Equal Service. Variations in types of service you offer to sellers and buyers may have discriminatory implications, or may appear to be based on "protected class" considerations. Service all buyers and sellers the same. Interview and financially prequalify all buyers using the same form and asking essentially the same questions.

Watch Your Language. Always remember that intentions really do not matter in a court of law hearing a fair housing complaint. Keep the conversation focused on the features of particular properties. A buyer may ask, "What is the neighborhood really like?" or "What kind of people live on this block?" Avoid entering into conversations that may quickly become discussions of racial or ethnic composition of various areas. Refer questions about racial composition, when they persist, to sources such as city planning or community relations departments or to area fair housing groups. A licensee's words or actions are violations if they limit integration or promote segregation, regardless of his or her "intentions."

AFFIRMATIVE MARKETING

In real estate sales, discrimination often takes the form of racial steering, directing buyers to or away from areas on the basis of race, where the effect is to limit housing choice and to promote segregation. Influencing white buyers to buy in all-white areas, or influencing minority buyers to buy in racially integrated areas are common forms of illegal racial steering. This practice was described in detail in the section on racial steering.

To avoid even unintentional racial steering, agents are advised to always seek to maximize the housing choices of customers. Make sure that prospects are offered and shown listings in a variety of areas in their price range. As a practical matter, you can avoid steering by always making sure minority customers are told about relevant listings in predominantly white areas and white customers are told about relevant listings in areas that are racially diverse or predominantly minority. This is consistent with the Federal Fair Housing Law and various court decisions.

Given the history of segregation, oftentimes buyers are unfamiliar with certain neighborhoods or communities within your market area, or they may assume that because of their race they will not be comfortable or welcome in a particular area. Remind buyers that all areas are open and that they should consider all their options before purchasing the home that best suits their lifestyle, fits their housing needs, and represents a good investment.

RECORD KEEPING

The best protection an individual or firm can have against allegations of discrimination are good records and proper documentation. What follows are some recommendations concerning record keeping:

1. Equal Service Report Form—Whether your office uses the one developed by a trade group, such as the NAR Prospect Equal Service Report (illustrated in Figures 7-2 and 7-3), or one devised by your office, use a form to be part of the transaction file that identifies prospect information (including minority or nonminority status), lists properties shown, and summarizes the criteria used in housing selection and the geographical location preference of the buyer. Inclusion of financial qualification information may also be made part of the form. Whatever form is used, it should be standardized throughout the office. This form insures equal professional service and constitutes a written record to respond, if necessary, to discrimination accusations.
2. Make notes of all appointments and any or all canceled or no-show appointments or showings, as well as homes where entry was denied, including the reasons for any denial.
3. Record correspondence with lenders, clients, customers, attorneys, etc.
4. Note why a customer rules out a property or certain areas of a community. Note any unusual comments or discussions.
5. Retain all offers and counteroffers and listing agreements, even if a contract does not materialize.
6. Follow up consistently and conscientiously with all prospects.
7. Keep records of open-house visitations.
8. Retain your Day-Timers and appointment books.
9. Retain records of all phone calls to or from prospects, including the times calls were made. This should include calls where there was no answer.
10. Use carbon message notebook pads and keep the spiral notebooks as a record of time and date of telephone calls.
11. Record follow-ups to open-house prospects.
12. Keep a record of property MLS computer printouts that you show or discuss with prospects.
13. Use some kind of client/customer follow-up form or Consumer Service Survey. This form should be sent routinely to prospects within 30 days after they have become inactive. This form can serve as a means to detect possible discrimination or perceptions of biased treatment, helping to ward off legal complaints and to correct or adjust discriminatory behavior. It is also a good method of determining the level and quality of service a firm is giving to all of its customers/clients.

STAFF DIVERSITY

Demographic trends through the 1990s will change the racial, ethnic, and gender makeup of the American work force. The U.S. Department of Labor projects that women, minorities, and immigrants will account for 80 percent of the labor force growth between now and 2000.

The growing diversity of our population and work force represents an opportunity—and perhaps a necessity—for real estate professionals to expand markets to remain successful. Real estate firms are strongly encouraged to diversify the racial and ethnic composition of their staffs to account for future trends.

Furthermore, the addition of minority agents and brokers throughout the marketplace can enhance consumer sensitivity to diversity and fair housing, reducing the likelihood of fair housing violations or allegations. Recognizing these trends, the National Association of REALTORS® recently produced a *Minority Recruiting Guide*. In this helpful guide, the NAR identified several reasons for minority outreach in real estate employment, including: positive reputation in the community; more creativity and innovation; and ability to capitalize on untapped and ethnic markets.

FIG 7-2

NATIONAL ASSOCIATION OF REALTORS®
Prospect Equal Service Report

Date: Sales Associate: Office:

PROSPECT INFORMATION

Name:			Name:		
Address:			Address:		
Home phone:	work phone:		Home phone:	work phone:	
Owns now	Rents now	Must sell to purchase?	Owns now?	Rents now?	Must sell to purchase?
Race: *			Race: *		

* For Affirmative Marketing purposes. Information on prospect race is sought to assist in the monitoring of the firm's commitment to equal professional service. Article 10 of the NATIONAL ASSOCIATION OF REALTORS® Code of Ethics states: **REALTORS® shall not deny equal professional services to any person for reasons of race, color, religion, sex, familial status, handicap, or national origin. REALTORS® shall not be parties to any plan or agreement to discriminate against a person or persons on the basis of race, color, religion, sex, familial status, handicap, or national origin.**

Prospect came to us as a result of	Walk in	Past Customer	Sign	Other
Referral	Ad (source)	Phone solicitation	Mail Solicitation	

PROSPECT NEEDS AND WANTS

Prospect wishes to	purchase	rent	possession date	
Prospect's price range preference		Purchase price range:	rental: (use rental form)	
Prospect requested locations:				
Type of home:		# Bedrooms:	# Baths:	Dining room / Family room
fireplace	garage	other features:		

Does prospect desire information regarding Housing for Older Persons?
if so, is any member of prospect's household over 55?

SERVICE PROVIDED

Was prospect asked questions regarding his/her finances? if yes, indicate information obtained	Income	Down payment	Other (specify)	
Was prospect offered information on financing options? indicate any rate information provided	Conventional/ fixed rate	Adjustable rate	FHA/VA	other (specify)

Did you financially qualify the prospect? ___Yes ___No ___not applicable
if yes, attach worksheets
if yes, Qualified Purchase Price:

Did you refer the prospect elsewhere for financial qualification? ___Yes ___No ___not applicable
if yes, to whom:
if yes, Qualified Purchase Price:

Contact dates and comments?

PROPERTY SHOWN - please complete the other side of this form and attach additional information needed

FIG 7-3

PROPERTY SHOWN

PART 1 - Did the prospect initially request information on or ask to view any specific property(s)? (Requests made prior to assistance being provided to the prospect.)

If yes, list address for each request, include street address, unit # and community. Use additional sheets if necessary.	Price	Was property shown?	If shown, Buyer's comments indicating preferences. If not, why not.	Was any written information provided?

PART 2 - Were additional properties or areas offered to the prospect for general consideration? list areas or properties	Was a computer generated or other list of properties provided? Describe and attach

If none, explain.

PART 3 - List properties shown or offered for consideration, including those selected by prospect. Include street address, unit #, and community. Use additional sheets if necessary. In the first column indicate who selected the property - P - prospect, A - real estate agent	Price	Was property shown?	If shown, Buyer's comments indicating preferences. If not, why not.	Was written information on property provided?

DISPOSITION

Please list materials (such as the REALTOR® Home Guide) provided:

Please attach additional information needed

TESTERS

Documentation of nondiscriminatory conduct becomes particularly important because of the increasing use of fair housing testers as a method for discovering discrimination. Testers are matched teams (individuals or couples), usually white and black or white and Hispanic, who pose as home seekers, separately visiting sales or rental offices to check for discriminatory behavior. Since they request the same type of housing and are matched in all other relevant home-seeker characteristics (such as income, down payment, area of interest, etc.), the object of the test is to determine whether their race—or some other protected-class factor being checked—influences the information or services offered by sales or leasing agents. Items such as their experiences when setting appointments; the number, price, and location of listings they were offered and/or shown; the type, number, and timing of the qualifying questions they were asked; and the type of service and follow-up provided are compared to determine whether any substantial difference in treatment has occurred.

Testing has been used by both public and private civil rights enforcement agencies and has been recognized by the Supreme Court of the United States as a legitimate method of gathering evidence of alleged or possible housing violations.

Testers are usually individual volunteers who have an interest in fair housing. They come from all walks of life and are usually paid a stipend for conducting tests. Their fee includes a written report in which they respond to objective questions and prepare a narrative. Another party—usually an audit supervisor—then compares the reports for possible differences in the information that was provided or differences in the treatment that occurred.

Testers may even sign sales contracts or leases as part of their investigations. When there has been an actual complaint by a bona fide home seeker, the complainant will purchase or rent the unit under the terms of the contract. Two further points:

1. Testers do not have to admit they are testers, even when asked. The fact that a tester may make misrepresentations concerning his or her purpose or status does not render his or her report inadmissible in court as the basis for a fair housing complaint.
2. Testers' pretense does not disqualify their testimony as a plaintiff for damages if they were misinformed about the availability of a property for reasons of race, color, religion, sex, or national origin, handicap, or familial status. Testers have legal standing to bring complaints if given unequal service or false information about housing availability.

Don't waste your time trying to discover testers. Giving all individuals fair, impartial, and objective treatment is the best policy for you and your office to follow.

ENFORCEMENT METHODS AND PROCEDURES

Let's take a look at the various ways federal, state, and local fair housing laws are enforced.

The federal law can be enforced: (1) by private civil suit—whereby a person engages an attorney to represent him or her in federal court; (2) through HUD; or (3) by the Justice Department, if a case represents a "pattern or practice" (a "general public importance" case). If a case is filed with HUD, and a "reasonable cause" determination is made, the case will proceed before an Administrative Law Judge (ALJ), unless either party elects to have the case heard in federal district court. The statute of limitations is two years for a private civil action, one year to file with HUD, and 18 months for an action by the Justice Department.

At the state level, likewise, if a case is filed with the Illinois Department of Human Rights and there is a "reasonable cause" finding made, the case will proceed before the Illinois Human Rights Commission (an adjudicative body), unless either party elects to have the case heard in state circuit court.

Local ordinances typically provide for an administrative process to receive, investigate, and seek resolution of complaints, and an adjudicative process to hear cases and issue findings of fact and orders for relief, if it is determined that discrimination occurred.

The Department of Professional Regulation is responsible for licensing and regulating real estate professionals, including investigating and resolving fair housing complaints. Possible outcomes in cases where violations are determined include: refusal to issue or renew a license; reprimand; license suspension or revocation; and fines up to $10,000.

Testing—the practice of using individuals to pose as home seekers—is a common investigative method. Other methods include interviews of relevant parties and reviews of relevant records and documents. Most enforcement processes provide an opportunity for the complainant to seek a "temporary restraining order" through the courts, to prohibit the defendant/respondent from renting or selling the unit in question—other than to the complainant—until the case can be heard. Conciliations and settlements are common means whereby parties resolve complaints. In such cases the parties mutually agree to a set of provisions for resolving the complaint. The overseeing court or administrative agency must then approve these terms.

The standard for proving a fair housing case turns on "a preponderance of evidence." Cases typically turn on circumstantial rather than direct evidence. And remember, in fair housing cases the party bringing the case does not necessarily have to show an intent to discriminate, but rather, only that the effect of a practice falls more heavily on one "protected class" than another. The burden of proof to establish a case of discrimination falls on the person bringing a case.

Where monetary damages are involved, a defendant can request a jury trial. All processes—judicial and administrative—must provide due process to all parties, including the right of appeal.

FINES, PENALTIES, AND THE RESULTS OF COMPLAINT PROCESSES

In HUD Administrative Law Judge (ALJ) cases, actual damages to the aggrieved party, injunctive or other equitable relief, and civil penalties can be ordered: $10,000 for a first offense, $25,000 for a second offense within five years, and $50,000 for more than two offenses within seven years. Attorney's fees and costs are also to be paid by the prevailing party.

In cases involving direct court action—private civil suits in federal court—actual (compensatory) damages, punitive damages, and equitable and affirmative relief can be awarded. There are no limits on punitive damages, which can be awarded in fair housing cases. A defendant's ability to pay and his or her economic condition are relevant to the size of awards.

Actual damages—including damages for "humiliation, embarrassment, and emotional distress"—have gone as high as $65,000 and more. Punitive damages—imposed to punish a defendant and to deter him or her or others from similar future incidents—grew considerably during the 1980s. Punitive awards of $10,000 to $50,000 are common; they have gone as high as $500,000.

Furthermore, courts can award attorney's fees and costs. Typically these fees and costs can amount to as much as or more than damages. In a recent Chicago case, the court awarded plaintiffs' attorneys $160,000 in fees and costs. And remember, broker/owners are usually liable for the acts of their agents.

The federal law does provide that the prevailing party is to pay legal fees and costs. Prevailing defendants will receive an award if it can be shown that the plaintiff's action was frivolous.

Monetary awards from state and local administrative agencies in fair housing cases tend to be smaller than court-ordered awards, ranging from the thousands to the tens of thousands of dollars. The size of these awards has grown in recent years, especially since enactment of the federal fair housing amendments in 1988. Administrative processes tend to provide for the payment of fines or civil penalties to a unit of government, rather than payment of punitive damages to the aggrieved party.

In addition to monetary awards, administrative and judicial bodies usually can order equitable or affirmative relief, taking the following forms:
1. access and occupancy of the dwelling;
2. access and provision of services connected with the dwelling;
3. prohibition against any future discrimination;
4. fair housing training for all staff;
5. affirmative advertising and marketing;
6. display of the fair housing logo or slogan in all advertising and promotional materials;
7. posting of the HUD or other fair housing posters;
8. affirmative employment practices;
9. reporting of progress to a monitoring agency.

Chapter 7 Fair Housing 133

WHAT TO DO IF FACED WITH DISCRIMINATION
In the event you, as a real estate professional, encounter an act or acts of discrimination while working with a minority buyer or tenant, taking the following actions could help you deal with the situation:
1. Tell the offending party that the action(s) is illegal and will not be tolerated.
2. Continue to make every reasonable effort to close the deal or pursue negotiations and/or showing of the property.
3. Distance yourself from the act of discrimination by making sure the buyer or tenant knows that you are not a party to the act.
4. Explain to the buyer(s) or tenant(s) that their rights may have been violated (and yours, too) and make clear your intention to cooperate with them in the securing of their rights.
5. Tell the buyers or tenant where they can go to file a complaint: local municipality (if there is a local fair housing ordinance), Illinois Department of Human Rights, U.S. Department of Housing and Urban Development, or the Leadership Council for Metropolitan Open Communities.
6. If there has been an act of harassment, the victim(s) should contact law-enforcement authorities as soon as possible.
7. Advise the prospective buyers or tenants that you will be a witness for them in any proceeding by providing affidavits and/or testimony as to what you know about the incident.
8. Immediately write down everything you have seen and heard relating to the incident of discrimination, including times and dates—and encourage the buyers or tenants to also record events related to the transaction.
9. Keep your broker or employer fully informed on all the details.
10. Continue to work with the buyers or tenants in the way in which you feel best serves *their* needs, including the right to the housing of their choice.
11. Report all incidents to your local real estate board or to other professional real estate associations of which you are a member so that they can take appropriate action.

RESOURCE GROUPS
The following groups are concerned and involved with fair housing education and/or handling complaints of "protected-class" discrimination or harassment:

United States Department of Housing
   and Urban Development
Region V, Fair Housing and Equal Opportunity
77 W. Jackson, 21st Floor
Chicago, IL 60604
312-353-7776

Illinois Department of Human Rights
100 W. Randolph, 10th Floor
Chicago, IL 60601
312-814-6200

Chicago Commission on Human Rights
500 N. Peshtigo Ct., 6th Floor
Chicago, IL 60611
312-744-2852

Illinois Association of REALTORS®
3180 Adloff Lane, Suite 400
Springfield, IL 62703
217-529-2600

National Association of REALTORS®
430 N. Michigan
Chicago, IL 60611
312-329-8200

Chicago Police Department
Human Relations Section
1121 S. State, Room 105
Chicago, IL 60605
312-747-5488

Leadership Council for Metropolitan
  Open Communities
401 S. State, Suite 860
Chicago, IL 60605
312-341-5678

Access Living
310 S. Peoria
Chicago, IL 60607
312-226-5900

Council for Disability Rights
343 S. Dearborn
Chicago, IL 60604
312-922-1093

Lawyers' Committee for Better Housing
1263 W. Loyola
Chicago, IL 60626
312-274-1111

Eighteenth Street Development Corporation
1839 S. Carpenter
Chicago, IL 60608
312-733-7315

United States Attorney's Office
219 S. Dearborn, 15th Floor
Chicago, IL 60604
312-353-5307

Cook County State's Attorney's Office
Community Unit
500 Richard J. Daley Center
Chicago, IL 60602
312-443-5598

United States Department of Justice
Community Relations Service
175 W. Jackson Blvd., Room 1113
Chicago, IL 60604
312-353-4391

NAACP
South Side Branch
7 E. 63rd
Chicago, IL 60637
312-363-8600

Chicago Urban League
4510 S. Michigan
Chicago, IL 60653
312-285-5800

ADDITIONAL READING MATERIAL

What Everyone Should Know about Equal Opportunity in Housing; National Association of REALTORS®.

Fair Housing—Issues, Approaches and a Model Ordinance; Northeastern Illinois Planning Commission, 1991.

Fair Housing Compliance Manual—for Multifamily Owners and Managers; National Association of Home Builders, 1990.

Housing Discrimination Study; HUD and the Urban Institute, 1991.

Credit by Color; Chicago Area Fair Housing Alliance, Calvin Bradford and William Peterman, 1991.

No Children Allowed: A report on the obstacles faced by renters with children in the Chicago rental housing market; Lawyers' Committee for Better Housing, Metropolitan Tenants Organization, Leadership Council for Metropolitan Open Communities.

Housing Discrimination—Law and Litigation; Robert Schwemm, 1990.

Community Residence Location Planning Act Compliance Guidebook; Dan Lauber, 1990.

Minority Recruitment Guide; National Association of REALTORS®, 1990.

CASES TO JUDGE

1. Defendants A.R.K. Partnership, owners and managers of certain rental apartments, appealed from an order of the Circuit Court of DuPage County denying their motion to dissolve a temporary restraining order entered against them. The restraining order prohibited the defendants from renting two of their apartments to any persons except the plaintiffs during the pendency of the plaintiffs' separate civil rights action against the defendants before the Illinois Human Rights Commission. That action was based on the plaintiffs' claim that the defendants' policy of refusing to rent apartments to unmarried couples of the opposite sex violates the prohibition against discrimination based on sex or marital status found in the Illinois Human Rights Act.

    The defendants argued that the trial court should have dissolved the temporary restraining order against them in that the act does not prohibit discrimination against unmarried cohabiting couples in real estate transactions.

    How should the appellate court rule? [*Mister v. A.R.K. Partnership*, 197 Ill.App.3d 105, 553 N.E.2d 1152, 143 Ill.Dec. 166 (1990)]

2. A United States citizen, born in Iraq and a member of the Muslim faith, was an associate professor at a private college in Pennsylvania. The college denied his request for tenure, and the professor filed a complaint against the college in the United States District Court. The complaint alleged that the college and its tenure committee violated the Civil Rights Act of 1866, which provides that all persons within the jurisdiction of the United States shall have the same right to make and enforce contracts as is enjoyed by white citizens. The District Court ruled that an action under the act could be maintained, since the complaint alleged denial of tenure because the professor was of the Arabian race. Another judge of the District Court, construing the complaint as asserting discrimination on the basis of only national origin and religion, granted the defendant's motion to dismiss.

    Although under current racial classifications, Arabs are Caucasians, should the professor have been permitted to maintain his claim? [*Saint Francis College v. Al-Khazraji*, 481 US 604, 95 L Ed2d 582, 107 S Ct 2022 (1987)]

3. The exterior of a synagogue was painted with anti-Semitic slogans, phrases, and symbols. The congregation and some of its members brought suit in the United States District Court alleging that the vandals of the synagogue had violated the Civil Rights Act of 1866, which guarantees all citizens of the United States the same right as is enjoyed by "white citizens" to inherit, purchase, lease, sell, hold, and convey real and personal property. The United States Court of Appeals held that discrimination against Jews was not racial discrimination, and that the 1866 Act was not intended to apply to situations in which a plaintiff was not a member of a racially distinct group but was merely perceived to be so by defendants.

    Was the appellate court correct in ruling that Jews were not a protected "race" under the Civil Rights Act of 1866? [*Shaare Tefila Congregation v. Cobb*, 481 US 615, 95 L Ed2d 594, 107 S Ct 2019 (1987)]

4. A lawsuit was filed in the United States District Court by three individuals and a nonprofit corporation against the owners of an apartment complex and one of its employees alleging that the defendants engaged in "racial steering" violative of the Fair Housing Act of 1968. It sought declaratory, injunctive, and monetary relief. One of the individuals was a black "renter" who attempted to rent an apartment from the owners. When he inquired about the availability of an apartment at the complex, he was falsely told that no apartments were available. The other two individuals were "testers" who, without an intent to rent an apartment, posed as renters for the purpose of collecting evidence of unlawful discriminatory practices. The testers were employed by the fair housing organization to determine whether the owners of the subject apartment building practiced racial discrimination. One of the testers was black, and on four separate occasions this tester made inquiries as to the availability of apartments and was told that no apartments were available. The other tester was white and was told that there were vacancies. The three individual plaintiffs (the renter and the two testers) claimed that they had been injured by the discriminatory acts of the defendant. The renter claimed that he had been denied the right to rent real property. All three plaintiffs alleged that the owner's practices deprived them of the important social, professional, business, economic, political, and aesthetic benefits of interracial associations that arise from living in integrated communities free from discriminatory housing practices. The black tester alleged that the misinformation given by the owner concerning the availability of apartments in the complex had caused specific injury. The organization asserted that the steering practices had frustrated its counseling and referral services, with a consequent drain on resources. On the defendant's motion, the District Court dismissed the claims of the two testers and the organization, holding that they lacked standing to sue.

    Which of the four plaintiffs should have been entitled to sue for the alleged discrimination? [*Havens Realty Corporation v. Coleman*, 455 US 363, 71 L Ed2d 214, 102 S Ct 1114 (1982)]

136   Chapter 7   Fair Housing

5. The defendant, Columbus Country Club (a branch of the Knights of Columbus, a Catholic men's organization), is a nonprofit membership organization that maintains a complex of 46 summer homes, a chapel, and other recreational facilities. Only an "annual member" of the club was permitted to own one of the 46 summer homes. An applicant for annual membership was required to submit a written recommendation from his or her parish priest stating that the applicant was a practicing Roman Catholic in good standing. The archbishop granted the club special permission to celebrate mass on the grounds, and he provided a priest for that purpose. The club, however, had no formal affiliation with the Catholic church. A member's daughter was refused membership on the basis of her sex, while her husband was denied membership on the basis of his religion. Both filed suit, claiming a violation of the Federal Fair Housing Act. The defendant claims that it is exempt under both the religious exemption and the private club exemption.

Under the circumstances, does either exemption apply? [*United States v. Columbus Country Club*, 915 F2d 877 (1990)]

10-QUESTION DIAGNOSTIC QUIZ

1. All of the following are Federal Fair Housing laws EXCEPT:
   A. Civil Rights Act of 1866.
   B. Civil Rights Act of 1968.
   C. Civil Rights Act of 1991.
   D. Illinois Human Rights Act.

2. Which of the following is NOT a protected class under the Federal Fair Housing Act of 1968 as amended in 1989?
   A. Race
   B. Age
   C. Sex
   D. Handicap

3. The purpose of the Americans with Disabilities Act is to:
   A. bar discrimination against Americans with physical and mental disabilities.
   B. provide financial assistance in housing to the disabled.
   C. provide educational assistance to the handicapped.
   D. provide job placement assistance to the mentally and physically impaired.]

4. In addition to being affected by the federal and state fair housing laws, brokers and salespeople are also affected by the:
   A. Illinois Real Estate License Act.
   B. codes of ethics of various professional real estate associations, societies, and institutes.
   C. local and municipal fair housing laws.
   D. All of the above

5. The practice of inducing one person to enter into a real estate transaction from which the first person may benefit by creating alarm that the neighborhood is changing racially is called:
   A. blockbusting.
   B. churning.
   C. mixing.
   D. neighborhood breaking.

6. The practice of channeling home seekers to particular areas based on race, color, religion, etc., is called racial:
   A. targeting.
   B. steering.
   C. balancing.
   D. conformity.

7. What Illinois statute makes it potentially illegal to solicit or "canvas" an area in regard to the listing, lease, purchase, or sale of residential real estate?
   A. Discrimination in Sale of Real Estate Act
   B. Illinois Human Rights Act
   C. Illinois Deceptive Practices Act
   D. Illinois Statute of Frauds

8. The Illinois Human Rights Act includes "classes"—in addition to those in the federal acts—for fair housing protection. These additional protected classes include:
   A. age.
   B. marital status.
   C. unfavorable military discharge.
   D. All of the above

9. Which of the following activities might a real estate *practitioner* engage in to protect himself or herself from allegations of illegal discriminatory practices?
    A. Advise all sellers, buyers, landlords, and tenants of fair housing laws and the responsibilities of licensees under these laws
    B. Provide equal service to all prospects
    C. Avoid any conduct that could be construed as blockbusting or racial steering
    D. All of the above

10. Which of the following activities might a real estate *office* engage in to protect itself from allegations of discriminatory practices?
    A. Use the fair housing logo on office stationery, business cards, advertising, and contracts
    B. Engage competent individuals to conduct fair housing educational sessions
    C. Include clauses that specially prohibit violation of local, state, and federal fair housing laws in all employment and independent contractor agreements
    D. All of the above

STUDENT NOTES

CHAPTER 8

AGENCY
(WHO'S ON FIRST?)

○ **CHAPTER OVERVIEW**

Purchasing or selling a property has never been easy; however, the real estate licensee is now facing new challenges as more and more suits are being filed against Illinois registrants relating to disclosure of agency relationships and property defects. This chapter explains in detail what agency disclosure means, who gives it, when, and how. Because the doctrine of *caveat emptor* (buyer beware) is no longer a valid defense for the used-home seller, sellers and their agents must now bear a greater responsibility for property disclosure. This chapter addresses that issue as well.

○ **LEARNING OBJECTIVES**

By the time you have finished studying this chapter, you should be able to:
1) Explain the duties an agent owes to a principal.
2) Differentiate between those who are called your CLIENTS and those who are your CUSTOMERS.
3) Understand the relationships between agents, subagents, and principals in the multiple listing service method of marketing property.
4) Explain the differences between the fiduciary relationship created in a SELLER AGENCY relationship and those in a BUYER AGENCY relationship.
5) Explain the potential problems arising from dual agency.
6) Understand when, to whom, and how agency disclosure must be given.
7) Discuss property disclosure and how it affects the parties in today's real estate transaction.
8) Determine the merits and the risks of employing unlicensed sales assistants.

○ **5 CASES TO JUDGE**

○ **10-QUESTION DIAGNOSTIC QUIZ**

CHAPTER 8

AGENCY
(WHO'S ON FIRST?)

Bud Abbott and Lou Costello, two of America's most beloved comics, had a classic comedy routine called "Who's on First?" You will remember that the routine began with Lou Costello asking the names of the players of the various positions on Bud Abbott's baseball team.

The result was a hilarious exchange of Bud's seemingly illogical and frustrating answers to Lou's simple question, "Who's on first [base]?"

The simple question, "Who's your client?" is also invoking some unexpected and confusing answers in today's real estate industry. Perhaps you'll want to study this very important chapter to get the answer to that and other important questions. Or, maybe you'll feel like saying, "I don't give a darn!" In which case Bud Abbott would probably reply, "Oh! He's our shortstop!"

Licensed real estate brokers and salespeople have a unique legal relationship with buyers, sellers, landlords, and tenants. This relationship falls within the domain of the body of law called "Law of Agency." This is a law of relationships that governs how one party, called a PRINCIPAL, and another party, called an AGENT, must act toward each other and to third parties, who are generally members of the public at large. Typically a SELLER (principal/client) hires a BROKER (agent) to find a ready, willing, and able BUYER (customer). However, anyone—buyer, landlord, or tenant—could hire a real estate broker to represent them as their agent.

FIDUCIARY RELATIONSHIP

This relationship between a principal and an agent is called a fiduciary relationship. This means that the agent owes the principal the duties of CARE, OBEDIENCE, ACCOUNTABILITY, LOYALTY, DISCLOSURE, and SERVICE. These duties can be further explained as:

Care. It is the duty of an agent to exercise reasonable care and skill while transacting the business which the principal has entrusted to him or her. An agent can be liable to the principal for any loss resulting from negligence or carelessness.

Example: If a broker took a listing at a price significantly less than the market value because the broker was unfamiliar with the area and did not take steps to educate himself or herself regarding similar property values, then the broker could be accused of negligence and be held liable to the seller for damages.

Obedience. The agent is required to follow the principal's instructions and to always act in good faith and within the scope of authority the principal has given him or her.

Example: The seller requested that his or her property continue to be marketed after the seller had accepted a contingency sales contract, even though the normal procedure in the area is to stop marketing a property when the sales contract was signed. An agent could be held liable for any subsequent loss in property value as a result of disobeying the seller and discontinuing the marketing efforts. The agent is not, however, required to obey unlawful or unethical instructions, like refusing to market the property to minorities. An agent cannot make decisions for the principal without the principal's consent or without having had previous authority to make certain decisions on the client's behalf.

Accounting. The agent is required to account for all monies or valuables entrusted to him or her.

Example: The agent may not use his or her principal's funds without permission and cannot commingle those funds with the agent's personal funds. Illinois license law requires the broker to "remit any documents or monies coming into the licensee's possession" and to "furnish copies upon request of all documents relating to a real estate transaction to all parties executing them."

Loyalty. The agent must place his or her principal's interests above those of others or those of the agent. An agent cannot disclose confidential information without the principal's consent.

Examples:
- A listing broker purposely does not disclose the true value of a property to a seller, and then purchases the property himself and resells it for a substantial profit; or
- An agent discloses to the buyer the fact the principal (seller) will accept a price lower than the listing price; or
- An agent discloses the financial condition of the buyer to the seller when the buyer was his or her principal.

Disclosure. The agent must keep the principal informed of any information and all facts which the agent has obtained that could affect the transaction or the principal's business decisions. In certain instances the agent may be liable for damages for failure to disclose.

Example: A broker fails to disclose to the seller information about the broker's interest in a corporation that is purchasing the seller's property or information about the broker's status as an Illinois real estate licensee.

Service. The agent must work diligently, professionally, and competently to accomplish the objectives of the principal. The fiduciary relationship is a relationship of trust and confidence, or, to put it in another perspective, the agent becomes the "alter ego" of the principal. Just as the agent would never purposely hurt himself or herself, he or she can never intentionally injure the principal. When a real estate broker accepts employment from a principal, both parties are obligated to conduct themselves within the confines of this fiduciary relationship. Typically, the principal is referred to as a CLIENT. If the seller were your client, then the buyer would be the CUSTOMER. Alternatively, if the buyer were the principal, then he or she would be your CLIENT. Do not refer to CUSTOMERS as CLIENTS.

Agent's Responsibilities to Third Parties. Even though the agent's primary responsibility is to the principal (CLIENT), the agent also has duties to the third parties with whom he or she deals. These duties include:
1. Reasonable care and skill in the performance of the agent's duties
2. Honest and fair dealing
3. Disclosure of all facts *known* to the agent that materially affect the value or the desirability of the property and that are *not* known to the buyer
4. Engaging third parties in a fair transaction
5. Trustworthiness

SUMMARY OF FIDUCIARY RESPONSIBILITIES

Seller's Agent or Subagent must:
- reveal ALL offers to purchase
- identify all potential buyers
- reveal any facts affecting the value of the property
- reveal facts about the buyer relating to ability to purchase/close
- reveal broker's or agent's interest as purchaser
- reveal buyer's intention to subdivide or resell
- reveal all information that would affect the seller's receiving the highest price or best terms

Buyer's Agent:
- willingness of seller to accept lower price
- seller's urgency
- relationship of licensee to seller
- facts affecting value
- time on the market, other offers or counteroffers
- licensee's interest as seller/owner
- other information that might affect buyer getting the lowest price and best terms

PENALTIES FOR BREACH OF AGENCY

When an agency has been created, the agent is authorized to act on behalf of the principal and is usually compensated for his or her efforts. Violating the agency relationship may cause the broker a loss of commission, the rescission of the contract, possible loss of licensure, and actual or punitive damages.

BROKER AS AGENT v. SALESPERSON AS AGENT

Before we explore the kinds, complexities, and legal requirements affecting those who are called "agents," let's clear up one of the more confusing questions in the brokerage field. That question is, "If they call salespeople 'agents,' doesn't that mean that salespeople are agents of the seller?" The answer is NO! Salespeople (employees or independent contractors) are hired by brokers to accomplish sales, leasing, and/or marketing activities on behalf of the broker. As a result, there exists a principal and agent relationship, but this one is between the *broker and salesperson*. The salesperson (agent) has a fiduciary relationship with the principal (*his or her employing broker*).

If the salesperson must represent the best interests of the broker, and if the broker is an agent for either the seller or buyer, then the salesperson also has a fiduciary relationship to the seller or buyer, vis-à-vis his or her relationship as agent to the broker. When salespeople are referred to as agents, it means agents of their employing broker, NOT agents of the seller, or, in the case of buyer brokerage, the buyer.

AGENCY RELATIONSHIPS IN REAL ESTATE

The question of who the broker licensee represents is becoming cloudier as the various kinds of agency relations are becoming more complex. Listed below are the more typical kinds of agency relationships that you will find in the practice of real estate today.

Subagents—licensees who act for and on behalf of agents (brokers). For instance, a salesperson is an agent to his or her employing broker and becomes a subagent of *each* of the sellers who have listed their property with their employing brokerage firm. In many Multiple Listing Services, cooperating brokers *also* become subagents of the listing broker. Sub-subagents are agents of subagents (salespeople of cooperating brokers). Check your local MLS rules (if you belong to one) regarding the subagency implications of cooperating offices and their sales staffs.

Listing Agent—the licensed broker (an individual, partnership, or corporation) who is employed by and represents only the seller/client in a real estate transaction, usually through some form of written employment or listing contact. In Illinois, all exclusive agency and exclusive right-to-sell listings should be in writing; however, Illinois does recognize oral "open" listings. (See Figure 8-1.)

Selling Agent—the cooperating broker who works with the buyer/customer, usually as a result of a multiple listing service arrangement between the brokerage offices, but who is a subagent of the listing broker and therefore has an obligation to represent the seller/client.

Buyer Agent—brokers who are employed by and represent only the buyer/client in a real estate transaction, regardless of whether the commission is paid by the buyer directly or by the seller through a commission split. In actuality, many buyer agents (brokers) also represent sellers as the occasion demands. They cannot, however, without proper written disclosure, represent *both* parties in the same transaction. That is called dual agency. (See Figure 8-2.)

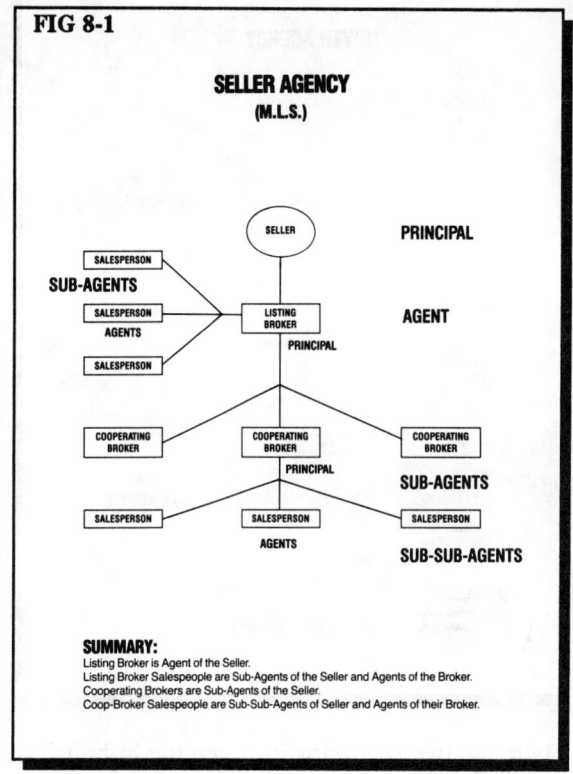

FIG 8-1

SELLER AGENCY
(M.L.S.)

SUMMARY:
Listing Broker is Agent of the Seller.
Listing Broker Salespeople are Sub-Agents of the Seller and Agents of the Broker.
Cooperating Brokers are Sub-Agents of the Seller.
Coop-Broker Salespeople are Sub-Sub-Agents of Seller and Agents of their Broker.

Dual Agents—licensees who attempt to represent BOTH buyer and seller in the same real estate transaction. Dual agency is not recommended in Illinois. The reason is based on the fact that it is almost impossible to serve "two masters" who have such different perspectives, interests, and goals. The seller, for instance, wants the highest price for the property; the buyer wants the lowest price. In Illinois, you may be a dual agent *only if both* of the parties to the transaction are informed of the dual agency and give you written permission. Dual agency may be categorized as:
- disclosed (legal, but dangerous);
- undisclosed (illegal and dangerous); and
- accidental or unintentional (illegal and dangerous).

In a recent National Association of REALTORS® *Homebuyer's Survey*, buyers and sellers were asked questions regarding the purchase and sale of homes. Seventy-one percent of the buyers who worked with cooperating agents (subagents to the seller) thought that the cooperating broker represented *them* as buyers. As shocking, 74 percent of the sellers interviewed *also* thought that the cooperating broker was the "buyer's broker." How would the sellers and buyers who deal with your office respond to the question, "Who represents you in a real estate transaction?" (See Figure 8-3.)

DISCLOSURE OF DUAL AGENCY
The "In-House" Transaction. An in-house transaction is one in which the listing office is also the selling office. This kind of transaction is the primary objective of most real estate firms, and well it should be. The reason, of course, is that the listing office keeps 100 percent of the commission because it did "both ends" of the transaction; therefore, no split is due a cooperating broker.

144   Chapter 8   Agency

FIG 8-2

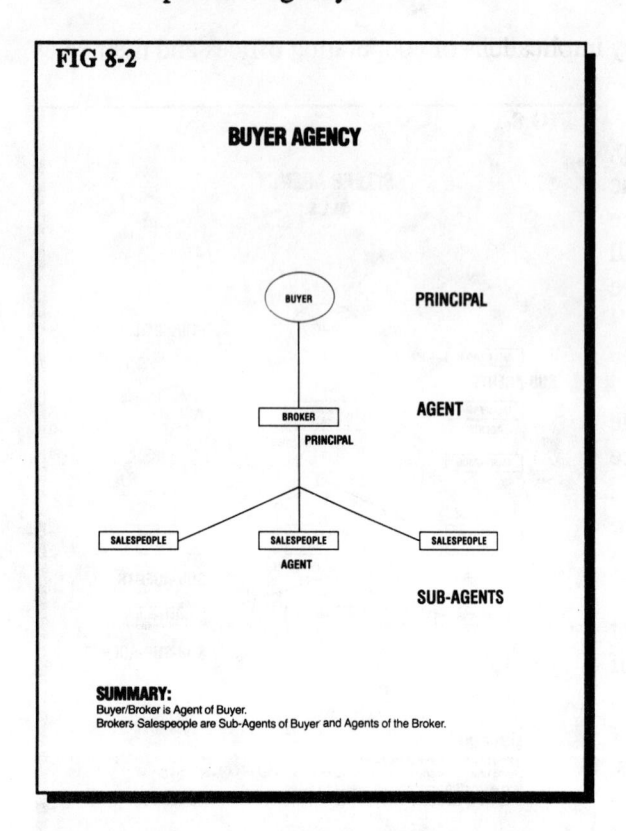

BUYER AGENCY

```
                    BUYER ───── PRINCIPAL
                      │
                    BROKER ──── AGENT
                   PRINCIPAL
         ┌──────────┼──────────┐
     SALESPEOPLE SALESPEOPLE SALESPEOPLE
                   AGENT
                                   SUB-AGENTS
```

SUMMARY:
Buyer/Broker is Agent of Buyer.
Brokers Salespeople are Sub-Agents of Buyer and Agents of the Broker.

FIG 8-3

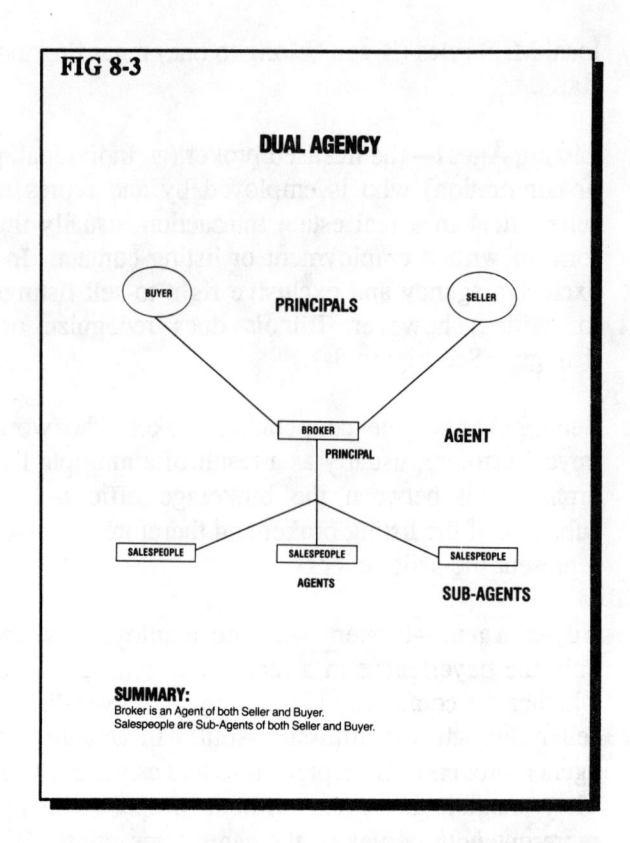

DUAL AGENCY

```
         BUYER ──── PRINCIPALS ──── SELLER
              \                    /
                    BROKER ──── AGENT
                   PRINCIPAL
         ┌──────────┼──────────┐
     SALESPEOPLE SALESPEOPLE SALESPEOPLE
                   AGENTS
                                   SUB-AGENTS
```

SUMMARY:
Broker is an Agent of both Seller and Buyer.
Salespeople are Sub-Agents of both Seller and Buyer.

There are two scenarios in which the in-house sale may invite a dual agency relationship; each presents important considerations for the licensee:

1. A buyer/customer working with the listing agent (or another sales agent in the listing office) purchases a company listing. As long as the agent makes proper disclosure to the buyer/customers that the agent is a seller's agent and behaves in the best interests of the seller, there is no problem here. Unfortunately, many sales agents establish close personal relationships with the buyers, giving them confidential seller information or acting as their advocate. In doing so, the sales agents create an implied and undisclosed dual agency, which is illegal for the selling salesperson and consequently illegal to his or her employing listing broker. Even if the undisclosed agency is unintentional, it is still illegal and has severe repercussions, which include, but are not limited to, rescission, forfeiture of commission, and actual or punitive damages.
2. The second scenario would present itself when a salesperson's buyer/client (represented under a buyer-broker agreement) purchases a property that has been listed by the salesperson's firm. This again is a dual agency for both the sales agent and broker, and may be a problem unless written disclosure is made to both the seller and the buyer.

In Illinois, an employing broker is responsible for all the acts of his or her salespeople who are acting within the scope of employment, and whose actions are done with the broker's knowledge and consent.

PROVISION FOR DUAL AGENCY

If a dual agency is allowed by company policy for "in-house" sales, a dual agency provision included in both the seller's listing contract or the buyer's agency agreement might be a good idea. The provision can be contained within these contracts or by separate provision. A provision simply notifies the client that a dual agency is a possibility and that should a buyer/client become interested in a firm's listing, then both parties will be required to sign a Dual Agency Consent Agreement. Dual agency may well be the answer for the sale of some real property transactions. If dual agency is attempted, all parties should be represented by attorneys and full disclosure and waiver must be in writing. The best policy, however, is probably to avoid dual agency. A dual agency disclosure addendum fulfilling the requirements of the foregoing discussion is set forth in Figure 8-4.

DUAL AGENCY AGREEMENT

A dual agency is not created, for instance, by the mere fact that a seller's agent (or subagent) is working with a buyer. In fact, if the proper disclosures are made to the buyer/customer *and* the agent acts in accordance with his or her fiduciary responsibility to the seller/client, then the agent should be protected.

In a Notice of Dual Agency, the following should be included:
1. A statement as to who will pay the commission or fee to the broker(s). Generally, the seller is amiable to any compensation package that will get his or her home sold without paying a higher brokerage fee than that provided for under a traditional MLS listing agreement. Therefore, the buyer's broker might be compensated by the listing broker from the seller's commission, just as they are currently compensated.

   Don't forget that it is the BUYER who brought the "funds" to the closing table, and it is from these "proceeds" that the commission is paid. The buyer could, of course, agree to compensate his or her agent under a separate agreement and terms, possibly even a flat fee for the buyer's broker's service. Another alternative might be to have the seller pay the buyer's broker at closing from the proceeds of the sale. For instance, assume a $200,000 sale at a 6 percent commission. Seller pays $6,000 to the listing broker and owes $6,000 to the buyer's broker at closing. The seller pays the same commission he or she would in a traditional sale, and the buyer can work the brokerage fee into the amount of his or her mortgage.

   The *source* of compensation to a broker, property manager, leasing agent, etc. does not determine who is the principal and agent. It is the *conduct* of the parties and the *agreements* between them (oral or written) that establish the fiduciary obligations. Remember, too, that commission rates, commission splits (between salespeople, brokers, property managers, leasing agents, etc.), and compensation agreements are always negotiable between the parties.

2. The *role* of the licensee in regard to the transaction.

3. An *acknowledgement* by the parties that the parties understand the role of the licensee and have no objection to the licensee acting in that capacity.

The "role" of the licensee should address the responsibility of the agent in regard to material information, and the duty of absolute fidelity to a client, as well as the fiduciary obligation agents owe their principals. As a dual agent, you are serving two masters. Therefore, you must make material disclosures, exhibit absolute fidelity, and owe the fiduciary responsibilities described earlier to BOTH parties to the transaction.

It would be wise when acting as a dual agent to provide in the dual agency agreement that the agent will act as a *facilitator* in the transaction rather than as an advocate for either party.

Although written disclosure and acknowledgment must be made, THE LICENSEE MUST THEN CONDUCT HIS OR HER ACTIVITIES CONSISTENT WITH TERMS OF THE DUAL AGENCY AGREEMENT.

FIG 8-4

NCR (No Carbon Required)

DUAL AGENCY DISCLOSURE ADDENDUM

In reference to the ☐ PURCHASE AGREEMENT, ☐ OTHER: _____
covering the real property commonly known as _____
dated _____, between _____
hereinafter referred to as BUYER and _____
hereinafter referred to as SELLER, the undersigned parties hereby agree as follows:

The Broker in this transaction, _____,
together with his associated salespersons, hereinafter collectively referred to as Broker, is hereby authorized by Seller and Buyer to represent both of them in this transaction as a dual agent.

Seller and Buyer understand that this dual agency creates conflicts of interest, and that Broker cannot represent the interests of one party to the exclusion or detriment of the interests of the other party.

The parties understand, and Broker acknowledges, that Broker will act as facilitator or intermediary and will endeavor to be impartial between Seller and Buyer. Except as expressly provided below, Broker in his capacity as a dual agent, shall disclose to both Seller and Buyer all known latent defects in the property, any matter that must be disclosed by law, and information which Broker believes may be material or might affect Seller's or Buyer's decisions with respect to this transaction.

The parties acknowledge that Broker has not disclosed and Broker agrees not to disclose:

A. To Buyer information about what price or terms Seller will accept other than the listed price or terms, without the express written permission of the Seller;
B. To Seller information about what price or terms Buyer will offer other than those offered in writing by Buyer without the express written permission of the Buyer;
C. Any information of a confidential nature which could harm one party's bargaining position or benefit the other's.

Both parties understand and agree that Broker has the right to receive _____ as compensation, agreed upon in the Exclusive Right To Sell Listing Agreement between Seller and Broker and that Broker shall not receive any compensation from Buyer unless it is disclosed and consented to by Seller.

In view of Broker's dual agency relationship, the parties understand they have the responsibility of making their own decisions with respect to the terms to be included in their agreement. The parties understand the implications of Broker's dual agency role as facilitator or intermediary, rather than that of advocate and exclusive representative, and have determined the benefits of entering into this transaction with Broker acting as dual agent outweigh said implications.

Therefore, Seller and Buyer both, and each of them individually, consent to Broker's dual agency and hereby waive any claims now or hereafter arising out of such conflicts of interest, or for breach of fiduciary duty.

Both parties are advised to seek competent legal advice with regard to this transaction, and with regard to all documents executed in connection therewith.

Seller and Buyer understand this document does not replace prior agreements entered into with Broker, i.e. the EXCLUSIVE RIGHT TO REPRESENT BUYER agreement signed by Buyer on _____, and the EXCLUSIVE RIGHT TO SELL agreement signed by Seller on _____. However, in any areas where this document contradicts or conflicts with those documents, this DUAL AGENCY DISCLOSURE AMENDMENT shall supersede.

The undersigned parties acknowledge that they have thoroughly read and approved this document and acknowledge receipt of a copy hereof.

Dated: _____ Time: _____ Dated: _____ Time: _____
Seller (print): _____ Buyer (print): _____
Seller's signature: _____ Buyer's signature: _____
Seller's signature: _____ Buyer's signature: _____
Address: _____ Address: _____
Phone: _____ Phone: _____

FORM 100-DA (9-91) COPYRIGHT © 1991, BY PROFESSIONAL PUBLISHING CORP. 122 PAUL DR. SAN RAFAEL CA 94903 (415) 472-1964

PROFESSIONAL PUBLISHING

BUYER AGENCY

Traditionally, residential real estate licensees have represented sellers, not buyers. This is largely due to the rules that many multiple listing services have enacted, whereby any sales agent who shows an MLS-listed property automatically accepts the "blanket" unilateral offer of subagency given by the listing broker. The subagent would have to *formally* reject the subagency, which most, if not all, do not. Seller representation is thus assumed.

The problem in the past has arisen from simple human behavior. Cooperating agents owe their loyalty to, in fact, *every* seller listed in the MLS, but because of the close relationship established with "their" buyers, salespersons tend to give the buyers advice and act as their advocates—and, in doing so, become their "implied agents."

The behavior of the real estate agent thus encourages buyers to believe that they are represented, yet at the same time the MLS rules assume the agent is representing the seller. An undisclosed dual agency is the result.

Even though all but the most careful agents have probably been guilty of undisclosed dual agency, few cases ever result in litigation. This is probably because the parties are satisfied with the result of the transaction or because they did not understand the "real" agency relationships and the attendant fiduciary obligations.

Examples of the types of behavior that can create an implied buyer agency might include:
- Advising buyers as to the lowest offer they should make on the property
- Advising the buyer to receive some compensation for defects found in the property during inspection
- Negotiating financing terms in which the seller carries back a note or pays for the buyer's loan discount points, etc.

These are all indications of an agency representing a buyer. Anytime the licensee becomes an "advisor and an advocate" for the buyer, an implied agency is created.

BUYERS WHO MUST BE CLIENTS

There are two categories where buyers "must" become the clients:
1. Licensee buying for his or her own account—No court could believe that an agent purchasing property for his or her own account could possibly represent the interests of the seller/client. Agents should consider entering into a dual agency agreement with the seller, or become a principal and hire their broker (or another salesperson) in the office to represent them in purchasing the property. Proper disclosure of license status and the proper agency disclosure will assure that all parties are adequately represented.
2. Buyers who wish anonymity—Any buyer who desires to remain anonymous must be a buyer/client, since a subagent is required to disclose to the seller the buyer's identity. Buyers who want anonymity are usually those who believe the seller's knowledge of their identity will weaken their negotiating position. Such buyers might include very wealthy people, corporations, speculators, or celebrities.

A buyer agency written agreement is always advisable, and a formal agreement setting forth the customary provisions of such an agency is set forth in Figure 8-5.

WHAT YOU CAN DO AND NOT CREATE A DUAL AGENCY

Suppose you decide that you do not want to be a buyer's agent or to enter into a dual agency relationship with buyer and seller. This is typically the way the residential real estate business has been transacted in the past, prior to all the heightened interest in buyer brokerage. The following is a brief list of some of the activities you can engage in while remaining loyal to the seller, and feeling confident that you have not violated any law relating to agency.

148 Chapter 8 Agency

FIG 8-5

☐ ZipForm™ Computer Alignment
NCR (No Carbon Required)

EXCLUSIVE RIGHT TO REPRESENT BUYER

DEFINITIONS

BROKER means exclusive agent of Buyer and includes all associated sales persons. **BUYER** means Broker's principal as purchaser, lessee, optionee, or exchanger of real property. **ACQUIRE** means purchase, lease, option or exchange. **SELLER** means owner of property to be acquired by Buyer. **DAYS** means calendar days unless otherwise specified. The **MASCULINE** includes the **FEMININE** and the **SINGULAR** includes the **PLURAL**. **ACQUISITION FEE** means compensation due Broker, **only** in the event Buyer is successful in acquiring a desired property under the terms of this agreement.

1. **EXCLUSIVE RIGHT.** The undersigned, _____, hereinafter designated as BUYER, hereby grants to _____, hereinafter designated as BROKER, the exclusive right and authority to represent Buyer, for the purpose of assisting Buyer in locating real property of a nature outlined in paragraph 3, or such other real property as may be acceptable to Buyer, and to negotiate terms and conditions acceptable to Buyer for the acquistion of such real property, and any personal property.

2. **TERM.** The term of this agreement shall commence this date and terminate at midnight of _____, 19____.

3. **PROPERTY:**
   TYPE OF PROPERTY: ☐ Residential, ☐ Residential Income, ☐ Commercial, ☐ Industrial, ☐ Vacant Land, ☐ Other:
   _____
   GENERAL NATURE OF PROPERTY: _____
   _____
   _____
   LOCATION: _____
   _____
   PRICE RANGE: _____
   PREFERRED TERMS: _____
   POSSESSION: _____
   OTHER REQUIREMENTS: _____
   _____
   _____

4. **BROKER'S OBLIGATIONS.** During the term of this agreement Broker agrees to:
   A. Become well informed in Buyer's objectives pursuant to paragraph 3;
   B. Assist Buyer with researching financing alternatives;
   C. Assist Buyer in locating and showing available properties in accordance with paragraph 3;
   D. Assist Buyer in obtaining available information relative to desired properties;
   E. Assist Buyer in preparing offers to acquire property and negotiating favorable terms;
   F. Assist Buyer in obtaining financing and monitoring closing procedures and deadlines.

5. **DISCLAIMER.** Buyer understands that a real estate broker is qualified to advise on matters concerning real estate, but is not expert in matters of law, tax, financing, surveying, structural conditions, hazardous materials, or engineering. Buyer acknowledges he has been advised by Broker to seek expert assistance for advice on such matters. In the event Broker provides names or sources for such advice or assistance, Buyer understands and acknowledges that Broker does not warrant the services of such experts or their products and cannot warrant the condition of property to be acquired, or guarantee that all property defects are disclosed by the seller. Broker does not investigate the status of permits, zoning, location of property lines, and/or code compliance and Broker does not guarantee the accuracy of square footage of a structure; Buyer is to satisfy himself concerning these issues.

6. **BUYER'S OBLIGATIONS.** During the term of this agreement Buyer agrees to:
   A. Provide upon request:
      [1] General nature, location, requirements and preferred terms and conditions relating to the acquisition of desired property;
      [2] Relevant personal and financial information, to assure Buyer's ability to obtain financing;
   B. Work exclusively with Broker and not with other real estate brokers, salespersons, or owners, with respect to viewing properties and to refer to Broker all inquiries in any form from any other real estate brokers, salespersons, prospective sellers, or any other source;
   C. Conduct in good faith all negotiations for property, described in paragraph 3, exclusively through Broker;
   D. Hold Broker harmless from any claims resulting from incomplete or inaccurate information provided by Buyer.

7. **POSSIBLE DUAL AGENCY.** A dual agency relationship would arise if Buyer wishes to acquire a property listed by Broker. In such event Broker will require the **prior written consent of both principals** (PPC Form 100-DA), and can act only as Intermediary between Buyer and Seller. Buyer understands that, in a dual agency relationship, the Broker as Intermediary could not legally disclose confidential information without express permission of the other party, such as disclosing to a buyer what the seller might accept, or disclosing to a seller what a buyer might be willing to pay.
   [_____] By initialling here, Buyer acknowledges that the above Dual Agency provision has been reviewed, understood and that Buyer hereby consents to a possible Dual Agency relationship.

8. **OTHER POTENTIAL BUYERS.** Buyer understands that other potential buyers may consider, make offers on, or acquire through Broker, the same or similar properties as Buyer is seeking to acquire. Buyer consents to Broker's representation of such other potential buyers **before, during and after the expiration of this agreement.**

FORM 100.1 (9-91) COPYRIGHT © 1991, BY PROFESSIONAL PUBLISHING CORP. 122 PAUL DR, SAN RAFAEL, CA 94903 (415) 472-1964

Page 1 of 2 pages

PROFESSIONAL PUBLISHING

- Give disclosure to the buyer that you represent the seller by requesting that the buyer sign a disclosure statement that your office uses.
- Show the buyer property (listed with your office or that of a MLS that you belong to) that meets his or her criteria of needs, wants, and affordability.
- Describe the property and make factual statements regarding the condition or status of the property.
- Transmit ALL offers in a timely manner.
- Complete preprinted contracts and riders by filling in blanks.
- Inform the buyer about financing, attorneys, home inspectors, and title companies.
- Disclose all material defects to the buyer as soon as possible. Do not violate your duty of confidentiality to the seller. If there is a conflict between what you think you should disclose and what the seller will allow you to disclose, document this and keep a copy in your transaction file. Give consideration to using a well-drafted property disclosure form.
- ALWAYS ACT IN THE BEST INTEREST OF YOUR CLIENT/SELLER.

BUYERS WHO SHOULD BE CLIENTS

There are seven categories of buyers who, because of their relationship to the agent or because of their inexperience, "should" become the client:

1. Relatives, spouses, parents, siblings, children, aunts, uncles, and cousins are all people who, along with the courts, could reasonably expect you to represent them as buyers.
2. Close friends—people whom you have known well for some time make up this category.
3. Business associates or partners. While this group probably does not include most members of a limited partnership or employees of large corporations, it does include anyone with whom you share a close business or financial relationship.
4. Former customers and clients. Buyers and sellers with whom you have worked in the past will generally consider you to be "their agent." Often when agency disclosure is made to them, they are surprised to learn you did not represent them in the prior transaction and may want to be absolutely sure that you represent them this time.
5. First-time buyers. Because of their naïveté and inexperience, it is often difficult not to behave as the agent for these buyers.
6. Out-of-town buyers. These may not be inexperienced buyers, but because they are probably uneducated to the marketplace and probably are not knowledgeable about the real estate transaction and/or state and local legal requirements, you may be tempted to give them advocacy or advice to the detriment of the seller.
7. Buyers who want to be represented. As a result of experience and/or education, more and more buyers understand agency relationships and obligations and will want an advocate on whom they can depend. If buyer agency is not an option for the real estate professional, then the obligations of subagency and the fiduciary relationship to the client/seller must be adhered to.

AGENCY DISCLOSURE

Section 18.2 of the Real Estate License Act of 1983, amended in 1989, provides:

> *Persons licensed under the Act shall disclose in writing to prospective buyers, the existence of an agency relationship between the licensee and the seller, or shall disclose in writing to sellers, or their agents, the existence of an agency relationship between the licensee and a prospective buyer at a time and in a manner consistent with the regulations established by the Department.*

Therefore, all real estate agents engaged in the brokerage business—whether they are seller's agents (including cooperating brokers) or buyer's agents (buyer's broker)—must make the proper agency disclosure to the opposite party.

The License Law does not distinguish between residential, commercial, industrial, or vacant land transactions. Therefore, the agency disclosure requirements apply to all of these purchase and sale transactions. All disclosures must be dated and in writing, and made at or before the FIRST SIGNIFICANT CONTACT. Review the disclosure form developed by the Illinois Association of REALTORS® that appears in Figure 8-6.

FIG 8-6

ILLINOIS ASSOCIATION OF REALTORS®
NOTICE OF AGENCY TO PROSPECTIVE PURCHASERS

Thank you for giving _____ (Name of Brokerage Firm) the opportunity to work with you. We feel it is important for you to know and be aware of the services that we can provide to you.

As members of the national, state and local Realtor® organizations and as fellow members of this community, we endeavor at all times to provide our customers with fair, honest and professional service.

As part of providing this service, we believe you should know that:

1. AS A LISTING OR COOPERATING BROKER ALL LICENSEES EMPLOYED BY OR ASSOCIATED WITH THE BROKERAGE FIRM WHO WILL WORK WITH YOU ARE THE AGENTS OF THE SELLER AS TO ALL PROPERTIES THAT WE WILL SHOW YOU.

2. As an agent of the seller, we have certain legal obligations to the seller, including the duties of loyalty and faithfulness.

As a part of our professional service to you, we can and will:

1. Treat you fairly and honestly.
2. Attempt to locate and show you available properties meeting criteria established by you.
3. Provide you with information and counseling about the financing of your purchase.

If you have any questions about our role, please feel free to ask. We look forward to having the opportunity to work with you and to provide you with our professional services.

The undersigned acknowledge receipt of this disclosure on the date indicated below.

THIS DISCLOSURE IS BEING PROVIDED AS REQUIRED BY STATE LAW

Date_____   Signature of Customer_____

Signature of Agent_____   Signature of Customer_____

Comments (if any)_____

(For use when acting as seller's agent only)

101 REVISED 6/90   COPYRIGHT© BY ILLINOIS ASSOCIATION OF REALTORS®

SELLER'S AGENT'S DISCLOSURE

For a seller's agent (including cooperating agents or subagents), the "first significant contact" is defined by the Department of Professional Regulation as the first of any the following:

A) the beginning of the showing of real property to the prospective buyer other than an open house or;

B) the beginning of the preparation of a sales contract on real property for the prospective buyer or; even if disclosure is a part of the contract

C) the beginning of an agent's pre-qualifications of a prospective buyer to determine the prospective buyer's financial ability to purchase real estate or the agent's request for specific information from a prospective buyer to determine ability to purchase or finance real estate in a particular price range.

The rule indicates that if the first significant contact is by telephone or in some similar manner, then oral disclosure should first be made and then confirmed in writing at a later date. This written disclosure is normally presented in person but could also be delivered by mail, facsimile, or other similar means. The disclosure form should have a place for the recipient of the disclosure to acknowledge receipt of the disclosure. While the recipient (seller or buyer) of the disclosure does *not* have to sign the acknowledgment, keeping a copy of the form acts a "receipt" or evidence of the licensee's actual delivery of the written disclosure. It is therefore advisable to request the party to whom disclosure is made to acknowledge receipt of the disclosure form. Should a buyer or seller refuse to acknowledge receipt of the disclosure, make a note of the person to whom disclosure was made, note the date and time of the delivery, and keep copies with the transaction file. Remember that "the employing broker shall retain a copy of the disclosure in the employing broker's file." Therefore, even if the transaction does *not* result in a sale, employing brokers must maintain a file of disclosures.

Some listing brokers are requiring that the cooperating agent submit a copy of the written disclosure to the buyer with the buyer's offer. They are concerned about their liability for the cooperating agent's failure to make a written disclosure to a buyer. Under agency disclosure regulations promulgated by the Department:

> *the listing office is NOT required to make disclosure to a prospective buyer unless the listing office has significant contact with the prospective buyer. The office that holds the listing is not required to ensure that a cooperating office has complied with the disclosure requirements of the Act. Buyer Agency disclosure to a seller can be done through seller's agent or subagent.*

SELLERS AS BUYERS

Suppose the seller that you are representing now wants to purchase property using your brokerage firm's services. Disclosure of agency must be made to him or her as well. Conversely, if your firm were going to represent this person as his or her buyer's broker, then notification of agency to prospective sellers must be made.

BUYER'S AGENT'S DISCLOSURE

A buyer's agent must disclose in writing to the seller or to the seller's agent the existence of his or her agency relationship with the buyer at the time of "the first significant contact with the seller, while acting on the buyer's behalf." In some circumstances, a real estate firm may be acting as a listing agent (and as such is an agent for the seller) and as a buyer's broker. The agent acting as a buyer's broker may also be showing the buyer one of his or her own listings. In that circumstance, different rules may apply.

To give guidance to the licensee when this type of issue arises, the Department has promulgated the following rules:

> *A written disclosure of agency must be made to a prospective buyer even though the licensee or licensee's employing broker has previously entered into a written agreement with the prospective buyer to represent the prospective buyer if the licensee acting as the agent of the seller in regard to a particular property or transaction in which the prospective buyer is involved.*
>
> *The written disclosure of agency to the seller or prospective buyer can be a general disclosure and does not need to be site or party specific unless:*
> 1. *As to a prospective buyer, the licensee is a seller's agent as to some properties and an agent of the buyer in regards to the purchase of other properties.*
> 2. *As to a seller, the licensee is a subagent or cooperating agent of the seller as to some prospective buyers and an agent of the buyer as to other prospective buyers.*

As stated earlier, if the first significant contact with the seller or seller's agent is by telephone or other similar methods, then an oral disclosure to the seller of your buyer agency should be made and then followed up and confirmed in writing.

EXCEPTIONS TO THE GENERAL DISCLOSURE RULES

Buyer Referrals. Licensees often refer buyers or sellers to other brokers in geographic areas where the referring agent does not service or as a result of the licensee working for a real estate referral company. In that circumstance:

> *no disclosure of an agency relationship need be made by a licensee when the licensee is merely making a referral of a prospective buyer or seller to another real estate brokerage entity even though consideration or compensation is or may be paid to the referring licensee, unless the licensee has significant contact with the prospective seller or buyer.*

If you are the *recipient* of a seller or buyer referral, then it is your obligation to discuss agency and present the proper paperwork. The licensee who has *made* the referral is not required to make agency disclosure unless "significant contact" with the seller or buyer has been made by the referring licensee. If the buyer is working with more than one person in your firm (perhaps multiple branch offices), you should still get the disclosure signed.

Auctions, Ownership Interest of Licensee, and Rental Transactions. If a property is sold at auction, you may make the required disclosure by including that disclosure in the advertising for the auction or in information sheets distributed to bidders at the time of the auction. No written agency disclosure is required to the ultimate purchaser of the property at the auction.

Additionally, from time to time a property may be marketed in which the licensee has an ownership interest. The Department has determined that the disclosure of your interest as a principal (seller or buyer) in the transaction satisfies the agency disclosure requirements of the law. The disclosure of interest should be made at first contact with the prospect.

FIG 8-7

AGENCY DISCLOSURE QUICK REFERENCE CHART

	If you are a SELLER'S AGENT	If you are a BUYER'S AGENT	If you are a DUAL AGENT
To whom must disclosure be made?	Prospective buyer	Seller/Seller's Agent	All parties
When must disclosure be made?	At the time of "first significant contact"	At the time of "first significant contact"	At the time of or before the creation of the dual agency
What is "first significant contact"?	The earlier of: A) the beginning of the showing of property (other than an open house); or B) preparation of offer to purchase; or C) prequalification of a prospective buyer or similar request for specific financial information	The first contact with seller or seller's agent on behalf of one or more prospective buyers concerning a property's: (a) availability; (b) price; (c) condition; or (d) showing instructions.	Not applicable
How must the disclosure be made?	In writing	In writing. (If first significant contact is by phone, then orally and followed up in writing.)	In writing and signed by all parties
How may the disclosure be delivered?	In person, by mail, fax, or similar means	In person, by mail, fax or similar means	By whatever means will produce a signed writing prior to the creation of the dual agency
Must the disclosure be signed by anyone?	No	No	Yes, by all parties
Must the disclosure be dated?	Yes	Yes	No
Must a copy of the disclosure be retained, and if so, for what period of time?	Yes, for 5 years	Yes, for 5 years	Yes, for 10 years
What transactions, if any, are exempt?	1. Lease or rental transactions, unless there is an option to purchase 2. Referrals, when the referring Licensee has no significant contact with the buyer or seller	1. Lease or rental transactions, unless there is an option to purchase 2. Referrals, when the referring Licensee has no significant contact with the buyer or seller	None

Many licensees also act as rental agents. Questions have arisen as to whether or not a licensee has to make written disclosure to a prospective tenant. The answer is NO, UNLESS *the lease or rental agreement also includes an option to purchase the real estate.*

DISCLOSURE ENFORCEMENT

Please note that as investigators for the Department are conducting interviews at real estate firms and offices, they will be making random checks to ensure that the proper disclosure forms are being prepared, presented, and filed.

We have already indicated that the prospective seller or buyer shall be provided with a copy of the disclosure and the employing broker shall retain a copy of the disclosure in the employing broker's files. The Department of Professional Regulation suggests that agency disclosure forms for *uncompleted transactions be kept for a minimum of one year and forms for completed transactions kept for a minimum of five years*. Since managing brokers have the primary responsibility to ensure compliance, they should make periodic checks to ensure that the proper disclosure forms are being prepared, presented, and retained by their sales agents.

DISCIPLINARY ACTION
Failure to disclose in a manner described above can result in the Department of Professional Regulation's suspension, revocation, or refusal of a license, including a civil penalty not to exceed $10,000.

PROPERTY DISCLOSURE
With growing frequency, and with expensive judgments resulting in some cases, disgruntled home purchasers are asserting claims against real estate agents involving allegations of misrepresentation, negligence, or fraud. While courts are quick to enforce the agent's duties of disclosure of *known* material defects in the property to prospective purchasers, a growing trend lurks on the horizon. This trend is to judge the real estate professional not only by what they know, but—more dangerously—by what they *should have known*.

> TWO THIRDS OF ALL LAWSUITS AGAINST REAL ESTATE BROKERS AND SALESPERSONS IN THE UNITED STATES ALLEGE MISREPRESENTATION OR FAILURE TO DISCLOSE PROPERTY DEFECTS.

Today's real estate professional might consider some of the following suggestions when representing sellers and their properties to prospective purchasers:
1. Do not ask any questions of the seller as to the material latent (hidden) defects on the property, and direct all questions in this regard to the sellers. Answer "I don't know, I will ask the seller!" if asked questions about property defects. While this is not very professional and may result in lost sales, it would protect most agents, their defense being they had no actual knowledge of defects. This should be of little comfort, of course, as the cost of litigation and the damage to one's professional reputation makes this a poor alternative.
2. Have the seller complete a thorough property disclosure form prior to listing the property, which would protect the agent from suits resulting from nondisclosure of material latent property defects. If the seller does not make a complete or thorough disclosure, then the seller and not the broker would be liable.
3. It may be advisable to also have a home inspection done *prior* to the listing of the property for the protection of both the seller and the broker.

Mandatory property disclosure is a growing trend in many states; however, currently only Maine and California have mandatory property disclosure laws. In those states, if a seller knows of a defect in a property but fails to disclose or mention it to the broker or buyer, the buyer can later demand that the seller make repairs or reparations.

A seller is responsible for revealing to a buyer any hidden or *latent* defects in a building. A *latent* defect is one that is known to the seller but not to the buyer and is not discoverable by ordinary inspection. Not to disclose is considered by the courts to be a type of fraud termed *fraudulent concealment*. Buyers have been able to rescind contracts or receive damages when such defects have not been revealed. Examples of such circumstances are cases in which a house was built over a ditch that was covered by decaying timber, a buried drain tile causing water to accumulate, a driveway built partially on an adjacent property, or problems of persistent flooding. Additionally, cases in which the seller neglected to reveal violations of building codes or zoning restrictions have also been decided in favor of buyers.

The current law on property disclosure in Illinois is that sellers have an obligation to disclose those defects known to them to their real estate agents and also to any prospective buyers. The key word here is *known*, because if the sellers are unaware of a defect then they may not be faulted. While Illinois does not require mandatory seller disclosure, except environmental disclosure on commercial properties, it does require sales agents to disclose defects that they are aware of. The sales agent is thus put between the proverbial rock and a hard place when, through salesperson investigation, he or she discovers a property defect and the seller requires that the sales agent be silent to third parties, such as a buyer. A salesperson, as a subagent of the seller, would do well to withdraw from the transaction, because this knowledge compels him or her to disclose the defects to the purchaser, but the sales agent cannot violate his or her fiduciary duties of obedience to the seller.

ILLINOIS COURTS' POSITION ON LIABILITY

Although the Illinois Legislature has restricted an aggrieved purchaser's cause of action against real estate brokers under the Consumer Fraud Act by requiring the broker's "knowledge" of property defects, the courts are still eager to frame most alleged misrepresentations as a deceptive act or practice for purposes of establishing liability. In addition, Illinois courts have honored well-pleaded complaints alleging fraud and misrepresentation in many of these cases. Illinois courts have also accepted agency theories of liability pursued by purchasers against brokers, even though brokers were paid by sellers.

The message from the courts is this: Brokers should investigate claims by sellers about conditions of the property and deal candidly with prospective purchasers if they wish to avoid liability.

Exhibited in Figures 8-8 through 8-10 is a sample property-disclosure form. Sales agents and their employing brokers might do well to use a disclosure form similar to this one when listing property. In this way, the seller and salesperson will have gone through a thorough discussion of the condition of the property. The salesperson can rest assured that his or her reliance on the seller's statement will hold the salesperson harmless from suit from a subsequent purchaser and that the matter of permission to disclose this information is settled.

PROPERTY DISCLOSURE AND THE LICENSE ACT

The Illinois Real Estate License Act requires that a licensee "should disclose all material information of which he has knowledge and which is not reasonably discoverable by inspection or the real estate. This does not require the licensee to violate his duties of agency."

Stigmatized Properties. Suppose the property has "defects" that are not of a physical nature, such as the occurrence of a murder or suicide, the presence of a deadly disease by the former owners, alleged appearances of ghosts, poltergeists, gremlins, demons, or other unusual circumstances surrounding the property? What are the licensee's duties of disclosure in these cases? Again, the Illinois Real Estate License Act states: "No action shall arise against a licensee for failure to disclose that the owner occupant was afflicted with AIDS or the property was the site of act or occurrence which had no effect on the physical condition of the premises."

Implied Warranty of Habitability. The Illinois Supreme Court decision in *Petersen v. Hubschman Construction Company*, 76 Ill 2d 31,389. N.E. 2d 1154 (1979) recognized the doctrine of *implied habitability* in the sale of the homes of builder-vendors. This applies to "part-time" builders as well as to "full-time" builders. The doctrine is a recent innovation designed to avoid the harshness of caveat emptor and to afford a degree of relief to buyers of NEW homes who subsequently discover latent defects. The warranty does not arise as a result of the execution of the purchase agreement between the buyer and seller. It exists as an independent implied promise or undertaking collateral to the covenant to convey. Therefore, unless waived by the purchaser, the builder-vendor is warranting that, when completed and conveyed to the purchaser, the new home would be reasonably suited for its intended use.

FIG 8-8

NCR (No Carbon Required)

SELLER'S PROPERTY DISCLOSURE STATEMENT
(Including the main structure and any outbuildings)

This document provides disclosures with respect to the property known to the Seller as of the date of this statement. It is not a warranty of any kind and is not a substitute for property inspections by experts which the Buyer may wish to obtain. Buyer understands and acknowledges that the broker(s) in this transaction cannot warrant the condition of the property or guarantee that all defects have been disclosed by the Seller.

PROPERTY ADDRESS _____
SELLER'S NAME _____

1. TITLE AND ACCESS
  a. Is the property currently leased? .... ☐ Yes ☐ No
  b. Has anyone right of refusal to buy, option, or lease the property? .... ☐ Yes ☐ No
  c. Do you know of any existing, pending or potential legal actions concerning the property or Owners Association? .... ☐ Yes ☐ No
  d. Has a Notice of Default been recorded against the property? .... ☐ Yes ☐ No
  e. Any bonds, assessments, or judgements which are liens upon the property? .... ☐ Yes ☐ No
  f. Do you own real property adjacent to, across the street from, or in the same sub-division as subject property? .... ☐ Yes ☐ No
  g. Any boundary disputes, or third party claims affecting the property (rights of other people to interfere with the use of the property in any way)? .... ☐ Yes ☐ No

2. ENVIRONMENTAL
Are you aware of the following with respect to the property?
  a. Any noises from airplanes, trains, trucks, freeways, etc.? .... ☐ Yes ☐ No
  b. Any odors caused by toxic waste, gas, industry, agriculture, animals, pets, etc.? .... ☐ Yes ☐ No
  c. Formaldehyde gas emitting materials, especially urea-formaldehyde foam insulation? .... ☐ Yes ☐ No
  d. Asbestos insulation or fireproofing? .... ☐ Yes ☐ No
  e. Elevated radon levels on the property? .... ☐ Yes ☐ No
  f. Elevated radon levels in the neighborhood? .... ☐ Yes ☐ No
  g. Use of lead-base paint on any surfaces? .... ☐ Yes ☐ No
  h. Contamination of well or other water supply? .... ☐ Yes ☐ No
  i. Any past or present flooding or drainage problems? .... ☐ Yes ☐ No
  j. Any past or present flooding or drainage problems on adjacent properties? .... ☐ Yes ☐ No
  k. Any standing water after rainfalls? .... ☐ Yes ☐ No
  l. Any sump pumps in basement or crawlspace? .... ☐ Yes ☐ No
  m. Any active springs? .... ☐ Yes ☐ No
  n. Is property located wholly or partially within Flood Hazard Zone, as determined by the National Flood Insurance Program? .... ☐ Yes ☐ No
  o. Is the house built on landfill (compacted or otherwise)? .... ☐ Yes ☐ No
  p. Is there landfill on any portion of the property? .... ☐ Yes ☐ No
  q. Any soil settling, slippage, sliding, or similar problems? .... ☐ Yes ☐ No
  r. Any sinkholes or voids on or near the property? .... ☐ Yes ☐ No
  s. Any depressions, mounds, or soft spots? .... ☐ Yes ☐ No
  t. Any pending real estate development in your area (such as common interest developments, planned development units, subdivisions, or property for commercial, industrial, sport, educational, or religious use)? .... ☐ Yes ☐ No
  u. Any federal or state areas once used for military training purposes, within one mile of the property? .... ☐ Yes ☐ No
  v. Traces of concrete, metal, or asphalt indicating prior commercial or industrial use? .... ☐ Yes ☐ No
  w. Proximity of property to former, current or proposed mines or gravel pits? .... ☐ Yes ☐ No
  x. Proximity of property to former or current waste disposal sites? .... ☐ Yes ☐ No
  y. Ravines or earth embankment that may indicate former dumping? .... ☐ Yes ☐ No
  z. Pipelines carrying oil, gas, or chemicals underneath or adjacent to the property? .... ☐ Yes ☐ No
  aa. Existence of pipeline rights-of-way or easements over or adjacent to the property? .... ☐ Yes ☐ No
  bb. Discoloring of soil or vegetation? .... ☐ Yes ☐ No
  cc. Oil sheen in wet areas? .... ☐ Yes ☐ No

3. STRUCTURAL
  a. Approximate age of the house: _____
  b. Do you know of any condition in the original or existing design or workmanship of the structures upon the property that would be considered substandard? .... ☐ Yes ☐ No
  c. Do you know of any structural additions or alterations, or the installation, alteration, repair, or replacement of significant components of the structures upon the property, completed during the term of your ownership or that of a prior owner without an appropriate permit or other authority for construction from a public agency having jurisdiction? .... ☐ Yes ☐ No
  d. Do you know of any violations of government regulations, ordinances, or zoning laws regarding this property? .... ☐ Yes ☐ No
  e. Do you know of any excessive settling, slippage, sliding, or other soil problems, past or present? .... ☐ Yes ☐ No
  f. Any problems with retaining walls cracking or bulging? .... ☐ Yes ☐ No
  g. Swimming pool out of level? .... ☐ Yes ☐ No
  h. Do you know of any past or present problems with driveways, walkways, sidewalks, patios (such as large cracks, potholes, raised sections)? .... ☐ Yes ☐ No
  i. Any significant cracks in any of the following: .... ☐ Yes ☐ No
     ☐ foundations, ☐ exterior walls, ☐ interior walls, ☐ ceilings, ☐ fireplaces, ☐ chimneys, ☐ decks, ☐ slab floors, ☐ garage floors?
  j. Any slanted floors? .... ☐ Yes ☐ No
  k. Any distorted door frames (uneven spaces between doors and frames)? .... ☐ Yes ☐ No
  l. Any sticking windows? .... ☐ Yes ☐ No
  m. Any sagging exposed ceiling beams? .... ☐ Yes ☐ No
  n. Any structural woodmembers (including mudsills) below soil level? .... ☐ Yes ☐ No
  o. Crawl space, if any, below soil level? .... ☐ Yes ☐ No
  p. Any structures (including play structures, tree house, etc.) that could be hazardous? .... ☐ Yes ☐ No

Seller(s) Initials [_____] [_____]
FORM 110.11 (10-91) COPYRIGHT © 1991, BY PROFESSIONAL PUBLISHING CORP. 122 PAUL DR. SAN RAFAEL, CA 94903 (415) 472-1964
Page 1 of 3 pages
PROFESSIONAL PUBLISHING

FIG 8-9

NCR (No Carbon Required)

Page 2 of 3 pages

Property Address _____

4. ROOF, GUTTERS, DOWNSPOUTS
 a. Type of roof: ☐ Tar and Gravel, ☐ Asphalt Shingle, ☐ Wood Shingle, ☐ Tile, ☐ Other _____. Age of roof: _____
 b. Has roof been resurfaced? _____ If so, what year? _____
 c. Is there a guarantee on the roof? _____ For how long? _____ By whom? _____
 d. Has roof ever leaked since you owned the property? _____
  If so, what was done to correct the leak? _____ ☐ Explanation attached.
 e. Are gutters and downspouts free of holes and excessive rust? _____
 f. Do downspouts empty into drainage system or onto splash blocks? _____
 g. Is water directed away from structure? _____

5. PLUMBING SYSTEM
 a. Source of water supply: ☐ Public, ☐ Private Well. If well water, when was water sample last checked for safety? _____
  Result of test: _____ ☐ Explanation attached.
 b. Well water pump: _____ Date installed: _____ Condition: _____ Sufficient water during late summer? _____
 c. Are water supply pipes copper or galvanized? _____
 d. Are you aware of below normal water pressure in your water supply lines (normal is 50 to 70 lbs.)? _____
 e. Are you aware of excessive rust stains in tubs, lavatories and sinks? _____
 f. Are you aware of water standing around any of the lawn sprinkler heads? _____
 g. Are there any plumbing leaks around and under sinks, toilets, showers, bathtubs, and lavatories? _____ If so, where? ☐ Explanation attached.
 h. Pool: Age: _____ Pool Heater: ☐ Gas, ☐ Electric, ☐ Solar. Pool Sweep: _____ Date of last inspection: _____
  By whom? _____ Regular maintenance? _____
 i. Hot Tub/Spa: _____ Date of last inspection: _____ By whom? _____
 j. ☐ City Sewer, ☐ Septic Tank: ☐ Fiberglass, ☐ Concrete, ☐ Redwood. Capacity: _____ Is septic tank in working order? _____

6. ELECTRICAL SYSTEM
 a. 220 Volt? .... ☐ Yes ☐ No
 b. Is the electrical wiring Copper? .... ☐ Yes ☐ No
 c. Are there any damaged or malfunctioning receptacles? .... ☐ Yes ☐ No
 d. Are you aware of any damaged or malfunctioning switches? .... ☐ Yes ☐ No
 e. Are there any extension cords stapled to baseboards or underneath carpets or rugs? .... ☐ Yes ☐ No
 f. Does outside TV antenna have a ground connection? .... ☐ Yes ☐ No
 g. Are you aware of any defects, malfunctioning, or illegal installation of electrical equipment in or outside the house? ... ☐ Yes ☐ No

7. HEATING, AIR CONDITIONING, OTHER EQUIPMENT
 a. Is the house insulated? .... ☐ Yes ☐ No
 b. Type of Heating System: _____
 c. Is furnace room or furnace closet adequately vented? .... ☐ Yes ☐ No
 d. Are fuel-consuming heating devices adequately vented to the outside, directly or through a chimney? ..... ☐ Yes ☐ No
 e. Heating Equipment in working order? .... ☐ Yes ☐ No
 f. Solar heating in working order? .... ☐ Yes ☐ No
 g. Air Conditioning in working order? .... ☐ Yes ☐ No
 h. Does Fireplace have a damper? .... ☐ Yes ☐ No
 i. Provision for outside venting of clothes dryer? .... ☐ Yes ☐ No
 j. Water Heater in working order? .... ☐ Yes ☐ No
 k. Is heater equipped with temperature pressure relief valve, which is a required safety device? .... ☐ Yes ☐ No
 l. Electric garage door opener in working order .... ☐ Yes ☐ No
 m. Burglar alarm in working order? .... ☐ Yes ☐ No
 n. Smoke Detectors in working order? .... ☐ Yes ☐ No
 o. Lawn Sprinklers in working order? .... ☐ Yes ☐ No
 p. Water Softener in working order? .... ☐ Yes ☐ No
 q. Sump pump: in working order? .... ☐ Yes ☐ No
 r. Are you aware of any of the above equipment that is in need of repair or replacement or is illegally installed? .... ☐ Yes ☐ No

8. BUILT-IN APPLIANCES
 a. Are you aware of any built-in appliances that are in need of repair or replacement? .... ☐ Yes ☐ No

9. CONDOMINIUMS — COMMON INTEREST DEVELOPMENTS
 a. Please check the availability of copies of the following documents: ☐ CC&Rs, ☐ Condominium Declaration, ☐ Association Bylaws, ☐ Articles of Incorporation, ☐ Subdivision Report, ☐ Current Financial Statement, ☐ Regulations currently in force.
 b. Does the Condominium Declaration contain any resale restrictions? _____
 c. Does the Homeowners Association have the first right of refusal? _____
 d. Please check occupancy restrictions imposed by the association, including but not limited to: ☐ Children, ☐ Pets, ☐ Storage of Recreational Vehicles or Boats on driveways or in common areas, ☐ Advertising or For Sale signs, ☐ Architectural or decorative alterations subject to association approval, ☐ Others: _____
 e. In case of a conversion, have you an engineer's report on the condition of the building and its equipment? _____
 f. Monthly/annual association dues:$ _____ What is included in the association dues? _____
 _____
 g. Has your association notified you of any future dues increases or special assessments? _____
  If so, give details: _____ ☐ Explanation attached.
 h. Are all dues, assessments, and taxes current? _____
 i. I shall provide a statement from the Condominium Homeowners Association documenting the amount of any delinquent assessments, including penalties, attorney's fees, and any other charges provided for in the management documents to be delivered to Buyer. _____
 j. Security: ☐ Inter-com, ☐ Closed circuit TV, ☐ Guards, ☐ Electric gate, ☐ Other: _____
 k. Parking: Does each unit have its own designated parking spaces? _____
 l. Sound proofing adequate? _____ Are there noisy trash chutes? _____
 m. Property Management Co. _____

Seller(s) Initials [_____] [_____]

FORM 110.12 (10-91) COPYRIGHT © 1991, BY PROFESSIONAL PUBLISHING CORP. 122 PAUL DR. SAN RAFAEL, CA 94903 (415)472-1964

PROFESSIONAL PUBLISHING

FIG 8-10

NCR (No Carbon Required)

Page 3 of 3 pages

Property Address _____

10. OWNERSHIP
a. Are you a builder or developer? .... ☐ Yes ☐ No
b. Are you a licensed real estate agent? .... ☐ Yes ☐ No
c. Have all persons on the title signed the listing agreement? .... ☐ Yes ☐ No
d. Please list all persons on the title who are not U.S. citizens: _____
_____

11. PERSONAL PROPERTY INCLUDED IN THE PURCHASE PRICE
a. The following items of personal property are included in the purchase price: _____
_____
b. Are there any liens against any of these items? _____ If so, please explain: _____

12. HOME PROTECTION PROGRAM
a. Do you want to provide a Home Protection Program at your expense? .... ☐ Yes ☐ No

13. REPORTS
a. Have you received or do you have knowledge of any of the following inspection reports or repair estimates made during or prior to your ownership?

REPORT	YES	NO	BY WHOM?	WHEN?	REPORT AVAILABLE?
Soils/Drainage					
Geologic					
Structural					
Roof					
Pest Control					
Well					
Septic					
Pool/Spa					
Heating					
Air Conditioning					
House Inspection					
Energy Audit					
Radon Test					
City/County Inspection					
Notice of Violation					

14. OTHER DISCLOSURES
a. In addition to the disclosure statements made herein, the following facts are known or suspected by me/us which may materially affect the value or desirability of the subject property, now or in the future: _____ ☐ Explanation attached

The foregoing answers and explanations are true and complete to the best of my/our knowledge and I/we have retained a copy hereof. I/we herewith authorize _____, the agent in this transaction, to disclose the information set forth above to other real estate brokers, real estate agents, and prospective buyers of the property.

Seller agrees to hold harmless all brokers and agents in the transaction and to defend and indemnify them from any claim, demand, action or proceedings resulting from any omission or alleged omission by Seller in this Disclosure Statement.

Dated: _____ Seller: _____ Seller: _____

The undersigned Buyer understands that this document is a disclosure of Seller's knowledge of the condition of the property as of the date signed by the Seller. It is not a warranty of any kind and is not a substitute for property inspections by experts which the Buyer may wish to obtain. Buyer understands and acknowledges that the brokers in this transaction cannot warrant the condition of the property or guarantee that all defects have been disclosed by the Seller.

I/we acknowledge receipt of this SELLER'S PROPERTY DISCLOSURE STATEMENT, including additional explanations, if any, attached hereto.

Dated: _____ Buyer: _____ Buyer: _____

I am satisfied with the above SELLER'S PROPERTY DISCLOSURE STATEMENT.

Dated: _____ Buyer: _____ Buyer: _____

I am NOT satisfied with the above SELLER'S PROPERTY DISCLOSURE STATEMENT and herewith rescind my offer to purchase above property.

Dated: _____ Buyer: _____ Buyer: _____

I reserve the right to have the property inspected by the following professional(s) _____
and to submit a copy of the inspection report(s) to Seller's agent on or before _____.

Dated: _____ Buyer: _____ Buyer: _____

FORM 110.13 (10-91) COPYRIGHT © 1991, BY PROFESSIONAL PUBLISHING CORP. 122 PAUL DR. SAN RAFAEL, CA 94903 (415) 472-1964

PROFESSIONAL PUBLISHING

158   Chapter 8   Agency

Special Compensation. This area of disclosure relates to the receipt of any compensation or remuneration that the licensee receives in the transaction. All fees, commissions, discounts, compensation, or other valuable consideration from brokers, lenders, attorneys, appraisers, title companies, or other persons must be disclosed to all parties in writing.

Special Interest. An Illinois licensee must disclose in writing his or her status as an Illinois registrant (having a real estate broker's or salesperson's license) and any and all interest he or she has or may have in the subject property either directly or indirectly.

Environmental Disclosure. Transfers of certain kinds of property in Illinois are subject to the Illinois Responsible Property Act of 1988. This act, effective November 1, 1989, requires sellers of nonresidential properties and residential properties containing underground storage tanks to disclose to potential buyers all they know regarding hazardous materials that are either present in the building or that may have seeped underground.

A "transfer" includes conveying property by a deed, a lease with a duration of more than 40 years, an assignment of more than 25 percent in the beneficial interest of a land trust, or a mortgage or collateral assignment of a beneficial interest in an Illinois land trust.

Under this law, the seller is responsible for filling out a disclosure form (Figures 8-11 through 8-14) that contains a checklist of chemicals and solvents considered to be hazardous by the Illinois Environmental Agency. The law requires only disclosure that any of these materials are present. It does not require that the seller clean up. The disclosure is made from information of which the seller knows. Thus, if the seller does not know any of the prior history of the property, the buyer, only relying on the seller's disclosure, could not purchase the property confident that the site is entirely free of hazardous material.

For this reason, it is a common practice for buyers and sellers to share the cost of a Level 1 Environmental Audit by hiring a professionally licensed environmental consultant.

UNLICENSED SALES ASSISTANTS

It has become increasingly popular for successful real estate agents to rely on administrative assistants to handle many of the details of a real estate transaction. To hire someone to act in a clerical or administrative capacity may not appear on the surface to represent a potential problem; however, it is extremely important that these unlicensed assistants do not hold themselves out to members of the public as having real estate expertise or that they are engaged in real estate activities as defined by the Illinois Real Estate License Act. The following individuals must be licensed: "Anyone who sells, exchanges, purchases, rents, or negotiates offers or leases; or who offers to list or collects rents or advertises real property for third parties." Additionally, anyone who ASSISTS in engaging in these activities must also be licensed.

What Unlicensed Sales Assistants Can Do. Placing signs on property, writing ads, typing correspondence, preparing prospecting lists, following up with attorneys, lenders, brokers, appraisers, tenants, landlords, etc., scheduling appointments, assisting with inspectors or appraisers—all these helpful and desirable activities can be the responsibilities of an assistant.

What Unlicensed Sales Assistants Cannot Do. Making "cold calls" (prospecting), giving property information to prospects in person or over the phone, showing property, measuring property, walkthroughs, negotiating and completing contracts, and unauthorized use of the MLS are among the activities that will cause the agent and his or her employer both loss of license and potential civil liability problems. For instance, an unlicensed person might be allowed to be a "house sitter" at an open house, with duties limited to handing out property information (previously prepared by a licensee) and registering potential prospects. However, if the assistant answers specific

Chapter 8 Agency 159

FIG 8-11

(Environmental Disclosure Document for Transfer of Real Property form, including Duty to Record notice, Seller/Buyer/Document No. fields, Property Identification section with address and legal description, Prepared by and Return to fields, and Section I. Liability Disclosure with Property Characteristics checklist.)

FIG 8-12

(Continuation of form: Section II. Nature of Transfer with questions about deed conveyance, assignment of beneficial interest in Illinois land trust, lease exceeding 40 years, and mortgage or collateral assignment; identification of Transferor and Transferee; Section III. Notification citing the Illinois Environmental Protection Act Sections 22.2(f), 4(q), 22.2(k), and 22.18(a).)

FIG 8-13

(Continuation: Section IV. Environmental Information — A. Regulatory Information During Current Ownership, with questions regarding operations involving hazardous substances, petroleum storage, specific waste management units (Landfill, Surface Impoundment, Land Treatment, Waste Pile, Incinerator, Storage Tank Above/Underground, Container Storage Area, Injection Wells, Wastewater Treatment Units, Septic Tanks, Transfer Stations, Waste Recycling Operations, Waste Treatment Detoxification, Other Land Disposal Area), permits, chemical safety plans, and Environmental Releases During Transferor's Ownership.)

FIG 8-14

(Continuation: additional questions 9–11 on sampling, monitoring, impaired usage, fumes, leaching; Section B. Site Information Under Other Ownership or Operation; Section V. Certification with signature lines for Transferor(s), Transferee(s), and Lender.)

questions about the property, price, terms, and contract conditions, then that would constitute a violation of the license law and result in a civil action against the employing broker.

Other Issues Concerning Unlicensed Sales Assistants. What about house keys, lock box keys, or apartment keys? The employing broker should be concerned about the potential liability of lost, stolen, or duplicated keys as a result of an unlicensed person's activities. Further, some MLS services prohibit the delivery of a lock box key to any unlicensed individual. Errors and omissions insurance may not provide coverage as a result of damages sought as a result of the actions of unlicensed individuals.

Business cards given to unlicensed individuals are permissible; however, precaution should be taken NOT to give the impression that the individual is employed directly by the company or is a licensed individual. The term *Administrative Assistant*, clearly visible on the card, is recommended. No insignia, logo, or designation of a trade group, association, or franchise should be used unless the unlicensed individual is, in fact, a member of the group or has written permission to use the logo, insignia, or designation.

Agents who engage the services of a personal secretary must also be sure that they adhere to all laws regarding withholding taxes and that they provide the required unemployment and workers' compensation insurance.

If your assistants have car accidents or injure themselves while performing services for you, questions of legal liability and insurance coverage arise. These questions should be anticipated by both the licensee and his or her employer PRIOR to engaging assistants. Every office should have clear-cut and definite polices regarding the employment of unlicensed individuals.

SALESPERSON'S BONUS
In order to effect a "quicker sale," some home sellers offer bonuses over and above the sales commission to induce salespersons to work harder. This notification of a bonus is found either on MLS sheets or in separate mailers to agents in the market area of the listing. Illinois statutes require that *fees or commissions can only be paid to the employing broker and not directly to the sales associate*. Commissions and bonuses must be paid to the employing broker, who may then direct monies to the associate.

SELLER AND BUYER INDUCEMENTS
It is no longer a violation of the License Act to offer cash or other types of inducement to a party to encourage them to list with your firm or to purchase property through your firm. For instance, a firm might offer a free tree to sellers who list their property with a firm, or the firm might give purchasers merchandise discount coupons if they purchase a home using a particular firm's services. It is illegal to offer compensation to an unlicensed person who refers business to any licensee. A broker must be certain that the inducement is going directly to the actual owner of the property or to bona fide purchasers. The License Act further requires that whenever a licensee advertises merchandise as being "free," all conditions of the offer must appear in the ad. This means that you cannot place a clause in the ad saying, "Call the office for more details" or "for further information." You must place all limiting conditions of your offer in any advertising or promotion, e.g., "This offer is contingent on the sale closing." A listing or selling office that offers an inducement to a buyer should notify the seller *in writing*, prior to submitting any offer to purchase, that the buyer will be receiving the cash or merchandise.

CASES TO JUDGE

1. The court heard a complaint from two purchasers against a broker for breach of fiduciary duty. In this case a brokerage office and salesperson were specifically retained by the purchaser to find a house for them. The salesperson found an acceptable house that had been listed by another brokerage firm within the cooperative listing service or MLS of which the firms were a member. An offer was submitted by the salesperson on the purchaser's behalf.

   Simultaneously, a competing offer was made on the same property through the same brokerage that the salesperson who was assisting the buyers worked for. Although the salesperson was aware of the competing offer, she did *not* inform the purchasers of the other interested purchasers. The other purchasers offered more for the property than the plaintiffs. The offer was accepted and the transaction completed.

   The purchasers then sued the defendant brokerage firm for breach of fiduciary duty for failing to disclose that a competing offer had been submitted. The brokerage firm argued that it was not an agent of the purchaser, but instead a subagent of the listing brokerage office, as a result of its MLS agreement. It said it owed its fiduciary obligation to the seller.

   Who was the client of the broker, the seller or the buyer? [*Stefani v. Baird & Warner, Inc.*, 157 Ill.App.3d 167, 510 N.E.2d 65 (1987)]

2. Purchasers conveyed confidential information to the defendant broker when the purchaser had submitted an initial offer of $1.5 million for a parcel of real property. The broker communicated that information to the seller, who was also his brother, and the seller counteroffered at $1.6 million. The purchaser accepted the higher counteroffer. The purchaser subsequently sued for breach of fiduciary duties by the broker.

   Was an agency relationship created? [*Conant v. Karris*, 165 Ill.App.3d 783, 520 N.E.2d 757 (1987)]

3. Purchasers sued a broker who failed to forward the second page of a termite inspection report to the purchaser's lender. This report would have disclosed extensive termite activity. The broker was aware that the purchasers would not be able to obtain financing in order to purchase seller's property if the lender had discovered termite infestation. This would then also negate the broker's commission. Additionally, the termite damage was so extensive that the purchasers had to abandon the premises.

   Is the broker liable for nondisclosure of a material defect? [*Warren v. LeMay*, 142 Ill.App.3d 550, 491 N.E.2d 464 (1988)]

4. Purchasers sued a broker under the Consumer Fraud and Deceptive Practices Act for failing to disclose that the property was on a flood plane. The salesperson pleaded he was not aware of the fact that the property was on a flood plane and therefore was not responsible for nondisclosure of a material fact.

   Is the broker responsible for nondisclosure? [*Riley v. Fair and Company REALTORS®*, 150 Ill.App.3d 597, 502 N.E.2d 45 (1986)]

5. Purchasers sued the broker for flooding problems that they had encountered after purchasing a house. The broker (salesperson) had stated that the water in the basement of the home was, to their knowledge, caused by a faulty check valve, not flooding. The broker believed the home to be free from flood problems, and the sellers had not indicated such trouble existed. The purchasers again noted that on the day before closing and during the final inspection (and the broker agreed) there appeared to be flooding problems. The broker told the purchasers at that time that they should contact their attorney.

   How did the court rule? [*Munjal v. Baird & Warner, Inc.*, 138 Ill.App.172, 484 N.E.2d 855 (1985)]

6. While purchasers were being shown residential property, they smelled an obnoxious odor. The broker stated that it was probably from a pile of dirty laundry that was located near the offending odor area. In actuality, the odor was a result of leaking sewer gas. The broker had offered to take the purchasers back to the property as often has they might wish prior to closing to be sure of the cause of the problem. The purchasers refused. In addition, little evidence was offered that would have linked the odor first smelled with the current odor in the home, which was found after the purchasers had moved in.

   Did the salesperson and broker act responsibly? [*Fischer v. G&S Builders*, 147 Ill.App.3d 168, 497 N.E.2d 1022 (1986)]

Chapter 8 Agency

7. Purchasers sued broker as a result of their finding termite infestation in the home after purchasing it. The sellers had gone to great lengths to conceal this problem from the broker and from potential purchasers.

   Did the court find the broker responsible for nondisclosure? [*Harkaka v. Widwood Realty, Inc.*, 200 Ill.App.3d 447, 558 N.E.2d 195 (1990)]

8. Buyers purchased a home from a builder while it was under construction. Although plaintiffs testified the building was not completed at closing, they took possession. Having found numerous defects (serious water problems and driveway repairs), they declared the property uninhabitable and moved out. Plaintiffs hired a general contractor and, for $1,628.50, made the necessary repairs. Buyers sued the builder for $1,628.50.

   What did the court rule? [*Weck v. A.M. Sunrise Construction Co.*, 36 Ill.App.2d 383, 184 N.E.2d 728 (1962)]

9. Buyers brought suit against the seller's failure to reveal a reevaluation of the real estate before closing. The contract between the parties called for proration based on the most recent tax bill. Before closing, seller received a reevaluation of property taxes increasing the assessed valuation by $10,000.

   Who was at fault?

10. Purchasers brought suit for violation of the implied warranty of a general contractor after it was shown that the builder-vendor was shown to be insolvent and incapable for remedying purchaser's complaint.

    How did the court rule? [*Minton v. Richards Group of Chicago*, 452 N.E.2d 835 (1983)]

10-QUESTION DIAGNOSTIC QUIZ

1. The Law of Agency requires a fiduciary relationship between the principal and agent that obligates the agent to duties of:
   A. care.
   B. accountability.
   C. loyalty.
   D. All of the above

2. Individuals holding an Illinois real estate salesperson's license are generally agents of:
   A. sellers.
   B. buyers.
   C. brokers.
   D. landlords.

3. In the real estate business, proprietors, corporations, or partnerships licensed as Illinois real estate brokers may represent as agents:
   A. sellers or buyers.
   B. landlords or tenants.
   C. exchangors or exchangees.
   D. All of the above

4. The agency disclosure and license status disclosure requirements of the Illinois Real Estate License Act do NOT apply to:
   A. any transaction that involves commercial, industrial, investment, or office property for sale or lease.
   B. a licensee who is selling or purchasing property for his or her own account.
   C. licensed builders in transactions of property owned or leased by them.
   D. any property sale or lease valued at under $100,000.

5. Which of the following is NOT important to creating an agency?
   A. Source or amount of agent's compensation
   B. The existence of a written contract creating the agency
   C. The existence of an oral contract creating the agency
   D. The conduct of the parties

6. A subagent:
   A. owes the same duties to the principal as the agent.
   B. does not owe any duties to the principal.
   C. can decide whom he or she represents at any time during the transaction.
   D. can be appointed as a result of membership in an MLS.

7. A seller's agent or subagent shall disclose in writing to a buyer, the existence of the agency relationship with the seller:
   A. at the beginning of the showing of the property to the prospective buyer.
   B. at the beginning of the preparation of a sales contract.
   C. at the beginning of the financial prequalification of the purchaser.
   D. All of the above

8. A buyer's agent or subagent shall disclose in writing to the seller or seller's agent, the existence of the agency relationship with the buyer:
   A. at the beginning of showing the purchaser property.
   B. after completion of the sales contract and all riders to the transaction.
   C. at the beginning of the preparation of the sales contract.
   D. at the time of the first significant contact with seller on buyer's behalf.

9. An unlicensed sales assistant can do all of the following EXCEPT:
   A. place signs on property.
   B. give specific information regarding price, terms, or condition regarding a property.
   C. follow up with attorneys, tenants, brokers, title companies, etc.
   D. write advertisements for the property.

10. A licensee must disclose all of the following EXCEPT:
    A. material information of which he or she has knowledge and which is not readily discoverable by inspection.
    B. any interest he or she has or may have in the property.
    C. any referral fees or remuneration he or she may receive from others, such as attorneys or title companies.
    D. the identities of the principal, even when instructed not to.

# STUDENT NOTES

CHAPTER 9

ANTITRUST
(NO! WE ALL CHARGE 7 PERCENT!)

○ **CHAPTER OVERVIEW**
Real estate education and training classes available to the real estate practitioner traditionally have been focused on licensing course work, as well as sales-training-type seminars. Increasingly important to the practitioner, however, are a firm understanding of and appreciation for the competitive environment in which one applies one's trade. It is therefore imperative that antitrust education be included in the real estate professional's course curriculum.

○ **LEARNING OBJECTIVES**
By the time you have finished studying this chapter, you should be able to:
1) Discuss the major federal antitrust acts that affect the real estate business, including the Sherman Act, the Federal Trade Commission Act, and the Clayton Act.
2) Describe the major categories of antitrust violations and their application to the real estate industry.
3) Identify the kinds of activities that could bring to a real estate practitioner allegations of antitrust practice.
4) Describe the two primary precipitating causes of antitrust suits alleging conspiracies.
5) Define price fixing and give examples of the various forms of price fixing that could be associated with the practice of real estate.
6) Describe the two forms of group boycotts and give examples of each.
7) Identify the kinds of individuals who might be considered "nontraditional" brokers and their relationship to group boycotts.
8) Determine the need for and the materials and programs available to develop an in-office antitrust compliance program.

○ **5 CASES TO JUDGE**

○ **10-QUESTION DIAGNOSTIC QUIZ**

CHAPTER 9

ANTITRUST
(NO! WE ALL CHARGE 7 PERCENT!)

RING! RING! RING!

Real Estate Office:	"Happy Acres Realty, may I help you?"
Caller:	"Yes, I am inquiring about marketing my property. Can you connect me with one of your sales associates?"
Real Estate Office:	"Of course. One moment, please."
Suzie Salesperson:	"This is Suzie Salesperson. May I help you?"
Caller:	"Can you tell me what your firm can do to market my property and how much you would charge?"
Suzie Salesperson:	"Most certainly. What is your name, please, and where are you located?"
Caller:	"Sara Seller, and the property is here in Glen Ellyn."
Suzie Salesperson:	"Let me tell you about some of the services Happy Acres Realty can offer you to market your property in the shortest time and at the highest price. Would that be of interest to you, Sara Seller?"
Sara Seller:	"Yes!"
Suzie Salesperson:	[Gives the seller vital information on herself and her firm and closes for the listing appointment.]
Sara Seller:	"And what is your commission rate for those services, Suzie?"
Suzie Salesperson:	"We charge 7 percent of the sales price of the property."
Sara Seller:	"I have called a number of real estate offices in town. Does anyone charge less?"
Suzie Salesperson:	"No! We all charge 7 percent!"

Every day in the real estate business, salespersons, brokers, leasing agents, and landlords are engaging in activities that, while seemingly innocent, are nevertheless endangering the entire profession. Antitrust activities are broad and ever present. It is imperative that all real estate professionals become knowledgeable about this topic and implement sound business practices to avoid potential lawsuits.

Suppose that the caller mentioned above was, in fact, not a prospective seller, but an investigator from the Federal Trade Commission. If so, you, your broker, and most probably every real estate professional in the market area that you serve are probably about to be accused of violation of antitrust activities pursuant to the Sherman Antitrust Act.

INTRODUCTION

The modern era in the application of antitrust laws to brokers began in 1950 with the Supreme Court opinion in the case of *United States v. National Association of Real Estate Boards*. Both criminal and civil actions had been brought against the Washington, D.C., Board of REALTORS® and the National Association of Real Estate Boards for price fixing under Article 3 of the Sherman Antitrust Act. At the conclusion of this case, the Supreme Court held that the broker members of the board had, over a wide range of brokerage services, maintained commission rates that had been fixed in a schedule of commission rates adopted by the board and that no business could be solicited at lower rates.

That practice constituted illegal price fixing, a *per se* unreasonable restraint of trade under the act. As a result, no Board or association of real estate practitioners can or should recommend a schedule of commission rates that its members should follow when conducting their business.

From that day to this, the real estate industry has come under federal and public scrutiny on the issues relating to antitrust, and it now faces the legal complexities and encounters associated with those issues.

FEDERAL LAWS

The government's purpose in federal antitrust laws is to preserve competition, discourage monopolies, and control the exercise of monopoly powers. This is the power that an individual, group of individuals, or group of companies has to fix prices and exclude competition in a particular market. By doing so, the government defends the production and distribution of goods and services in the most economical and efficient manner by preserving free and competitive markets. In this way, we protect our free enterprise economic system by promoting consumer fairness, which ultimately gives American consumers a wider choice of products and services of the highest quality and at the lowest price.

THE SHERMAN ANTITRUST ACT OF 1890

Section 1 of this federal antitrust legislation (see Figure 9-1) provides that *every* contract, combination in the form of a trust or otherwise, or conspiracy in restraint of trade or commerce among the states or with foreign nations, is declared illegal. Every person who shall monopolize or attempt to monopolize, or combine or conspire with another person to monopolize any part of trade or commerce among the several states, or with a foreign nation, shall be deemed to be guilty. On the following page are the sections of the Sherman Act applicable to the real estate industry. Exemptions to the act are those industries that are affected by being in the public interest and/or regulated by other government agencies, such as the power, banking, insurance, airlines, radio, and television industries, union activities, agricultural cooperatives, and exporters.

The Sherman Act specifically has jurisdiction over only interstate (between states) activities. While it is true that most real estate transactions are local (intrastate) in nature, the Supreme Court has ruled that they still fall under the Sherman Act because the companies that finance and insure the titles in real estate transactions are usually involved in interstate commerce (*McClain v. Real Estate Board of New Orleans*).

Rule of Reason. Rather than making a literal interpretation of the act that would strike down each and every restraint, the U.S. Supreme Court has applied a reasonableness test in ascertaining illegality in many situations. In effect, the rule of reason permits the court to examine the reasons the defendant's business engaged in the activities that appear to be in violation of the Sherman Act. The rule of reason encompasses the "nature" of the alleged restraint, its effect on market conditions, and the purpose the restraint is intended to serve.

Per Se Illegality. Opposite the rule of reason is conduct that would violate a federal act *per se* (in and of itself), which means that some conduct is illegal based on the act itself and does not need to be subjected to a case-by-case analysis and inquiry as to whether there are reasonable means of accomplishing an objective without unduly suppressing trade. Agreements to establish and maintain prices, agreements to refuse to deal with third parties (boycotts), agreements to allocate market share, and agreements to require tie-in sales (the customer must purchase an unwanted item in order to purchase the product the customer wants) are all considered illegal *per se* violations.

FIG 9-1 SHERMAN ACT

Sec. 1. Every contract, combination in the form of trust or otherwise, or conspiracy, in restraint of trade or commerce among the several States, or with foreign nations, is hereby declared to be illegal: *Provided*, That nothing herein contained shall render illegal, contracts or agreements prescribing minimum prices for the resale of a commodity which bears the label or container or which bears the trademark, brand, or name of the producer or distributor of such commodity and which is in free and open competition with commodities of the same general class produced or distributed by others, when contracts or agreements of that description are lawful as applied to intrastate transactions, under any statute, law, or public policy now or hereafter in effect in any State, Territory, or the District of Columbia in which such resale is to be made, or to which the commodity is to be transported for such resale, and the making of such contracts or agreements shall not be an unfair method of competition under section 5, as amended and supplemented, of the act entitled "An Act to create a Federal Trade Commission, to define its powers and duties, and for other purposes," approved September 26, 1914: *Provided further*, That the preceding proviso shall not make lawful any contract or agreement, providing for the establishment or maintenance of minimum resale prices on any commodity herein involved, between manufacturers, or between producers, or between wholesalers, or between brokers, or between factors, or between retailers, or between persons, firms, or corporations in competition with each other. Every person who shall make any contract or engage in any combination or conspiracy hereby declared to be illegal shall be deemed guilty of a misdemeanor, and, on conviction thereof, shall be punished by fine not exceeding one million dollars, or by imprisonment not exceeding one year, or by both said punishments, in the discretion of the court.

Sec. 2. Every person who shall monopolize, or attempt to monopolize, or combine or conspire with any other person or persons, to monopolize any part of the trade of commerce among the several States, or with foreign nations, shall be deemed guilty of a misdemeanor, and, on conviction thereof, shall be punished by fine not exceeding one million dollars, or by imprisonment not exceeding one year, or by both said punishments, in the discretion of the court.

Sec. 3. Every contract, combination in form of trust or otherwise, or conspiracy, in restraint of trade or commerce in any Territory of the United States or of the District of Columbia, or in restraint of trade or commerce between any such Territory and another, or between any such Territory or Territories and any State or States or the District of Columbia, or with foreign nations, or between the District of Columbia and any State or States or foreign nations, is declared illegal. Every person who shall make any such contract or engage in any such combination or conspiracy, shall be deemed guilty of a misdemeanor, and, on conviction thereof, shall be punished by fine not exceeding one million dollars, or by imprisonment not exceeding one year, or by both said punishments, in the discretion of the court.

Sec. 4. The several district courts of the United States are hereby invested with jurisdiction to present and restrain violations of this act; and it shall be the duty of the several district attorneys of the United States, in their respective districts, under the direction of the Attorney General, to institute proceedings in equity to prevent and restrain such violations. Such proceedings may be by way of petition setting forth the case and praying that such violation shall be enjoined or otherwise prohibited. When the parties complained of shall have been duly notified of such petition the court shall proceed, as soon as may be, to the hearing and determination of the case; and pending such petition and before final decree, the court may at any time make such temporary restraining order or prohibition as shall be deemed just in the premises.

Sec. 5. Whenever it shall appear to the court before which any proceeding under section four of this act may be pending, that the ends of justice require that other parties should be brought before the court, the court may cause them to summoned, whether they reside in the district in which the court is held or not; and subpoenas to that end may be served in any district by the marshall thereof.

Sec. 6. Any property owned under any contract or by any combination, or pursuant to any conspiracy (and being the subject thereof) mentioned in section one of this act, and being in the course of transportation from one State to another, or to a foreign country, shall be forfeited to the United States, and may be seized and condemned by like proceedings as those provided by law for the forfeiture, seizure, and condemnation of property imported into the United States contrary to law.

Sec. 8. That the word "person," or "persons," wherever used in this act shall be deemed to include corporations and associations existing under or authorized by the laws of either the United States, the laws of any of the Territories, the laws of any State, or the laws of any foreign country.

FEDERAL TRADE COMMISSION ACT OF 1914
This act, passed by Congress, created the Federal Trade Commission and empowered it to identify any anti-competitive behavior that should be prohibited as "unfair methods of competition" and to proceed against violators of the Sherman and Clayton Acts. The FTC is only authorized to issue cease-and-desist orders, directing the respondent to terminate conduct deemed to restrict competition unfairly or to deceive consumers. Unlike the Sherman Act, under the FTC Act, a company or individual cannot recover damages and/or attorney's fees.

CLAYTON ACT OF 1914
The Clayton Act was passed by Congress to supplement and augment the Sherman Act by specifically outlawing certain practices that had been ruled by the courts not to be barred by the Sherman Act. Section 3 of the Clayton Act makes it unlawful for any person engaged in interstate commerce to *fix a price for commodities,* or to engage in *tying contracts* or *exclusive dealing contracts.*

Because Section 3 applies only to commodities, it does not apply to exclusive dealing agreements or tying contracts in agreements involving real estate, intangibles, or services. Such agreements must be challenged under the Sherman Act. Section 7 of the act was amended in 1950, making the statute much more stringent in the regulation of mergers. Congress intended the Clayton Act to be a preventative measure. As a result, only a *probability* of significant antitrust competitive effect must be shown for most Clayton Act violations. Because the Clayton Act deals only with probable harms to competition, there are no criminal penalties for violating its provisions. Private plaintiffs, however, can sue for treble damages or injunctive relief if they are injured or threatened with injury by a violation of the act's provisions.

Tying Agreements. These are agreements that require a buyer to purchase one product (the tied product) from a seller as condition of purchasing another product from the seller (the tying product). This, therefore, would prevent the buyer from purchasing the tied product from the seller's competitors.

Exclusive Dealing Arrangements. When buyers agree to purchase one of seller's products or services exclusively from seller, they are in effect agreeing not to purchase similar items from seller's competitors. Not all exclusive dealing agreements are illegal; only those that "substantially lessen competition."

ROBINSON-PATMAN ACT
This antitrust act was passed by Congress in 1936 for the purpose of greatly expanding the original prohibition against price discrimination, which was contained in the Clayton Act. Section 2(a) of this act makes it unlawful for any person engaged in *interstate commerce to discriminate in price between purchasers of commodities of like grade and quality.* The act also specifically applies to price discrimination of commodities. Price discrimination of intangibles, like real estate services, must be challenged under the Sherman Act as a restraint of trade or attempt to monopolize, or it must be challenged under the FTC Act (as an unfair method of competition.)

CLASS ACTION SUITS
Rule 23 of the Federal Rule of Civil Procedures allows lawsuits to proceed on behalf of a class or group of persons similarly situated or harmed. Rule 23 has been frequently invoked in antitrust cases involving the real estate business by individuals who, as a class, are accusing price conspiracy or commission fixing by real estate brokers.

SANCTIONS
Violators of the federal antitrust laws found guilty under the Sherman Act may be subject to injunction, forced divisions or divestitures of assets, and/or government seizure of property. Criminal penalties against individuals can result in maximum fines of $100,000 and/or up to three years in jail. Penalties against corporations can include fines of up to $1 million. Additionally, TREBLE damages (three times the loss) in actual damages plus attorney's fees and court costs may be assessed the offending party.

ENFORCEMENT

The following bodies enforce and or bring suit against violators of the federal antitrust laws:

U.S. Department of Justice. Actions can be both civil, whereby the FTC seeks to enjoin future illegal activity, and criminal, whereby the FTC seeks to impose both fines and imprisonment.

Private Parties. Any individual or class of individuals (competitors, sellers, buyers) harmed by the activity can bring suit seeking treble damages.

Federal Trade Commission. Created and enforced by the Federal Trade Commission Act, the commission is an independent federal agency, headed by five commissioners appointed by the President and confirmed by the Senate. The FTC has a variety of legal devices for ensuring compliance with federal statutes and for punishing violators of those statutes. The three most common devices are voluntary compliance, issuance of trade regulation rules, and adjudicative proceedings.

Antitrust Improvements Act of 1976. State Attorneys General were given authority to act in the capacity of *parens patriae* (protector of the citizens). They can sue on behalf of a general class of citizens believed to have been wronged by price fixing. The group of persons does not have to be specifically identified, as in a class action suit, and members do not have to give permission for a suit to be filed. If an award is made, members of the public can later file a claim for their portion. All unclaimed monies accrue to the state treasury.

Interstate Commerce. In actions brought under the federal law, plaintiffs must show the violation's effect on interstate commerce in order to establish federal court jurisdiction. The first jurisdictional test is the "in commerce test"—does the alleged violation of the act occur within the flow of interstate commerce? The second test is whether the local activity, allegedly violative of the act, substantially affects interstate commerce—the "substantial effect test."

Most antitrust violations, particularly real estate price fixing, would probably meet one or the other test and would therefore be a federal matter. However, some courts have held that membership rules that exclude a broker from access to an MLS do not come under the laws of interstate commerce. These types of cases tend to be tried on the state level.

State Laws. The Illinois laws regarding antitrust activities are similar to the federal laws and are enforced by the Illinois Attorney General.

AVOIDING MISCONDUCT

The real estate business has at its foundation the service of bringing together parties to a real estate transaction whose objectives are to transfer, lease, exchange, or otherwise accomplish a conveyance of rights in real property between parties for compensation. As a result, a network of cooperating interests has developed for the accomplishment of the broker's goals in delivering service on behalf of client's and customer's interests. Simultaneously, the real estate practitioner is competing to offer his or her specific real estate service to customers and clients.

This dual tradition of cooperation and competition presents opportunities for antitrust misconduct, almost on a daily basis. The major antitrust areas of concern in the real estate business of which real estate professionals must be aware are: conspiracies, price fixing, group boycotts, territorial allocations, list-back agreements, third-party purchase contacts, condominium sales, full-service companies, home-purchase contracts, and comparative advertising. It is important that, as you study this chapter on antitrust, you draw parallels from the information you are studying to how these concepts might manifest themselves in your daily activities. *Keep in mind that antitrust issues do not only apply to the residential broker or salesperson, but to all real estate practitioners.*

Therefore, when reading this chapter, the word *commission* could also mean management fee, appraisal fee, home inspection fee, or leasing fee. The word *board* could mean any association of real estate competitors, including appraisal associations, management associations, and/or commercial/investment brokerage associations. A *licensee* could be a broker, salesperson, appraiser, property manger, leasing agent, or home inspector.

CONSPIRACIES

A conspiracy occurs when two or more competitors agree to conspire or to act in concert to accomplish some objective that has the effect of fixing prices or in some other way lessening competition. This constitutes a *per se* violation of antitrust laws. Conspiracies are unlawful agreements, which may be oral or written, formal or informal, expressed or implied, and may be proved on the basis of circumstantial evidence or may be inferred from a course of conduct. In the real estate business, there are two primary precipitating causes of antitrust suits alleging conspiracy:

1. A substantial degree of uniformity in the commission rates or other price changes for brokerage or other real estate services in a given marketplace.
2. A substantial degree of uniformity in the amount of a real estate commission for fee that is offered to a cooperating broker in a cooperative sale for his or her services in a given marketplace.

If rates in real estate industry have been stable over time, this may give the impression that the fees are set pursuant to commission schedules. It is important that sales agents and brokers present their firm's commission rates or management fees in such a manner as to confirm that the rates were set *independently* by their real estate firm. *Never* refer to the pricing policy of competitors or *any other organization or association as setting, prohibiting, or recommending a commission schedule or compensation amount.*

The keys to avoiding antitrust vulnerability based on the fees a broker establishes are:
- Establish the fee unilaterally without consultation or discussion with persons affiliated with any competing firm.
- Insure that when the company's brokers or salespersons discuss fees with actual or potential clients, they use words that convey the impression to the listener that the company is pricing its services independently.
- Never announce to any competitor, however casually, your intention to adjust your fees prior to your action.

Commission rates and fees may indeed result in uniformity, because most commission rates charged reflect a common economic result in the marketplace and are merely paralleling activity by competitors.

The licensee should therefore point out (to those inquiring about the amount of commission or fee) the relation of the commission to the value of the services the client will receive, and how the commission or fee paid by the client will benefit the client (by a faster transaction and competent, professional service). Learn to sell your service and to explain why the fees or commissions you charge justify that service.

No group of competitor brokers should recommend or make mandatory commission splits or referral arrangements between cooperating members. Listing contracts, sales contracts, and other real estate business forms or publications created by individuals or by Boards of REALTORS®, MLSs, or any other group of industry competitors should *not* include preprinted commission rates, cooperating commission splits, or other "terms" that might create an inference that a conspiracy exists to encourage a customary, fixed, or recommended split or commission.

PROTECTION FROM CHARGES OF CONSPIRACY

Brokers or their employees must never discuss or reveal their intention concerning fees or other competitive business activities with or to competitors. While salespersons and brokers working for the same firm or company can discuss commission rates, splits, and other pricing policies relating to *their* office among themselves, they should never discuss these items with any competitor. To avoid the appearance of impropriety, all decisions relating to changes in the firm's commission rates charged to members of the public should be clearly documented as a necessary business decision based on the economic condition of a particular real estate firm.

Price Fixing. Price fixing is a subset of the issue of conspiracy and includes all agreements that have the effect of "raising, depressing, fixing, or stabilizing prices." The commission rates, management fees, tenant fees, appraisal fees, home inspection fees, or other compensation are not the only "price" that may be fixed. Price fixing can also be extended to include an agreement to fix the economic term of the listing or management agreement. This includes the length of time of the listing contract or management contract, the type of listing taken (exclusive right-to-sell, open, or exclusive agency), or the formula upon which compensation will be based (flat fee, percentage of sale price, or other variable percentage). Firms must have established polices on the length, type, or variability of commission rates and other fee structures. These listing-term fee structures and other contract conditions cannot be made company policy *because other firms are following them*. Licensees and their agents must learn to explain these kinds of policies as those of their office and not as a result of concerted efforts among competitors in the marketplace.

Subagency Splits. While most of the time we think of price fixing as relating to the amount or price we charge a customer or client, it can also apply to the price one pays for goods and services. In the real estate business, this has been extended to include conspiracies among competitors to fix the compensation paid for the cooperative efforts of other brokers, which would be a *per se* violation of the antitrust laws.

Brokers must determine their cooperative compensation policies in the same unilateral and independent manner that they establish their commission fees charged to clients. Listing and cooperating brokers may discuss or negotiate the compensation they pay each other, but they should never discuss this in the presence of third parties, and never as the policy of any association of real estate professionals.

Independent Contractor and Employee Compensation. A licensee is free to determine what kinds of compensation polices he or she will offer to those that work for him or her. Every licensee who is engaged in activities under the Illinois License Act must have a written employment/independent contractor agreement with his or her employing broker. These agreements typically spell out terms of employment, including compensation structure, fees paid, duties and responsibilities, and other terms and conditions relating to the hiring and dismissal of staff. These contracts should be developed independently from any other competitor and not with any consultation or discussion with a competitor. Fees and compensation paid to employees are strictly a matter of internal office or firm policy. Like the cooperating commission splits arrangement, if the compensation that you are paying an employee should be adjusted, then this decision should be made for independent business reasons and documented to the licensee's employees and retained in the firm's records.

GROUP BOYCOTTS

Allegations of group boycotts are the most common antitrust claims to be asserted against real estate brokers, and they are held to be *per se* violations of the antitrust laws. A group boycott can take one of two forms:
  1. Denying a business access to goods or services necessary for it to compete in the marketplace. (For example, all the brokers in a given area refuse to advertise their listings in the local paper because they feel the paper's rates are too high. By banding together they feel they can get the newspaper to lower its rates.)

2. When two or more brokers agree to refuse to cooperate or maintain a relationship with a third party for the purpose of inducing the third party to conform its behavior to the desires of the boycotters. (For example, two brokerage firms, Apple Realty and Orange Realty, agree not to show the listings of Tree Realty, because Tree Realty's cooperating commission splits are less than 50/50. The boycott agreement will last until Tree Realty's splits are at a more "acceptable" division.)

Refusal to Deal with Third Parties or Nontraditional Broker. A third party or "nontraditional" broker might be one who:
1. does not affiliate with a particular association/board or group of real estate professionals.
2. charges a flat fee for his or her services or is a competitor who discounts commissions that are charged to clients or customers.
3. assists "For Sale By Owners."
4. has a variable commission policy.
5. has a less traditional commission split policy with cooperating brokers or a nontraditional compensation policy with his or her salespersons or employees.

APPLICABILITY OF BOYCOTT LAWS TO THE OPERATION OF REAL ESTATE ASSOCIATIONS
Real estate industry members may combine to form a trade association to upgrade industry standards or to increase industry efficiency. Furthermore, a trade association that has these purposes and objectives may also adopt reasonable rules and regulations designed to implement them. Thus, when a trade organization demonstrates that its activities are not designed to reduce or eliminate competition, the validity of its rules and membership criteria will be judged by the rule of reason, even if enforcement of those rules will produce an effect resembling a boycott on competitors who cannot or will not comply with the association's membership criteria or rules.

The legality of nearly every facet of operation of a Board or association of REALTORS® or real estate professionals depends on application of this doctrine. A Board or association of real estate professionals faces a threat of alleged boycott whenever it applies its membership criteria, enforces its ethical codes of conduct, conducts arbitration proceedings, or denies a nonmember access to its MLS or any other service or benefit offered by the association rules.

A Board or other real estate association should NEVER:
1. establish or even recommend a commission rate schedule.
2. establish or even recommend a schedule of commission splits between competitors who are cooperating in a real estate transaction.
3. boycott any nontraditional competitor.
4. establish minimum amounts of time, commission rates, or fees or splits to be charged a client or customer for any member services that the Board or association offers, e.g., MLS.
5. establish or recommend the division of the marketing area between competitors/members.
6. restrict any member from comparative advertising services.

Two prominent cases involving group boycotts where certain boards refused to allow MLS services to nonmembers are summarized below and indicate the trend that courts seem to be taking regarding this antitrust issue.

THE *GRILLO* CASE
Historically, the connection between the local brokerage Board and the MLS has been close; most MLSs, in fact, are subsidiary corporations of the Board. Some Boards were established for the sole purpose of operating an MLS.

The leading case testing the propriety of local Board control over an MLS is *Grillo v. Board of REALTORS® of Plainfield Area.* The plaintiff, who was not a member of the local Board, sought membership in the local multiple listing service but was several times denied admission. He did not seek a judgment compelling the board to admit him. In his petition, he sought to enjoin the prohibition on nonmembers using the Board's MLS and asserted that the Board's "restriction on membership [is] an important element in the success of those business methods which . . . are illegal and harmful to him and to other licensed brokers who are not members of the board."

After reviewing the conditions of Board membership, the Supreme Court of New Jersey stated that "the Plaintiff and others who are nonmembers are placed at a competitive disadvantage as a result of the defendant's action in combination." The court characterized the restrictions to MLS access as tending toward a concerted refusal to deal with, or a group boycott of, the plaintiff. The court decided that a rule of reason rather than a *per se* rule applied in this case.

Under the rule of reason the court ruled that the argument of the Board that it was protecting the public from unqualified brokers, would not prevail as against "the public harm produced by the alleged combination." [*Grillo v. Board of REALTORS® of Plainfield Area*, 91 N.J.Super. 202, 219 A.2d 635, 644 (1966), noted at 21 Rutgers L. Rev. 547 (1967)]

THOMPSON v. DEKALB COUNTY (GEORGIA) BOARD OF REALTORS®
In September 1991, the 11th Circuit Court of Appeals handed down a landmark ruling that could jeopardize the link between mandatory REALTOR® Board membership and access to REALTOR® owned and operated multiple listing systems. The lawsuit was brought in 1988 by non-REALTOR® Fletcher Thompson and the Empire Board of Real Estate Brokers (a group of independent brokers) against the Metropolitan Multi-List Inc., a subsidiary of the DeKalb County (Georgia) Board of REALTORS®. The independent brokers argued that the Metro Multi-List, by insisting that MLS members also belong to the DeKalb REALTOR® Board, were engaged in a discriminatory boycott.

The court agreed and held for the plaintiffs, and directed all REALTOR® Boards in the states of Georgia, Mississippi, and Florida that they could no longer require individual real estate brokers and salespeople to be members of the local REALTOR® Boards as a requirement to receiving MLS services. This would mean that individuals in those states would not have to pay membership dues to *both* the Board and the MLS, but in fact could join the MLS separate and apart from joining the REALTOR® association.

Thus, the link between the MLS and the requirement to join and pay dues for NAR, state, and local Boards of REALTOR® membership has been broken. The National Association of REALTORS® has asked the U.S. Supreme Court to overturn the ruling, which if allowed to stand could open up every REALTOR®-owned multiple listing system in the country to nonmembers, jeopardizing the economic health of local REALTOR® Boards everywhere and potentially eroding the clout of the world's largest trade association. [*Thompson, et al. v. DeKalb Board of REALTORS® Inc. et al.* 1990-2 Trade Cases (CCH) 69,173 (N.D. GA. 1990)]

TERRITORIAL ALLOCATIONS
When competitors eliminate or reduce competition between them with agreements to limit or restrict territories in which they market their goods or services, they create a *per se* violation of the antitrust acts.

Several brokers, for instance, might agree to divide the market into exclusive territories, which would preclude the parties in the agreement from taking listings and/or cooperating in the sale of listings located in another broker's territory. While such agreements are theoretically possible in the real estate business, they would practicably be unlikely.

The more likely source of antitrust concern for real estate broker Boards of REALTORS® lies in the NAR's assignments of Board territorial jurisdictions. Most boards limit participation in their MLS to Board members. Similarly, most Boards have a membership criterion that requires that an active member applicant have an office within the board's territorial jurisdictional boundaries. The combined effect of these two rules is to require a broker who desires access to a Board's MLS to open an office within the Board's jurisdiction.

In some cases, however, offices on the far boundaries of a Board are required to join the Board whose jurisdiction they lie in, even though the Board's jurisdiction does not conform to the office's natural market area. Thus, the firm must also join another contiguous Board, where the firm would get the benefit of a MLS. Boards have, until now, effectively handled these situations by allowing for nonresident membership. In the new age of antitrust and real estate associations, these practices are sure to be challenged.

TYING CONTRACTS

Any contact for sale of land that requires a buyer to also purchase other goods or services from the seller or some other person raises tying issues. One of the Supreme Court's most exhaustive opinions concerned the legality of tying arrangements involving the sale of land. In 1870, Congress granted to the Northern Pacific Railway over 40 million acres of land to facilitate construction of a railroad. Over the next three quarters of a century, the railroad sold or leased most of its holdings. In a large number of the sale or lease contracts, the railroad included a provision requiring that all commodities produced or manufactured on the land be shipped over the Northern Pacific Railroad lines. In a case brought by the government, the Supreme Court held that these preferential routing clauses were illegal tying arrangements. [*Northern Pacific Railway Co. v. United States, 356 U.S. 1 (1958)*]

List-Back Agreements. As a result of the Northern Pacific case, real estate brokers should treat with caution any contract for the sale of land that conditions the sale on the buyer's agreement that the purchaser must engage the services of the seller or some other person. An example of the type of sales contract that may be vulnerable to a tying attack is a contract for the sale of subdivision lots, which contains a "list-back" clause in it. Under a typical list-back clause, a developer who also happens to be a real estate broker will place a condition on the sale of a new home in one of his or her subdivisions that the buyer will list the home with the builder's brokerage company if and when the home is sold by the buyer.

Third-Party Purchase Contracts. Relocation companies typically agree to purchase a transferee's home at a price equal to the average of two or more appraisals. The relocation firm then assists the transferee in selecting and purchasing another home in a new location.

A tying contract might be created in this instance if the relocation firm requires, as a condition of acquiring the transferee's existing home, that the transferee also agree to purchase a new home through a brokerage firm owned by or affiliated with the relocation firm. The "tying" service would be the acquisition of the transferee's home and the "tied" service would be the brokerage services required to be used by the transferee in purchasing a new home.

Condominium Sales. A number of lawsuits have been filed against developers and licensees alleging that the sale of a condominium unit has been "tied" to the lease of specific recreational facilities or to the use of a specific management agent to manage the units in the condominium complex. A condominium unit sale might be tied to the lease of a swimming pool or parking area or to the owner's acceptance of the developer's choice of a particular management agent. For instance, in order to purchase the unit, you must lease a particular parking area (or recreational facility), or after you purchase a unit, the condominium units' homeowners association must accept the developer's choice of a management agent. Most court cases have found that these types of so-called tying arrangements were not illegal—particularly where the developers did not have any ownership interest in the property-management company.

The real estate practitioner should be aware that no precise formula exists for determining the antitrust legality of a contract for sale of real estate that binds the buyer to use other services provided by the seller or some other person or firm. Questions concerning whether the contract involves the sale of one or two products whether the seller has "market power" in the land to which the other services are tied, or whether the defendant has an economic interest in the sale of both the tied and tying products, are questions of fact that must be determined on the merits of each individual case.

Full-Service Home Purchase Companies. Another potential tying problem in the real estate industry is the apparent trend toward "full-service" real estate companies. These are firms that combine brokerage services with mortgage services, title or homeowner's insurance, termite inspection, home inspection, home protection contracts, or even legal services. While antitrust statutes do not prohibit a firm from offering these services separately or as a package, the antitrust laws could be invoked if a firm conditioned the sale of one or more of these services on a customer's agreement to buy another service.

Comparative Advertising. Federal and state courts have generally held that the advertising of professional services and fees benefits the potential customers or clients and generally encourages competition. Real estate trade associations, therefore, would be advised not to restrict their member activities as they relate to marketing and promotion of services or fees to the public. Trade associations could, however, set ethical standards that members must follow, that relate to truthful or deceptive advertising practices.

Office Compliance Programs. Brokers and salespeople must keep in mind that the broker is responsible for the acts of the salespersons employed by him or her whether the salespersons are independent contractors or employees. The fact that a broker did not authorize a salesperson to act in a particular manner or did not have actual knowledge of the salesperson's conduct will not relieve the broker from liability in a antitrust case. Ignorance is never an excuse for any violation of the law. It is the duty and responsibility of all brokers and salespersons to know, understand, and keep continually informed about current antitrust laws and practices.

To protect themselves against allegations of antitrust activity, all real estate licensees and the offices they are associated with should participate in continuous and practical educational office training seminars relating to antitrust topics. Too many licensees feel that the issue of antitrust is an issue only involving the firm, their broker, or others in the real estate business and does not affect them as practitioners. Nothing could be further from the truth.

ANTITRUST TRAINING AND EDUCATIONAL MATERIALS

The National Association of REALTORS® has developed materials for use by all real estate industry practitioners pertaining to information on the topic of antitrust and real estate. These excellent educational materials can be used in office antitrust training programs.

Antitrust and Real Estate—Revised and Updated for the 90s is a comprehensive examination of antitrust laws and the implications on real estate brokerage and organized real estate. Topics include price fixing, group boycott, territorial allocations, tying contracts, and strategies for compliance. An instructor training kit and videotape are included with this program.

Antitrust Reference Manual is an easy-to-use and easy-to-understand 68-page handbook designed for use by brokers, association leadership, legal counsel, and real estate instructors. Call 1-800-874-6500 to order these materials by phone.

DANGEROUS WORDS OR PHRASES

The following are some examples of words or phrases that real estate professionals sometimes use and the probable category of antitrust violation into which they fall. It is strongly recommended that no licensee should ever use these statements.

Price Fixing

"Our office would like to charge a lower commission [fee], but the local Board [real estate association] has a rule that we all charge the same amount."

"The MLS will not accept any listing for less than 90 days."

"Commission rates [real estate fees] are recommended by the Illinois Real Estate Commission."

"X percent is the going rate in our area."

"Shop around, but it won't do any good, because all the firms in the area charge the same amount."

Group Boycott

"Don't list with XYZ Company; they're not members of the real estate association [MLS], and no one will show your property."

"The best way to deal with XYZ Company is to boycott him and not show any of his listings."

"The local real estate association requires that all broker member offices force their salespeople to join."

Territorial Allocation

"If your firm wants to take the north side of town, mine will take the south side."

"Their firm is from out of the area and isn't located in our Board [MLS] jurisdiction."

"You're not from our area, so I can't allow you to present the contract."

Tying Contract

"This agreement provides that after you purchase the home, you are required to list it with our company when it is sold."

"If you purchase your home through our company, you must also use the mortgage and title services that we offer."

"As an out-bound transferee, you are required to purchase a new home from our company in the town you are being transferred to."

Conspiracy

"Something has got to be sour about that company; nobody can pay their salespeople that kind of split and still make any money."

"When I see XYZ Company's signs, I drive my prospects down another street."

"If she were really a professional, she would join the local real estate association."

"He doesn't have an MAI [GRI, CRB, CRS] designation, so you should not do business with him."

CASES TO JUDGE

1. Plaintiff was a real estate appraiser and a member of the American Institute of Real Estate Appraisers, a subsidiary of the National Association of REALTORS®. He was involved with a disciplinary proceeding brought about by the state chapter of the Association and was expelled from membership in the Institute. He thereafter brought an antitrust suit alleging restraint of trade (a group boycott) by Institute members who found him unqualified to do appraisal work for the largest mortgage lenders in the state. Plaintiff alleged that the alleged agreement among Institute members to keep for themselves the appraisal business generated by large lenders amounts to an unlawful group boycott of appraisers like himself who are not members in good standing of the Institute. The Institute disputes the existence of the alleged agreement. The district court dismissed the boycott claim.

    Were they right? [*McDonnell v. Michigan Chapter No. 10 Am. Inst. of Real Estate Appraisers of the Natl. Assn. of REALTORS®*, 587 F. 2nd 7, 8(6th Cir. 1978)]

2. A leading broker in the county invited five competitors, all from the largest broker firms in the county, to a dinner at his country club. After dinner, he announced that his firm was going to raise its brokerage commission by 1 percent. His announcement provoked a discussion. Subsequently, all of the firms represented did in fact raise their commission rates by the 1 percent announced at the dinner.

    Any problem with antitrust? [*Montgomery County Real Estate Antitrust Litigation*, 542 F. Supp. (D.Md. 1978), settlement confirmed 83 F.R.F. 305 (1979)]

3. A California broker decided to change his commission schedule from a percentage of the selling price to a "flat fee of $1,200." As a result of this, the flat-fee broker would pay other brokers $400 of his $1,200 if those brokers procured a buyer for the flat-fee broker's listings. In retaliation, the other brokers in the Board (who customarily split 50/50 on a 6 percent commission with cooperating brokers) notified the flat-fee broker that henceforth they were going to pay him only $400 as a subagency com-mission rather than the customary 50 percent of the 6 percent commission.

    Did the court find conspiracy in this case? [*People v. National Association of REALTORS®* (San Diego Board of REALTORS®)].

4. The National Society of Professional Engineers' Code of Ethics had prohibited Society members from engaging in competitive bidding for engineering projects. The Society contended that the ethical injunction against bidding was reasonable because it protected the public from inferior engineering work that might result if engineers were permitted to compete on price.

    In your opinion, was the Society's ethical standard a violation of the Sherman Act? [*Professional Engineers v. United States*, 435 U.S. 679 (1978)]

5. Two home builders and a real estate broker formed a corporation that acquired a tract of land. The corporation subdivided the tract and sold lots to builders for use as home sites. The corporation appointed one of its builder/shareholders as the exclusive marketing agent for the subdivision and included a clause in the sales contract of each lot requiring the marketing agent to be paid a 6 percent commission on the sales price of the finished house constructed on the lot. Subsequently, purchasers contracted with the other builder/shareholders to build a house and, even though they paid the required commission at closing, they also filed suit alleging that the required commission represented a conspiracy among the corporation's shareholders to artificially inflate the price of the home.

    Would this be considered an illegal tying arrangement and a violation of the antitrust laws? [*Ballo v. James S. Black Co., Inc., et al.*, 39 Wn.App.21, 692 P.2d 182 (1984)]

10-QUESTION DIAGNOSTIC QUIZ

1. Commission rates for the sale of property are usually determined by:
   A. the local association/Board of REALTORS®.
   B. the local MLS.
   C. the Department of Professional Regulation.
   D. mutual agreement between seller and broker.

2. The "going listing" commission rate in your area for listing real property is:
   A. 5 percent.
   B. 6 percent.
   C. 7 percent.
   D. negotiable in every instance between seller and broker.

3. Which of the following is NOT a violation of the Antitrust Act?
   A. A prospective seller, who wishes to negotiate the commission rate charged when listing her property, is told by the listing salesperson, "The commission rate we charge is the same as all of the other firms in town."
   B. Broker Smith calls a meeting of his salespersons and announces that because of rising operating and marketing costs for his firm, his office's new policy will mean raising commission rates to prospective sellers by 1 percent.
   C. Salesperson Jansen receives an offer on a property that is listed in the MLS of which she is a member. She knows that the selling office with the offer is not a member of her MLS, and she refuses to present it.
   D. Broker Adams charges a flat fee to any seller who lists with his office. Because of this, all the other brokers in the area mutually agree to split any cooperating commissions with him on a 30/70 basis—but 50/50 for the brokers who charge the "going" percentage rate.

4. The primary federal law regulating antitrust, restraint of trade monopolistic practices, and price fixing in the real estate business is the:
   A. Clayton Act.
   B. Federal Restraint of Trade Act.
   C. Sherman Antitrust Act.
   D. Robinson-Patman Act.

5. Which of the following may bring court action or suit against a real estate firm, real estate association, or an individual real estate practitioner for violations of antitrust laws?
   A. Federal Trade Commission
   B. State Attorney General's Office
   C. Individual citizens
   D. All of the above

6. MLS services may:
   A. set reasonable standards for membership.
   B. prohibit the taking of "open" or nonexclusive listings.
   C. determine what splits will be permissible between cooperating brokers or their salespersons.
   D. determine the commission rates members must charge sellers.

7. The penalties for a conviction of violating the antitrust laws include:
   A. liability for treble damages.
   B. payments of attorney's fees and court costs.
   C. up to ten years of court supervision for the offending business entity.
   D. All of the above

8. Antitrust in the real estate industry includes:
   A. price fixing.
   B. group boycotts.
   C. tying agreements.
   D. All of the above

9. Restraint of trade in the real estate business might include all of the following EXCEPT:
   A. a refusal of two or more real estate firms to deal with brokers who are not members of a particular group or association of brokers.
   B. refusal to do business with individuals or firms that have a nontraditional commission rate.
   C. refusal to do business with a nontraditional broker who assists "by owners."
   D. All of the above

10. The first and foremost case relating to the prohibiting of MLS services for nonmembers is the:
    A. *Grillo* case.
    B. *Brillo* case.
    C. *Sherman* case.
    D. *Clayton* case.

STUDENT NOTES

CHAPTER 10

FINANCE DEVELOPMENTS
(ALL THAT GLITTERS)

○ CHAPTER OVERVIEW
Nothing changes faster in the real estate business than the ways and means of financing the purchase and sale of real property. This chapter will update you on all the latest financing requirements, techniques, and issues, better equipping you to function in today's dynamic real estate environment.

○ LEARNING OBJECTIVES
Upon completing the study of this chapter, you should be able to:
1) Discuss FIRREA, its activities, and its organization.
2) Detail the important changes implemented by FNMA, GNMA, and FHLMC affecting maximum loan limits and loan application requirements.
3) Discuss the major changes in FHA/HUD regulations for 1992.
4) Calculate the maximum amount of Insured Commitment on FHA loans.
5) Discuss the major VA loan regulatory changes for 1992.
6) Become familiar with the Illinois Affordable Housing Program and the activities of the Illinois Housing Development Authority.
7) Explain the advantages of the Mortgage Certificate Programs available in Illinois.
8) Discuss the elements of the adjustable-rate mortgage, its advantages and disadvantages.
9) Explain some of the more popular alternative financing sources, including the shared appreciation mortgage, the reverse annuity mortgage, and the buydown.
10) Explain the new reporting requirements for credit information services.

○ 5 CASES TO JUDGE

○ 10-QUESTION DIAGNOSTIC QUIZ

CHAPTER 10

FINANCING DEVELOPMENTS
(ALL THAT GLITTERS)

REAL ESTATE FINANCING IN TODAY'S TRANSACTION
The real estate business is predicated on the Golden Rule: "He who has the Gold, Makes the Rule." The more familiar the real estate practitioner is with financing, the more service he or she will be able to provide to customers and clients. More than any one topic, knowledge of real estate financing is the quickest way to distinguish yourself as a successful professional and to make more gold of your own. The following is intended to brief the finance student on important new changes in the arena of real estate finance and is guaranteed to have a profound effect on your future real estate transactions.

FIRREA
As a result of biased lending decisions, poor management, and the negative effects of the Tax Reform Act of 1986 on real estate investments, over half of the nation's 4,600 thrift institutions (savings and loans) began disappearing or facing bankruptcy since deregulation of the lending industry began in 1988. At that time 57 percent of all residential loans were originated by savings and loans associations; today it is less than 23 percent.

Congress enacted the Financial Institutions Reform, Recovery and Enforcement Act (FIRREA) on August 9, 1989, to deal with the crisis. The principal thrust of FIRREA was to influence the lending activities of commercial banks and savings and loans by introducing new capital-requirement thresholds and by restructuring the regulatory levels of the thrift industry. One of the principal missions of the act is to close insolvent savings and loan associations and sell or reorganize those on the brink of failure. It is possible that two thirds of the 2,150 existing savings associations will be sold or merged over the next several years. The Resolution Trust Corporation (RTC) was created as the agency responsible for running the failed thrifts, then disposing or selling their estimated $400 billion in leftover real estate and other assets.

It is encouraging to note that as of the end of 1991, 1,800 of the thrifts are making money and enjoying their most profitable year since 1986. Only 64 thrifts remain in the "high risk" or "likely to fail" category.

Note that under FIRREA, the Federal Deposit Insurance Corporation (FDIC), which primarily insured deposits at commercial and savings banks, has been given increased responsibilities, which include management of two subsidiaries: the Bank Insurance Fund (BIF), which insures deposits of banks, and the Savings Association Insurance Fund (SAIF), which insures deposits of savings and loans. FSLIC, the predecessor of SAIF, has been eliminated.

FNMA/FHLMC
Most lenders' loan-underwriting guidelines come from their own board of directors' policies. But because federal and private agencies like Fannie Mae (FNMA), Ginnie Mae (GNMA), and Freddie Mac (FHLMC) are so influential in the secondary market (they purchase many of the loans originated by banks, savings and loans, mortgage bankers, etc.), they also have a profound effect on the lending policies to which lenders will agree.

UNIFORM RESIDENTIAL LOAN APPLICATION
One of the important changes is the revision of the Fannie Mae 1003/Freddie Mac 65 residential loan application. Use of this form has been optional in the past, but as of January 1, 1992, it became mandatory for all residential

loans. The new form, entitled "Uniform Residential Loan Application," is for all loans secured by one-family to four-family properties, including FHA and VA loans.

LOAN LIMITS

Recently the standards for conventional loan limits set by Fannie Mae and Freddie Mac have been increased. What this "limit "means is that neither Fannie Mae nor Freddie Mac will purchase loans that exceed that limit. It does not limit the loan originators unless they choose to sell their loans to one of the two agencies. Because most lending institutions do not hold all their loans in their own portfolios, changes in the FNMA/FHLMC loan limits affect their lending practices.

The Illinois 1992 loan limits are:

Number of units	FNMA/FHLMC Max. Loan Limits
1	$202,300
2	$258,800
3	$312,800
4	$388,800
Second Mortgages	$101,150

FNMA will not purchase a loan where the purchaser owns more than five dwelling units. The rule refers to units owned in one-family to four-family properties only, and is based not just on properties with loans sold to FNMA, but on all properties held. For example, two single-family dwellings and one triplex would be combined to reach the five-unit maximum.

Loans that exceed the maximum limits are termed "jumbo" loans and usually carry a higher interest rate than the lower "conforming" loans. FNMA will also purchase these loans. The "two-part" jumbo loan is really two loans in one: one fixed-rate loan for the maximum allowed, and a second in the form of an adjustable mortgage up to the balance. In this way, the rate of the adjustable mortgage is lower than on the fixed mortgage, allowing for easier qualifying. The fixed-rate mortgage helps to lessen the blow should the adjustable rates begin to rise.

FNMA allows for another market option program, that of the FNMA balloon. This has helped to increase the popularity of the balloon loan to the point where it is becoming more popular than the adjustable-rate loan.

ENVIRONMENTAL INFORMATION

Both Fannie Mae and Freddie Mac are requiring certain environmental information on the property appraisal submitted with a loan eligible for them to buy. The appraiser must comment on any known environmental conditions that would adversely affect the property's value. This includes asbestos and urea-formaldehyde foam insulation. Further information is required on the proximity of the mortgaged property to industrial sites, waste or water treatment facilities, and commercial establishments using chemicals or oil products.

Loan documents are beginning to require environmental covenants restricting the borrower from using hazardous materials and promising to abide by state and federal environmental laws. The borrower must notify the lender if an investigation or lawsuit is filed against the mortgage property. The form is illustrated in Figures 10-1 through 10-4.

FIG 10-1

Uniform Residential Loan Application

This application is designed to be completed by the Borrower(s) with the Lender's assistance. The Co-Borrower Section and all other Co-Borrower questions must be completed and the appropriate box(es) checked if ☐ another person will be jointly obligated with the Borrower on the loan, or ☐ the Borrower is relying on income from alimony, child support or separate maintenance or on the income or assets of another person as a basis for repayment of the loan, or ☐ the Borrower is married and resides in, or the property is located in, a community property state.

I. TYPE OF MORTGAGE AND TERMS OF LOAN

Mortgage Applied for: ☐ VA ☐ FHA ☐ Conventional ☐ FmHA ☐ Other:

Agency Case Number

Lender Case No.

Amount $

Interest Rate %

No. of Months

Amortization Type: ☐ Fixed Rate ☐ GPM ☐ Other (explain): ☐ ARM (type):

II. PROPERTY INFORMATION AND PURPOSE OF LOAN

Subject Property Address (street, city, state, & zip code)

No. of Units

Legal Description of Subject Property (attach description if necessary)

Year Built

Purpose of Loan ☐ Purchase ☐ Refinance ☐ Construction ☐ Construction-Permanent ☐ Other (explain):

Property will be: ☐ Primary Residence ☐ Secondary Residence ☐ Investment

Complete this line if construction or construction-permanent loan.

Year Lot Acquired	Original Cost	Amount Existing Liens	(a) Present Value of Lot	(b) Cost of Improvements	Total (a + b)
	$	$	$	$	$

Complete this line if this is a refinance loan.

Year Acquired	Original Cost	Amount Existing Liens	Purpose of Refinance	Describe Improvements ☐ made ☐ to be made
	$	$		Cost: $

Title will be held in what Name(s)

Manner in which Title will be held

Estate will be held in: ☐ Fee Simple ☐ Leasehold (show expiration date)

Source of Down Payment, Settlement Charges and/or Subordinate Financing (explain)

III. BORROWER INFORMATION

Borrower	Co Borrower
Borrower's Name (include Jr. or Sr. if applicable)	Co-Borrower's Name (include Jr. or Sr. if applicable)
Social Security Number / Home Phone (incl. area code) / Age / Yrs. School	Social Security Number / Home Phone (incl. area code) / Age / Yrs. School
☐ Married ☐ Unmarried (include single, divorced, widowed) ☐ Separated / Dependents (not listed by Co-Borrower) no. ages	☐ Married ☐ Unmarried (include single, divorced, widowed) ☐ Separated / Dependents (not listed by Borrower) no. ages
Present Address (street, city, state, zip code) ☐ Own ☐ Rent ____ No. Yrs.	Present Address (street, city, state, zip code) ☐ Own ☐ Rent ____ No. Yrs.

If residing at present address for less than seven years, complete the following:

Borrower	Co Borrower
Former Address (street, city, state, zip code) ☐ Own ☐ Rent ____ No. Yrs.	Former Address (street, city, state, zip code) ☐ Own ☐ Rent ____ No. Yrs.
Former Address (street, city, state, zip code) ☐ Own ☐ Rent ____ No. Yrs.	Former Address (street, city, state, zip code) ☐ Own ☐ Rent ____ No. Yrs.

IV. EMPLOYMENT INFORMATION

Borrower	Co Borrower
Name & Address of Employer ☐ Self Employed / Yrs. on this job / Yrs. employed in this line of work/profession	Name & Address of Employer ☐ Self Employed / Yrs. on this job / Yrs. employed in this line of work/profession
Position/Title/Type of Business / Business Phone (incl. area code)	Position/Title/Type of Business / Business Phone (incl. area code)

If employed in current position for less than two years or if currently employed in more than one position, complete the following:

Borrower	Co Borrower
Name & Address of Employer ☐ Self Employed / Dates (from - to) / Monthly Income $	Name & Address of Employer ☐ Self Employed / Dates (from - to) / Monthly Income $
Position/Title/Type of Business / Business Phone (incl. area code)	Position/Title/Type of Business / Business Phone (incl. area code)
Name & Address of Employer ☐ Self Employed / Dates (from - to) / Monthly Income $	Name & Address of Employer ☐ Self Employed / Dates (from - to) / Monthly Income $
Position/Title/Type of Business / Business Phone (incl. area code)	Position/Title/Type of Business / Business Phone (incl. area code

Freddie Mac Form 65/Rev. 5/91 Page 1 of 4 Fannie Mae Form 1003/Rev. 5/9`

FIG 10-2

V. MONTHLY INCOME AND COMBINED HOUSING EXPENSE INFORMATION

Gross Monthly Income	Borrower	Co-Borrower	Total	Combined Monthly Housing Expense	Present	Proposed
Base Empl. Income *	$	$	$	Rent	$	
Overtime				First Mortgage (P&I)		$
Bonuses				Other Financing (P&I)		
Commissions				Hazard Insurance		
Dividends/Interest				Real Estate Taxes		
Net Rental Income				Mortgage Insurance		
Other (before completing, see the notice in "describe other income" below)				Homeowner Assn. Dues		
				Other:		
Total	$	$	$	Total	$	$

* Self Employed Borrower(s) may be required to provide additional documentation such as tax returns and financial statements.

Describe Other Income *Notice:* Alimony, child support, or separate maintenance income need not be revealed if the Borrower (B) or Co-Borrower (C) does not choose to have it considered for repaying this loan.

B/C		Monthly Amount
		$

VI. ASSETS AND LIABILITIES

This Statement and any applicable supporting schedules may be completed jointly by both married and unmarried Co-Borrowers if their assets and liabilities are sufficiently joined so that the Statement can be meaningfully and fairly presented on a combined basis; otherwise separate Statements and Schedules are required. If the Co-Borrower section was completed about a spouse, this Statement and supporting schedules must be completed about that spouse also.

Completed [ ] Jointly [ ] Not Jointly

ASSETS Description	Cash or Market Value	Liabilities and Pledged Assets. List the creditor's name, address and account number for all outstanding debts, including automobile loans, revolving charge accounts, real estate loans, alimony, child support, stock pledges, etc. Use continuation sheet, if necessary. Indicate by (*) those liabilities which will be satisfied upon sale of real estate owned or upon refinancing of the subject property.		
Cash deposit toward purchase held by:	$	**LIABILITIES**	Monthly Payt. & Mos. Left to Pay	Unpaid Balance
		Name and address of Company	$ Payt./Mos.	$
List checking and savings accounts below				
Name and address of Bank, S&L, or Credit Union				
		Acct. no.		
Acct. no.	$	Name and address of Company	$ Payt./Mos.	$
Name and address of Bank, S&L, or Credit Union				
		Acct. no.		
		Name and address of Company	$ Payt./Mos.	$
Acct. no.	$			
Name and address of Bank, S&L, or Credit Union				
		Acct. no.		
		Name and address of Company	$ Payt./Mos.	$
Acct. no.	$			
Name and address of Bank, S&L, or Credit Union				
		Acct. no.		
		Name and address of Company	$ Payt./Mos.	$
Acct. no.	$			
Stocks & Bonds (Company name/number & description)	$			
		Acct. no.		
		Name and address of Company	$ Payt./Mos.	$
Life insurance net cash value	$			
Face amount: $				
Subtotal Liquid Assets	$			
Real estate owned (enter market value from schedule of real estate owned)	$	Acct. no.		
Vested interest in retirement fund	$	Name and address of Company	$ Payt./Mos.	$
Net worth of business(es) owned (attach financial statement)	$			
Automobiles owned (make and year)	$			
		Acct. no.		
		Alimony/Child Support/Separate Maintenance Payments Owed to:	$	
Other Assets (itemize)	$	Job Related Expense (child care, union dues, etc.)	$	
		Total Monthly Payments	$	
Total Assets a.	$	Net Worth (a minus b) $	Total Liabilities b.	$

Freddie Mac Form 65/Rev. 5/91   Page 2 of 4   Fannie Mae Form 1003/Rev. 5/91

FIG 10-3

VI ASSETS AND LIABILITIES (cont.)

Schedule of Real Estate Owned (If additional properties are owned, use continuation sheet.)

Property Address (enter S if sold, PS if pending sale or R if rental being held for income)	Type of Property	Present Market Value	Amount of Mortgages & Liens	Gross Rental Income	Mortgage Payments	Insurance, Maintenance, Taxes & Misc.	Net Rental Income
		$	$	$	$	$	$
	Totals	$	$	$	$	$	$

List any additional names under which credit has previously been received and indicate appropriate creditor name(s) and account number(s):

Alternate Name	Creditor Name	Account Number

VII DETAILS OF TRANSACTION

a. Purchase price	$
b. Alterations, improvements, repairs	
c. Land (if acquired separately)	
d. Refinance (incl. debts to be paid off)	
e. Estimated prepaid items	
f. Estimated closing costs	
g. PMI, MIP, Funding Fee paid in cash	
h. Discount (if Borrower will pay)	
i. **Total costs (add items a through h)**	
j. Subordinate financing	
k. Borrower's closing costs paid by Seller	
l. Other Credits (explain)	
m. Loan amount (subtract j, k & l from i) (exclude PMI, MIP, Funding Fee financed)	
n. PMI, MIP, Funding Fee financed	
o. Loan amount (add m & n)	
p. Cash from/to Borrower (subtract o from i)	

VIII DECLARATIONS

If you answer "yes" to any questions a through l, please use continuation sheet for explanation.

	Borrower Yes	Borrower No	Co-Borrower Yes	Co-Borrower No
a. Are there any outstanding judgments against you?	☐	☐	☐	☐
b. Have you been declared bankrupt within the past 7 years?	☐	☐	☐	☐
c. Have you had property foreclosed upon or given title or deed in lieu thereof in the last 7 years?	☐	☐	☐	☐
d. Are you a party to a law suit?	☐	☐	☐	☐
e. Have you directly or indirectly been obligated on any loan which resulted in foreclosure, transfer of title in lieu of foreclosure, or judgment? (This would include such loans as home mortgage loans, SBA loans, home improvement loans, educational loans, manufactured (mobile) home loans, any mortgage, financial obligation, bond, or loan guarantee. If "Yes," provide details, including date, name and address of Lender, FHA or VA case number, if any, and reasons for the action.)	☐	☐	☐	☐
f. Are you presently delinquent or in default on any Federal debt or any other loan, mortgage, financial obligation, bond, or loan guarantee? If "Yes," give details as described in the preceding question.	☐	☐	☐	☐
g. Are you obligated to pay alimony, child support, or separate maintenance?	☐	☐	☐	☐
h. Is any part of the down payment borrowed?	☐	☐	☐	☐
i. Are you a co-maker or endorser on a note?	☐	☐	☐	☐
j. Are you a U.S. citizen?	☐	☐	☐	☐
k. Are you a permanent resident alien?	☐	☐	☐	☐
l. Do you intend to occupy the property as your primary residence?	☐	☐	☐	☐

IX. ACKNOWLEDGMENT AND AGREEMENT

The undersigned specifically acknowledge(s) and agree(s) that: (1) the loan requested by this application will be secured by a first mortgage or deed of trust on the property described herein; (2) the property will not be used for any illegal or prohibited purpose or use; (3) all statements made in this application are made for the purpose of obtaining the loan indicated herein; (4) occupation of the property will be as indicated above; (5) verification or reverification of any information contained in the application may be made at any time by the Lender, its agents, successors and assigns, either directly or through a credit reporting agency, from any source named in this application, and the original copy of this application will be retained by the Lender, even if the loan is not approved; (6) the Lender, its agents, successors and assigns will rely on the information contained in the application and I/we have a continuing obligation to amend and/or supplement the information provided in this application if any of the material facts which I/we have represented herein should change prior to closing; (7) in the event my/our payments on the loan indicated in this application become delinquent, the Lender, its agents, successors and assigns, may, in addition to all their other rights and remedies, report my/our name(s) and account information to a credit reporting agency; (8) ownership of the loan may be transferred to successor or assign of the Lender without notice to me and/or the administration of the loan account may be transferred to an agent, successor or assign of the Lender with prior notice to me; (9) the Lender, its agents, successors and assigns make no representations or warranties, express or implied, to the Borrower(s) regarding the property, the condition of the property, or the value of the property.

Certification: I/We certify that the information provided in this application is true and correct as of the date set forth opposite my/our signature(s) on this application and acknowledge my/our understanding that any intentional or negligent misrepresentation(s) of the information contained in this application may result in civil liability and/or criminal penalties including, but not limited to, fine or imprisonment or both under the provisions of Title 18, United States Code, Section 1001, et seq. and liability for monetary damages to the Lender, its agents, successors and assigns, insurers and any other person who may suffer any loss due to reliance upon any misrepresentation which I/we have made on this application.

Borrower's Signature	Date	Co-Borrower's Signature	Date
X		X	

X INFORMATION FOR GOVERNMENT MONITORING PURPOSES

The following information is requested by the Federal Government for certain types of loans related to a dwelling, in order to monitor the Lender's compliance with equal credit opportunity, fair housing and home mortgage disclosure laws. You are not required to furnish this information, but are encouraged to do so. The law provides that a Lender may neither discriminate on the basis of this information, nor on whether you choose to furnish it. However, if you choose not to furnish it, under Federal regulations this Lender is required to note race and sex on the basis of visual observation or surname. If you do not wish to furnish the above information, please check the box below. (Lender must review the above material to assure that the disclosures satisfy all requirements to which the Lender is subject under applicable state law for the particular type of loan applied for.)

BORROWER

☐ I do not wish to furnish this information

Race/National Origin: ☐ American Indian or Alaskan Native ☐ Asian or Pacific Islander ☐ Black, not of Hispanic origin ☐ Hispanic ☐ White, not of Hispanic origin

Sex: ☐ Female ☐ Male

CO-BORROWER

☐ I do not wish to furnish this information

Race/National Origin: ☐ American Indian or Alaskan Native ☐ Asian or Pacific Islander ☐ Black, not of Hispanic origin ☐ Hispanic ☐ White, not of Hispanic origin

Sex: ☐ Female ☐ Male

To be Completed by Interviewer		
This application was taken by:	Interviewer's Name (print or type)	Name and Address of Interviewer's Employer
☐ face-to-face interview	Interviewer's Signature — Date	
☐ by mail		
☐ by telephone	Interviewer's Phone Number (incl. area code)	

Freddie Mac Form 65/Rev. 5/91 — Page 3 of 4 — Fannie Mae Form 1003/Rev. 5/91

Chapter 10 Finance Developments 187

FIG 10-4

Continuation Sheet/Residential Loan Application

	Borrower:	Agency Case Number:
Use this continuation sheet if you need more space to complete the Residential Loan Application. Mark B for Borrower or C for Co-Borrower.		
	Co-Borrower:	Lender Case Number:

I/We fully understand that it is a Federal crime punishable by fine or imprisonment, or both, to knowingly make any false statements concerning any of the above facts as applicable under the provisions of Title 18, United States Code, Section 1001, et seq.

Borrower's Signature:	Date	Co-Borrower's Signature:	Date
X		X	

188   Chapter 10   Finance Developments

HUD/FHA CHANGES
The Housing and Urban Development Reform Act of 1989 changed several policies and lending standards affecting the single-family home loan program. The following is a summary of nine important changes. Real estate licensees should keep current with HUD/FHA regulations through either their local HUD Field Office or FHA-approved lenders. The Chicago Area HUD Field Office (which includes all of Illinois) is located at 77 West Jackson Blvd., Suite 2200, Chicago, Illinois 60604 (phone: 312-353-5682).

CHANGE 1. Rules for assumption of FHA mortgages made on or after February 15, 1989, were tightened to require credit checks from all HUD/FHA-approved mortgage assumers prior to conveyance of title. Failure to comply will result in acceleration of the note. HUD/FHA will not release the original mortgagor from liability when the mortgage is assumed; only the lender may do that. The lender cannot refuse to release the original borrower if an acceptable substitute assumes the loan. Note that there are different rules regarding assumptions for loans that were originated prior to December 1, 1986, and different rules for loans originated between December 1, 1986, and December 15, 1989.

CHANGE 2. While there are currently 18 different types of FHA-approved programs, the primary single-family program is the Section 203(b) loan. This loan program provides mortgage insurance, which protects the lender in case of default, thus encouraging lending on high loan-to-value ratio loans, and thereby assisting home buyers in the purchase of new and existing one- to four-family dwellings. The 203(b) program is available for use in both rural and urban areas provided a market exists for the property and the property meets HUD's minimum property standards.

CHANGE 3. The maximum FHA loan amounts insurable by the FHA continue to change and vary from area to area to reflect FHA's perception of regional differences in housing costs. The maximum loan limits for FHA-insured loans in Illinois by county and number of units is found later on in this chapter.

In the past, determining the maximum insured commitment (maximum amount a lender will lend a borrower on an FHA-insured loan) was not very difficult. The new procedure for calculating the maximum insured commitment, however, requires two separate calculations: one with closing costs added, and one without. The lesser of the two calculations is the correct insured commitment. Note that in the calculation that includes closing costs, HUD has limited the amount to 57 percent of the Good Faith Estimate (GFE) of the closing costs. Note also that different percentage limitations apply to houses priced either above or below $50,000.

For Properties *Exceeding* $50,000

First calculation:

Take the lesser of the sales price or the appraised value *plus closing costs* as the value for mortgage insurance purposes. Remember that only 57 percent of the GFE of closing costs will be allowed. The insured commitment is 97 percent (100 percent for an eligible veteran) of the first $25,000 of the value for mortgage-insurance purposes plus 95 percent of the remaining amount.

Second calculation:

Multiply the LESSER of the sales price or appraised value (do NOT add closing costs) by 97.75 percent.

Example 1: Assume a sales price (and appraisal) of $90,000. The Good Faith Estimate (GFE) of closing costs amounts to $2,000. What is the value of the property for FHA insurance purposes, assuming the figures do not exceed the maximum mortgage limit for your particular area?

First calculation:

$90,000	Lesser of sales price or appraised value
+$1,140	Add 57% of the $2000 GFE
$91,140	Value for calculating insurance

$25,000 × .97 = $24,250
$66,140 × .95 = $62,833
$87,083   Maximum Insured Commitment

Second calculation:

$90,000	Lesser of sales price or appraised value
× 97.75%	DO NOT add closing costs
$87,975	

In the above example the first calculation produces the lesser amount of $87,083 rounded down to $87,050, the Maximum Insured Commitment. Remember: the borrower is only financing 57 percent of closing costs, and not 100 percent as borrowers once did.

For Properties *of $50,000 or less*

Assume the sales price (appraisal) this time is $48,000. Use the same calculations as for the more expensive houses but with two important changes: (1) The first calculation uses a flat 97 percent of the property value; and (2) the second calculation uses 98.75 percent (instead of the 97.75 percent that applies to the larger houses).

First calculation:

$48,000	Lesser of the sales price or appraisal
+ $855	Add 57% of the $1,500 GFE
$48,855 × .97 = $47,389	

Second calculation:

$48,000	Lesser sales price or appraisal
0	DO NOT add closing costs
$48,000 × 98.75% = $47,400	

In this case the lesser amount is rounded down to $47,350, which becomes the Maximum Insured Commitment.

CHANGE 4. There are now two calculations needed for Mortgage Insurance Premiums. One is the a one-time Up-Front Mortgage Insurance Premium (UFMIP) and the other is the Annual Premium.

UFMIP—The amount of the UFMIP is based on a percentage of the loan amount, and that percentage will decline over the next five years, depending on when the loan was originated. The UFMIP may be paid in cash or added to the loan amount.

Up-Front Premium	Fiscal Year of Origination
3.80%	1991-1992
3.00%	1993-1994
2.25%	1995-beyond

Annual Premium—The annual premium is a 0.50 percent premium calculated at each annual anniversary date of the loan on the loan's outstanding unpaid principal balance. The term of the annual premium is based on the year of loan origination, as well as the loan-to-value ratio. One twelfth of the annual premium is added to the monthly payment and must be included in the proposed monthly housing expense at the initial qualification of the borrower's income. Annual premiums are nonrefundable, and if there is prepayment or termination of the mortgage, the final annual premium must be prorated to the closing date.

YEAR OF ORIGINATION	BELOW 90%	90% - 95%	ABOVE 95%
1991-92	5 YEARS	8 YEARS	10 YEARS
1993-94	7 YEARS	12 YEARS	30 YEARS
1995-ON	11 YEARS	30 YEARS	30 YEARS

The loan-to-value ratio is calculated as the base loan amount (without UFMIP) divided by the value, excluding closing costs.

CHANGE 5. Investor mortgagors were eliminated. Effective December 15, 1989, private investors were banned from the FHA Single-Family Programs. HUD/FHA will no longer insure mortgages for investors to acquire or construct property.

CHANGE 6. Gross effective income has replaced net effective income for the calculation of a borrower's qualifying income, via the housing expense ratio. Income taxes no longer will be deducted from gross income before calculating the two ratios.

CHANGE 7. The Housing Expense Ratio (sometimes referred to as the "front-end ratio") may not exceed 29 percent (monthly housing expenses, which can include association fees in addition to PITI, divided by monthly gross income). Utility expenses and maintenance costs of the house are no longer included in the calculation of the housing expense ratio.

CHANGE 8. Total Fixed Obligation Ratio (monthly housing expenses PLUS all other fixed obligations divided by monthly gross income) has been changed to a maximum of 41 percent of gross income. This is sometimes referred to as the "back-end ratio." It is interesting to note that the back-end ratio for conventional loans is 36 percent. Debt extending beyond six months is now considered a fixed obligation (long-term, nonhousing debt). Previously it was debt beyond 12 months.

CHANGE 9. The FHA began collecting the up-front mortgage insurance premium (UFMIP) on FHA loans made after September 1983. The assumption was that the average FHA loan would be "alive" for 12 years. Therefore, if a loan was paid off (or property sold) before the 12-year period, then the borrower is entitled to a refund of the unexpired premium. In other words, the borrower paid for 12 years of mortgage insurance protection and did not use the full 12 years. The refund is payable to the person or persons who own the property insured by the FHA at the time the loan was paid off. If an FHA loan is assumed, than the party assuming the loan would be entitled to the refund. The refund is automatic in that the lender with the FHA loan is required to notify the FHA of the payoff, which in turn would cause the FHA to issue a refund. The FHA borrower should sign a refund form (HUD-2344) at the payoff of the FHA loan (closing), which is then forwarded to the FHA. FHA loans made prior to September 1983 are not entitled to a refund. Inquiries can be directed to Mortgage Insurance Accounting Insurance Operation Division, HUD, 451 Seventh St. SW, Washington, DC 20410 (phone: 202-708-0616).

SUMMARY of HUD/FHA CHANGES

As a result of the above changes in the FHA rules, conventional financing may be more attractive to many first-time buyers. However, FHA underwriting requirements are still more lenient than for a conforming conventional loan. FHA still permits higher debt ratios, requires modest down payments (4 percent to 5 percent) and allows a portion of the closing costs to be financed. For those borrowers who must opt for more-lenient underwriting, FHA financing is still a viable alternative. As of September 1991, 6 percent of all loans were insured FHA loans, down substantially from the 15 percent in 1985. FHA for multifamily buildings remains a great loan program, because the 5 percent down payment for two-, three-, and four-flats is still below the conventional 10 percent to 20 percent down. Remember that while most single-family residences can qualify for FHA/VA insurance/guarantees, condominiums, townhouses and PUDs must be approved by HUD on an individual basis. Buyers, sellers, and "others" (brokers) may now pay points on the sellers' behalf on FHA-approved financing. On VA financing, only the seller may pay points.

FHA MAXIMUM MORTGAGE LIMITS	1 UNIT	2 UNITS	3 UNITS	4 UNITS
AURORA-ELGIN, IL KANE COUNTY KENDALL COUNTY	$124,875	$140,600	$170,200	$197,950
CHICAGO, IL COOK COUNTY DUPAGE COUNTY MCHENRY COUNTY	$120,500	$135,700	$164,850	$190,250
DAVENPORT-ROCK ISLAND-MOLINE, IA-IL HENRY COUNTY & ROCK ISLAND COUNTY	$72,750	$81,900	$99,550	$114,850
JOLIET, IL WILL COUNTY & GRUNDY COUNTY	$107,600	$121,200	$147,250	$169,950
LAKE COUNTY, IL LAKE COUNTY	$124,875	$140,600	$170,200	$197,950
ROCKFORD, IL BOONE COUNTY WINNEBAGO COUNTY DEKALB COUNTY	$74,500 $77,400	$83,950 $87,200	$102,050 $106,400	$117,750 $122,800
ALTON-GRANITE CITY, IL JERSEY COUNTY & MADISON COUNTY	$85,500	$96,300	$117,000	$135,000
BLOOMINGTON-NORMAL, IL MCLEAN COUNTY	$79,500	$89,500	$108,750	$125,500
CHAMPAIGN-URBANA-RANTOUL, IL CHAMPAIGN COUNTY	$99,950	$112,600	$136,800	$157,850
EAST ST. LOUIS-BELLEVILLE, IL CLINTON COUNTY & ST. CLAIR COUNTY	$85,500	$96,300	$117,000	$135,000
SPRINGFIELD, IL MENARD COUNTY SANGAMON COUNTY	$74,250	$83,600	$101,600	$117,200
ST. LOUIS, MO-IL MONROE COUNTY	$99,150	$111,650	$135,650	$156,550
ALL OTHER ILLINOIS COUNTIES REMAIN AT BASIC MAXIMUM LIMITS:	$67,500	$76,000	$92,000	$107,000

Chapter 10 Finance Developments

VA CHANGES

Several important facets of VA loans have changed as a result of the passage in 1989 of the Veterans Home Loan Indemnity and Restructuring Act and the 1990 Budget Bill passed by Congress. These include:

1. The Veterans Administration was elevated to a cabinet rank and called the Department of Veterans Affairs; however, it is still officially called the VA. Title and loan documents should refer to the "Secretary of Veterans Affairs" rather than the "Administrator of Veterans Affairs."

2. The current limits for the VA guaranty are based on the following sliding scale:

Loan Amount	Guaranty
$45,00 or less	50% of loan
$45,001 to $56,250	$22,500
$56,251 to $90,000	40% of loan
$90,001 to $144,000	$36,000
$144,001 to $184,000	25% of loan
$184,001 and up	$46,000

    If you consider the $46,000 guaranty as a "down payment," then the veteran has "put down" 25 percent of the loan. Therefore, a veteran could borrow as much as $184,000 with no real down payment out of his or her pocket. We have to assume the veteran could qualify to make mortgage payments based on this amount at the VA interest rate.

3. Virtually all veterans must now pay a "funding fee" for VA guaranteed loans based on the size of the down payment and calculated as a percentage of the loan amount. The fee schedule in effect as of *October 1, 1991*, is as follows:

Down Payment	Funding Fee
Less than 5%	1.250 points
5% but less than 10%	0.75 points
10% or more	0.50 points
Loan Assumptions	0.50

    The funding fee can be added to the loan amount and financed over the life of the loan, or paid in full at closing. Disabled veterans are not required to pay a funding fee. For Vendee loans and Section 1812 manufactured home loans, the 1-point funding fee remains unchanged.

4. Gross income replaced net income as the amount used to calculate the VA total monthly obligations ratio (total monthly expenses divided by gross monthly income).

5. All VA guaranteed loans originated after March 1, 1988, can only be assumed after the substitute mortgagor is found creditworthy following a credit check. Loans originated prior to that date may still be assumed without the credit check. Lenders are permitted to charge an assumption (transfer) fee up to maximum of $500, and the DVA requires a payment of a fee of one half of one percent (0.50%) to assume the loan. The total population eligible for VA housing benefits (war veterans, including those who served in the Persian Gulf and the Merchant Marine, spouses, widows [not remarried, including those of MIAs and others]) is *58 million* people. However, only 11 million have used their benefits. There are two principal reasons for this: (1) veterans don't know enough about their benefits; and (2) neither do real estate professionals.

VA loan programs include 30-year and 15-year fixed, as well as buydowns and GPMs. The Veterans Administration sets the maximum interest rate a lender can charge on the guaranteed VA loan. Typically this is below conventional interest rates.

Common myths about VA loans:
Myth #1:   Sellers should fear "low-ball" appraisals.
Reality: In the past when the VA used "staff" appraisals, this was probably true; however, today most VA appraisals are done by independent "fee" appraisers.
Myth #2:   Loan processing time is too long.
Reality: With lenders using the "VA automatic approval," the process has been speeded up and typically takes four weeks.
Myth #3:   Sellers will not pay discount points.
Reality: Sellers are still required to pay discount points, which equal 1 percent of the amount of the loan; however, a full-price sale should remedy this concern. Buyers cannot pay sellers' discount points.

FEDERAL and STATE AFFORDABLE HOUSING PROGRAMS

FIRREA. One of the provisions of FIRREA is that each of the 12 Federal Home Banks contributes 5 percent of its net annual income in 1990 as a subsidy for "affordable housing." The member lending institutions make application twice a year to receive subsidized advancements. Projects sponsored by state, local, or not-for-profit housing authorities are eligible for subsidy. The goal is $100 million by 1995.

Illinois Affordable Housing Authority. The Affordable Housing Program was established and became effective in 1989. This program authorizes the Illinois Housing Development Authority (IHDA) and the Department of Commerce and Community Affairs (DECCA) to develop a plan in relation to the use of tax incremental financing for affordable housing for moderate-, low-, and very low-income households. The program is funded by a 0.25/$500 Illinois Real Estate Transfer Tax on the taxable consideration paid by Illinois sellers of each real estate sale in Illinois. The program administrator of the Affordable Housing Trust Fund distributes money from the fund to make grants, mortgages, or other loans for acquisition, rehabilitation, construction, or rental subsidies to low-income qualifiers. Proprietorships, partnerships, for-profit and not-for-profit corporations, and units of the government are all eligible to receive funds. Applicants seeking money from the fund must make application to the authority on forms provided by the authority with a $250 nonrefundable application fee. The maximum mortgage loan is $500,000 for each application, and the maximum term of a mortgage loan is 40 years.

Several times a year the Illinois Housing Authority will announce special low-interest-rate programs available through the program, generally to first-time buyers. Borrower eligibility will include a maximum yearly income level, minimum down payment, and low closing costs. Typically the availability of an offering will receive media attention. Call the Authority's toll-free number, 1-800-942-8439, to get a brochure listing the names, locations, and phone numbers of participating lenders.

Individuals interested in: IHDA's single-family programs should call 312-836-5241
                            Low-income housing credit information should call 312-836-5246
                            Loans and housing partnerships should call 312-836-5318
                            Multifamily housing development should call 312-836-5352

Mortgage Credit Certificate Program. The Tax Reform Act of 1984 authorized the Mortgage Credit Certificate (MCC) Program as a new concept for providing housing assistance to home buyers. Available to home rule communities in Illinois, the MCC Program benefits low-income and middle-income home buyers in their purchase of moderately priced homes. The MCC allows first-time home buyers to obtain a tax credit of $2,000 or 20 percent to 25 percent of the annual mortgage interest, whichever is less, against federal income tax owed. To report the tax credit borrowers must use IRS Form 8369 to calculate the credit and file it with their 1040 form. By reducing the amount of federal income tax a buyer pays, the buyer has more income available to qualify for a mortgage.

How the MCC Program works :

Purchase Price	$77,500
Loan Amount (LTV = 95%)	$73,625
Interest Rate	10%
Interest Year 1	$7,344.08
MCC Tax Credit	$1,836.02 (25% of yearly interest or $2,000, whichever is less)
Monthly Payment Comparison	
Monthly Payment (PI)	$646.11
Monthly Value of MCC	$153.00 (MCC Tax Credit divided by 12)
Net Monthly Payment After MCC Credit	$493.11

The following Illinois communities have introduced MCC programs the last few years: Aurora, Calumet City, Decatur, DeKalb, Evanston, Freeport, Lansing, Moline, North Chicago, Oak Forest, Park Forest, Pekin, Rantoul, South Holland, Urbana, Joliet, and Berwyn.

ADJUSTABLE-RATE MORTGAGES (ARMs)

In the early 1980s, lenders discovered that when interest rates reach a certain level, buyers refuse to obtain mortgages for the purchase of homes. To combat that problem, lenders introduced a new "product" to the marketplace called the graduated payment mortgage, the forerunner to the adjustable-rate loan. While fixed-rate loans might be at 13 percent, a borrower could take advantage of the initially low interest rate of a GPM. Later the rates of the GPM would be increased above 13 percent to give the lender the net return on its investment. The idea is that later in the term of the loan buyers would have more income by promotions, raises, etc., and buyers would pay off bills relating to the home purchase (furniture, appliances, etc.) and be in a better position to pay the higher rates. The following is a brief description of today's ARMs and the various ARM programs the residential real estate practitioner should be familiar with.

The primary elements of the ARM that distinguish it from a fixed-rate mortgage are:
1. Index
2. Lender's margin
3. Calculated interest rate
4. Interest-rate cap
5. Yearly payment cap

Index. The index is a measuring device to determine the buyer's payment on the payment adjustment date. If the index goes up or down, the buyer's payment will follow. The only requirement is that the index is verifiable by the buyer, approved by the lender's regulator, and beyond the control of the lender. The two most popular indexes are the Cost of Fund Index prepared by the 11th District Federal Home Loan Bank, and the One-Year Treasury Bill Index prepared by the Federal Reserve Board.

HISTORICAL RECORD OF INDEXES*			
YEAR	COST OF FUNDS	CONTRACT RATE	ONE-YEAR TREASURY
1981	11.58	15.53	12.85
1982	10.43	13.44	8.91
1983	9.90	11.94	10.11
1984	9.92	12.26	9.33
1985	8.48	10.70	7.67
1986	7.28	9.29	7.73
1987	7.11	8.86	5.78
1988	7.40	9.61	6.99
1989	7.92	9.69	7.72
1990	7.59	9.58	7.05
1991	8.78	6.59	4.89

*Percentages as of December each year.
Source: Mortgage Bankers Association, Economics Department

Lender's Margin. The lender's margin or spread is a percentage added to the index and is intended to cover all lender's costs plus profit. While indexes may move up and down, the lender's margin percentage should remain constant.

Calculated Interest Rate. This is the interest rate that the lender would base its return on over the life of the loan. It is computed by adding the selected index to the lender's margin (calculated interest rate equals index plus margin). It is the rate on which future adjustments and caps apply. Lenders will sometimes forgo their first-year earnings by discounting the initial interest rate. While this helps to qualify potential buyers at artificially low interest rates (teaser rates), these rates may be *too* low, and when the first interest-rate adjustments are made, borrowers may not be able to afford the monthly payments in the second year of the loan. It is best for ARM borrowers to ask for the *Annual Percentage Rate (APR)*. This is the true cost of borrowing money expressed as a yearly rate. In the case of an ARM mortgage, the APR is a "composite rate." It is a very serious offense for the lender not to disclose the APR, and the Federal Trade Commission will prosecute violating lenders.

Interest-Rate Cap. To protect borrowers against unacceptable increases in the interest-rate adjustment, lenders and regulators have established standards calling for ceilings on increases. The three most common caps used to limit increases in the calculated interest rates of ARM loans are:
1. The amount of the increase that can be applied at the first adjustment.
2. The amount of increase that can be applied during any one adjustment interval (for example, no more than a 2 percent increase over any one-year period). (The lender might be adjusting the interest rate quarterly, and sometimes even monthly, based on the yearly cap.)
3. The total amount of interest that may be increased over the life of the loan (for example, no more than 5 percent over 30 years).

Yearly Payment Cap. Rather than interest-rate caps, many lenders offer payment caps each year. This cap refers to the buyer's monthly payment, not his or her interest rate. The cap most widely referred to is 7.5 percent annually. Example: If the buyer had an initial monthly payment of $800 for principal and interest, then the buyer's payment increases (or decreases) would be limited to $60. Lenders might also give the borrower the additional protection of a "life of the loan" interest-rate cap.

ADDITIONAL FEATURES OF ARMs
Convertible Feature—Some lenders allow a buyer with a 3-year or 5-year ARM to convert to a fixed-rate mortgage for the balance of the term after initial adjustment period is complete.

No Prepayment Penalty—ARM loans should not contain penalties for early payoff. This consumer protection feature allows the buyer to obtain more-suitable financing at a later date.

Refinance Option—As long as an ARM does not contain a prepayment penalty, the buyer can always refinance his or her ARM with another lender or fixed-rate mortgage. A general rule is to convert an existing ARM to a fixed-rate mortgage whereby the borrower will recoup his or her investment (loan origination fees) within two years as a result of a lower fixed-rate payment.

REFINANCING CHART

<u>Example Column</u>: The figures used in the column below are typical for refinancing a $100,000, 30-year mortgage, if an existing loan at 10.5 percent is replaced by an 8.5 percent loan. The costs will vary among lenders.

COSTS OF REFINANCING		EXAMPLE
Application Fee	$_____	$350
Origination Fee	$_____	500
Credit Check	$_____	70
Discount Points	$_____	1,500
Appraisal Fee	$_____	400
Inspection Fees	$_____	350
Title Search Fee	$_____	100
Title Insurance	$_____	400
Repayment Penalty (Existing Mortgage)	$_____	0
Attorney Review Fee (Owner's)	$_____	250
Attorney Review Fee (Lender's)	$_____	250
Miscellaneous Fees	$_____	500
Estimate of Other Costs	$_____	250
Total of All Costs	$_____	4,920
Current Mortgage Payment (P & I Only)	$_____	915
Less New Mortgage Payment	$_____	(769)
Monthly Savings		$146

To determine the number of months to recover costs, divide the total costs by the monthly savings amount:
$4,920 ÷ $146 = 33.7
In the above example, it will take 34 months to recover the costs of refinancing.

Buyer Qualification—Lenders are allowed to qualify buyers on the first-year mortgage payment, rather than on future payments. This rule allows a buyer to substantially increase the loan amount, thereby purchasing a home with a greater value; however, more lenders today are now using the SECOND year's interest rate as the qualifier on Graduated Payment Mortgages. Both Fannie Mae and Freddie Mac loans require borrowers with less than 20 percent down payment on a one-year adjustable-rate loan to be qualified at the initial interest rate plus 2 percent. When deciding whether to apply for an ARM or a fixed-rate loan, a borrower should compare the two loans for a five-year period, which is about how long the average homeowner lives in a home.

COMPARISON OF AN ARM AT 8% AND A CONVENTIONAL LOAN AT 10.5%				
YEAR OF LOAN	ARM (8%) PAYMENT	FIXED (10.5%) PAYMENT	DIFFERENCE	
			MONTHLY	YEARLY
1	$734	$915	$181	$2172
2	$878	$915	$37	$2616
3	$1029	$915	($114)	$1248
4	$1185	$915	($270)	($1992)
BOTH LOANS ARE FOR 30 YEARS; ARM HAS 2% ANNUAL CAP AND 5% LIFE-OF-LOAN CAP				

In the above example, the borrower would reach his or her "break-even point" in May of year 4 and may wish to consider refinancing. At that time, the ARM would begin to be more expensive than the fixed rate, and the borrower would have lost the principal advantage of the ARM's lower monthly payments.

When advertising ARMs for Regulation Z purposes, an adjustable-rate or variable-rate mortgage is defined as one that includes at least one future interest-rate change not known at the time of the transaction.

Advertisements for ARMs must include the APR. This appears difficult when future rates are uncertain. The law therefore allows for some assumptions of future rates based on payment caps. The ad must state that the rate is subject to future change. The simple starting interest rate must be shown, but unlike ads for buydowns, the ad need not show the simple interest rate for the remainder of the loan. The reduction in the payment amount may be shown without triggering the need for other disclosures.

Additionally, the licensee should be aware of how ARMs function and how the payments may change in future years. A worst-case example of how high the prospect's payments may go should be provided. A disclosure of the historic movement of the selected index over the past ten years and how it would affect the payments on a $10,000 loan would be suggested.

ERRORS IN ARM ADJUSTMENTS
A not-for-profit service bureau has found that 47.5 percent of the 9,000 ARMs audited in 1991 had ERRORS. This amounted to an average *overcharge to customers of $1,588.* Three quarters of these mistakes were caused by the lender using the wrong index value to determine the mortgage rate or computing the new payment from the wrong time or from the wrong place. Companies like Consumer Loan Advocates in Lake Bluff, Illinois, and Loan Tech, a mortgage auditing firm (1-800-888-6781), will check your adjustable-rate payments for a fee. A borrower may want to check the payments before refinancing and closing out the loan. Overpayments must be refunded by the mistaken lender.

VA GPM AND FHA ARMs

The Veterans Administration GPM program starts with lower initial monthly payments and increases the payments 7.5 percent per year for five years and levels off for the next 25. These loans are limited to veterans on single-family owner-occupied units, including VA-approved condominiums. VA mobile homes have not as yet been approved.

Down payments will vary from 2.5 percent on new construction (covered by homeowner's warranty insurance) and as much as 12 percent on resale properties. The down payments are typically below conventional rates and are about 5 percent. The subject property of the loan must have at least a 30-year remaining economic life.

YEAR OF LOAN	VA/GPM PAYMENT COMPARISONS					
	$60,000		$90,000		$135,000	
	VA LEVEL	GPM LEVEL	VA LEVEL	GPM LEVEL	VA LEVEL	GPM LEVEL
1	505	391	757	587	1135	880
2	505	421	757	631	1135	946
3	505	452	757	678	1135	1017
4	505	486	757	729	1135	1094
5	505	522	757	783	1135	1176
6	505	562	757	842	1135	1265

VA LEVEL PAYMENT AT 9.5%, VA GRADUATED AT 9.75%
PAYMENTS INCLUDE PRINCIPAL AND INTEREST

FHA GPM—SECTION 245(a)

The FHA GPM Program was designed to allow more buyers to be able to buy homes. It can significantly reduce buyers' mortgage payments in the early years, helping them to be able to budget and qualify for a home they might not able to obtain under other financing terms. The buyer receives lower payments for the first five (5) years and then makes up for the lower payments by having higher payments from year 6 through the balance of the term. Because the reduced early payments are at a lesser rate than what's necessary to fully amortize the loan, the payment shortfall (negative amortization) is added back on to the principal balance of the loan. There are five plans to choose from. Plan 3 is the most popular.

Plan 1—Payments increase 2.5 percent each year for five years.
Plan 2—Payments increase 5 percent each year for five years.
Plan 3—Payments increase 7.5 percent each year for five years
Plan 4—Payments increase 2 percent each year for ten years.
Plan 5—Payments increase 3 percent each year for ten years.

FHA GPM PLAN COMPARISON
PRINCIPAL AND INTEREST—30 YEARS—$90,000 LOAN

YEAR	CONVENTIONAL FIXED	FHA FIXED	FHA GPM 1	FHA GPM 2	FHA GPM 3	FHA GPM 4	FHA GPM 5
1	824	790	736	672	614	718	676
2	824	790	755	706	660	732	696
3	824	790	773	741	709	747	717
4	824	790	793	778	763	762	739
5	824	790	813	817	820	777	761
6	824	790	834	858	881	792	784
7	824	790	834	858	881	808	807
8	824	790	834	858	881	824	832
9	824	790	834	858	881	841	857
10	824	790	834	858	881	858	882
11 & AFTER	824	790	834	858	881	875	909

CONVENTIONAL LOAN 10.5%; FHA FIXED RATE 10%; FHA GPM'S 10.25%

The down payment for these loans varies widely depending on the plan and the interest rate, but typically is between 5 percent and 6 percent. The maximum loan amount is identical to the FHA-level payments, between $67,500 and $124,875, depending on the area in Illinois in which the property is located. The programs are only for owner-occupied single-family residences. No investor loans, unless purchasing with a related owner-occupant. No duplexes, triplexes, or fourplexes are allowed. Condominiums may be financed if owner-occupied and if approved by the FHA.

FHA ARM—SECTION 251

The FHA does provide an ARM program whereby the buyer's payment is fixed for the first year and the payment would be adjusted according to the one-year Treasuries index. The buyer's payment would not be increased or decreased by more than 1 percent interest in any one year. Additionally, the overall interest rate may not increase or decrease by more than 5 percent over the life of the loan. Negative amortization is not allowed under this ARM. While these loans are assumable, loans made after February 1, 1988, carry a due-on-sale clause for the first year.

Negative Amortization. Negative amortization is the opposite of amortization. Rather than decreasing the principal balance of your loan, negative amortization, also referred to as deferred interest, has the effect of *increasing* the loan's principal balance. While there are many benefits to the negative amortization of ARM loans (more cash flow to borrower through lower monthly payments, the buyer gets the house the buyer wants, mortgage interest tax breaks, and appreciation), deferred interest is still a concern to borrowers and should be explained thoroughly by the lending institution.

ALTERNATIVE FINANCING METHODS

Buydowns. A buydown is money that is paid by someone (seller, builder, employer, investor, buyer) to a lender in return for lower interest rates and monthly payments. The payment in dollars or discount points lowers the buyer's payments either for the entire mortgage term (which is called a "permanent buydown") or for a lesser

200 Chapter 10 Finance Developments

period, such as three to five years (which is termed a "temporary buydown"). A temporary buydown will have a more dramatic effect on the purchaser's ability to buy, as more of the buydown dollars are used to reduce the payment in the early years of a loan. For example, if a seller/builder paid discount points to a lender on a $60,000, 30-year mortgage, a permanent buydown would allocate $3,600 over 350 payments and might only reduce the monthly payments by $10. However, if the 6 percent discount was allocated at 3 percent for year one and 2 percent for year two and 1 percent for year three, then the $3,600 would be allocated such that each of the first year's monthly payments would be reduced by $150, year two's monthly payments by $100, and year three's monthly payments by $50.

While builders across the county have overwhelmingly employed temporary buydowns, home sellers have not. Most home sellers would "buydown" the buyer's mortgage by reducing the sales price by $3,600, in effect giving a permanent buydown to the buyer. Sellers might consider a full-price sale and give the buyer a 3-2-1 temporary buydown, pledging the $3,600 from the sale proceeds in an interest-bearing account (better for the seller and the buyer).

Temporary v. Permanent Buydowns. There are three ways to compute the cost of a buydown. You can calculate the cost in interest, dollars, or discount points. Calculating the cost of temporary buydowns in dollars is probably the simplest method, and using a financial calculator or amortization payment book is all you need. For temporary buydowns, simply calculate the payments each year for the mortgage without the buydown and then calculate the lower payment with the buydown. The difference between the payments is the gross buydown amount needed. Many lenders will credit back interest over the buydown period (or do a present value calculation) to lower the amount of money required. Don't hesitate to ask the lender for some interest credit, because most lenders will earn some interest on the unused buydown funds.

Interest-Rate Buydown
1. Use a financial calculator or amortization schedule to calculate the Monthly Payments without the buydown. Enter this amount in Column A.
2. Determine from the seller how much money is available for a buydown. Enter the monthly and annual amounts in Columns C & D.

   Let's say $4,500. Then, since 3 + 2 + 1 = 6, 3/6 = 50%, 2/6 = 33%, 1/6 = 17%
   50% of $4,500 = $2,250 Year 1 buydown ÷ 12 for monthly $188
   33% of $4,500 = $1,500 Year 2 buydown ÷ 12 for monthly $125
   17% of $4,500 = $750 Year 3 buydown ÷ 12 for monthly $62.50
   $4,500 $4,500 Total buydown

3. Subtract Column A from C for Column B

YEAR	A PAYMENT WITHOUT BUYDOWN	B PAYMENT WITH BUYDOWN	C MONTHLY DIFFERENCE	D ANNUAL DIFFERENCE
\$72,000 MORTGAGE—30 YEARS—10%					
1	632	444	188	2250
2	632	507	125	1500
3	632	569.50	62.50	750
4	632	632	-	-
5	632	632	-	-

GROSS BUYDOWN AMOUNT: $4500

Assume a sales price of $90,000, and an 80 percent loan-to-value ratio. It would be *better* for the purchaser to pay *full price* of $90,000 and receive a 3-2-1 buydown of $4,500 than for seller to reduce the price $4,500 to $85,500, because the buyer's payment would then be only $600.26 (80% × $85,500 = $68,400 mortgage).

Advertising Buydowns. Advertising requirements for Regulation Z buydowns are not too complicated. What needs to be disclosed (along with the lower initial effective rate of interest) are:
1. how long the lowered rate will last;
2. what the simple interest rate will be for the remainder of the loan; and
3. the Annual Percentage Rate (APR).

REVERSE ANNUITY MORTGAGE
Under legislation that took effect on January 1, 1992, Illinois joined the majority of states in permitting the RAM. This mortgage loan allows homeowners 62 and over to convert the equity in their home to cash without making monthly repayments or having to sell the property. The RAM loan involves a definite time period and payback obligation. The RAM loan is intended to provide older homeowners (over 1.4 million in Illinois) the use of their homes while enjoying use of the equity that has been built up over the years.

Over 75 percent of homeowners over 65 years of age own their homes free and clear. The RAM program is especially designed for these people. Typically a RAM borrower may obtain up to 80 percent of the home's appraised value. The amount borrowed is paid to the homeowner in monthly installments over a five-year to 15-year period based on actuarial years from life insurance statistics. A RAM at 10 percent on an $80,000 equity home for eight years might yield a monthly advance of $400 to the homeowner ($38,400 total advances).

Assuming a 3 percent appreciation factor, the homeowner would still have more than $42,000 of equity remaining *after* paying the loan's principal and interest, eight years later. At the end of the term or at the death of a homeowner, whichever occurs first, the loan must be paid or the loan renegotiated. While only about 2,000 such loans have been made so far, the RAM is growing in acceptance by lenders. The FHA will now insure these mortgages, and it has expanded the number of approved lenders to include all 6,000 FHA lenders. Fannie Mae has agreed to buy $2 billion worth (approximately 25,000 loans) through September 1995, and servicing corporations have been started to assist lenders who originate these loans. Illinois law requires lenders to give RAM applicants a statement regarding the advisability and availability of independent counseling, at HUD-approved counseling centers, when they make loan application. Counselors also alert homeowners to other options, including home sharing, room rental, subsidized housing, free meals, tax deferrals, and home equity loans.

RAM QUICK FACTS
- RAM mortgages are available to any homeowner aged 62 or older whose house or condo is completely paid for or substantially paid for. Jointly owned homes require that both homeowners must be at least 62.

- FHA maximum loan amounts vary by area. Income and credit rating are not considered when qualifying.

- Homeowners can choose between receiving monthly payments, a line of credit, or a single lump sum.

- The payments do not affect Social Security or Medicare Benefits. Loan proceeds are not taxable as income.

- Mortgages do not allow the lender to force a sale if the principal owed should exceed the value of the property. FHA insurance covers any balance due lender.

- One payment of the principal balance is due within 12 months of either: homeowner's death, sale of home, or otherwise vacating the home.

SHARED APPRECIATION MORTGAGE

The shared appreciation mortgage should, for the sake of accuracy, be called the "shared equity mortgage." The SAM/SEM plan makes a relative, lender, or investor a partner (or borrower) by sharing the down payment, monthly payments, and other expenses with the purchaser. The partner is then permitted to share in the property's appreciation at some future point. For example, the investor (e.g., parents) might pay half the down payment and half the monthly payments for a condominium with their son, who pays the other half. In addition, the son will pay the investors (parents) half of a fair market rent for the half the house the son uses but does not own. For the investors, the half interest represents an interest in income-producing real estate. The IRS will permit the investor to write off one half of the depreciation of the house, together with one half of the mortgage interest, property taxes, and expenses for repairs or improvements. The son also gets 50 percent of the mortgage interest and property taxes he pays, but cannot claim depreciation because he resides in the property. He also cannot claim depreciation for repairs. When the property is sold, the profits will be divided according to the ownership interest of each. FHA has a SAM program.

15-YEAR MORTGAGES

Fannie Mae has established programs with guidelines to buy 10-, 15-, and 20-year mortgage loans. Perhaps one of six borrowers opts to make a larger down payment and wants quicker equity buildup in contrast to the traditional 30-year amortization period. The 15-year mortgage will save them almost half the interest of a 30-year loan and, because it is for a shorter period of time, it carries an interest rate between 0.25 percent and 1.00 percent less. The drawbacks to the 15-year loan are the larger initial down payment and the larger monthly payments. A 30-year $80,000 mortgage at 11 percent interest will cost a borrower about $762 per month and $194,000 in interest. The same loan over 15 years at 11.5 percent would be $935 per month and cost $88,000 in interest.

A borrower may consider converting a 30-year mortgage to a 15-year mortgage by making an annual 13th (extra) payment on the loan, designating on the payment to apply it all to principal.

On the opposite page is a mortgage payment "Quick Check" for those of us who are still not using financial calculators when computing monthly payment of principal and interest for the buyer. It is a quick and easy method of computation.

BIWEEKLY

Imagine that instead of making 12 monthly payments each year on your 30-year mortgage, you make 26 payments (one every other week). By attacking the principal balance this way, the borrower can substantially reduce both interest and the loan payoff period. One drawback to the biweekly is that until recently, the secondary market did not purchase them. Another is that it takes a complete reworking of the lender's automated bookkeeping systems to compute and track the payments. Also, if the borrower misses just one payment, he or she would technically be in default of the loan. Most lenders will not convert existing 30-year mortgages to a biweekly, principally because the loan has already been set up for 30-year amortization and, most probably, has been sold to investors. Lenders do, however, encourage borrowers to make additional payments to apply strictly to principal.

AFL-CIO UNION PRIVILEGE FINANCING

Two nationwide programs recently announced by the AFL-CIO will assist union members in Illinois in buying a home. The Housing Investment Trust, which invests AFL-CIO union pension funds in a variety of residential projects, has initiated a $7 million pilot program in Illinois.

In one of the programs, the trust selects a new all-union construction project and makes money available to a qualified participating union member/purchaser of the project; usually single-family homes, townhomes, or condominiums. These loans are fixed-rate, 30-year loans usually at or below market rates. Points may be charged. The Housing Investment Trust predicts it could invest over $300 million in Illinois and the Chicago area in 1992.

QUICK CHECK—A METHOD OF QUICKLY COMPUTING MONTHLY LOAN PAYMENTS

Multiply the amount of buyer's loan (in thousands) by the dollar per thousand from the table below. For example, how much would the buyer pay each month for principal and interest on a $60,000 loan at 8.5 percent for 25 years? The answer: 60 × 8.052 = $483.12 monthly payment (principal and interest).

EQUAL MONTHLY PAYMENT TO AMORTIZE A LOAN OF $1000
YEARS IN TERM

RATE	1	2	3	4	5	6	7	8	9	10	15	20	25	30
6.000%	86.07	44.32	30.42	23.49	19.33	16.57	14.61	13.14	12.01	11.10	8.439	7.164	6.443	5.996
6.125%	86.12	44.38	30.48	23.54	19.39	16.63	14.67	13.20	12.07	11.17	8.506	7.237	6.520	6.076
6.250%	86.18	44.43	30.54	23.60	19.45	16.69	14.73	13.26	12.13	11.23	8.574	7.309	6.597	6.157
6.375%	86.24	44.49	30.59	23.66	19.51	16.75	14.79	13.32	12.19	11.29	8.643	7.382	6.674	6.239
6.500%	86.30	44.55	30.65	23.72	19.57	16.81	14.85	13.39	12.25	11.35	8.711	7.456	6.752	6.321
6.625%	86.35	44.60	30.70	23.77	19.62	16.87	14.91	13.45	12.32	11.42	8.780	7.530	6.830	6.403
6.750%	86.41	44.66	30.76	23.83	19.68	16.93	14.97	13.51	12.38	11.48	8.849	7.604	6.909	6.486
6.875%	86.47	44.72	30.82	23.89	19.74	16.99	15.03	13.57	12.44	11.55	8.919	7.678	6.988	6.569
7.000%	86.53	44.77	30.88	23.95	19.80	17.05	15.09	13.63	12.51	11.61	8.988	7.753	7.068	6.653
7.125%	86.58	44.83	30.93	24.00	19.86	17.11	15.15	13.70	12.57	11.68	9.058	7.828	7.148	6.737
7.250%	86.64	44.89	30.99	24.06	19.92	17.17	15.22	13.76	12.63	11.74	9.129	7.904	7.228	6.822
7.375%	86.70	44.94	31.05	24.12	19.98	17.23	15.28	13.82	12.70	11.81	9.199	7.980	7.309	6.907
7.500%	86.76	45.00	31.11	24.18	20.04	17.29	15.34	13.88	12.76	11.87	9.270	8.056	7.390	6.992
7.625%	86.82	45.06	31.16	24.24	20.10	17.35	15.40	13.95	12.83	11.94	9.341	8.133	7.472	7.078
7.750%	86.87	45.11	31.22	24.30	20.16	17.41	15.46	14.01	12.89	12.00	9.413	8.210	7.553	7.164
7.875%	86.93	45.17	31.28	24.35	20.22	17.47	15.52	14.07	12.95	12.07	9.485	8.287	7.636	7.251
8.000%	86.99	45.23	31.34	24.41	20.28	17.53	15.59	14.14	13.02	12.13	9.557	8.364	7.718	7.338
8.125%	87.05	45.28	31.39	24.47	20.34	17.59	15.65	14.20	13.08	12.20	9.629	8.442	7.801	7.425
8.250%	87.10	45.34	31.45	24.53	20.40	17.66	15.71	14.26	13.15	12.27	9.701	8.521	7.885	7.513
8.375%	87.16	45.40	31.51	24.59	20.46	17.72	15.77	14.33	13.21	12.33	9.774	8.599	7.968	7.601
8.500%	87.22	45.46	31.57	24.65	20.52	17.78	15.84	14.39	13.28	12.40	9.847	8.678	8.052	7.689
8.625%	87.28	45.51	31.63	24.71	20.58	17.84	15.90	14.46	13.35	12.47	9.921	8.758	8.137	7.778
8.750%	87.34	45.57	31.68	24.77	20.64	17.90	15.96	14.52	13.41	12.53	9.995	8.837	8.221	7.867
8.875%	87.39	45.63	31.74	24.83	20.70	17.96	16.03	14.59	13.48	12.60	10.07	8.917	8.307	7.956
9.000%	87.45	45.68	31.80	24.89	20.76	18.03	16.09	14.65	13.54	12.67	10.14	8.997	8.392	8.046
9.125%	87.51	45.74	31.86	24.94	20.82	18.09	16.15	14.72	13.61	12.74	10.22	9.078	8.478	8.136
9.250%	87.57	45.80	31.92	25.00	20.88	18.15	16.22	14.78	13.68	12.80	10.29	9.159	8.564	8.227
9.375%	87.63	45.86	31.97	25.06	20.94	18.21	16.28	14.85	13.74	12.87	10.37	9.240	8.650	8.318
9.500%	87.68	45.91	32.03	25.12	21.00	18.27	16.34	14.91	13.81	12.94	10.44	9.321	8.737	8.409
9.625%	87.74	45.97	32.09	25.18	21.06	18.34	16.41	14.98	13.88	13.01	10.52	9.403	8.824	8.500
9.750%	87.80	46.03	32.15	25.24	21.12	18.40	16.47	15.04	13.94	13.08	10.59	9.485	8.911	8.592
9.875%	87.86	46.09	32.21	25.31	21.19	18.46	16.54	15.11	14.01	13.15	10.67	9.568	8.999	8.684
10.000%	87.92	46.14	32.27	25.36	21.25	18.53	16.60	15.17	14.08	13.22	10.75	9.650	9.087	8.776
10.125%	87.97	46.20	32.33	25.42	21.31	18.59	16.67	15.24	14.15	13.28	10.82	9.733	9.175	8.868
10.250%	88.03	46.26	32.38	25.48	21.37	18.65	16.73	15.31	14.21	13.35	10.90	9.816	9.264	8.961
10.375%	88.09	46.32	32.44	25.54	21.43	18.72	16.80	15.37	14.28	13.42	10.98	9.900	9.353	9.054
10.500%	88.15	46.38	32.50	25.60	21.49	18.78	16.86	15.44	14.35	13.49	11.05	9.984	9.442	9.147
10.625%	88.21	46.43	32.56	25.66	21.56	18.84	16.93	15.51	14.42	13.56	11.13	10.07	9.531	9.241
10.750%	88.27	46.49	32.62	25.72	21.62	18.91	16.99	15.57	14.49	13.63	11.21	10.15	9.621	9.335
10.875%	88.32	46.55	32.68	25.78	21.68	18.97	17.06	15.64	14.56	13.70	11.29	10.24	9.711	9.429
11.000%	88.38	46.61	32.74	25.85	21.74	19.03	17.12	15.71	14.63	13.78	11.37	10.32	9.801	9.523
11.125%	88.44	46.67	32.80	25.91	21.80	19.10	17.19	15.78	14.70	13.85	11.45	10.41	9.892	9.618
11.250%	88.50	46.72	32.86	25.97	21.87	19.16	17.25	15.84	14.76	13.92	11.52	10.49	9.982	9.713
11.375%	88.56	46.78	32.92	26.03	21.93	19.23	17.32	15.91	14.83	13.99	11.60	10.58	10.07	9.808
11.500%	88.62	46.84	32.98	26.09	21.99	19.29	17.39	15.98	14.90	14.06	11.68	10.66	10.16	9.903
11.625%	88.67	46.90	33.04	26.15	22.06	19.36	17.45	16.05	14.97	14.13	11.76	10.75	10.26	9.998
11.750%	88.73	46.96	33.10	26.21	22.12	19.42	17.52	16.12	15.04	14.20	11.84	10.84	10.35	10.09
11.875%	88.79	47.02	33.15	26.27	22.18	19.49	17.59	16.18	15.11	14.27	11.92	10.92	10.44	10.19
12.000%	88.85	47.07	33.21	26.33	22.24	19.55	17.65	16.25	15.18	14.35	12.00	11.01	10.53	10.29
12.125%	88.91	47.13	33.27	26.40	22.31	19.62	17.72	16.32	15.25	14.42	12.08	11.10	10.62	10.38
12.250%	88.97	47.19	33.33	26.46	22.37	19.68	17.79	16.39	15.33	14.49	12.16	11.19	10.72	10.48
12.375%	89.02	47.25	33.39	26.52	22.43	19.75	17.85	16.46	15.40	14.56	12.24	11.27	10.81	10.58
12.500%	89.08	47.31	33.45	26.58	22.50	19.81	17.92	16.53	15.47	14.64	12.33	11.36	10.90	10.67
12.625%	89.14	61.27	33.51	26.64	22.56	19.88	17.99	16.60	15.54	14.71	12.41	11.45	11.00	10.77
12.750%	89.20	47.42	33.57	26.70	22.63	19.94	18.06	16.67	15.61	14.78	12.49	11.54	11.09	10.87
12.875%	89.26	47.48	33.63	26.77	22.69	20.00	18.12	16.74	15.68	14.86	12.57	11.63	11.18	10.96

Under another program, qualifying union member borrowers can obtain financing for as low as 3 percent for the first-time buyer and 5 percent for other applicants. Mortgage rates can be locked in for up to 90 days for existing housing and up to six months for newly constructed union-built housing. Low application fees and closing costs are also included in the program. At present 18 unions have agreed to provide this service to their memberships. Eventually 92 AFL-CIO union members may have access to the Union Privilege Mortgage Program (UPMP). Union members can receive more information about the program through their participating local union office.

The following example shows the comparison of a conventional mortgage and the UPMP for a family with a yearly income of $35,000 who is purchasing an $80,000 home.

	UPMP	Conventional
Mortgage Payment	$77,600	$76,000
Down Payment	2,400 (3%)	4,000 (5%)
Points	0	1,520 (2)
PMI	543	760
Escrows	0	1,614
Closing Costs	550	550
Total Up-Front Cost	$3,493	$8,444
UPMP Savings	**$4,951**	

FHA 203(K)

A little-known federal loan program issued by HUD and known as the 203(K) Rehabilitation Mortgage Insurance Program is a cheaper way to pay for repairs and to modernize while spending less money up front when buying or refinancing a home. Loans are available for individuals or investors for residential properties of one to four units up to a maximum mortgage of $124,875. The program allows buyers to get a "handyman's special" at a low price and still qualify for a mortgage that includes all renovation costs.

Buyers save money, because they avoid having to get a separate construction loan at rates about 2 percent higher than mortgages. They put down less money, because 203(K) allows financing up to 100 percent of closing costs. Regular FHA loans limit financing to 57 percent. Buyers can include up to six months of mortgage payments in the loan so they don't have to make mortgage payments until the work is completed. Below is a comparison between the 203(K) and an FHA direct endorsement loan.

	203(K)	FHA Direct Endorsement
Sale Price	$50,000	$75,000
Renovations	25,000	0
Value	75,000	75,000
Closing Costs	2,550	1,050
Mortgage	77,550	76,050
Down payment	3,500	5,700
Monthly Payment	652	640

Loans are both at 9.5 percent for 30 years.
One hundred percent of closing-cost financing with 203(K) versus only 57 percent with conventional FHA.

With the 203(K) you save $1,700 in down payment and, for an additional $12 per month, you have a modernized home. You also avoid a separate construction loan, which may be as high as 11.5 percent. To obtain financing, the property would have to be located in a viable area, where the market value after renovations would exceed repair costs. Any type of renovation, e.g., bathrooms, kitchens, room or garage additions, wiring, heating, and plumbing, can be financed—providing the cost is over $5,000 and the work is not just cosmetic (painting or wallpapering). The program will not finance luxuries like saunas and swimming pools. For homeowners considering refinancing mortgages, the program lets them save on interest costs and pay for renovation with a single loan.

4/26, 5/25, 7/23 HIKE!!

No . . . this is not a play being called by the Chicago Bears. These programs are balloon loans, where the rates are fixed for the first time frame and then adjusted for the duration of the 30 years. The 4/26 balloon would carry an interest rate of 8 percent for the first four years and then rise 2.5 percentage points above the weekly Treasury Bill Index at the end of the 48th month. There are usually no conversion costs, title search, or additional underwriting preformed at the time of conversion on these balloons.

MTx ALTERNATIVE FINANCING SYSTEM

A new PC-based automated loan-origination system is now on line that will significantly increase opportunities for the estimated 20 percent of all home buyers who do not qualify for standard financing. Through the Mortgage Trading Exchange, or MTx, buyers will be able to choose from hundreds of nontraditional alternative mortgages offered by some of the country's largest lenders.

Alternative mortgages or "nonconforming" loans are those that do not conform to the strict underwriting guidelines of FNMA or FHLMC, the two federally charted private companies that supply the lion's share of the nation's mortgage money. An estimated 80 percent of all mortgages fit Fannie Mae and Freddie Mac credit standards. But dozens of the top national lenders deal in the other 20 percent of the mortgage market, which includes jumbo loans above the agency limit, first and second mortgages, and refinance loans.

MTx is programmed to select an exact match between what the borrower needs and want the lender requires. And if there is more than one match, it shows the best choice in terms of interest rates and points. More important, by using "fuzzy logic" it also selects several other additional loan possibilities that the buyer may also wish to consider. This technological breakthrough allows lenders to review loan applications that would never have come to their attention and bend otherwise rigid rules if the buyers generally fit their loan criteria.

CREDIT REPORTS

Because of the abuse and errors found in the credit reporting system and their reports issued by the National Credit Repositories, the three major companies involved in credit reporting have agreed to improve their handling of credit data. To check your own credit file, submit your full name, spouse's name, current address, Social Security number, year of birth, and addresses for the past five years. By law you are entitled to a FREE copy of your credit report within 30 days of a credit denial, but you must ask for it.

The three major companies and their charges are:

TRW Consumer Assistance Center   Price: $7.50 until April 30, 1992; free thereafter
P.O. Box 749029
Dallas, Texas 75374
Phone: 214-235-1200

Eqifax Information Service Center   Price: $3 to $15
Wildwood Plaza
7200 Windy Hill Road Suite #500
Marietta, Georgia 30067
Phone: 800-685-1111

Trans Union Consumer Relations Center
25249 Country Club Blvd.
P.O. Box 7000
North Olmstead, Ohio 44070

Price: $3 to $20

Phone: Check Yellow Pages under "Credit Reporting Agencies"

CASES TO JUDGE

1. Plaintiff's mother, Ivory Anderson, died on October 7, 1977, leaving him as the surviving joint tenant of certain real estate located in Kankakee County, the value of which was approximately $15,000. Plaintiff desired to provide his mother with a funeral and requested Defendant's assistance in raising the funds necessary, which approximated $1,500. Defendant was a half-brother of the decedent and the Plaintiff's half-uncle.

   Defendant accompanied Plaintiff in his efforts to borrow the necessary funds for his mother's funeral, but they were unsuccessful. Plaintiff and Defendant then entered into an agreement whereby in return for Defendant's paying the funeral bill for Plaintiff's mother, Plaintiff would deed the premises to Defendant.

   Plaintiff and Defendant went to Defendant's attorney's office, where Plaintiff signed a paper he thought was a contract to pay Defendant $115 a month for 15 months ($1,725). A warranty deed was prepared by Defendant's attorney and signed by Plaintiff when he went to the lawyer's office on October 9, 1977, two days after his mother's death. The next day, Defendant paid the funeral bill in the sum of $1,473.75.

   Plaintiff made one payment to Defendant before losing his job and generally falling on hard times by drinking heavily. No further payments were made to Defendant. Plaintiff and his family made temporary use of the premises on several occasions after delivery of the deed to Defendant at his lawyer's office. Defendant conceded he did not go to the house after his half-sister died. Plaintiff continued to keep the property in good repair and to pay the 1978 and 1979 taxes on the property, and Defendant made no attempt to pay any taxes on the property until October 1980, when his check was returned indicating that the taxes had already been paid. In January 1980, Plaintiff had offered to pay Defendant the balance of the debt, but Defendant refused payment. In June 1980, Defendant recorded the deed.

   Defendant never used the property or interfered with Plaintiff's use until June 1980, when Plaintiff discovered that Defendant was attempting to list the property for rent with a real estate broker. Plaintiff contacted an attorney, discovered the warranty deed, and filed the instant suit to quiet title.

   Under these facts and circumstances, what interest, if any, does the Plaintiff have in the real estate? [*McGill v. Biggs*, 105 Ill.App.3d 706, 434 N.E.2d 772, 61 Ill.Dec.417 (1982)]

2. On July 31, 1907, a couple by the name of Smith signed a $5,000 one-year note and mortgage on an 80-acre tract of land. The mortgage was recorded on August 7, 1907. On July 31, 1941, the Smiths signed a new note for $500 that recited that it was secured by the 1907 mortgage. In 1943, both Smiths died intestate and the lender sought to foreclose the mortgage. If the lender were permitted to foreclose, its claim against the estate would be superior to other estate claims. Otherwise, it would share the assets of the estate proportionately with the other creditors.

   Should the lender be permitted to foreclose? [*Trustees of Zion Methodist Church v. Smith*, 335 Ill.App. 233, 81 N.E.2d 649 (1948)]

3. In 1975, Slevin Container Corp. (Slevin) borrowed from Provident Federal Savings & Loan Association of Peoria (Provident) $468,000 and executed and delivered in return therefor a promissory note, which provided in part: (a) "The undersigned (Slevin) reserve the right to prepay this note in whole or in part at any time, but the Association (Provident) may require payment of not more than six (6) months' advance interest on that part of the aggregate amount of all prepayments on the note in one year, which exceeds twenty percent (20%) of the original principal amount of the loan"; (b) "[I]n the event the undersigned's interest in said real estate is transferred without the consent of the Association, the Association may increase the interest rate to 8 percent per annum or declare the entire unpaid balance of this note due, or both, by giving the undersigned written notice."

   On June 14, 1980, the property was sold, and the bank was notified of the sale. It was asked to inform the new owner of its election to accelerate or increase the interest rate to 8 percent. The bank responded with notice of acceleration and demanded a prepayment penalty.

   The balance due without the penalty was paid and a lawsuit was filed seeking to establish whether the prepayment penalty could be charged.

May a lender accelerate the maturity of a note upon the sale of the premises and also collect a premium or penalty for prepayment? [*Slevin Container Corp. v. Provident Federal Savings and Loan Association of Peoria*, 98 Ill.App.3d 646, 424 N.E.2d 939, 54 Ill.Dec. 189 (1981)]

4. The plaintiff bank was given a mortgage dated October 4, 1974, which was recorded on October 25, 1974, at 9:28 a.m. The defendant finance company was given a prior mortgage dated September 16, 1974, which was also recorded on October 25, 1974, at 3:07 p.m.

The finance company's mortgage stated that the amount of the initial debt was $30,000, but the mortgage contained a clause that permitted unlimited advances of additional funds. The bank's mortgage did not reflect the amount of the debt at all.

State law requires that in order for a mortgage to give constructive notice of a party's interest in real estate, the document must state the amount of the indebtedness.

Under these circumstances, which mortgage is the prior lien against the real estate? [*Northridge Bank v. Lakeshore Commercial Finance Corporation*, 48 Ill.App.3d 82, 365 N.E.2d 382, 8 Ill.Dec. 144 (1977)]

5. Defendants appealed a judgment of foreclosure, claiming that the plaintiff bank should not be permitted to accelerate the mortgage debt because of waiver, estoppel, and/or laches.

On April 4, 1977, defendants entered into a partnership agreement, and on July 1, 1977, they mortgaged the subject real estate to plaintiff. Thirty-five days after the mortgage was signed, the real estate was transferred by the partnership to a land trust. The transfer was recorded on September 2, 1977. Although there was conflicting evidence, by early 1978 the plaintiff bank was or should have been aware of the land trust transfer based on the defendant's having given the bank year-end accounting records disclosing that one of the partners had sold out.

In October 1978, defendants sought plaintiff's consent to a transfer of the property to a new owner by the name of Dr. Clark. Plaintiff committed to permit the transfer, subject to certain conditions. When the bank's terms and conditions were not accepted, on February 19, 1979, the bank accelerated the note on the basis of the September 2, 1977, transfer and proceeded to foreclose.

Should the bank be permitted to foreclose even though it accepted payments for approximately 12 months after it became aware of the transfer? [*First National Bank of Lincoln v. Brown*, 90 Ill.App.3d 215, 412 N.E.2d 1078, 45 Ill.Dec. 496 (1980)]

10-QUESTION DIAGNOSTIC QUIZ

1. The agency created under the Financial Institutions Reform, Recovery, and Enforcement Act to run failed thrifts and dispose of their real estate assets is called the:
   A. RTC.
   B. RTA.
   C. RTZ.
   D. RTS.

2. All of the following are participants in the secondary mortgage market EXCEPT:
   A. VA.
   B. FNMA.
   C. GNMA.
   D. FHLMC.

3. The current maximum one-unit loan limit on loans purchased by FNMA/FHLMC is:
   A. $202,300.
   B. $100,000.
   C. $50,000.
   D. There is no limit on the loans these organizations will purchase.

4. Calculating the maximum insured commitment on an FHA loan:
   A. requires different calculations for properties over $50,000 and under $50,000.
   B. requires two different calculations after determining the maximum mortgage amount.
   C. is fairly confusing to calculate.
   D. All of the above

5. FHA loans can be:
   A. fixed-rate loans.
   B. variable-rate loans.
   C. assumable loans.
   D. All of the above

6. VA loans are available on all of the following EXCEPT:
   A. one-family to four-family dwellings.
   B. cooperatives.
   C. condominiums.
   D. large apartment complexes.

7. Adjustable-rate mortgages can be an advantage over a fixed-rate mortgage:
   A. when the purchaser will own the home for a short time before selling.
   B. by allowing the purchaser to qualify for a larger loan amount.
   C. by keeping payments smaller in the early years of the loan.
   D. All of the above

8. Adjustable-rate mortgages can be a disadvantage over a fixed-rate loan:
   A. when the buyer will own the property for a long time and does not want to refinance.
   B. for borrowers who have a fixed income.
   C. for borrowers who want to maximize their equity buildup in the early years of the loan.
   D. All of the above

9. An alternative financing method about which real estate salespeople may wish to become more knowledgeable is the:
   A. reverse annuity mortgage.
   B. shared appreciation mortgage.
   C. buydown.
   D. All of the above

10. A potential source of financing for individuals—and of financial assistance for builders and developers for low-income housing—is the:
    A. Illinois Housing Authority.
    B. Federal Reserve Board.
    C. Resolution Trust Corporation.
    D. League of Savings and Loans.

CHAPTER 11

TAXATION
(ONE OF LIFE'S CERTAINTIES)

○ **CHAPTER OVERVIEW**
One of the two certainties of life (taxation--death, of course, is the other) is detailed in this chapter. A licensee should stay abreast of the most important and relevant areas of taxation, which are discussed in this chapter.

○ **LEARNING OBJECTIVES**
When you have completed studying this chapter, you should be able to:
1) Explain and distinguish between the types of income.
2) Highlight three changes affecting real estate as a result of recent tax acts.
3) Explain what is meant by a *capital gain* as it applies to real property.
4) Explain what is meant by the terms *basis* and *adjusted basis*.
5) Name and be familiar with three methods of disposing of real property.
6) Describe what is meant by the *rollover rule* in principal residence ownership.
7) Know the key elements of the *55-or-over rule*.
8) Explain the purpose for using the installment-sale method.
9) Explain what is meant by *points* and when they are deductible.
10) Explain what *depreciation* for tax purposes means as it applies to real estate.
11) Explain what *passive activities* are and state their relationship to tax sheltering.
12) Cite two new transaction-closing requirements imposed by the IRS.

○ **5 CASES TO JUDGE**

○ **10-QUESTION DIAGNOSTIC QUIZ**

CHAPTER 11

TAXATION
(ONE OF LIFE'S CERTAINTIES)

Our Constitution is in actual operation; everything appears to promise that it will last; but in this world nothing is certain but death and taxes.
—Benjamin Franklin (1706-1790)

The purpose of this chapter is to familiarize licensees with *selected highlights* and current aspects of federal income taxes affecting real estate. The purpose is NOT the development of expertise. The real estate licensee's role is *not* to give professional tax advice, but to be knowledgeable about basic tax information and important recent changes in tax laws to be able to alert clients to their need for professional tax and legal advice *before* they purchase or sell real property. In Colorado, a real estate broker lost a negligence suit because the seller was not advised of the tax implications of the transaction and was not advised to seek the help of a tax expert. Fortunately, a similar claim in Illinois was rejected; however, the court, for technical reasons, did not thoroughly consider the issue.

The federal government first levied an income tax from 1862 to 1872 to help pay for the Civil War. In 1894, Congress passed a new income tax law, which was declared unconstitutional by the U.S. Supreme Court. The 16th Amendment to the Constitution, adopted in 1913, made possible the present system of federal income taxes.

RECENT FEDERAL TAX ACTS

The Tax Reform Act of 1986 (TRA '86), the most sweeping overhaul in the history of the income tax, required a totally new look at one's personal tax, retirement planning, business tax, and investments. The impact was and is enormous. Since its passage, write-offs (deductions) have become nearly as scarce as Republicans in Chicago's City Hall.

Although the Revenue Act of 1987 (RA '87) did not have the impact of the Tax Reform Act of 1986, it was aptly named, because its purpose was and is to raise revenue. Of particular interest to real estate licensees are the changes affecting "qualified residence interest" and "installment sales."

The Technical and Miscellaneous Revenue Act of 1988 (TAMRA '88) puts into the Tax Code the "Taxpayer Bill of Rights." It provides tax benefits to individual taxpayers, many of which are retroactive (a taxpayer who might benefit can file an amended return).

The Revenue Reconciliation Act of 1989 contained several items affecting real estate, primarily in regard to tax-deferred exchanges and the low-income housing credit.

Toward the end of 1990, Congress passed a deficit-reduction package that made extensive changes to late-1980s tax legislation. Three of the important provisions affecting real estate licensees, each effective January 1, 1991, are: the maximum tax rate on income was lowered from 33 percent to 31 percent, a new maximum capital-gain tax rate of 28 percent was established, and the alternative minimum tax rate was raised from 21 percent to 24 percent.

The art of taxation consists of so plucking the goose as to obtain the largest amount of feathers with the least possible amount of hissing.
—J. B. Colbert (1619-1683), controller general of finance to Louis XIV of France, the "Sun King"

TAX BASICS

Currently, three income tax brackets exist: 15 percent, 28 percent, and 31 percent. An individual taxpayer's *marginal rate* is the highest rate at which a portion of income is taxed. Net capital gain is taxed at a maximum rate of 28 percent.

TYPES OF INCOME
Ordinary income is an amount earned. It consists of three types:
   a) *Active income*—salary, wages, bonuses, tips, commissions, income from activities in which the taxpayer *materially participates* (involved in on a regular, continuous, and substantial basis).
   b) *Passive income*—gain from an activity conducted for profit (including an activity that is not a trade or business) in which the taxpayer does *not* "materially" participate; income from most limited partnerships or from rental activities where payments are primarily for the use of tangible property (includes net lease of property) regardless of whether the taxpayer materially participates in these two situations. Determining whether a particular activity is a "rental activity" is complex—early tax counsel is essential.
   c) *Portfolio income*—interest, dividend, royalty or annuity income; gains and losses from the disposition of (1) property held for investment and not used in a passive activity and (2) property that normally produces interest, dividend, royalty, or annuity income.

Capital-gain income is gain or profit derived from the sale of a principal residence, investment property, property used in a trade or business, or income-producing property. Capital gains (and losses) are characterized as *short-term* if the holding period of the property is 12 months or less and as *long-term* if the holding period is more than 12 months.
   a) If a *net gain* results, the full net gain is added to taxable income.
   b) If a *net loss* results, up to $3,000 may be deducted in any one tax year. Unlimited *carryover* is permitted in subsequent years. Net long-term capital losses, as well as net short-term capital losses, also offset taxable income dollar for dollar.

DETERMINATION OF A GAIN OR LOSS
In the sale or exchange of property, a seller's gain or loss is the difference between the amount realized and the adjusted basis of the property. Good records are a necessity!

Amount realized is selling price minus selling expenses. *Selling expenses* are the actual costs of selling the residence, such as brokerage commission, title insurance, seller's attorney's fees, appraisal fees, survey costs, state, county, and municipal transfer taxes, and points paid by the seller to the buyer's lender.

Adjusted basis is purchase price or basis of the property plus additions (buying expenses and capital improvements) minus deductions.
   a) *Basis* is the amount paid for the property (or the basis "carried over" from a previously owned property).
   b) *Additions* include: (a) buying expenses, such as municipal transfer taxes, buyer's attorney's fees, appraisal fees, survey fees, and title insurance costs; and (b) capital improvements, such as a new central heating/air-conditioning system, a new room, landscaping, new floors, or a pool.

c) *Deductions* include nontaxable (deferred) gain from the sale of a previous residence, depreciation (when allowed), and deductible casualty losses.

Example: Dora bought her first home for $50,000, spent $10,000 for a room addition, and suffered casualty losses of $2,000. Her adjusted basis is $58,000 ($50,000 + $10,000 − $2,000). If she sells the property for $75,000 and has selling expenses of $5,000, the amount realized is $70,000. Her gain would be $12,000 ($70,000 − $58,000).

SELLING OR EXCHANGING PROPERTY

In general, when real property is sold or exchanged, significant tax consequences usually occur. Because of this impact on principals and clients, licensees need to be familiar with different ways of disposing of property and the resulting reporting of gain (or loss) for income tax purposes.

SALE AND REPLACEMENT OF PRINCIPAL RESIDENCE: ROLLOVER RULE

Tax laws give preferred treatment to taxpayers who sell their principal residence. A *principal residence* is the primary place in which one lives. The owner-occupied principal residence may be a house, condominium, cooperative, mobile home, houseboat, or the like. A taxpayer may reside in more than one residence but can only have one principal residence.

Deferring the tax on the gain from the sale of a principal residence by purchasing a replacement residence is called *nonrecognition of gain* or *rollover of gain* (Internal Revenue Code, Section 1034). As a general rule, if a homeowner sells his or her principal residence and replaces it with a new principal residence (either an existing or a newly constructed dwelling) and physically occupies it, all within 24 months before *or* after the sale of the old residence, then the taxpayer may "defer recognition of the gain" (postpone paying tax on the gain). If the cost (purchase price plus buying expenses) of the new residence is equal to, or greater than, the adjusted sales price of the old residence, the taxpayer may defer (rollover) all gain. (*Note*: The IRS is not interested in the cash involved or in mortgages on either house. It simply compares the cost of the new residence with the adjusted sales price of the old residence.) The *adjusted sales price* is the amount realized (selling price minus selling expenses) minus fix-up expenses; it is the minimum cost of a new residence to avoid recognition of all gain.

Selling expenses include broker's commissions, legal fees, advertising costs, and loan charges paid by the seller.

Fix-up expenses are costs paid to make a principal residence easier to sell (painting, repairs, cleaning, etc.). Such work must be performed within 90 days before the contract to sell and paid for no later than 30 days after the date of the sale of the old residence. Fix-up expense is a unique cost—it is not deductible on the income tax return and it is not a capital improvement that increases the adjusted basis of the property. Fix-up expenses affect only the adjusted sales price, which is used to determine whether any of the gain will be deferred.

If the new home costs less than the "adjusted" selling price of the old home, tax is paid (must be "recognized") on the lesser of (1) the gain from the sale *or* (2) the portion of the adjusted sales price that exceeds the cost of the new home. (A loss on a principal residence is not deductible.) This gain may be reported using the installment-sale method. Any deferred gain will reduce the basis of the new residence. If no replacement residence is purchased, all *realized gain* (actual gain) must be reported for tax purposes.

Example: A 50-year-old client sells his home for $160,000. The home was purchased ten years earlier and has an adjusted basis of $138,800. The sales commission is 7 percent. There are qualified fix-up expenses of $3,800. Determine the realized gain and the adjusted sales price.

Selling price of old residence	$160,000
Sales commission	− 11,200
Amount realized on sale	$148,800
Adjusted basis of old residence	−138,800
Realized gain	$ 10,000
Amount realized on sale	$148,800
Fix-up expenses	− 3,800
Adjusted sales price	$145,000

Imagine that your client plans to purchase a home within the next two months and he or she will meet the requirements of the rollover rule. The following table illustrates how four different costs of a new residence will affect the gain that will be recognized and that must be deferred.

	(a) Realized Gain from Sale of Old Residence	(b) Adjusted Sales Price of Old Residence	(c) Sample Cost of New Residence	(d) Recognized (Taxable) Gain* (b - c)	(e) Deferred Gain (a - d)	(f) Basis of New Residence (c - e)
(1)	$10,000	$145,000	$150,000	none	$10,000	$140,000
(2)	$10,000	$145,000	$145,000	none	$10,000	$135,000
(3)	$10,000	$145,000	$141,000	$ 4,000	$ 6,000	$135,000
(4)	$10,000	$145,000	$130,000	$10,000**	none	$130,000

   * Applies only if the adjusted sales price of the old residence is greater than the cost of the new residence.
  ** Taxable gain cannot be more than the realized gain.

Capital improvements made within 24 months of the sale of an old residence may be added to the basis of the new residence. This can decrease recognition of gain (lower the amount subject to tax) on the old residence. (*Improvements* add to the value of the property; *repairs* merely maintain the current value.) If, in the previous table, capital improvements are made to New Residence #3 totaling $4,000 or more within the replacement period, then all of the gain would be deferred for tax purposes. The total cost of New Residence #3 would then be $145,000 ($141,000 + $4,000) and would equal the $145,000 adjusted sale price of the old residence.

Temporarily renting either the old or the new principal residence will not necessarily disqualify either property from gain deferral. The primary purpose of the rental must be for security and maintenance and not for rental income. In order to qualify, the taxpayer must personally occupy both the new and the old principal residences within the prescribed period (usually 24 months).

When more than one principal residence is bought or sold within a replacement period, the determination of which is the replacement residence and which qualifies for deferral of gain falls under special rules. A taxpayer should seek tax advice when ownership of more than two homes in a two-year period is involved.

In the year that a personal residence is sold, if part of the home qualifies for the "office-in-the-home deduction," then deferral (or exclusion) of the gain on that portion of the home is not allowed. Any business depreciation claimed in the current or previous years must be subtracted from the tax basis of the home, which will increase the taxable profit at the time of sale.

A widow or widower can defer tax on the gain from the sale of the family home even though his or her spouse died before a new home was acquired, *if* the requirements for gain deferral are met *plus* (1) the couple was married on the date the spouse died and (2) the new residence is used as the principal residence. This rule applies whether the title to the old residence was in only one spouse's name or was held jointly.

SALE OF PRINCIPAL RESIDENCE: 55-OR-OVER RULE
The current exemption for homeowners 55 years of age or older who sell their principal residence is $125,000. This 55-or-over rule allows a qualified seller to elect a once-in-a-lifetime home-sale tax exemption (exclusion) on the profits (gain) of up to $125,000 *provided* the taxpayer meets three tests:
   a) "Age test": The taxpayer is 55 years of age or older on the day of title transfer.
   b) "Ownership and use test": The taxpayer has owned and used the property as the principal residence for at least three years during the five-year period ending on the date of sale. The ownership and use requirements need not be met simultaneously as long as both are met during the five-year period ending on the date of the sale. Short temporary absences, such as vacations or other seasonal absences, may be counted as periods of use. An exception applies to individuals who become physically or mentally incapable of self-care.
   c) "Exclusion test": Neither the taxpayer nor the spouse (if married on the date of sale) has ever taken an allowable exclusion from the sale or exchange of a residence after July 26, 1978.

A married couple is treated as one person for the purpose of this $125,000 exclusion. *One* co-owner spouse must qualify, but both must sign the election to claim the exclusion (Form 2119). When the home is not jointly owned, the spouse whose name is on the deed must qualify. No additional tax exemption is available if both spouses are over 55. When filing separately, each spouse is entitled to only half of the full exclusion (currently $62,500). A qualified single person may take the full $125,000 exemption. If the home is owned jointly with a person other than a spouse (for example, a child or parent), each joint owner who qualifies is entitled to a full $125,000 exclusion of the portion of the gain attributable to his or her interest in the home.

Many homeowners have bought and sold progressively more expensive homes over the years, deferring the tax on profit by using the rollover rule. If a homeowner has made more than the $125,000 profit, tax is paid on the excess over $125,000 *unless* another home is bought. Using this $125,000 exemption, there may be no tax to pay even though no home is bought or a less expensive home than the one that was sold is bought.

While the ownership and usage rules apply to the latest principal residence sold, the realized gain (profit) includes all unrecognized gain from past sales. If the profit to date adds up to less than $125,000 and the homeowner elects to use this tax exemption to exclude a gain of $90,000, for instance, the exclusion cannot be used again to claim the remaining balance in a later transaction.

The use of this 55-or-over rule may be combined with the preferential tax treatment received under the rollover rule (deferral of tax on gain) and/or an installment sale (spreading tax on gain over time). The gain allowed to be excluded using the 55-or-over rule is never taxed. [Internal Revenue Code, Section 121]

REPORTING SALE OF PRINCIPAL RESIDENCE
The sale of a principal residence must be reported on Form 2119, "Sale of Your Home," in the year of sale, even though none of the gain is subject to tax. Form 2119 has two functions: (1) to show details of the sale of the old principal residence and the purchase of the replacement residence, and (2) to elect to exclude all or part of the gain

from the sale of the principal residence of an over-55 taxpayer. Call the IRS at 1-800-424-3276 and request Publication 523, "Tax Information on Selling Your Home."

POSTRETURN PROCEDURES
If a new residence is acquired after the taxpayer files the return but within the replacement period, and the new residence costs at least as much as the adjusted sales price of the old residence, the taxpayer should send written notification to the IRS Center where the return is filed and attach another Form 2119 for the year of sale. If the new residence costs less than the adjusted sales price of the old residence, or if the taxpayer does not buy or start construction of a new residence within the replacement period, an amended return, Form 1040X, must be filed for the year of sale. The gain must also be reported on Schedule D together with Form 2119.

If the taxpayer elects on the income tax return to exclude gain on the sale of the residence, the election may be revoked by the taxpayer by filing an amended return (Form 1040X) within the time applicable for refund claims.

INSTALLMENT-SALE METHOD
The basic concept of the *installment-sale method* is that it relieves the seller of paying tax on gain not yet collected. Generally, the installment method calls for the gain on an installment sale to be reported only as payments actually are received, with each payment treated as part profit and part recovery of investment in the property sold. If an installment sale results in a loss, the seller may *not* use the installment method to report the loss for tax purposes. A *qualified* loss must be reported (recognized) in the year of sale.

Unstated ("imputed") interest is considered to exist when the sales contract either makes no provision for the payment of interest or provides for a low interest rate. In addition, the sales price must be more than $3,000 and at least one payment must be due more than six months after the date of sale. When interest is imputed, part of each of the deferred payments is treated as interest both to the seller and to the buyer.

The *imputed interest* rule applies even if: (1) there is a loss on the sale; (2) all or part of the gain or loss is postponed; or (3) one elects out of using the installment-sale method. The rate and manner in which interest will be imputed depends on the type of property sold, the selling price, the type of installment, the length of the contract, as well as to whom the property is sold. An installment sale works well in many cases, but calculating imputed interest is one of many problems that can complicate an installment sale.

Many buyers like to deal with sellers who will carryback financing. Similarly, many property sellers want to finance the sale of their homes to earn interest income. They offer easy financing, obtain a quick sale, and spread their profit tax over the years that payments are received. There are, however, many pitfalls (for example, what if the buyer defaults?) and many complexities (such as imputed interest) to an installment sale. Form 6252, "Computation of Installment Sale Income," must be used. Early tax counsel is mandatory.

LIKE-KIND EXCHANGE
When business or investment property (other than inventory, personal property, or securities) is *exchanged* solely for "like-kind property," then gain (or loss) must be deferred (it is not elective). This enables a taxpayer to realize immediately the benefits of investments and their appreciation while paying taxes later.

Like-kind refers to the nature of the property rather than its grade or quality. Thus, improved real estate can be traded for unimproved real estate, city real estate can be swapped for a ranch or farm, and an apartment building can be exchanged for an office building. Foreign and U.S. real property are no longer like-kind property. If cash or other *unlike property* (boot) is received in a like-kind exchange, gain may have to be recognized (reported) up to the value of the boot (loss is not recognized).

Tax-deferred exchanges are subject to close scrutiny by the IRS; any transaction attempted should be carefully structured, timed, calculated, and executed. Obtain competent tax counsel when an exchange opportunity appears. [Internal Revenue Code, Section 1031]

TAX STATUS OF INHERITED PROPERTY

For inherited property, an heir's basis is the fair market value on the date of the decedent's death. An heir's basis is not the same as the decedent's basis.

For example, suppose a relative paid $50,000 for a parcel of land. He leaves it to you in his will. The land now is worth $150,000. Your basis would be $150,000. If you sell the land for $150,000, you would owe no federal capital-gains tax. The $100,000 capital gain your relative would have had if he had sold the parcel during his lifetime is forgiven by the IRS. That's why death can be called the "ultimate tax shelter."

PROPERTY DISPOSITION TO RELATED PARTY

Regardless of the method of disposition, special rules apply when a transaction occurs between specified "related parties," including spouses, parents, children, grandchildren, brothers, sisters, half brothers, half sisters, or any ancestors or lineal descendants or various controlled corporations, partnerships, or trusts. In such transactions, favorable tax benefits may be denied. For example, a deductible loss may become nondeductible or a gain may not be able to be deferred.

INTEREST DEDUCTIBILITY

Interest (payment for the use of borrowed money) may be deductible when computing income tax. For interest to qualify as a possible deduction, the taxpayer is generally legally liable for the debt. Both the lender and the borrower must intend that the loan be repaid. The deductibility of such interest depends on the type of debt that causes the interest. Separate bank accounts and records for each type of loan transaction should be kept so the loan can be traced from its original source to its final use.

Personal interest is the expense on debts incurred by individuals for personal (consumer) use and is not deductible.

Trade or business interest is expense on debts incurred in a trade or business in which the taxpayer "materially participates," and it is generally deductible.

Investment interest is defined as interest paid to purchase or carry property for investment. (This includes interest allowable to portfolio income, but it does not include interest from a passive activity, nor from a rental real estate activity in which the taxpayer actively participates. Such interest is treated as a passive activity deduction.) The deduction for investment interest is limited to the amount of net investment income. Any interest disallowed as a current deduction may be carried over indefinitely to subsequent years.

Passive activity interest is a charge for the use of money for an activity conducted for profit in which the taxpayer generally does not materially participate. (Limited partnerships and rental real estate are considered passive activities even if the taxpayer materially participates.) It is deductible only against income from passive activities.

Qualified-residence mortgage interest is interest paid on a loan secured by a mortgage on a qualified residence. A *qualified residence* can include both a principal home and one second home. Mortgage interest can be deducted even though the taxpayer did not live in the home, as long as the home is not rented. If the second home is rented for any time during the tax year, it qualifies only if the taxpayer used it for more than the greater of 14 days or 10 percent of the rental days in the tax year. This provision is retroactive to January 1, 1987. Under RA '87 for tax years beginning after 1987, such mortgage interest is deductible on up to $1 million (*acquisition debt*) spent to acquire, construct, or substantially improve a qualified residence (includes funds borrowed and secured within 90 days after acquisition), plus on up to $100,000 of *home equity indebtedness* (may be used for any purpose). Qualified indebtedness created prior to October 14, 1987, is not subject to the $1 million loan limit. It is treated, however, as acquisition indebtedness and reduces the amount available for new acquisition debt; it does not affect the amount available as home equity debt. The amount of acquisition debt cannot be increased by refinancing. Also, interest deductibility on home-mortgage or home-equity debt that is not "qualified" or is in excess of the set limit will be determined by the use of the loan proceeds. Penalty payments made for the privilege of prepaying a mortgage debt are deductible as interest in the year paid.

Points are one of a number of possible loan-processing charges. One point equals 1 percent of the amount borrowed. Points, when paid by the buyer for the use of money rather than for specific services, are deductible as interest. To establish the interest amount, it is important for a financing agreement to separately list interest, commissions, and service changes, rather than lumping them together as a single "loan charge."

When points are paid for a loan to purchase or improve a principal residence, they are deductible in the year they are paid by the buyer/taxpayer: (1) if the charging of points is an established lending practice in the area; (2) if no more than the number of points generally charged locally is paid; and (3) if the points are paid in cash from sources other than from the lender.

If the points are paid with funds from the lender (that is, the point cost is included in the face amount of the loan but is withheld from the loan proceeds), they are not considered paid and may be deducted only over the life of the loan. When paid for a loan on business or investment property or to refinance a principal residence, points are considered prepaid interest (payment of future years' interest) and must be amortized (deducted in equal amounts over the time to which the loan pertains). For example, if a homeowner pays $2,400 in points to refinance a 240-payment loan, that homeowner/borrower can deduct the equivalent of $10 for each monthly payment (subject to qualified-residence rules). However, when the property is sold, that portion of the points not yet deducted can then be deducted.

OTHER FACTORS AFFECTING REAL PROPERTY OWNERSHIP

REAL PROPERTY TAXES
These *ad valorem* (according to the value) taxes generally are deductible in the year that they are due and paid, even if the taxes cover a period after the payment, regardless of the type of property involved.

DEPRECIATION
Depreciation as a tax concept (as opposed to an appraisal concept), is an income tax deduction for the estimated wear, tear, and obsolescence of real and personal property. It is a noncash deduction that is allowed even though a property might be appreciating in market value. The net result is that depreciation may serve to "shelter" income from taxation.

Depreciation is a means for deducting, over a specified period of time, the cost of improvements to land, but not the cost of the land itself. Depreciation is allowed only for business property—this includes income-producing property. Depreciation is not allowed for inventory property or for a personal residence.

To determine the amount that may be depreciated, the *basis* (total cost of the property) must be allocated between the depreciable and the nondepreciable components of the property, based on the respective market values of each.

The Tax Reform Act of 1986 created the fourth new depreciation schedule in five years and is less generous than the previous methods! For properties placed in service after 1986, the Modified Accelerated Cost Recovery System (MACRS) increases the depreciation period to 27.5 years for residential rental property and 31.5 years for nonresidential real property. "Alternative MACRS" allows a recovery period of 40 years for both types of property. While previous rates produced bigger deductions in the early years of ownership, both MACRS and alternative MACRS require that residential rental and nonresidential properties be written off using *straight-line depreciation* with the "mid-month convention." This depreciation method produces equal deductions over the entire write-off period and treats property as being placed in service (or disposed of) on the midpoint of a month.

Example: An apartment building is purchased for $250,000 on October 8, 1990.

There are additional acquisition costs of $5,000. An appraisal indicates that the market value of the land is $50,000, while the market value of the building is $200,000. As the building represents 80 percent of the cost ($200,000 ÷ $250,000), 80 percent of the acquisition costs may be allotted to the building cost. Therefore, the basis for depreciation of the building is:

Building cost	$200,000
Additional costs (80% × $5,000)	+ 4,000
Depreciable basis	$204,000

(The remaining 20 percent of the purchase and acquisition costs is allocated to the land and is not depreciable.)

Using MACRS, determine the depreciable amount for 1991 (full year) and 1990 (2.5 months).

1991: $204,000 ÷ 27.5 years = $7,418 (allowable depreciable amount)

1990: $7,418 per year ÷ 12 months = $618 per month
$618 per month × 2.5 months = $1,545 (allowable depreciable amount)

Although the new law replaces previous systems of depreciation, it does not eliminate them. Property being depreciated under earlier methods will continue to use those methods. The IRS provides optional tables with recovery periods and rates for computing allowable depreciation deductions.

TAXABLE INCOME

Release from a legally binding debt produces an "economic benefit" that is subject to federal income tax. When a lender offers to reduce the balance due on a mortgage if paid off early, tax will be due on the discount received (amount of reduction). Also, if a property is foreclosed and a person is legally released from repaying the mortgage amount due at the time, the amount of that mortgage must be included as taxable income.

TAX SHELTERS—PASSIVE ACTIVITIES AND AT-RISK RULES

A *tax shelter* is an investment "designed" to lower an investor's current taxes. Well-chosen real estate always has met the criteria for what constitutes a "good" tax shelter: profitability, minimum risk, and tax relief. Unfortunately, many tax shelters in the past have concentrated on tax relief. TRA '86 completely changed the value of tax shelters and deductions. Formerly, virtually every viable real estate investment paid investors more in after-tax savings than the investment itself cost to own. Changes in the depreciation rules now make the economic benefits of the investment, such as cash flow, more important. Combined with the limitation on losses from "passive" rental activity and the drop in tax rates, return on investment (ROI) now may depend solely on rising market values (appreciation).

TRA '86 specifies a tough loss-limitation rule under which tax shelters, including limited partnerships and real estate, generally are considered *passive activities*. Losses from passive activities can be deducted only against income from other passive activities. Unused passive losses are "suspended" and may offset (be deducted from) passive income in future years. When a passive activity is completely disposed of in a fully taxable transaction, the "suspended losses" are subtracted first from passive income and then from active income.

An exception to this loss-limitation rule applies to rental real estate in which a taxpayer "actively participates." Up to $25,000 of loss from all such activities is allowed to be deducted each year from nonpassive (active) income. The $25,000 allowance is systematically phased out for taxpayers with adjusted gross incomes of between $100,000 and $150,000. *Actively participates* means being significantly involved in management decisions or in arranging for others to provide services.

One common characteristic of tax shelters is that they generally involve the use of *leverage* (financing the majority of the investment with borrowed money), often with "nonrecourse loans" (financing for which the taxpayer is not personally liable). *At-risk rules* provide that deductions from business and income-producing activities are limited to the amount that the taxpayer has at risk (amount invested plus personal liability for financing). TRA '86 extended this rule to real property placed in service after 1986. An important exception was made for real estate that also allows deductions attributable to "qualified" nonrecourse financing. Generally, *qualified nonrecourse financing* is financing: for which no one is personally liable for repayment, that is secured by real property used in the activity, and that is provided by a lending organization. In addition, qualified nonrecourse financing can be provided by a person related to the taxpayer if the financing is commercially reasonable and substantially on the same terms as loans involving unrelated persons. If nonrecourse financing is not considered "qualified," losses would not be deductible against that portion of the debt—for example, nonrecourse-seller financing.

VACATION HOME

Vacation homes include single-family dwellings, apartments, condominiums, mobile homes, boats, and timeshares. In addition to providing pleasure, a vacation home provides deductions for property taxes for all owners and mortgage interest for most owners. (Interest may be subject to qualified-residence rules.) A vacation home also can be a source of extra income when rented—income that may be tax-free when deductions are taken.

A home qualifies as a vacation home if it is used *personally for the greater of* 14 days in a given year *or* 10 percent of the time it is rented out *and* it is rented for more than 14 days. The owner can then use the rent-related deductions to offset up to the total amount of rental income. The mortgage interest and property taxes related to the rental period must be deducted from income first, then other rent-related deductions may be deducted. Lastly, depreciation up to the total amount of rental income may be deducted. The portions of the interest and taxes related to the personal use of the vacation home may be taken as itemized deductions.

If an owner rents his or her qualified vacation home for 14 days or less during a given year, the rent does not have to be included as income. The mortgage interest and property taxes are deductible as itemized deductions.

If the second home is rented out, even for one day, and does not meet the above personal-use requirements, it is treated as a rental (and not as a vacation home) and none of the interest allocated to personal use is deductible as home-mortgage interest. The deduction will be subject to the passive activity rules, and up to $25,000 of rental losses may be deducted against other income if the taxpayer "actively participates." Use by family members is treated as personal use.

ALTERNATIVE MINIMUM TAX (AMT)

To help ensure that all taxpayers with income pay a certain amount of federal income tax (despite their allowable use of exclusions, deductions, and credits), some individuals are subject to an "alternative minimum tax." The *alternative minimum tax* provides a formula for tax computation that, in effect, ignores certain "preferential tax treatments" that are allowed under law. By eliminating these preferential deductions and credits, a tax liability may be created for a taxpayer who otherwise would pay little or no income tax. In this case, the income is taxed at the flat rate of 24 percent (previously 21 percent) as opposed to the 15 percent, 28 percent, or 31 percent brackets. The alternative minimum tax is paid when it exceeds the taxpayer's regular tax.

ADDITIONAL REPORTING TO THE IRS

CLOSING INFORMATION

Sales and exchanges of *reportable real estate* must be reported to the IRS on Form 1099-S (or a suitable substitute) between January 1 and February 28 (29) following the calendar year in which the transaction occurred. The 1099-S may be given to the seller on or before the day of closing, but it cannot be delivered later than January 31 of the following calendar year. "Reportable real estate" means any present or future "ownership interest" in: land, including air rights; buildings (residential, commercial or industrial); condominium units; and cooperative housing corporation stock. *Ownership interests* include fee simple interests, life estates, reversions, remainders, perpetual easements, and rights to possession or use, such as leaseholds, easements, or time-shares if the possession right has a remaining time of at least 30 years, including renewal options. To be subject to reporting, the transaction must be in whole or in part a "sale or exchange" as defined under federal tax laws. It is irrelevant if the gain is or is not taxable (for example, rollovers, exclusion of gain, like-kind exchanges).

To report the transaction, a qualified individual (person responsible for closing the transfer, buyer's attorney, seller's attorney, or disbursing title company) should be designated in a written and format-conforming agreement. Form 1099-S is not required for sales by certain "exempt sellers": corporations, governmental units, and certain high-volume sellers.

ALIENS SELLING U.S. PROPERTY

Real estate licensees must be aware of a government regulation that concerns the purchase of real property in the United States from foreign sellers ("transferors"). In order to prevent foreigners from avoiding the payment of federal taxes on the sale of real property, the IRS requires buyers ("transferees") to withhold 10 percent (10%) of the amount to be realized by the foreign seller (including cash and debt assumed by the buyer), usually equal to the selling price. The buyer must report the purchase and pay the IRS any amount withheld by the tenth day after the closing. While a few exceptions to this rule allow the buyer to avoid the withholding of funds, all licensees should consult the IRS or a tax specialist regarding the application of this rule or face the danger of new liability.

To indicate how seriously some closing agents are taking this IRS requirement, an "affidavit of nonforeign status" is being used at closings to attest to the fact that the seller is not a nonresident alien for purposes of U.S. income taxation. This document then "covers" the closing agent should a question be subsequently raised by the IRS.

TAX STATUS OF REAL ESTATE LICENSEES

Licensed real estate salespersons who are "independent contractors" are classified by the IRS as self-employed persons. This means that licensees are not subject to employer withholding and employment taxes *provided* two conditions are met:

1. Substantially all of their income for services as real estate agents is directly related to sales or other similar output activities, rather than, for example, to the number of hours worked or supervisory duties, *and*
2. Their services are performed under a *written* contract that calls for them not to be treated as "employees" for federal income tax and employment purposes, and they are responsible for paying their own estimated income and self-employment taxes.

This estimated tax total is generally paid quarterly and is due on the 15th day of April, June, and September (of the current year) and on the 15th day of January (in the following year).

Additionally, the qualified-real-estate-agent classification includes individuals who are engaged in appraisal activities connected with real estate sales and who realize income dependent on sales or other output activities. [Internal Revenue Code Section 3508]

TAX TIDBITS

Copies of your old federal income tax returns can be obtained from the IRS. To request a copy, fill out Form 4506 (available at local IRS Centers). The cost is currently $4.25 for each year you request. The form requesting the copy must be filed at the IRS Center where that year's return originally was filed.

Use Form 8822 to notify the IRS if you change your mailing address. To obtain a copy of Form 8822, call the IRS at 1-800-424-3276. Mail the completed change-of-address form, as soon as you move, to the IRS Center that you used for your old address. If you are changing both your home and business addresses, you will need to complete two separate forms. If you simply file an income tax return using your new address, the IRS may not note the change. In addition, ordinary letters to the IRS that report address changes are often misprocessed. Last year, more than $40 million in refunds went undelivered because the IRS could not locate eligible taxpayers!

Never send the IRS originals of valuable tax documents. In a case where the IRS lost all of an individual's records, the Tax Court ruled that the individual still had the obligation of proving that the disputed tax wasn't owed!

A recommendation made by many experts is to file your income tax return by certified mail, return receipt requested. An increasing number of returns are lost and the IRS denies ever having received them. The Tax Code states that a certified or registered mail receipt is proof of delivery to the IRS, but the IRS will *not* accept a postage meter mark, a receipt from a delivery service, or an Express Mail receipt as proof of filing!

Here's a tactic that might save you some grief. Whenever you write to the IRS, include with your letter a copy of that same letter, along with a self-addressed, stamped return business envelope. Request that the IRS agent mark the copy "Received on _____ [date]" and return the copy to you in the envelope you enclosed. What you gain is specific proof of correspondence received; a postal receipt proves only that you sent "something" to the IRS; it is not proof of what you actually wrote.

Automobile expenses are deductible if the vehicle is used in business or in the production of income. The IRS authorizes two methods that taxpayers can use in computing their car expenses: the actual cost and the standard mileage rate methods. The mileage method may be used provided the vehicle is owned by the taxpayer. For business auto expenses incurred in 1991, the standard mileage rate is 27.5 cents per mile for *all* miles of business travel. The allowable rate is no longer reduced after the first 15,000 miles of business use.

SOME FINAL THOUGHTS

As the opening paragraph of this chapter clearly states, the purpose of focusing here on federal income taxes affecting real estate is *familiarization, NOT development of expertise*. The attempt is to highlight certain features that are applicable to the real estate practitioner in order that he or she might better serve each principal and customer.

The need for licensees to become better informed is forcefully brought home by the fact that there continues to be a significant increase nationwide in the number of negligence suits *against* real estate practitioners. Real estate licensees are failing to inform buyers and/or sellers of the tax consequences of the buyers' and sellers' actions. In addition, licensees are trying to act as tax experts instead of advising their buyers and sellers to seek professional advice in real estate transactions.

Federal income taxes greatly affect the benefits that may be obtained from the purchase, ownership, and disposition of real property. Since every real estate transaction has some definite tax impact, real estate licensees need to be familiar with the effect of federal income taxes on the various real estate transactions.

Note: For IRS tax information in Illinois, call 1-800-829-1040.
In the 312 area, call 435-1040.

SUMMARY: SELECTED FEDERAL TAX *CHANGES* AFFECTING REAL ESTATE

Tax Provision	Present Status	Effect
Mortgage interest	Deductible on: acquisition debt (used to purchase, construct, or improve principal and second residence) up to $1 million, plus home equity debt up to $100,000 used for any purpose. (Total debt not to exceed fair market value of home[s].)	Deduction no longer unlimited; refinancing or all-cash purchase could further limit this deduction.
Net capital gain	Maximum rate is 28 percent.	Tax savings for those above the 28 percent bracket.
Net long-term capital gain	No capital-gains deduction.	Loss of deduction means higher taxes.
Net long-term capital loss	Entire resulting loss can offset income up to $3,000 per year.	Increased deduction should lower taxes.
Installment sale	Rules tightened.	Tax advantages reduced or eliminated, in some instances
Investment interest	Deductible only against investment income (phase-in period ended December 31, 1990).	Does not affect rental real estate (passive activity).
Depreciation	Straight-line method: 27.5 years for residential rental property; 31.5 years for nonresidential real property.	Smaller yearly deduction combined with lower tax rate means less tax savings.
Losses from passive activities	Only deductible against passive income ($25,000 exemption for small investors).	Eliminates main source of real estate tax shelter for nonpassive income.
At-risk rule	Now applies to real estate, with significant exception for qualified nonrecourse financing.	Makes nonrecourse (not personally liable) seller financing uneconomical.
Alternative minimum tax	Flat rate of 24 percent.	Applies to more taxpayers.
Time of sale: closing agents and foreign sellers	New rules for closing agents and for buyers dealing with foreign sellers.	Additional responsibilities at closing.

CASES TO JUDGE

1. Under the Internal Revenue Code, a homeowner may deduct from gross income losses that arise from "fires, storms, shipwreck or other casualty..." The taxpayers (the Fays) appealed an adverse ruling denying them a deduction on their income tax returns for a "casualty loss" caused by termite damage. The taxpayers' home was built in 1913, and in 1935 it was discovered that termites had destroyed the wooden framework of their porch. The evidence indicated and the court observed that "the insects had obviously been at work for a long time, and the loss had therefore in fact taken place gradually although it was not discovered until it was complete." The tax court had previously treated as "casualties," losses found to be (a) accidents or (b) sudden occurrences. Previous decisions had approved deductions for such losses as freezing waterpipes, the bursting of a boiler, sink holes, and (of course) fires, floods, hurricanes, and other sudden losses caused by nature. Since the Fays' loss took place over a number of years and could have been discovered through reasonable maintenance, the tax court held that the termite damage was not a casualty loss.

   Should a homeowner be entitled to deduct as a casualty loss damages caused by termites over a substantial period of time? [*Fay v. Helvering*, 120 F2d, 235 (1938)]

2. Art Rosenburg appealed a decision of the tax court that disallowed a casualty loss deduction he had claimed on his tax return for termite damage. The tax court held that even though the damage had been done over a relatively short period of time (eight months) the loss was not a casualty loss within the meaning of the Internal Revenue Code. Rosenburg claimed that the damage was sudden and should qualify as an "other casualty" for which a deduction could be properly claimed. Rosenburg purchased the property in April 1946 for $38,500. Prior to purchasing the property, he had the property inspected to determine whether there were termites. The inspector, who had more than 15 years' experience, thoroughly checked the premises and was satisfied that the home was free of termite infestation. Relying on the inspection, Rosenburg purchased the property and moved in during September 1946. In April 1947 termites were discovered; however, the degree of infestation had been confined to a small area. The total amount expended for treatment and repairs to the property amounted to $1,800, and Rosenburg claims that his loss was distinguishable from the loss suffered by the Fays in the previous case in that the damages had been done over a very short period of time and should qualify as a casualty.

   Should the appellate court follow its earlier decision and deny the taxpayer's claimed casualty loss, or is Rosenburg's loss distinguishable? [*Rosenburg v. Commissioner of Internal Revenue*, 198 F2d, 46 (1952)]

3. Samuel E. Bogley and Anita C. Bogley (the Bogleys) sought a review of a tax court decision denying them the benefits of nonrecognition of gain relating to the sale and purchase of a home. The Bogleys sold their home and three of the original 13 acres of land on December 1, 1950, and retained the remaining ten acres of the original tract only because an immediate purchaser was not available for the residence and all 13 acres of land. The retention of the ten acres was not for investment or trade purposes. In June and August of 1951, the Bogleys sold the remaining ten acres in two separate transactions of five acres each. The majority of the tax court judges reasoned that since the rollover rule applied only to a "residence," the taxpayers' sale of the ten remaining acres was a sale of unimproved land upon which they did not reside; therefore, the value received from the sales of the remaining ten acres were not sales of the taxpayers' "principal residence" or "old residence" to which the rollover rule applied.

   Where taxpayers sold their previous residence in three separate transactions should they be permitted to "rollover" the gain only on that portion of the real estate that was improved by their home? [*Bogley v. Commissioner of Internal Revenue*, 263 F2d, 746 (1959)]

4. On May 8, 1957, the taxpayers, Dr. and Mrs. Sheahan, sold their home in Missouri for $270,000 in anticipation of Dr. Sheahan's imminent retirement from the army. The Sheahans planned to buy a home in Atlanta, Georgia, and live there with their daughter, Mrs. D. T. Lauderdale, and her family. The army, however, notified Dr. Sheahan that he would be retained in his position for a year. Following the sale of their previous home, the Sheahans searched for a new principal residence in Atlanta in order to move there promptly following Dr. Sheahan's release by the army. During this time they resided with a second daughter in Godfrey, Illinois. Mrs. Sheahan made several trips to Atlanta in search of a new home, and on March 31, 1958, the taxpayers entered into a contract to purchase a partially completed home in Atlanta. The new house was to be completed and the agreement closed on May 1, 1958, but bad weather caused several delays, and the final contract of sale was not signed until May 8, 1958, precisely one year after the sale of the taxpayers' St. Louis home. No one actually slept in the house, however, until May 10, the date when the moving van brought the large pieces of furniture. The Lauderdale family moved in at that time. Mrs. Sheahan did not spend any time in the house until that summer, and although Dr. Sheahan spent two weeks there in June, he did not move in permanently until April 1959. There was no question, however, but that as early as March

1958, the Sheahans intended to make the new house in Atlanta their principal place of residence and to live there with their daughter and her family. The tax court jury determined that Dr. Sheahan was entitled to roll over the gain on the sale of his Missouri home. The IRS appealed the decision, claiming that the gain may not be deferred because the taxpayers did not purchase *and use* their new principal residence within 12 months (now 24 months) of the sale of their previous home.

Should the Sheahans be permitted to roll over the gain on the sale of their previous home where they purchased a new home within the statutorily prescribed time period but failed to use the home until after the expiration of the stated time? [*United States v. Sheahan*, 323 F2d, 383 (1963)]

5. Taxpayers were married two years ago and Husband moved into the Wife's home, which she had owned for 20 years. Under state law the home belonged to the wife. Upon the taxpayers' marriage in 1990, Wife transferred the property into joint tenancy with her husband, and they have resided in the home since that time. In 1992, Husband will reach the age of 55 (Wife will be 50), and they would like to sell the home and take advantage of the $125,000 senior citizen capital-gains exclusion upon the sale of the home.

Are they entitled to the exclusion? [LTR RUL 8989 020]

10-QUESTION DIAGNOSTIC QUIZ

1. In the rollover rule, the "adjusted sales price" of the old residence is:
   A. needed to determine the amount of gain that can be excluded from taxation.
   B. the selling price minus the sales commission.
   C. equal to the basis of the new residence.
   D. the amount realized minus fix-up expenses.

2. J. J. Jones is single and qualifies for the "55-or-over rule." One month after his 55th birthday, he sold his principal residence for $190,000 and has a realized gain of $130,000. He does not plan to purchase another home. How much can Jones exclude from federal taxation?
   A. $0
   B. $62,500
   C. $125,000
   D. $130,000

3. When a real estate sales contract makes no provision for the payments of interest or provides for an exceptionally low interest rate in an installment sale, the IRS will:
   A. disallow the use of the installment-sale method.
   B. apply the imputed-interest rule.
   C. require tax to be paid in the year of sale on the entire profit.
   D. apply the rate used for all installment sales.

4. A homeowner was required to pay $3,000 in points by separate check to refinance a 25-year loan on her qualified principal residence. The IRS will allow the homeowner/taxpayer to deduct:
   A. the equivalent of $10 per month over 25 years.
   B. up to a maximum of $120 per month until amortized.
   C. $3,000 for the year in which the points were paid.
   D. nothing pertaining to the cost of the points.

5. Depreciation as an income tax deduction is:
   A. allowed if paid in cash.
   B. not allowed if the property is appreciating.
   C. not allowed on the cost of the land itself.
   D. allowed on real, but not personal, property.

6. In order to postpone the entire tax on the gain in the sale of one's principal residence, the homeowner must:
   A. be 55 years of age or older.
   B. purchase a new home within 24 months at a cost equalling the gain.
   C. have occupied the home for at least five years.
   D. make an election to postpone the gain by filing the appropriate form (2119).

7. Ted Miller is 55 and his wife, Natalie, is 21. If Ted and Natalie sell their principal residence:
   A. they will not be able to claim the "55-or-over" exclusion.
   B. the tax on the gain will be based on 40 percent of the realized gain.
   C. they may qualify for a "age-split" tax concession.
   D. their age difference is immaterial to any tax computations.

8. Interest expenses on which of the following would reduce a real estate salesperson's taxable income?
   A. Qualified vacation home
   B. Business debt
   C. Personal credit card
   D. Home mortgage

9. Which of the following would be the LEAST important consideration in establishing whether, for income tax purposes, a salesperson was an employee or an independent contractor?
   A. The total number of hours worked
   B. The terms of a written contract between the parties
   C. Whether there was a direct relationship between income earned and the number of hours worked
   D. Whether the salesperson agreed in her contract to pay her own income and employment taxes

10. A closing agent is responsible for reporting sales of real estate to the IRS on form:
    A. W-2.
    B. 1040.
    C. 2119.
    D. 1099.

CHAPTER 12

ILLINOIS APPRAISAL LAW
(UNCLE SAM WANTS YOU)

○ **CHAPTER OVERVIEW**
The real estate professional interfaces on a daily basis with many other professionals. The appraiser is one of these. Appraisal is a new ball game, and the licensee should be familiar with the new rules and players.

○ **LEARNING OBJECTIVES**
After completing your study of this chapter, you should be able to:
1) Explain what is meant by a voluntary two-tier system of real estate appraisers.
2) Define the terms *state certified appraiser* and *state licensed appraiser*.
3) State the requirements for state-certified and state-licensed appraiser applicants.
4) State the education/experience requirements applicable to both state-certified and state-licensed appraiser categories.
5) Explain why a real estate licensee should exercise caution in using the terms *licensed* and *appraisal services* in real estate advertising, business cards, and other promotional materials.
6) Explain what a contingent fee is and under what circumstances an appraiser may enter into such a fee arrangement.
7) Recall the statute of limitations for violations of the License Act.
8) Recognize the potential drawbacks of holding a real estate license and either an appraiser's license or certificate.

○ **5 CASES TO JUDGE**

○ **10-QUESTION DIAGNOSTIC QUIZ**

CHAPTER 12

ILLINOIS APPRAISAL LAW
(UNCLE SAM WANTS YOU)

Statement of purpose. The intent of this Article of the Real Estate License Act of 1983 is to enable real estate appraisers in this State to voluntarily obtain a real estate appraiser's license or real estate appraiser's certificate for the purpose of enabling real estate appraisers to conduct appraisals which are required to be performed by a State licensed or State certified appraiser under the provisions of Title XI of the federal Financial Institutions Reform, Recovery, and Enforcement Act of 1989 (12 U.S.C., Chapter 34A), as now or hereafter amended. It is the intent of the General Assembly that this Act shall be consistent with the provisions of Title XI of the federal Financial Institutions Reform, Recovery, and Enforcement Act of 1989, as now or hereafter amended.

Nothing in this Act shall preclude a person who is not certified or licensed under this Article from appraising real estate in this State for compensation.
—Real Estate License Act of 1983, Section 36.01

INTRODUCTION

Appraisers were partially to blame for the savings and loan fiasco of the early and mid-1980s. Some appraisers had rendered faulty and fraudulent appraisals that were relied on by lenders in making investment decisions. Prior to the collapse of the thrift industry, only a handful of states had undertaken legislation aimed at the regulation of appraisers. For the most part, the few states that had enacted legislation simply required that all persons holding themselves out as an appraiser must have a real estate license. Due to the federal legislation mentioned in the introductory quotation from the License Act, all states, virtually overnight, scurried to enact appraisal laws that would conform to the as-yet unwritten and unpublished standards required by federal law.

As many know, the hurry was to try to avoid a total collapse of the real estate business within each state, which would have come about if no appraisers were qualified to appraise property that would be financed by a federally related loan or lender. The first deadline set by FIRREA was July 1, 1991. (Illinois had no certified appraisers as of that date.) The July 1 date was extended to December 31, 1991 (we had 15 certified and 32 licensed appraisers by then—hardly enough to service the entire state), and a subsequent extension further delayed the effective date to December 31, 1992.

Illinois hastily adopted the first appraisal act in 1990; in 1991 the legislature made extensive revisions to the act. At the time of this writing, Rules for the Administration of the Act were not expected for several months. This chapter, then, will set forth the appraisal act in its entirety, following the order that appears in the act. Where appropriate, we have added comments that appear in boxes within the relevant section or paragraph. These comments highlight and, where appropriate, explain important considerations to the real estate practitioner. These comments may also be of interest to the prospective candidate for appraisal licensure, since the act is not generally part of the curriculum for the required appraisal courses.

As alluded to in this chapter's subtitle, Uncle Sam wants to regulate appraisal practices to protect consumers, who, for years to come, will be picking up the tab for the bankers who hired dishonest and unqualified appraisers. Melding federal law, federal agency regulations, state law, and state regulations together is at best a nightmare. To do so in less than two years verges on the superhuman, and we submit that the Department of Professional Regulation, its Director, and the Commissioner have done an admirable job in complying with Uncle Sam's demands. Two years ago there was no appraisal law, and the reader should therefore realize that this is a rapidly changing area that will merit your continued attention.

APPRAISAL CERTIFICATION

§36.1 **Definitions.** As used in this Article:

(a) "Appraisal" or "real estate appraisal" means an analysis, opinion or conclusion relating to the nature, quality, value or utility of specified interests in, or aspects of, identified real estate, for or in expectation of compensation. An appraisal may be classified by purpose into either a valuation or an analysis. A "valuation" is an estimate of the value of real estate or real property. An "analysis" is a study of real estate or real property other than estimating value.

(b) "Appraisal assignment" means an engagement for which an appraiser is employed or retained to act, or would be perceived by third parties or the public as acting as a disinterested third party in rendering an unbiased analysis, opinion, or conclusion relating to the nature, quality, value, or utility of specified interests in, or aspects of, identified real estate. The term "appraisal assignment" may apply to valuation work and to analysis work.

(c) "Appraisal report" means any communication, written or oral, of an appraisal.

(d) "Appraiser" or "real estate appraiser" means any person who inspects, analyzes, or renders an opinion or conclusion relating to the nature, quality, value or utility of specified interests in, or aspects of, identified real estate, for or in expectation of compensation.

(e) "Department" means the Department of Professional Regulation.

(f) "Federally related transaction" means any real estate related financial transaction that:

(1) a federal financial institution's regulatory agency or the Resolution Trust Corporation engages in, contracts for, or regulates and requires the services of an appraiser; or

(2) any other real estate related financial transaction for which a licensed or certified real estate appraiser is required under federal law or regulations.

(g) "Real estate related financial transaction" means any transaction involving:

(1) the sale, lease, purchase, investment in or exchange of real property, or the financing thereof;

(2) the refinancing of real property or interests in real property; or

(3) the use of real property or interests in property as security for a loan or investment, including mortgage-backed securities.

(h) "Federal financial institutions regulatory agencies" means the Board of Governors of the Federal Reserve System, the Federal Deposit Insurance Corporations, the Office of the Comptroller of the Currency, the Office of Thrift Supervision, and the National Credit Union Administration.

(i) "Financial institution" means an insured depository institution as defined in Section 3 of the Federal Deposit Insurance Act or an insured credit union as defined in Section 101 of the Federal Credit Union Act.

(j) "Real Estate" means an identified parcel or tract of land, including improvements, if any.

(k) "Real Estate Appraisal Committee" or "Committee" means the Real Estate Appraisal Committee established in this Article.

(l) "Real property" means one or more defined interests, benefits, and rights inherent in the ownership of real estate.

(m) "State certified real estate appraiser" means a real estate appraiser who holds a current, valid real estate appraiser's certificate issued under Article 2 of this Act.

(n) "State licensed real estate appraiser" means a real estate appraiser who holds a current, valid real estate appraiser's license issued under Article 2 of this Act.

> As is fully covered in Sections 36.10 and 36.11 below, Illinois has a voluntary "two-tiered" appraisal structure. The structure is similar to the two-tiered real estate license structure in which the "licensed appraiser" (like a salesperson) is a less experienced and educated appraiser, whereas the "certified appraiser" (similar to a broker) will be more experienced and will require additional training. There are considerable dissimilarities between the two categories; however, the foregoing analogy may enable you to keep them straight.

§36.2 Use of terms

(a) No person, other than a State certified real estate appraiser, shall assume or use that title or any title, designation, or abbreviation likely to create the impression that the person is a State certified real estate appraiser.

(b) No person, other than a State licensed real estate appraiser shall assume or use that title or any title, designation, or abbreviation likely to create the impression that the person is licensed as a real estate appraiser by this State.

(c) This Article does not preclude a person who is not certified or licensed as a real estate appraiser from appraising real estate in this State for compensation.

> The real estate licensee must be extremely cautious in avoiding the use of business cards, stationery, advertising materials, and other promotional materials that fail to clearly adhere to the provisions of this particular section. Statements relating to "licensed broker" or "Illinois licensed salesperson," if used in any advertising materials, should not lead the reader to possibly conclude that the appraisal services offered in the same advertisement are to be done by a licensed appraiser, unless of course the broker is in fact a licensed appraiser. Likewise, the use of the word *certified* or any similar verbiage should be avoided lest the licensee be charged with misleading or untruthful advertising.

§36.3 Real Estate Appraisal Committee

(a) There is hereby established the Real Estate Appraisal Committee which shall consist of the following 10 voting members appointed by the Governor:

(1) Seven members shall be real estate appraisers who have been engaged in the practice of real estate appraising in the State of Illinois for not less than 5 years immediately preceding their appointment.

(A) At least 2 of the 7 members appointed under this paragraph (1) shall be representatives of a statewide real estate trade organization. One member shall be appointed to an initial term to expire on January 15, 1993. The other member appointed under this item (A) of paragraph (1) shall be appointed to an initial term to expire on January 15, 1996.

(B) After the date when federal law requires real estate appraisals for federally related transactions in Illinois to be performed by a State certified or licensed real estate appraiser, appraiser appointments to the Committee shall be made so that at least 2 of the real estate appraiser members hold a valid certificate and that all noncertified members hold a valid license.

(C) Members of the Committee appointed before and serving on the effective date of this amendatory Act of 1991 shall be allowed to complete their appointed terms.

(2) One member shall be a representative of a financial institution, as defined in Section 36.1 of this Act, that engages primarily in residential real estate lending services. The initial member so appointed shall serve a term to expire on January 15, 1992.

(3) One member shall be a representative of a financial institution, as defined in Section 36.1 of this Act, that engages primarily in commercial lending services. The initial member so appointed shall serve a term to expire on January 15, 1995.

(4) One member shall be a member of the general public. The public member initially appointed shall serve a term to expire on January 15, 1992.

(b) In meeting the appointment criteria prescribed in this Section, each appointee shall be attributed as being a member of the committee from only one of the 4 specified classifications.

(c) The Commissioner of Real Estate shall act as a member of the Committee, but shall not vote.

(d) Except for initial appointments to the Committee, members shall be appointed to 4 year terms. Appointments to fill vacancies shall be made in the same manner as original appointments and shall be for the unexpired portion of the term. A member may be reappointed for successive terms, but no member shall serve more than 10 years in his or her lifetime. Upon expiration of their terms, members of the Committee shall continue to hold office until the appointment and qualification of their successors.

(e) The membership of the Committee should reasonably reflect representation from the various geographic and demographic areas of the State.

(f) The Committee shall meet as often as agreed upon to conduct its business. Dates and places of future meetings shall be decided by the vote of members at meetings. Written notice shall be given to each member of the time and place of each meeting of the Committee at least 10 days before the scheduled date of the meetings.

(g) A quorum of the Committee shall be 6 voting members.

(h) The voting members of the Committee shall annually elect a chairman from among the voting members to preside over meetings. The member so elected as chairman shall serve as chairman for a term of one year. A member may serve as chairman more than once, but no person shall serve as chairman consecutively for more than 2 terms.

(i) Each member shall receive a per diem stipend as the Director shall determine. Each member shall be paid his or her necessary expenses while engaged in the performance of his or her duties. Such compensation and expenses shall be paid out of the Real Estate License Administration Fund.

(j) The Governor may terminate the appointment of any member for cause which in the opinion of the Governor reasonably justifies such termination. Cause for termination shall include, but not be limited to, misconduct, incapacity, neglect of duty or missing 4 committee meetings during any one calendar year.

§36.4 **Powers and duties of the Committee.** The Real Estate Appraisal Committee has the following powers and duties:

(a) The Committee shall conduct hearings on charges against State certified and State licensed real estate appraisers for violations of this Article and shall report its findings on such charges to the Department.

(b) The Committee shall make recommendations to the Department on rules, regulations, and procedures implementing the provisions and policies of this Article.

> The proposed Rules for the Administration of the Act have been drafted and redrafted seven times and are not expected to be adopted until, at the earliest, June 1992. Similar to the Real Estate Administration and Disciplinary Board for real estate licensing, this committee will be the arbiter of disciplinary complaints and, as seen below, will also suggest the adoption of Rules for the Administration of the Act.

§36.5 **Powers and duties of the Department**

(a) None of the functions, powers, or duties enumerated in Sections 36.13, 36.18, 36.19, 36.20, or 36.21 shall be exercised by the Department except upon the action and report in writing by the Committee.

(b) The Department, after considering the recommendations of the Committee, may promulgate rules and regulations consistent with the provisions of this Article as it applies to State certified and State licensed real estate appraisers for its administration and enforcement of this Article.

(c) The Department has the following additional powers and duties:

(1) to receive applications for State certification and State licensing;

(2) to establish the administrative procedures for processing applications for State certification and State licensing;

(3) to approve or disapprove applications and issue certificates and licenses;

(4) to maintain a registry of the names and addresses of State certified and State licensed real estate appraisers and to transmit the registry, along with the federal registry fees collected under Section 36.6 of this Act, to the Federal Financial Institutions Examination Council in a manner consistent with Title XI of the federal Financial Institutions Reform, Recovery and Enforcement Act of 1989;

(5) to retain these records and all application materials submitted to it;

(6) to assist the Committee in such other manner as the Committee may request.

(d) The Director has the power to refuse to issue or renew a certificate or license or to suspend, revoke, reprimand, place on probation, or otherwise discipline the certificate or license of any State certified or State licensed real estate appraiser upon recommendation of the Committee pursuant to the disciplinary proceedings provided for in this Article.

The Director shall give due consideration to all recommendations of the Committee on questions involving standards of professional conduct, discipline, and examination of candidates under this Article.

If the Director disagrees with or takes action contrary to a recommendation of the Committee, the Director shall provide the Committee with a written and specific explanation of the disagreement or action.

(e) The Department, after considering the recommendations of the Committee, shall promulgate rules for establishing reasonable minimum standards of educational requirements for State certified and State licensed real estate appraisers.

(f) Without in any manner limiting the power of the Department to conduct investigations, the Committee may recommend to the Director that one or more State certified or State licensed real estate appraisers be selected by the Director to conduct or assist in any investigation pursuant to this Article. Such State certified or State licensed real estate appraisers may receive remuneration as determined by the Director.

§36.6 Fees

(a) Except as otherwise specified in this Section, the following fees, which are nonrefundable, shall be charged and deposited in the Real Estate License Administration Fund created by Section 17 of this Act:

(1) The application fee for obtaining a license as a real estate appraiser is $100, plus any fees required pursuant to federal regulations or laws. Of the $100 fee, $5 shall be deposited in the Real Estate Research and Education Fund.

(2) The application fee for certification as a real estate appraiser is $150, plus any fees required pursuant to federal regulations or laws. Of the $150 fee, $5 shall be deposited in the Real Estate Research and Education Fund.

(3) The Department shall fix the cost of examination and reexamination for appraiser certification and licensing at the cost of providing such examination.

(4) The fee for renewal of a real estate appraiser's license is $50 per year, plus any fees required pursuant to federal regulations or laws.

(5) The fee for renewal of certification as a real estate appraiser is $75 per year, plus any fees required pursuant to federal regulations or laws.

(6) An additional fee of $20 shall be assessed for the delinquent renewal of a certificate or license.

(7) The Department shall provide by rule for reasonable application and renewal fees for approval of pre-licensing education, pre-certification education, and continuing education schools and instructors.

For those interested in becoming licensed/certified, the chart below summarizes the original licensure fee structure, examination costs, and estimated educational costs for the prerequisite courses. The listed costs for the educational expenses are based on tuition and books at $20 per hour.

§36.7 Certification and licensing process
(a) The Department shall issue a license or certificate to each applicant entitled to a license under this Act

	LICENSE	CERTIFICATE
Original fees (payable to the State of Illinois)	$ 100	$ 150
Examination fee (payable to ASI)	42	42
Subtotal	$ 142	$ 192
Educational expenses (tuition and books)	$1,500	$3,300
TOTAL EXPENSES	$1,642	$3,492
Renewal fees ($50 or $75 per year)	$100	$150

in the form and size as shall be prescribed by the Department. Applications for original certification or licensing, renewal certification or licensing, and examinations shall be made in writing to the Department on forms approved by the Department.

(b) Appropriate fees, as fixed by the Department pursuant to Section 36.6 shall accompany all applications for original certification or licensing, renewal certification or licensing, and examination. Such fees are nonrefundable.

(c) At the time of filing an application for certification or licensing, each applicant shall sign a pledge to comply with the provisions in this Article and state that he or she understands the types of misconduct for which disciplinary proceedings may be initiated against a State certified or licensed real estate appraiser, as set forth in this Article.

§36.8 Classes of certification.
Applications for original certification, renewal certification and examination shall specify the classification of certification being applied for or previously granted.

§36.9 Examination requirement
(a) An original certification as a State certified real estate appraiser shall not be issued to any person who has not demonstrated, through a comprehensive written examination process provided by rule, competence to transact the business of a State certified real estate appraiser in such a manner as to safeguard the interests of the public.

(b) An original license as a State licensed real estate appraiser shall not be issued to any person who has not demonstrated, through a comprehensive written examination process provided by rule, competence to transact the business of a State licensed real estate appraiser in a manner that safeguards the interests of the public.

(c) The Department, or its designated testing service, shall conduct exams for appraiser certification and licensing at such times and places as the Department may determine.

See the following page for examination information.

The examination administered by the Department is conducted by Assessment Systems, Inc. (ASI), an independent testing agency. Exams are given at a number of testing locations throughout the state. The following outline details the content of the appraisal examinations.

CONTENT CATEGORY	LICENSE EXAM Approximate % Questions		CERTIFICATE EXAM Approximate % Questions	
Influences on Real Estate Value	3%-4%	4	2%-3%	3
Legal Considerations in Appraisal	6%-8%	7	7%-8%	9
Types of Value	3%-5%	4	2%-3%	3
Economic Principles	7%-9%	9	3%-5%	5
Real Estate Market & Analyses	5%-7%	5	5%-7%	7
Valuation Process	4%-6%	5	2%-4%	4
Property Description	2%-4%	3	2%-4%	4
Highest and Best Use	5%-7%	7	5%-7%	5
Appraisal Statistical Concepts	1%-3%	1	3%-5%	5
Sales Comparison Approach	21%-24%	22	10%-12%	14
Site Value	4%-6%	6	3%-5%	6
Cost Approach	8%-10%	10	9%-12%	14
Income Approach	7%-9%	7	20%-24%	27
Valuation of Partial Interests	1%-3%	1	4%-6%	7
Appraisal Standards & Ethics	7%-11%	9	7%-11%	12
TOTAL	100%	100	100%	125

§36.10 Examination prerequisites

(a) Certification. As a prerequisite to taking the examination for certification as a State certified general real estate appraiser, an applicant shall present evidence, satisfactory to the Department, that he or she has successfully completed not less than 150 classroom hours or its equivalent, as provided by rule, of courses in subjects relating to real estate appraisal, plus 15 classroom hours relating to standards of professional practice and the provisions of this Article, from one or more of the following entities, approved by the Department:

    (1) a college or university;

    (2) a community college or junior college;

    (3) a real estate appraisal or real estate related organization;

    (4) a trade association or organization that consists in whole or in part of members engaged in real estate appraising; or

    (5) any other providers approved by the Department.

> Pending the adoption of rules that vary the current policy with respect to approved curriculum, the Department has approved the following series of courses for certification: Standards of Professional Practice and the Act (15 hours); Foundations of Real Estate Appraisal (30 hours); Appraising the Single-Family Home (30 hours); Real Estate Appraisal Methods (30 hours); Principles of Capitalization (30 hours); and Real Estate Appraisal Applications (30 hours).

(b) Licensing. As a prerequisite to taking the examination for obtaining a license as a State licensed real estate appraiser, an applicant shall present evidence satisfactory to the Department that he or she has successfully completed not less than 60 classroom hours or its equivalent, as provided by rule, of courses in subjects relating to real estate appraisal, plus 15 classroom hours relating to standards of professional practice and the provisions of this Article, from one or more of the following entities, approved by the Department:

(1) a college or university;
(2) a community college or junior college;
(3) a real estate appraisal or real estate related organization;
(4) a trade association or organization that consists in whole or in part of members engaged in real estate appraising; or
(5) any other providers approved by the Department.

> Currently approved for licensing are: Standards of Professional Practice and the Act (15 hours); Foundations of Real Estate Appraisal (30 hours); and Appraising the Single-Family Home (30 hours).

§36.11 Experience requirement

(a) A real estate appraiser's certificate shall not be issued to any person who does not possess 2 years of experience, or the equivalent thereof as provided by rule. For the purposes of this Section, one year of experience is defined as 1,000 hours of experience.

> Simple arithmetic (50 weeks × 40 hours per week = 2,000 hours) forces one to conclude that there must be a mistake. It's not a mistake, just poor draftsmanship. The rules to be adopted and the application clarify the requirements, but they are too complicated and extensive to reprint here. In a nutshell, to satisfy the experience requirement, only 1,500 hours may be claimed per year. Thus, essentially, in order to qualify, an applicant must have worked in the field for two of the immediately preceding five years and have accumulated no more than 1,500 of the 2,000 hours during any one given year.

Approved experience shall include fee appraisal, staff appraisal, mass appraisal, ad valorem tax appraisal, mass ad valorem tax appraisal, review appraisal, appraisal analysis, highest and best use analysis, feasibility analysis or study, real estate sales and brokerage, real estate counseling, real property management, teaching approved appraisal courses, and other related experience approved by the Department. Nevertheless, the amount of experience granted for this experience shall be equivalent to the amount of credit that may be granted for the experience under Title XI of the federal Financial Institutions Reform, Recovery and Enforcement Act of 1989.

The applicant for a certificate shall provide to the Department on forms prescribed by rule a summary of the level and type of experience for which the applicant is claiming credit. To obtain experience credit for the preparation of a written appraisal report, the applicant shall provide in the experience summary the date the appraisal was prepared, the type of property, the approximate size of the property (land and improvements), and general location of the property. Nothing in this Section shall require, as a condition of obtaining experience credit, that a real estate appraiser disclose the identity of the client for whom the appraisal was performed, the specific address of the property, or the value arrived at in the appraisal. The Department may require that an applicant provide samples of the applicant's work for which experience is claimed.

Of the 2,000 hour experience requirement, at least 1,000 hours must be earned in one or more of the following areas: fee appraisal, staff appraisal, ad valorem tax appraisal, mass ad valorem tax appraisal, review appraisal, or appraisal analysis.

(b) An applicant who has been engaged in appraising real property for ad valorem tax purposes as a local assessment officer, as defined in Section 1 of the Revenue Act of 1939, including deputies and employees of a local assessment officer, shall receive experience credit for the number of hours the applicant was engaged in:

(1) the analysis and establishment of the value of properties through the cost, income, and market sale appraisal techniques;

(2) model development and calibration in relation to mass ad valorem tax assessments; and

(3) the review and analysis of appraisals employing cost, income, and market sale appraisal techniques.

Such applicant shall provide to the Department an affidavit that sets forth in detail the experience for which credit is being claimed and the length of time the applicant has been employed as a local assessment officer. The experience under this subsection (b) shall not be required to be set forth in the form of the experience summary provided in subsection (1) of Section 36.11, but shall be documented by reports certified by the local assessment officer and by reference to assessment records available under Section 98.1 of the Revenue Act of 1939 or the Freedom of Information Act. Upon submission of the affidavit and certified documentation, the Director shall grant the experience credit set forth above. Notwithstanding other provisions of this Act, the amount of experience credit granted for appraising real property for ad valorem tax purposes as a local assessment officer, or deputy or employee thereof, shall be equivalent to the amount of credit that may be granted for that experience under the provisions of Title XI of the federal Financial Institutions Reform, Recover and Enforcement Act of 1989.

(c) Of the 2,000 hour experience requirement, at least 1,000 hours must be approved experience relating to nonresidential real estate. For the purposes of this Section, nonresidential real estate shall include, but is not limited to, property used for commercial, industrial or agricultural uses, multi-family residential property with 5 or more dwelling units, and other properties considered to be nonresidential under the provisions of the federal Financial Institutions Reform, Recovery, and Enforcement Act of 1989.

(d) The Department may provide by rule for an experience requirement for applicants for a real estate appraiser's license if the experience is required to be recognized as a licensed real estate appraiser under the federal Financial Institutions Reform, Recovery and Enforcement Act of 1989. Any appraisal experience which meets the requirements of subsection (a), (b), or (c) of this Section shall be deemed approved experience under this subsection (d).

When is a competitive market analysis (CMA) an appraisal? Answer: when done by a state licensed/certified appraiser. CMAs will not provide acceptable proof of experience; however, there is growing support for the position that a dual licensee (real estate salesperson/broker and appraiser) may *NOT* do a typical CMA but must conform the CMA to a "full blown" appraisal. The sticky issue follows from a thorough reading of Section 36.1(a) (definition of an appraisal, which a CMA clearly falls within) and various provisions of Section 36.18 (disciplinary infractions), which is set forth below. Opinions on this issue are divided and, unless clarified by legislation or administrative rule, may be cause for considerable disappointment to the real estate licensee who acquires an appraiser license/certificate and then must conform his or her CMAs to the standards of an appraisal or face possible concurrent disciplinary charges under both the real estate and appraiser acts.

---

§36.12 Term of certificate and license. The Department shall issue a license or certificate as a real estate appraiser, as the case may be, to any person who meets the requirements for certification under this Article 2. The term of a certificate and the term of a license issued under this Article shall be established by rule. The expiration date of the certificate or license shall appear on the certificate or license. The Department shall establish by rule procedures for the issuance of renewal notices and procedures for the renewal of a certificate or license under this Article.

> As noted above, the Rules will not be effective until adopted by the Department; however, the proposed Rules call for the renewal of licenses and certifications biannually by June 30 of each odd-numbered year.

§36.13 Nonresident certification and reciprocity; nonresident licensure and reciprocity

(a) A nonresident may be certified under this Article upon complying with all the provisions and conditions required for certification in this State. Any person who is certified as a real estate appraiser in another state, territory of the United States, or the District of Columbia, who, in the opinion of the Department, meets the qualifications and requirements for certification in this State, is entitled to receive certification hereunder upon submission of a duly certified copy of his or her certification from such other state, territory of the United States, or the District of Columbia, and any other information the Department may require, and upon payment of the appropriate fee; provided, however, that the laws of such state, territory, or District of Columbia accord substantially equivalent reciprocal rights to a State certified real estate appraiser in good standing in this State who desires to practice his or her profession in such state, territory, or the District of Columbia, and further provided that no proceeding is pending or unresolved against such appraiser under the laws of such other state or territory. In any such application for certification, all questions of the academic and experience requirements of other states, territories or the District of Columbia shall be determined by the Department and, at the discretion of the Department, the reciprocal or nonresident certification applicant must comply with additional requirements specified by rule.

(b) A nonresident certificate holder shall not be required to maintain a place of business in this State if he or she maintains an active place of business in the state of domicile. Every nonresident certificate holder shall file an irrevocable consent that suits and actions arising out of any appraisal work in this State may be commenced against such certificate holder in the circuit court of any county of this State in which the cause of action arose or in which the plaintiff resides, by the service of legal process on the Commissioner, such consent agreeing that such service on the Commissioner shall be acknowledged in all courts to be valid and binding as if personal service of process had been made upon the nonresident in this State. In case any process herein mentioned is served upon the Commissioner, it shall be his or her duty to forward a copy of the process by registered mail to the last known address of the certificate holder against whom the process is directed.

(c) A nonresident may be licensed under this Article upon complying with all the provisions and conditions required for obtaining an appraisal license in this State. Any person who is licensed as a real estate appraiser in another state, territory of the United States, or the District of Columbia, who, in the opinion of the Department, meets the qualifications and requirements for licensure in this State, is entitled to receive a license under this Article upon submission of a duly certified copy of his or her license from the other state, territory of the United States, or the District of Columbia and any other information the Department may require, and upon payment of the appropriate fee if the laws of that state, territory, or District of Columbia accord substantially equivalent reciprocal rights to a State licensed real estate appraiser in good standing in this State who desires to practice his or her profession in such state, territory, or District of Columbia, and if no proceeding is pending or unresolved against the appraiser under the laws of the other state or territory. In any application for a license, all questions of the academic and experience requirements of other states, territories, or the District of Columbia shall be determined by the Department and, at the discretion of the Department, the reciprocal or nonresident applicant for licensure must comply with additional requirements specified by rule.

(d) A nonresident licensed appraiser shall not be required to maintain a place of business in this State if he or she maintains an active place of business in the state of his or her domicile. Every nonresident licensed appraiser shall file an irrevocable consent that suits and actions arising out of any appraisal work in this State may be commenced against the licensed appraiser in the circuit court of any county of this State in which the cause of action arose or in which the plaintiff resides by the service of legal process on the Commissioner, the consent agreeing that service on the Commissioner shall be acknowledged in all courts to be valid and binding as if personal service of process had been made upon the nonresident in this State. In case any process mentioned in this Section is served upon the Commissioner, it shall be his or her duty to forward a copy of the process by registered mail to the last known address of the licensed appraiser against whom the process is directed.

(e) The Department shall adopt rules consistent with Title XI of the Financial Institutions Reform, Recovery, and Enforcement Act of 1989 permitting nonresident licensed or certified appraisers to practice in Illinois on a temporary basis.

§36.14 Renewal certificate

(a) The Department shall issue regulations establishing procedures for the renewal of certification upon completion of the continuing education requirements specified in Section 36.18 [*Note: The legislature intended to insert "36.17"*]. Such regulations shall extend the term of the certificate if failure to meet the requirements for renewal is through mistake, misunderstanding, or circumstances beyond the control of the applicant, as defined by rule.

(b) If a person fails to renew a certificate as a State certified real estate appraiser prior to its expiration or within a period of extension granted by the Department pursuant to this Article, the person may obtain a renewal certificate by satisfying all of the requirements for renewal and paying a late renewal fee.

§36.15 Certificate

Each State certified real estate appraiser shall place his or her certificate number adjacent to or immediately below the title "State Certified Residential Real Estate Appraiser" or "State Certified General Real Estate Appraiser" when used in an appraisal report or in a contract or other instrument used by the certificate holder in conducting real property appraisal activities.

§36.16 Prohibition on licensing or certification of other than individuals

(a) The term "State certified real estate appraiser" or "State licensed real estate appraiser" may only be used to refer to a person certified or licensed as an appraiser under this Article and may not be used following or immediately in connection with the name or signature of a firm, partnership, corporation, or group, or in such manner that it might be interpreted as referring to a firm, partnership, corporation, group or anyone other than an individual holder of the certificate or license.

(b) No certification or license shall be issued under this Article to a corporation, partnership, firm or group. This shall not be construed to prevent a State certified or licensed appraiser from signing an appraisal report on behalf of a corporation, partnership, firm or group practice.

(c) Nothing in this Article shall be construed as prohibiting an employee of a financial institution or any other entity from performing appraisals or being licensed or certified under this Article.

§36.17 Continuing education

(a) As a prerequisite to renewal of a certificate or license, a State certified or licensed real estate appraiser shall present evidence satisfactory to the Department, as provided by rule, of having completed not less than 10 hours per year of continuing education, or its equivalent as provided by rule, from one or more of the following entities approved by the Department:

(1) a college or university;

(2) a community college or junior college;

(3) a real estate appraisal or real estate related organization;

(4) a trade association or organization that consists in whole or in part of members engaged in real estate appraising; or

(5) such other providers approved by the Department.

The Department may provide by rule for the temporary waiver of such continuing education requirement for good cause.

(b) In lieu of meeting the requirements of subsection (a) of this Section, an applicant for renewal of a certificate or license may satisfy all or part of the requirements by presenting evidence of the following:

(1) Completion of an educational program of study determined by rule to be equivalent, for continuing education purposes, to courses approved pursuant to subsection (a); or

(2) Participation, other than as a student, in educational processes and programs approved pursuant to subsection (a) which relate to real property appraisal theory, practices or techniques, including, but not limited to, teaching, program development and preparation of textbooks, monographs, articles, and other instructional materials.

§36.18 Disciplinary proceedings. Pursuant to the action and report in writing of the Committee, the Department may suspend, revoke, place on probation, or reprimand the certificate or license of any State certified or licensed real estate appraiser, or may refuse to issue or renew a certificate or license, or may impose a civil penalty not to exceed $10,000 upon the holder of a certificate or license, or the holder of a certificate or license may be otherwise disciplined for any of the following acts or omissions:

(1) Procuring or attempting to procure a certificate or license by knowingly making a false statement, submitting false information, refusing to provide complete information in response to a question in an application for certification or licensure or through any form of fraud or misrepresentation.

(2) Failing to meet the minimum qualifications for certification or licensure as an appraiser established by this Article.

(3) Paying money, other than for the fees provided for by this Article, to any member or employee of the Committee or Department to procure a certificate or license under this Article.

(4) A conviction, including conviction based upon a plea of guilty or nolo contendere, of a crime which is substantially related to the qualifications, functions, and duties of a person developing real estate appraisals and communicating real estate appraisals to others.

(5) An act or omission involving dishonesty, fraud or misrepresentation with the intent to substantially benefit the certificate or license holder or another person, or with intent to substantially injure another person.

(6) Violation of any of the standards for the development or communication of real estate appraisals as provided in Section 36.21 of this Act.

(7) Failure or refusal without good cause to exercise reasonable diligence in developing an appraisal, preparing an appraisal report or communicating an appraisal.

(8) Negligence or incompetence in developing an appraisal, in preparing an appraisal report, or in communicating an appraisal.

(9) Willfully disregarding or violating any of the provisions of this Article or the rules or regulations promulgated for the administration and enforcement of this Article.

(10) Accepting an appraisal assignment for valuation when the employment itself is contingent upon the appraiser reporting a predetermined estimate, analysis or opinion, or where the fee to be paid is contingent upon the opinion, conclusion, or valuation reached, or upon the consequences resulting from the appraisal assignment.

(11) Violation of the confidential nature of governmental records to which he or she gained access through employment or engagement as an appraiser by a governmental agency.

(12) Adjudication of liability in a civil proceeding on grounds of fraud, misrepresentation or deceit in the making of any appraisal of real property. In a disciplinary proceeding based upon a finding of such civil liability, the State certified or licensed real estate appraiser shall be afforded an opportunity to present mitigating and extenuating circumstances, but may not collaterally attack the civil adjudication.

(13) Engaging in misleading or untruthful advertising, or using any trade name or insignia of membership in any real estate appraisal or real estate related organization of which the certificate or license holder is not a member.

> As with the same section of the License Act, Section 36.18 will be of critical importance to an appraiser's continuing education. A violation of the appraisal act will become part of the news release issued by the Department, and it remains to be seen whether a violation will subject the offender to concurrent discipline under the "unworthiness or incompetency" provisions of Section 18 of the Real Estate License Act (see Chapter 6).

§36.19 Due process

(a) Upon the motion of either the Department, or the Committee, or upon the verified complaint in writing of any person setting forth facts which, if proven, would constitute grounds for suspension, revocation, or other disciplinary action against a State certified or licensed real estate appraiser or applicant for a certificate or license, the Department shall cause to be investigated the actions of any person so accused who holds, represents to hold, or has applied for a certificate or license under this Article.

(b) Before taking any disciplinary action or suspending or revoking any certificate or license pursuant to action by the Committee, the Department shall notify the holder of the certificate or license, in writing, of the charges that are the basis of such disciplinary action at least 20 days prior to the date set for the hearing and shall afford him or her an opportunity to be heard in person or by counsel.

(c) The written notice may be served personally or sent by registered or certified mail to the last known business address of the holder of the certificate or license.

(d) The Department has the power to issue subpoenas and subpoenas duces tecum to bring before it any person in this State to take testimony by deposition or to require production of any records relevant to any inquiry or hearing by the Committee in the same manner as prescribed by law in judicial proceedings in the courts of this State.

§36.20 Hearing

(a) The hearing on the charges shall be held at a time and place prescribed by the Committee and in accordance with the provisions of the Illinois Administrative Procedure Act.

(b) If the Committee determines that a State certified or State licensed real estate appraiser is guilty of a violation of any of the provisions of this Article, it shall prepare a finding of fact and a recommendation that the appraiser be reprimanded, placed on probation, or otherwise disciplined, or that his or her certificate or license be suspended or revoked or otherwise disciplined. The Director shall give due consideration to the recommendations of the Committee and shall then enter a decision and order in the matter. In the event the Director takes action contrary to the recommendation of the Committee, the Director shall file with the Committee in writing the action taken and the specific reasons for his action contrary to the recommendation.

(c) Any final administrative decision of the Director is subject to judicial review pursuant to the provisions of the Administrative Review Law, as now or hereafter amended.

(d) Beginning 3 years after the effective date of this amendatory Act of 1989, an appraisal certificate or license that has been revoked as a result of disciplinary action by the Department shall not be reinstated unless the applicant presents evidence of completion of the continuing education required by this Article. This requirement of evidence of continuing education shall not be imposed upon an applicant for reinstatement who has been required to successfully complete the examination for State certified or State licensed real estate appraiser as a condition for reinstatement of the certificate or license.

(e) Notwithstanding the provisions of this Article concerning the conduct of hearings and recommendations for disciplinary actions, the Department has the authority to negotiate agreements with State certified and State licensed real estate appraisers or applicants for such certification or licensure resulting in disciplinary consent orders. Such consent orders may provide for any of the forms of discipline provided in this Act. Such consent orders shall provide that they were not entered into as a result of any coercion by the Department, Commissioner or Committee. Any such consent order shall be filed with the Director along with the Committee's recommendation and accepted or rejected by the Director in a timely manner.

(f) At any time after the suspension or revocation of any certificate or license, the Director may restore it to the accused person without examination, upon the written recommendation of the Committee.

> The disciplinary procedures will be essentially identical to the procedures and proceedings for the discipline of real estate licensees, which are fully discussed in Chapter 6.

§36.21 Standards of practice

(a) A State certified real estate appraiser must comply with standards of professional appraisal practice promulgated by the Department at the recommendation of the Committee. The Department may adopt, as its own rules, the Uniform Standards of Appraisal Practice as published from time to time by the Appraisal Foundation as defined in this Act. The Department shall consider federal laws and regulations regarding the certification or licensure of real estate appraisers prior to adopting its own rules for administration of this Article.

(b) All written appraisal reports signed by a State licensed or State certified real estate appraiser shall indicate whether the appraiser is licensed or certified, and shall bear the appraiser's license or certificate number.

§36.22 Contingent fees

(a) A client or employer may retain or employ a State certified real estate appraiser to act as a disinterested third party in rendering an unbiased estimate, value or analysis. A client or employer may also retain or employ a State certified real estate appraiser to facilitate the client's or employer's objectives. In either case, the appraisal and the appraisal report must comply with the provisions of this Article.

(b) A State certified real estate appraiser may not accept a fee for an appraisal assignment that is contingent upon the State certified real estate appraiser reporting a predetermined estimate, analysis or opinion or is contingent upon the opinion, conclusion or valuation reached, or upon the consequences resulting from the appraisal assignment. A State certified real estate appraiser who enters into an agreement to perform specialized appraisal services may be paid a fixed fee or a fee that is contingent on the results achieved by the specialized appraisal service. If a State certified real estate appraiser enters into an agreement to perform specialized appraisal services for a contingent fee, this fact shall be clearly stated in each written and oral appraisal report. In each written appraisal report, this fact shall be clearly stated in a prominent location in such report and also in each letter of transmittal and in the certification statement made by the State certified real estate appraiser in such report.

> A simple example of a contingent fee is an arrangement whereby the client agrees to pay the appraiser a fee representing say, 1 percent of the estimated fair market value of the property. There are many other examples; however, it should be obvious that such a fee arrangement creates a conflict of interest between the appraiser's best interests and his or her final estimate of value, i.e., the greater the value, the greater the fee. For the protection of the client and others who will rely on the appraiser's opinion of value, contingent fees are not permitted. Special appraisal services for which contingent fees have been permitted are instances where the appraiser becomes an *advocate*, such as in real estate tax assessment appeal proceedings whereby a client seeks a reduction in his or her assessed value. Typically, appraisers doing this type of work take a percentage of the reduction of the client's tax bill.

§36.23 Retention of records.

A State certified or State licensed real estate appraiser shall retain for 5 years, originals or true copies of (a) all written contracts engaging his or her services for real property appraisal work, and (b) all appraisal reports and supporting data assembled and formulated by the appraiser in preparing the appraisal reports. This 5 year period for retention of records is applicable to each engagement of the services of the State certified or licensed real estate appraiser and shall commence upon the date of the submittal of the appraisal to the client unless, within such 5 year period, the State certified or licensed real estate appraiser is notified that the appraisal or appraisal report are involved in litigation, in which event the 5 year period for the retention of records shall commence upon the date of the final disposition of such litigation.

§36.24 Statute of limitations. No action may be taken under this Article against any State certified or licensed real estate appraiser unless the action is commenced within 5 years after the occurrence of the alleged violation. A continuing violation will be deemed to have occurred on the date when the circumstances first existed which gave rise to the alleged continuing violation.

§36.25 The provisions of this Act are severable under Section 1.31 of the Statute on Statutes.

CASES TO JUDGE

1. A real estate broker was subpoenaed to appear before the Real Estate Disciplinary Board and provide certain records in connection with a complaint concerning the broker's appraisals of several parcels of real estate. The broker performed appraisal services as well as practiced real estate, and the complaint concerning the real estate appraisals was not connected to any real estate transactions; however, the Department claims that the improper appraisal practices have a bearing on his trustworthiness and competency to act as a broker. The broker claims that since a license to appraise real estate is not required and his conduct was not related to his real estate practice, the court should quash (cancel) the subpoena.

    Should the State be able to investigate the broker for activities falling outside his real estate practice? [*Blackmore v. Shaffer*, 512 N.Y.S.2d 421 (A.D. 2 Dept. 1987)]

2. An owner of real estate that was condemned for railroad purposes appealed the judgment of the trial court claiming that the trial judge had erred in not permitting testimony from the owner's witness as to the value of the property for a particular purpose--a nursery. The court instructed the jury to consider the value of the property for all lawful purposes and cautioned them not to consider a particular purpose for which a buyer might desire to use the property.

    Should a jury have been permitted to consider the value of the property for particular purposes or, as the trial court ruled, for all purposes? [*Sacramento Southern R. Co. v. Heilbron*, 156 Cal. 408, 104 Pac. 979 (1909)]

    Note: Until recently, the foregoing case was credited and is best known for its enunciation of the definition of market value. That definition was "...the highest price estimated in terms of money which the land would bring if exposed for sale in the open market, with reasonable time allowed in which to find a purchaser, buying with knowledge of all of the uses and purposes to which it was adapted and for which it was capable." Recently, the appraisal industry has adopted the *probable* sales price of the property as opposed to the *highest* price of the property as its definition of market value.

3. In a condemnation proceeding, the defendant was awarded a judgment of $600,000 and the plaintiff appealed, claiming that the trial court's refusal to admit the testimony of its witness, who would have testified that the land's market value was $58,000, was improper. The trial court refused to permit the expert opinion of a licensed Illinois real estate broker, who devoted full time to appraising and had been so occupied for 30 years. The expert for the plaintiff was on the governing council and editorial board, chairman of the rural technical committee of the American Institute of Real Estate Appraisers, and also a member of the Society of Real Estate Appraisers. The appraiser had taught courses relating to real estate appraising at five universities, including the University of Illinois. The appraiser had examined the premises in question and, prior to the trial court's refusal to permit further testimony, the appraiser testified that he was familiar with real estate conditions in Henry County (the county where the property was located) and that he was experienced with mineral lands generally. He had made seven appraisals of mineral lands in northern Illinois for both private owners and governmental agencies, including one or more that had been made in Henry County. The trial court ruled the appraiser incompetent on the basis that he had not participated as a buyer, seller, or broker in northern Illinois real estate transactions involving property of the kind under consideration.

    Based on the foregoing, should the trial court have permitted the plaintiff's expert witness to testify? [*Department of Public Works and Buildings v. Oberlaender*, 42 Ill.2d 410, 247 N.E.2d 888 (1969)]

4. A portion of the parking lot of a property improved with a restaurant was condemned for road purposes. The jury awarded the property owner $7,500 for the land taken and $68,000 for damages to the remaining property. The Department appealed the award because the trial court permitted testimony as to the value of the property under both the income and cost approaches to value. The Department based its claim on the general rule that in

condemnation proceedings where property is owner-occupied, the market comparison approach must be used unless the property is a special-purpose building, such as a church, school, or post office. All of the expert witnesses who testified agreed that there were no comparable sales that could be relied upon and therefore the only accurate approaches were the income and cost approaches to value.

Under these circumstances, should evidence of the cost and income approaches be admitted? [*People ex rel. Dept. of Transportation v. Quincy Coach House, Inc.*, 29 Ill.App.3d 616, 332 N.E.2d 21 (1975)]

5. The Lombard Park District appealed the trial court's decision ordering a new trial because of the court's conclusion that it had erred in not permitting testimony as to the value of the property based on a highest and best use that was not permitted by existing zoning. The sole issue on appeal was the extent to which an expert valuation witness may base his or her opinion on a highest and best use that was not permitted by existing zoning regulations. Under what circumstances should a court permit testimony as to market value for a use that is not permitted in the area where the condemned land is located? [*Lombard Park District v. Chicago Title and Trust Co.*, 103 Ill.App.2d 1, 242 N.E.2d 440 (1968)]

10-QUESTION DIAGNOSTIC QUIZ

1. In order to qualify under state and federal law to appraise commercial property for a "federally related loan or lender," an appraiser must provide satisfactory evidence of his or her experience in nonresidential appraising of how many hours?
   A. None
   B. 500
   C. 1,000
   D. 2,000

2. In order to provide a competitive market analysis (CMA) for a potential client's listing, the analysis must be done by:
   A. a "licensed" appraiser.
   B. a "certified" appraiser.
   C. a "qualified" appraiser.
   D. a real estate licensee.

3. An infraction of the appraisal act may subject the offender to all of the following penalties EXCEPT:
   A. up to a $10,000 fine.
   B. imprisonment.
   C. license revocation.
   D. license suspension.

4. An appraiser will be required to complete how many hours of continuing education prior to the renewal of his or her license/certificate?
   A. None
   B. six hours per year
   C. ten hours per year
   D. 15 hours per year

5. An applicant for "state certification" must provide satisfactory proof of all of the following EXCEPT:
   A. 2,000 hours of experience.
   B. 165 hours of approved appraisal courses.
   C. having passed a state-administered exam.
   D. that he or she is 21 years of age.

6. The major difference between a "state-licensed," "state-certified," and an uncertificated appraiser is:
   A. the amount of experience each actually has.
   B. the amount of training each actually has.
   C. the types of property each may appraise.
   D. their respective abilities to do appraisals for federally related loans and lenders.

7. The term of an appraiser's license is:
   A. unknown.
   B. one year.
   C. two years.
   D. variable; licensed appraisers renew by April 30 of odd-numbered years and certified appraisers renew February 28 of even-numbered years.

8. Corporations and general and limited partnerships:
   A. may not be licensed or certified under the appraisal act.
   B. may engage in the appraisal business only if "registered" by the state.
   C. may be certified if at least 49 percent of the officers/partners are certified appraisers.
   D. may be licensed if 10 percent of the officers/general partners are certified.

9. A certified appraiser may charge a contingent fee:
   A. under no circumstances.
   B. if disclosure of the arrangement is made to and approved by the Department.
   C. if the agreement relates to "specialized appraisal services" and the fee is contingent on the result achieved by the specialized appraisal services.
   D. if such fee is in accordance with the Elwood Tables.

10. The statute of limitations under the appraisal act is:
    A. two years.
    B. four years.
    C. five years.
    D. ten years.

Get the Performance Advantage on the job...*in the classroom*

	Order Number	Real Estate Principles and Exam Prep	Qty.	Price	Total Amount
1.	1510-01	Modern Real Estate Practice, 12th edition	___	$34.95	___
2.	1510-02	Study Guide for Modern Real Estate Practice, 12th edition	___	$13.95	___
3.	1961-01	Language of Real Estate, 3rd edition	___	$28.95	___
4.	1610-07	Real Estate Math, 4th edition	___	$15.95	___
5.	1512-10	Mastering Real Estate Mathematics, 5th edition	___	$25.95	___
6.	1970-04	Questions & Answers To Help You Pass the Real Estate Exam, 4th edition	___	$21.95	___
7.	1970-06	Real Estate Exam Guide: ASI, 3rd edition	___	$21.95	___
8.	1970-09	Guide to Passing the PSI Real Estate Exam	___	$21.95	___

Advanced Study/Specialty Areas

9.	1520-02	ADA Handbook: Employment and Construction Issues Affecting Your Business	___	$29.95	___
10.	1560-08	Agency Relationships in Real Estate	___	$25.95	___
11.	1978-03	Buyer Agency: Your Competitive Edge Real Estate	___	$25.95	___
12.	1557-10	Essentials of Real Estate Finance, 6th edition	___	$38.95	___
13.	1559-01	Essentials of Real Estate Investment, 4th edition	___	$38.95	___
14.	1556-10	Fundamentals of Real Estate Appraisal, 5th edition	___	$38.95	___
15.	1556-14	How to Use the Uniform Residential Appraisal Report	___	$24.95	___
16.	1556-15	Introduction to Income Property Appraisal	___	$34.95	___
17.	1556-11	Language of Real Estate Appraisal	___	$21.95	___
18.	1557-15	Modern Residential Financing Methods, 2nd edition	___	$19.95	___
19.	1556-12	Questions & Answers to Help You Pass the Real Estate Appraisal Exams	___	$26.95	___
20.	1551-10	Property Management, 4th edition	___	$35.95	___
21.	1560-01	Real Estate Law, 3rd edition	___	$38.95	___
22.	1556-18	Uniform Standards of Professional Appraisal Practice	___	$19.95	___

Sales & Marketing/Professional Development

23.	1913-04	Close for Success	___	$18.95	___
24.	1907-06	How to Develop a Six-Figure Income in Real Estate	___	$22.95	___
25.	1916-11	Finding & Buying Your Place in the Country	___	$24.95	___
26.	1909-06	New Home Selling Strategies: A Handbook for Success	___	$24.95	___
27.	1913-01	List for Success	___	$18.95	___
28.	1922-06	Negotiating Commercial Real Estate Leases	___	$34.95	___
29.	1913-11	Phone Power	___	$19.95	___
30.	1907-05	Power Real Estate Advertising	___	$24.95	___
31.	1926-03	Power Real Estate Letters	___	$29.95	___
32.	1907-01	Power Real Estate Listing, 2nd edition	___	$18.95	___
33.	1907-04	Power Real Estate Negotiation	___	$19.95	___
34.	1907-02	Power Real Estate Selling, 2nd edition	___	$18.95	___
35.	1965-01	Real Estate Brokerage: A Success Guide, 3rd edition	___	$35.95	___
36.	1913-13	The Real Estate Sales Survival Kit.	___	$24.95	___
37.	1978-02	Recruiting Revolution in Real Estate	___	$34.95	___
38.	1903-31	Sold! The Professional's Guide to Real Estate Auctions	___	$32.95	___
39.	2703-11	Time Out: Time Management Strategies for the Real Estate Professional	___	$19.95	___
40.	1909-04	Winning in Commercial Real Estate Sales	___	$24.95	___

NEW! Audio Tapes

41.	1926-06	Power Real Estate Listings	___	$19.95	___
42.	1926-05	Power Real Estate Selling	___	$19.95	___
43.	1926-04	Staying on Top in Real Estate	___	$14.95	___

Book total ___
Tax ___
Shipping and Handling ___
Less $1.00 off if you fax order ___
Total amount ___

Shipping/Handling Charges:
$0-24.99 — $4
$25-49.99 — $5
$50-99.99 — $6
$100-249.99 — $8

Order shipped to the following states must include applicable sales tax: CA, FL, IL & NY

R92005

Real Estate Education Company
Where Experts Begin

a division of Dearborn Financial Publishing, Inc.
520 North Dearborn Street, Chicago, IL 60610-4354

Place your order today! **By FAX: 1-312-836-1021**. Or call **1-800-437-9002, ext. 650**. In Illinois, call 1-312-836-4400, ext. 650. Mention code R92005. Or fill out and mail this order form to: **Real Estate Education Company,** 520 North Dearborn Street, Chicago, Illinois 60610-4354

Your Satisfaction is Guaranteed!

All books come with a 30 day money-back guarantee. If you are not completely satisfied, simply return your books in saleable condition and your money will be refunded in full.

☐ Please send me the Real Estate Education Company catalog featuring your full list of titles.
Prices are subject to change without notice.

**Fill out form and mail today!
Or Save $1.00 when you order by Fax:
312-836-1021.**

Name _____
Address _____
City/State/Zip _____
Telephone _____

Payment must accompany all orders (check one):
☐ Check or money order (payable to Dearborn Financial Publishing, Inc.)
520 North Dearborn Street, Chicago, Illinois 60610-4354
☐ Charge to my credit card: ☐ VISA   ☐ MasterCard
Account No. _____ Exp. Date _____
Signature _____
(All charge orders must be signed.)

12/92

Return Address:

_____

_____

BUSINESS REPLY MAIL
FIRST CLASS   PERMIT NO. 88176   CHICAGO, IL

POSTAGE WILL BE PAID BY ADDRESSEE:

Real Estate Education Company
a division of Dearborn Financial Publishing, Inc.

Order Department
520 North Dearborn Street
Chicago, Illinois 60610-9857

No Postage Necessary if Mailed in the United States

IMPORTANT • PLEASE FOLD OVER • PLEASE TAPE BEFORE MAILING

NOTE: This page, when folded over and taped, becomes a postage-free envelope, which has been approved by the United States Postal Service. It is provided for your convenience.

IMPORTANT • PLEASE FOLD OVER • PLEASE TAPE BEFORE MAILING